THE Frankfurt SCHOOL ON RELIGION

Key
Writings
by the
Major
Thinkers

EDITED BY
EDUARDO MENDIETA

ROUTLEDGE
NEW YORK AND LONDON

"Eduardo Mendieta has put together a fascinating collection of eye-opening essays by the leading figures of the Frankfurt school that adds still one more important voice to the ongoing conversation concerning the 'return of religion,' that is, to the growing consensus that religious discourse and practices are irreducibly important human phenomena that cannot be dismissed by outdated reductionistic critiques of religion. No one interested in the renewed interest philosophers today are showing in religion can fail to be instructed by this first rate collection."

—John D. Caputo, Thomas J. Watson Professor of Religion and Humanities,
Syracuse University

"The critique of religion that Marxism once called for and the reappraisal of religion—in its historical definition and modern semantics, rhetoric, pragmatics, imaginary—as itself perhaps the most powerful archive and potential for critique (indeed, in our days, of far more than religion alone) go hand in hand in the writings of the theorists of the so-called Frankfurt School and their intellectual allies. This volume presents an excellent selection from some of the most representative statements on religion as social critique of this diverse and original group of thinkers. Eduardo Mendieta's thoughtful introduction situates their writings in the present-day intellectual context and spells out the reasons why a full assessment of their intellectual legacy has only just begun."

—Hent de Vries, Professor of Modern European Thought,
The Humanities Center, Johns Hopkins University

"*The Frankfurt School on Religion* is an invaluable collection of the most important essays on religion by members of the Frankfurt School and by those in dialogue with it. Many of the texts are 'classics.' They represent a broad spectrum of diverse opinions. To have them in one collection makes this volume indispensable for any course on critical theory and religion."

—Francis Schussler Fiorenza, Stillman Professor,
Harvard Divinity School

"For all its insistence on the this-worldly nature of redemption, the Frankfurt School has always taken seriously the subversive impulses hidden beneath the affirmative facade of organized religion. Through the editorial efforts of Eduardo Mendieta, we can now appreciate for the first time the full range of their critical appropriation of theological and religious motifs, which extends even into the resolutely secular theory of Habermas."

—Martin Jay, Sidney Hellman Ehrman Professor of History,
University of California, Berkeley

"*The Frankfurt School on Religion* is an indispensable resource for all critical social and political theorists who want to rethink 'the religious' beyond Marx's suspicion of it as an opiate of the masses and Nietzsche's condemnation of it as a nihilistic or slave morality. Mendieta's anthology rescues in yearnings of the present age a reservoir of postsecular hope and dangerous memory, redemptive expectation as well as ruthless critique of injustice."

—Martin Beck Matuštík,
author of Jürgen Habermas: A Philosophical-Political Profile

Published in 2005 by
Routledge
270 Madison Avenue
New York, NY 10016
www.routledge-ny.com

Published in Great Britain by
Routledge
2 Park Square
Milton Park, Abingdon
Oxon OX14 4RN U.K.
www.routledge.co.uk

Printed in the United States of America on acid-free paper.

10 9 8 7 6 5 4 3 2 1

Library of Congress Cataloging-in-Publication Data

The Frankfurt School on religion : key writings by the major thinkers / edited by Eduardo
Mendieta.
    p. cm.
ISBN 0-415-96696-5 (hardcover : alk. paper) — ISBN 0-415-96697-3 (pbk. : alk. paper)
1. Religion and sociology. 2. Frankfurt school of sociology. I. Mendieta, Eduardo.
BL60.F68 2004
200—dc22
                                                        2004019354

Contents

Acknowledgments   vii

Introduction: Religion as Critique: 1
Theology as Social Critique and Enlightened Reason
   Eduardo Mendieta

Part I Ernst Bloch

1   On the Original History of the Third Reich   21
2   Not Hades, But Heaven on Earth   41
3   Hunger, "Something in a Dream," God of Hope, Thing-For-Us   49
4   Marx and the End of Alienation   52

Part II Erich Fromm

5   The Dogma of Christ   61

Part III Leo Löwenthal

6   The Demonic: Project for a Negative Philosophy of Religion   101

Part IV Herbert Marcuse

7   A Study on Authority: Luther, Calvin, Kant   115

Part V Theodor W. Adorno

8   Reason and Sacrifice   149
9   Reason and Revelation   167
10 Meditations on Metaphysics   175

Part VI Max Horkheimer

11 Theism and Atheism   213
12 The Jews and Europe   225
13 Religion and Philosophy   243
14 Observations on the Liberalization of Religion   251

Part VII Walter Benjamin

15 Capitalism as Religion   259
16 Theological-Political Fragment   263
17 Theses on the Philosophy of History   265

Part VIII Johann Baptist Metz

18 Productive Noncontemporaneity   277
19 Anamnestic Reason: A Theologian's Remarks   285
    on the Crisis of the Geisteswissenschaften

Part IX Jürgen Habermas

20 Israel and Athens, or to Whom Does Anamnestic Reason Belong? 293
21 Transcendence from Within, Transcendence in this World   303
22 Faith and Knowledge   327
23 On the Relation between the Secular Liberal State and Religion 339

Part X Helmut Peukert

24 Enlightenment and Theology as Unfinished Projects   351

Part XI Edmund Arens

25 Religion as Ritual, Communicative, and Critical Praxis   373

Permissions Credits   397

Index   401

Acknowledgments

This book was conceived before its companion, *Religion and Rationality: Essays on Reason, God and Modernity* (Polity, 2002), a collection of essays by Jürgen Habermas that I edited back in 2001. However, due to the size of the project, it got delayed. The project received an enthusiastic response by Damon Zucca, who made sure that Routledge acquired it. I am sorry that he is no longer at Routledge to see it published. Martin Jay guided me with his prodigious scholarship on the Frankfurt School. He made comments on early versions of the introduction and saved me from egregious errors. David Kaufmann and Hent de Vries responded to queries concerning their important essays on religion and the Frankfurt School. Jürgen Habermas was extremely generous with this time, suggestions, and responses. He considered contributing something original to the book, but world events over took us all. Still, he provided me with an unpublished manuscript he produced for an encounter with Cardinal Joseph Ratzinger, which appears here for the first time in any language. Edmund Arens, who arguably has been the premier theologian to take up the work of the Frankfurt School, and Habermas' in particular, was my teacher at Union Theological Seminary in the 90s. He has written and edited several volumes on the subject. His pioneering work guided me in thinking about how to organize this collection. I also thank him for taking time from his busy administrative work schedule to write something original for this volume. I want to thank all the translators that contributed to the transmission and preservation of the Frankfurt School's work into English, especially those who worked on translations for this volume: Matthias Fritsch and Chad Kautzer. Jeff Hall and Lynn Goeller masterfully guided the manuscript through production, and Azucena Cruz helped with the index and the proofs.

Eduardo Mendieta
Stony Brook University

Introduction
Religion as Critique
Theology as Social Critique and Enlightened Reason

Eduardo Mendieta

Introduction

This anthology provides the reader with an overview, as well as samplings, of the contributions that the Frankfurt School made to the study and critique of religion. The Frankfurt School was not the original name of the school, nor was it a school per se. Rather, this intellectual institution and school of thought began in 1923 as the Institute for Social Research in Frankfurt and was affiliated with the Goethe University in the city of Frankfurt am Main, Germany. The director of the Institute was also to be appointed to the university faculty. During the early 1920s, the Institute for Social Research was affiliated with the Marx-Engels Institute in Moscow, and contributed to the publication of the up to then unknown Marx manuscripts. With the rise of the Nazis to power in 1933, the Institute went into exile, first in Switzerland, where an affiliated office had been established, and then in 1934 to New York. During World War II, the Institute set up offices in a building next to Columbia University, where it proceeded to engage in empirical research on "prejudice" and "anti-Semitism." In 1951 the Institute for Social Research returned to Frankfurt. Fredrick Pollack, Max Horkheimer, and Theodor W. Adorno returned to conduct research under the auspices of the Institute, to teach at the Goethe University in Frankfurt, and to have a very active public intellectual life in Germany, while most of the other members remained in the United States, notably Herbert Marcuse, Leo Löwenthal, Franz Neumann, and Otto Kirchheimer. These are the most elemental historical facts, but they hardly begin to tell us anything about the profound and epochal mark that the Institute for Social Research has left on the intellectual landscape of the twentieth and twenty-first centuries.[1] In this introduc-

1

tion I will give a general characterization of what the Institute accomplished intellectually and of what it contributed specifically to the study of religion.

Critical Theory

Just as it is almost impossible to think of the intellectual physiognomy of Western culture without the French *philosophes* of the Enlightenment,[2] it is also almost impossible to think of Western culture today without the tradition of inter-disciplinary, critical, and philosophically informed social research developed by the eponymous called Frankfurt School. The comparison to the French philosophers of the Enlightenment is neither exaggerated nor frivolous. Just as for the former reason was to be liberated from the shackles of dogmatism and superstition, thus allowing reason to spread its liberating light, for the latter reason was to be liberated from the rigid grip of a reifying and mystifying idolatry of technology and the market. If for the *philosophes* reason was to be rescued from the church and theology, for the Frankfurt School theorists reason was to be liberated from the church of positivism and the theology of the market. The comparison, as we will see, is most felicitous.

The Frankfurt School contributed extensively to many fields. From its inception, the members of the Institute contributed at different levels with varying degrees of consistency. There was an evident division of labor. The members created a fruitful cross-fertilization of barely inaugurated research methods and approaches. In many cases, the contributions of the members of the Institute were germinal and helped to determine future investigation. Indeed, without the particular approach and commitment to what we today call inter-disciplinary research, many of the most taken-for-granted disciplines and forms of analysis that orient our thinking today, would not have developed, or would have developed quite differently.[3] The Frankfurt School will undoubtedly be identified with what we now call "cultural studies."[4] One of the main areas of investigation for the members of the Frankfurt School was what they called the "culture industry"[5] and mass or popular culture. The study of the mass production of a mass culture was pursued in terms of what are called media studies, the study of the way in which different media convey through their very form, i.e., technological and material mediation, different cultural norms and ideological messages. The culture industry was studied in its diverse materializations: literature, music, movies, as well as the mass ornaments of a consumer culture that instigates consumption by bestowing on the commodity the aura of a symbolic power not reducible to the use value that the commodity embodies. The study of mass culture and the culture industry was central to the theoretical and research agenda, as it offered another clue in the processes of the psychology of assimilation and resignation that undermined the revolutionary fervor of the working classes in industrialized nations. Yet, as the Frankfurt School sought to understand how culture contributed to the domestication and pacification of the masses, it also sought to understand those products that both mediated and gave expression to yearning and hopes not exhausted and totally commodified by the culture industry; such products were thought to be the objects of art. For this reason, as the other side of its studies in reification and alienation, the Frankfurt School paid equal attention to the study of the aesthetic, and thus sought to develop a critical theory of art.

Another central area of research for the Institute was the socio-psychological process of integration in post-liberal societies. In other words, in light of the rise of mass movements of genocidal racism, orchestrated and choreographed with the emergent advertising industry at the service of dictators, the question became what kinds of social processes have developed, becoming both operative and dysfunctional, that allowed the rise of particular personality profiles that are either resistant or easy prey to totalitarian propaganda. A twin area of research was the psychosocial development of individuals in terms of ego and family development. Thus, early on, members of the Frankfurt School used elements from Sigmund Freud's psychoanalytical theories of ego development to study the rise of what they called the "authoritarian personality." This personality type was linked to a weak ego, a despotic alter ego, and a weakened or marginalized family structure. Thus, if the focus on the processes of social integration into modern societies traced the phylogenesis of certain psychosocial patterns of social behavior, the focus on ego and family structures traced the ontogenesis of individual developmental stages of moral and psychological autonomy. Both areas of investigation, namely the intra- and extra-psychic, the internal and the social, the private and the public, as well as their mediation by a commodified and mass culture, were always studied under the shadow of a culture of "resignation," of accommodation, of paralyzing cynicism and regressive tolerance. Close to these studies on social psychology, were studies on political will formation, and the interaction between democracy and the rule of law, justice, and voting practices. Such studies were pursued not just with reference to Germany, in particular, but also to Western political systems in general. The "totalitarian state" became a shibboleth for a thorough critique of the totalitarian tendencies in modern legal and political forms of organization. Thus, the history of political theory in the twentieth century cannot circumvent the contributions of Herbert Marcuse, Franz Neumann, Otto Kirchheimer, and more recently of Jürgen Habermas, to the development of post-totalitarian and post-liberal forms of democratic self-legislation and political justice.[6]

Yet another central area of research for the Frankfurt School was what we now call science studies, or the philosophy of technology. Indeed, any course in the philosophy of technology, or any curriculum in science studies, would be incompetently incomplete without the inclusion of the studies of Max Horkheimer, Theodor W. Adorno, Herbert Marcuse, and Jürgen Habermas on technology and science.[7] For the members of the Frankfurt School, attention to technology and science was a *sine qua non*, for science and technology embodied the noblest ideals of the Enlightenment. In science and technology the pursuit of objectivity and truth for the sake of the improvement of the human condition met its most evident materialization. Yet, these very ideals were also betrayed by both science and technology, for both were used for legitimating the most obnoxious forms of racism, as well as the most devastating technological means for the extermination of humanity. Technology, which promised a cornucopia of utopian amenities, had turned into a demonic machine used for crushing skulls and decimating the earth. At the center of the Frankfurt School's analysis of technology was the question whether technology as such was, in its structure and very operation, determined to be a tool of devastation, or whether it had been sequestered into its obliterating mission by an ideological perspective, or world view, that injected technology with its particular orientation and mood. In other words, for the Frankfurt School the question was whether another form of science and technology was possible that not just preserved it from its dehumanizing effects, but also rescued it from its pejorative ideological neutralization. In this way, then, the Frankfurt School was fundamentally concerned with the critique of positivism, if by positivism we understand all forms of thinking that taken for granted the idea of an objective reality that is accessible through the study of facts by putative transparent methods of quantification. Thus, the Frankfurt School had not just a research agenda, but also a particular philosophical orientation that criticized both the naïveté of all forms of positivism as well as their ideological effects. As a general outlook, positivism contributed to concealing the way in which science and technology are informed by values, but also contributed to concealing what values were guiding present science and technology. As a critique of positivism, and in tandem with the formulation of a critical theory of science, the critical theory that the Frankfurt School developed was also a critique of deforming and deformed processes of the rationalization of society. Succinctly, the Frankfurt School sought to develop a theory of rationality, one that sought to point to its pathological implementation through forms of mystifying positivism, and that sought to rescue reason from its imprisonment in the iron cage of capitalist economy.

What at first blush may seem like a laundry list of areas of research is actually held together by a very particular theoretical orientation that has been called "interdisciplinary materialism."[8] This historicized and historicizing materialism is aimed at understanding social reality along three axes of consolidation: political economy, social psychology, and the theory of culture.[9] The anachronistically, or rather, retrospectively assigned name of "interdisciplinary materialism" underscores how the Frankfurt School departed from a very general "historical materialist" perspective that always focused on the material production of society, at different levels, though partly autonomous but always mutually determining, spheres of social integration and production. The political economy axis focused on post-liberal bourgeois society in which the production and accumulation of capital had been exacerbated by capitalism's advancement into a higher stage of finance capital. This latest form of capitalism had not only attained new forms of monopolization and consolidation on a continental and even global scale, but had also achieved the neutralization of socialist and social democratic movements during the early part of the twentieth century. With the expansion of markets, and the development of mass cultures, and capitalist concessions to workers in terms of minimum wages, through the stabilizing measures of the Welfare State, there also came about a generalization of the commoditization of all social life. Under capitalism in its latest forms, we have the triumph of the commodity form, the type of conceptual and practical orientation that reduces everything to quantity and eviscerated identity. The social-psychological axis focused on the psychic life of the social, and the social life of the psychic, which would be a more contemporary way of phrasing what we earlier referred to as the phylogenesis of the social and the ontogenesis of the individual, where neither is to be thought without the other. As a bridge between the very historically indexed production and reproduction of society at the level of the material and technologically production of social wealth, and the socio-psychological unfolding of structures of selfhood, and social interaction, is the axis of the analysis of culture. Culture mediates the interaction between the material and the mental, the economic and the socio-political. Culture is the medium for symbolic continuity and the reproduction of webs of meaning that give coherence to our private and public dramas and narratives. But culture itself is branded by the context of its material production; it is also mediated and determined by the commodity form, the coin of the market. Thus, the culture industry, and its products, mass culture and mass consumption, themselves became elements in the symbolic reproduction of commodified subjectivities that are empty of any normative and thus moral content.

The Frankfurt School was not just an innovative research agenda; it was also the locus for the appropriation and transformation of many intellectual traditions. When one speaks of Frankfurt School "critical theory," one is also making reference to a whole encyclopedia of philosophical and conceptual approaches. At the most basic level, as was already noted, the Frankfurt School sought to appropriate and transform "historical materialism" into a viable and expanded form of social research that would be historically specific and critical of its own limitation. In order to appropriate the most fruitful elements of Marxism, the Frankfurt School also had to engage in a genealogical analysis of Marxism that traced its roots to Hegel, in particular, but also to German idealism in general, and more broadly to the radical traditions of the European Enlightenment.[10] Another current of thought that converged in the critical theory of the Frankfurt

School is what has been called an atheistic Jewish Messianism, which was very unique and particular to assimilated central European Jews, especially those of Germany, where the Jews, paradoxically, had achieved the greatest assimilation.[11] The convergence of what Georg Lukács called "romantic anti-capitalism"[12] that was expressed as a relentless and obsessive critique of the corrosive effects of capitalism's leveling of all social life, with the paradoxically secular and atheistic forms of Jewish apocalyptic and Messianic critique synthesized with a Marxist critique of commodity fetishism, gave shape to a form of social critique that was trans-disciplinary, even anti-disciplinary. That is to say, it gave shape to a form of social analysis that did not fit comfortably under any of the traditional rubrics that categorized forms of thinking and social research. This form of social critique rejected the acceptance of social reality as pure positivity, while it paid attention to every fragment and detail of social life as possible ciphers of both resistance and utopian projection. Social reality is the ruin of human life. It is unacceptable, except to deluded and ideological thought, that it is the expression of all that humans can be and have been. Thus, key phrases in the lexicon of social and philosophical analysis of the Frankfurt School thinkers were "negative," "dialectics," and "the wholly other." Negative dialectics, which became another name for critical theory, was a form of thinking that dwelled on the edge of reason, not because reason is not to be found in the world and the only alternative is irrationalism, but because reason is always being exiled from the world by the reifying power of identity thinking and commodity fetishism.

What is significant, however, about the critical theory tradition inaugurated by the Frankfurt School is precisely this attempt to rescue the Enlightenment, and with it reason, by means of a refusal to grant immanence the last word. Refusing to give the last word, also meant refusing the disciplinary boundaries of any fixed status. Disciplines and faculty boundaries are as much a result of the specialization of knowledge as they are a product of the intellectual division of labor; often at the mercy of the technological development of the productive forces, and the level of exacerbation of the conflicts of social relations. It is this critical attitude toward the very tools of critique and social analysis that have led the Frankfurt School to be identified with "critical theory" *en toto*. Critical theory is not just critical of social reality, but it is also critical of theory *tout court*, and the concept and medium itself in which theory lives. It is a form of thinking that is always trying to give an account of the logic by which social reality has become what it is, but also of itself, its standpoint. For this reason, we may think of critical theory as a form of "meta-philosophy," as a type of thinking that is trying to think the very possibility, viability, and legitimacy of the concepts in which and through which thinking thinks itself. As a meta-philosophy, critical theory aims to think with the concept against the concept. For concepts themselves become an impediment, and an obstacle in the way to that which they seek to grasp: human social existence. As Adorno put it in the

Negative Dialectics, philosophy "must strive, by way of the concept, to transcend the concept."[13] For this reason, in all of the critical theory tradition, there is persistence on thinking of key concepts, *inter alia*, self, subject, society, the object, civilization, concept, work, and freedom. Critical theory, then, is reason criticizing itself. And it is this critical impetus, this fastidious self-reflexivity that is so exemplarily exhibited by the work of the best-known representative of the Frankfurt School in the last half of the twentieth century, namely Jürgen Habermas. In his work, the most recent, as well as most complex and demanding, theoretical approaches are brought together into theoretical perspectives that refuse to reconcile reason with the world. As the early Frankfurt School brought together Karl Marx, George Lukács, Ernst Bloch, George Simmel, Arthur Schopenhauer, Friedrich Nietzsche, Sigmund Freud, names that metonymically stand for disciplines and approaches (historical materialism, social psychology, phenomenology, skepticism, romanticism, phenomenology, etc.), in its most recent incarnations we have also witnessed a determination to rescue the critical impetus of the Enlightenment by confronting the most recent theoretical and philosophical developments in the works of Niklas Luhmann, Talcott Parsons, George Herbert Mead, Richard Rorty, Hans-Georg Gadamer, Lawrence Kohlberg, Michel Foucault, Jacques Derrida, and so on (systems theory, pragmatism, phenomenology, developmental, moral, and cognitive psychology, deconstruction, structuralism, and so on). In the recent work on what are now beginning to be called a second and third generation of Critical Theorists (not just Habermas, but also Albrecht Wellmer and Axel Honneth), there is also a very deliberate confrontation with the very roots, tasks, and accomplishments of the tradition itself. Thus, in Habermas as well as in Honneth, we find some of the harshest and acute criticisms of the critical theory tradition they inherited from the early Frankfurt School.[14]

With the critical latitude that temporal distance grants us, we may be in a position to access the impact and accomplishments of the tradition. In their collected works, those that continue to appear, as in the case of Theodor W. Adorno, and those that remain to be gathered, as in Habermas' case, we find one of the richest encyclopedic compendiums not just of the disasters and triumphs of the twentieth century, but also of the retreats and advances made by Enlightenment thought. In breath and depth, the works of the Frankfurt School remain some of the most impressive accomplishments of the human mind. They are also indispensable testimonies to the tragedy and catastrophe that was unleashed upon the Jewish people during the darkest of centuries in the annals of human history. Just as the transition from the Medieval and Renaissance periods to modernity are to be negotiated through the portal of the French philosophes, a transition to a new Enlightenment, a new form of enlightened and enlightening reason, is hardly to be negotiated without passing through the majestic portals of the Frankfurt School's critical theory.

Religion as Critique

The Enlightenment declared the triumph of reason by vanquishing theology and segregating religion into domesticated subjectivity. Today the Enlightenment lives on by recruiting the services of theology to rescue reason through religion by unmasking the idolatry and fetishism of the market and technology, and by returning to the subject of subjective freedom. Alternatively, but just as pointedly precise, it is only in a "secularized world that theology, and religion, can be seen in their truth."[15] This is the paradoxical situation that the critical theory of the Frankfurt School most eloquently addresses and tries to think through. This is what the present anthology seeks to illustrate and prove beyond contestation. Just as philosophy, to echo the first lines from *Negative Dialectics*, "lives on because the moment of its realization was missed," today religion lives on because its promise and complaint, its yearning and sigh, have remained unfulfilled and unheard. At the heart of the Frankfurt School critical theory we find not just an incidental or ancillary attention to religion, but a central, deliberate, and explicit confrontation with both religion and theology. This concern with religion and theology was not just a function of the encyclopedic and comprehensive thoroughness of the Frankfurt School thinkers; rather, like art and the culture industry, religion had to be a major field of study. For just like art and the culture industry, religion registers both the level of technological development society has achieved, and the degree of pathological socialization and reification individuals have undergone. But like art and the products of mass culture, religion also becomes the site for the negotiation of critique, remembrance, and emancipatory projections.

Throughout the works of the Frankfurt School theorists we are able to discern different ways in which religion was viewed. Religion was neither reductively nor simplistically analyzed. Rather, it was viewed as a heterogeneous phenomenon that intersects at many different levels with social existence.[16] On one level, religion was viewed as a fundamental part of the lifeworld, for it mediates and constitutes it. Religion is an institution, not just because it coalesces into churches, sects, and proselytizing movements, but also because it provides societies with *lingua francas*, common languages through which to address their hopes and discontents. Religion is both an institution, one that augured the very rationalization that gave birth to modernity, and also a world view that inflects and refracts every lived movement within the lifeworld. In this way, it is saddled between what Habermas has called the lifeworld and the systems level of the social totality. For the Frankfurt School theorists, religion, and all the aspects that constitute religion, is integral to social evolution, yet it is not exhausted or abolished by this evolution. In all of their writings, as is evident in the readings here collected, there is a concern with the way in which religion provided the fertile soil for ideas of autonomy, authority, power, and development of critical thinking, but at the same time how, under the pressure of new forms of socialization, personality development and the production of culture. Religion was thereby indoctrinated into the service of new and more acute forms of domestication and pacification.[17]

Religion, on another level, has been analyzed by Critical Theorists as a language that antecedes metaphysics and ontology, but which nonetheless instigated the very demise and relativization of all metaphysical and ontological vocabularies.[18] Religion gives words to non-conceptual experiences that *philosophemes* and *theologoumenon* preserve in a provisionary and non-exhaustive way. In this way, religion harbors a lexicon of transcendence and anti-fetishism. Religious language therefore is both inexhaustible, albeit always succumbing to decay and forgetfulness, and renewable via new experiences of the liminal and numinous, albeit gropingly searching for words beyond the quotidian and the hyperbolic. Religious language, as well as its institutions, is the medium in which that from which it flows is both accessed and hindered from being encountered. The concept becomes the wall between the subject and the non-conceptual. Religious language gets in the way of the subject and the religious experience. Thus, religion is to be secured by means of the relentless criticism of religion. In the Frankfurt School we find a *non-secular critique*[19] of religion for the sake of religion. It is a critique that uses reason against religion, not so as to reject religion, for reason can no more do this than it can reject itself, but for the sake of reason itself.

In critical theory we find the conviction that all attempts to understand religion through theology miss religion's truth content, yet, without theology this truth content would have remained blind and speechless. In tandem, we find the accompanying conviction that theology lives on as an asymptotic approximation to the luminous and the liminal experience of religion because reason has retreated from the world as this has ossified into the totems of the commodity form. Thus, in critical theory we find not just a deliberate attempt to think religion *with* religion and *against* religion, but also the urge to rescue theology for the sake of reason. As with Karl Marx's critique of religion, the criticism of theology does not merely seek to pluck the "imaginary flowers" from a mystified social reality, but theology is criticized so that the living flower of reason may be plucked from the thorn bush of calamitous historical reality.[20] As David Kaufmann has very perceptively noted, "'Theology' as Adorno construes it [this applies equally to Walter Benjamin and Max Horkheimer]— the dialectical overcoming of a mythic sense of subjection to alien (and in truth merely alienated) powers—takes the place that reason was supposed to fill in the thought of Enlightenment writers. It reveals the falseness of superstition and helps deliver fate to freedom."[21] This theology, however, can be neither positive nor confessional, much less fideistic. In contrast with the traditional idea that theology is faith-seeking understanding, for the thinkers of the

Frankfurt School theology is reason in search of itself by way of the demysti-fication of social reality. Therefore, in contrast to Immanuel Kant, who grounded religion in the moral, and G. W. F. Hegel, who assimilated religion into a develop-ment sequence that relegated it to the early stages of human cognitive development, the Frankfurt School approaches religion as a thoroughly con-temporary phenomenon that seats next to art and philosophy, neither seeking to replace nor be replaced by these. In the Frankfurt School's critique of religion, religion offers not just consolation, but also the conceptual and epistemological elements with which to criticize a world that has made humanity disconsolate and superstitious.[22]

Critical theory's theology can only be a form of "negative theology"—a theology that begins with the absence of God, or of a God that has been exiled from creation by the disaster that history has turned. At the very least, it is an inverse theology that rejects both theodicy and divine history mendaciously turned progress. As inverse theology it rejects the idea that human history has been benevolently guided by a *Heilsgeschichte*, for in the image of Walter Benjamin, progress is but a storm and catastrophe. Progress has been a sham, for the earth is "radiant with triumphant calamity."[23] And just as this theology cannot reconcile God to a world that betrays and belies everything it stands for, nor can it be a reconciliation with a foreclosed world, in which a *Heilsgeschichte* is both analepsis and prolepsis, a return to genesis, the beginning. Theodicy, whether in the form of Augustine, Spinoza, or Hegel, exiles justice from the world, just as it ontologically forecloses the new, the absolute *Novum*. A God that is reconciled with the misery and suffering of the world already prefigured at the moment of creation vitiates human creativity. It is what Hannah Arendt called *natality*, and what makes God divine, the power to generate and create *ex nihilo*, and *ad novo*. For God, in this type of Jewish apocalyptic Messianism, is the meta-onto-logical problem of two fundamental mysteries: redemption and the new.[24] Thus, theology cannot be an apologia but a *Summa Theologica con-tra immanentes*, for social reality is rent asunder by a suffering than has not lessened but grown more intense as the mechanisms for the torture of the self and the flesh have become more sophisticated, and memory, which is the con-dition of possibility of justice, is, in turn, only made possible by a God that remains not just *absconditus*, but forthcoming, yet to be. For this atheistic nega-tive theology, God is the cipher of a dual negativity: what negates the present Golgotha, and what negates the delusional self-sufficiency of the concept that betrays reason to positivistic pieties. In Adorno's words, ". . . God, the Absolute, eludes finite beings. Where they desire to name him, because they must, they betray him. But if they keep silent about him, they acquiesce in their own im-potence and sin against the other, no less binding, commandment to name him."[25] This inverse, or negative theology, must reject and refute God, for the sake of God, and it must also reject and refute religion for the sake of what the religious prefigures and recalls. In an age in which religion itself is continuously sequestered into the service of totalitarian ends, only that religion which is useless is true, and if it is useful it is not true.[26] The motto that hangs over the Frankfurt School's negative theology, is one that Ernst Bloch articulated thus: "Only an atheist can be a good Christian; only a Christian can be a good atheist."[27]

This negative theology, then turns into a redemptive and hopeful theology, for which the two central theologemes are memory and hope, remembrance and utopia. The goal, to underscore, is not faith, but truth and reason. Negative, *qua* redemptive, theology is not faith in search of reason, *Deus* in quest of justification, but reason in quest of its possibility, hope, and truth.[28] As Horkheimer notes, "Faced with the sciences and the entire present situation, my idea of expressing the concept of an omnipotent and benevolent Being no longer as a dogma, but as longing that unites all men so that the horrible events, the injustice of history so far would not be permitted to be the final, ultimate fate of the victims, seems close to the solution of the problem."[29] This longing that Horkheimer also calls the *yearning for the wholly other*, is a yearning for a truth whose condition of possibility is the just society. Theology, as the medium in which religion is able to speak and disclose its truth content, is at the service of a critical social theory, although this last one can neither replace it nor dispense with it.

The Frankfurt School's critique of religion turns religion into a source of social critique that transverses the traditional disciplinary boundaries that have been used to gerrymander religion. The critical theory's approach is neither a sociology of religion, nor is it exactly a philosophy of religion, nor is it a mere theological approach. Its approach is neither functionalistic, nor phenomenological, nor existentialist. It is also not denominational, or confessional; although its sources can be traced to the atheistic Messianic Judaism, crisis theology, and Christian Socialism of the early part of the twentieth century. This is what makes the Frankfurt School's approach to religion and theology particular fertile and generative today. For in the Frankfurt School's critical theory of religion we find a dual confrontation with the religious sources of modern, European, and Western Culture, sources that unleashed a fateful dialectic of introjected and sacrificial violence, and an attempt to rescue what makes the religious not just a source of alienation and negation of the world, but also of remembrance, hope, redemption, and utopia. This dual perspective that seeks to render explicit the ways in which modernity, and the West in general, could not become what it became without the perennial confrontation among Athens, Rome, and Jerusalem,[30] opens up a line of dialogue with other religious world views and lifeworlds, in which religion can be both a source of reification and opium, but just the same, of memory, hope, and yearning that may from within instigate new forms of Enlightenment and Cosmopolitanism.[31]

A final note on the selection of the texts included in this volume is in order. Ernst Bloch was not a member of the Institute for Social Research. Yet, his work was determinant for the development of the Frankfurt School's thinking about religion, theology, and Judaism. Bloch's *The Spirit of Utopia,* published in 1918, along with Georg Lukács' *The Theory of the Novel,* was formative and foundational as some of the essays reprinted here attest; as was the prodigious correspondence among members of the Institute on these works. Bloch followed a parallel line of intellectual development. He immigrated to the United States during World War II but returned to Germany (soon to be divided) after the war. In 1949 he returned to East Germany, to the University of Leipzig, where he taught with great distinction. In 1961, while he was in West Germany, the Berlin Wall started to be erected. Completely disillusioned with the East, he asked for political asylum. Until his retirement, he taught at the Tübingen University.[32] Bloch, like Benjamin, forms part of the train of Adorno's negative dialectics. Without Bloch, Adorno's resolute negativity would turn into nihilism and irrationalism. As David Drew notes perspicaciously, "The consummate and unflinching negativity of Adorno's post-war philosophy, including his philosophy of New Music, delineates with the utmost clarity the mirror images of *Geist der Utopie* and *Das Prinzip Hoffnung.*"[33] In Adorno's own words, "consummate negativity, once squarely faced, delinates the mirror-image of its opposite."[34] Adorno's negative dialectics is met halfway by Bloch's principle of hope. And, just as in Adorno and Horkheimer we are to discern what David Kaufmann has called a "redemptive ontology,"[35] in Bloch we discern a dialectical materialism that also seeks to redeem matter, and to give voice to a negative anthropology that in Habermas' terms makes Bloch into a Marxist Schelling.[36] Nonetheless, the extent to which Bloch influenced the Frankfurt School is perhaps to be gauged by a dialogue that was held in 1964 between Adorno and Bloch in which the mutuality of their perspective is explicitly acknowledged.[37] The texts here included, however, are contemporary with some of the works produced by the Frankfurt School on religion and theology. Even when they are not explicitly discussed, they form the back-drop against the ruminations and explorations of the Frankfurt School. These texts ought to be read in tandem with the Frankfurt School's criticisms on the mendacious and deleterious uses of religion by the fascists. The essays here excerpted from *Heritage of Our Times,* a book from 1935, should be read jointly with the section "Elements of Anti-Semitism: Limits of Enlightenment" in the *Dialectics of Enlightenment.* The selections from Bloch's *Atheism in Christianity* (1968), correspond to the most explicit formulations of the relationship between Marxism and Christianity that as if by proxy say what Adorno could not say explicitly, or in the same language.[38]

Erich Fromm was an early member of the Institute for Social Research, and the essay included here belongs to the period when he was affiliated with the

Institute. This early essay of Fromm's clearly left its traces on the Frankfurt School's critique of religion, as is attested by the early works on authority by Herbert Marcuse and the sociological analysis of superstition and religious speech undertaken by the Institute in the United States during its exile. The break between Fromm and the Institute came about because of the widening gap between his interpretation of Freud and psychoanalytic theory in general, and the more "orthodox" reading that Horkheimer, Adorno, and Marcuse espoused of Freud's theory of the instincts.[39]

The essay by Leo Löwenthal appears here for the first time in English. It is a very unique find, as it gives explicit testimony to the Jewish, apocalyptic, atheistic Messianism that characterized the work of the Frankfurt School. This work also makes evident not only how in the 1920s the intellectual atmosphere in Frankfurt was suffused with the critical reception of Lukács and Bloch, but also how the cultural romanticism was given expression through a religious language. The Adorno selections span his philosophical career. The excerpt from his Kierkegaard book belongs to the earliest of Adorno's philosophical works. What is notable is that this book was submitted as his *Habilitation* to Paul Tillich, who accepted it.[40] The section on Adorno concludes with selections from Adorno's magnus opus, *Negative Dialectics*. This section could have included selections from his sociological writings, but these are more easily accessible and also would have unduly overburdened the text with Adorno selections. The selections from Max Horkheimer's work contain hitherto untranslated essays that belong to the latter part of his intellectual production.[41] The Benjamin pieces are classics and they are *sine qua non* for all thinking about religion by the Frankfurt School. I have included a hitherto little know piece by Benjamin that is a gem of prescient thinking. Johann Baptist Metz, although not a member of the Frankfurt School, has been one of the most influential German theologians to make theologically fruitful the critique of religion and religion as critique that the Frankfurt School developed.[42] Helmut Peukert, a theologian in the tradition of Metz, Dorothe Sölle, and Jürgen Moltmann's political theology, has gone a step beyond Metz, and has sought to develop a fundamental theology on the basis of a communicative theory of action and rationality.[43] The same is to be said of Edmund Arens, whose contribution was specifically written for this volume, and, who like no one else, has doggedly pursued the appropriation of not just the early Frankfurt School's work on religion, but also especially the theoretical insights of Jürgen Habermas. One last note is in order: Prof. Habermas was to have contributed an original piece for this collection, but historical events overtook us.[44] The explosion of the terror of war and the Machiavellian deployment of unmatched military power, unfettered by alliances and the sanctioning of the court of reason, has created a deep rift between the United States and Europe, but also between the West and non-Western societies. As a consummate Enlightenment figure and an engaged public intellectual, Habermas' attention has turned to a criticism of the lawless violence of an Empire no longer constrained by the ideals that first give it its birth certificate: the rule of law and democratic self-legislation.[45] In an age of so-called religious violence, and religious terror, we have to be self-reflexive of how our own forms of violence are also deeply religious. It is not that "theirs" is a religious terror, while ours is selfless and enlightened. Our imperial violence is itself a form of a religious crusade animated by an intolerant fundamentalism. It is to this new form of fundamentalism and religious intolerance that the Frankfurt School's critique of religion can speak so eloquently in light of its confrontation with other imperial ambitions.

Notes

1. The most comprehensive history and study of the Institute for Social Research is the massive book by Rolf Wiggerhaus, *The Frankfurt School: Its History, Theories, and Political Significance*, trans. Michael Robertson (Cambridge, MA: The MIT Press, 1994). An early, but still indispensable study of the school is by Martin Jay, *The Dialectical Imagination* (Boston: Little, Brown & Co., 1973). For a brief overview of the Frankfurt School see the beautiful introduction by Wolfgang Schirmacher to his edition of *German 20th Century Philosophy: The Frankfurt School* (New York: Continuum, 2000), vii–xx.
2. See Peter Gay, *The Enlightenment: An Interpretation. The Rise of Modern Paganism* (New York: Alfred A. Knopf, 1966), 3–19.
3. See Craig Calhoun and Joseph Karaganis, "Critical Theory" in George Ritzer and Barry Smart, eds., *Handbook of Social Theory* (London: Sage Publications, 2001), 179–200. The following analysis of the Frankfurt School's six main areas of research is indebted to Jürgen Habermas, *The Theory of Communicative Action, Volume Two. Lifeworld and System: A Critique of Functionalist Reason*, trans. Thomas McCarthy (Boston: Beacon Press, 1987), 378–83.
4. See Douglas Kellner, "Cultural Studies and Social Theory: A Critical Intervention" in George Ritzer and Barry Smart, eds., *Handbook of Social Theory*, 395–409. See also the introduction by J. M. Bernstein to Theodor W. Adorno, *The Culture Industry: Selected Essays on Mass Culture* (London and New York: Routledge, 1991).
5. See Max Horkheimer and Theodor W. Adorno, *Dialectics of Enlightenment: Philosophical Fragments*, trans. Edmund Jephcott (Stanford: Stanford University Press, 2002 [1947]), the chapter entitled "The Culture Industry: Enlightenment as Mass Deception." See also Theodor W. Adorno, *The Culture Industry* (London and New York: Routledge, 1991).
6. See James Bohman, "Critical Theory and Democracy" in David M. Rasmussen, ed., *The Handbook of Critical Theory* (Cambridge, MA: Blackwell Publishers Ltd., 1996), 190–219. In the same volume, see also Rainer Forst, "Justice, Reason, and Critique: Basic Concepts of Critical Theory," 138–67.
7. Two extremely important works that illustrate this are Andrew Feenberg, *Questioning Technology* (New York: Routledge, 1999), and Steven Vogel, *Against Nature: The Concept of Nature in Critical Theory* (Albany: SUNY Press, 1996).
8. Termed coined by W. Bonss and N. Schindler in "Kristische Theorie als interdisziplinäre Materialismus" in W. Bonss and A. Honneth, eds., *Sozialforschung als Kritik.* (Frankfurt am Main: Suhrkamp, 1982), 31ff.
9. See Axel Honneth, "Critical Theory" in Axel Honneth, *The Fragmented World of the Social: Essays in Social and Political Philosophy* (Albany: SUNY Press, 1995), 61–91.
10. See Nicolae Tertulian, "Lukács, Adorno and German Classical Philosophy" in *Telos*, no. 63 (Spring 1985), 79–96.
11. The best study on this phenomenon remains Michael Löwy, *Redemption and Utopia: Jewish Libertarian Thought in Central Europe. A Study in Elective Affinity* (Stanford: Stanford University Press, 1992). See also Martin Jay, *Permanent Exiles: Essays on the Intellectual Migration from Germany to America* (New York: Columbia University Press, 1985), espe-

cially the first part: "The Frankfurt School." Anson Rabinbach, *In the Shadow of Catastrophe: German Intellectuals between Apocalypse and Enlightenment* (Berkeley: University of California Press, 1997), especially chapter 1: "Between Apocalypse and Enlightenment: Benjamin, Bloch, and Modern German-Jewish Messianism," 27–65.

12. Georg Lukács, *The Theory of the Novel*, trans. Anna Bostock (Cambridge, Massachusetts, 1971), 19. See Axel Honneth, "A Fragmented World: On the Implicit Relevance of Lukács Early Work" in A. Honneth, *The Fragmented World of the Social*, 50–60.

13. Theodor W. Adorno, *Negative Dialectics*, trans. E. B. Ashton (New York: Continuum, 1983), 15.

14. For Habermas' criticisms see Jürgen Habermas, *The Theory of Communicative Action. Volume 1. Reason and the Rationalization of Society*, trans. Thomas McCarthy (Boston: Beacon Press, 1984), especially chapter IV: "From Lukács to Adorno: Rationalization as Reification." See also J. Habermas, *The Philosophical Discourse of Modernity*, translated by Frederick Lawrence (Cambridge, MA: The MIT Press, 1987). For Honneth, see *The Fragmented World of the Social*, especially chapters 5 and 6.

15. David Kaufmann, "Correlations, constellations, and the Truth: Adorno's Ontology Redemptive" in *Philosophy & Social Criticism*, vol. 26, no. 5: 62–80 (at 78).

16. See Jonathan Z. Smith, "Religion, Religions, Religious" in Mark C. Taylor, ed., *Critical Terms for Religious Studies* (Chicago & London: The University of Chicago Press, 1998), 269–84. This wonderful article traces the historicity of the term religion and how it has been linked up with Eurocentric and Civilizational struggles.

17. The empirical research agenda of the Frankfurt School during the early forties follow this line of approach. See in particular the writings now collected in volume 9, parts 1 and 2, of Theodor W. Adorno's *Gesammelte Schriften* (Frankfurt: Suhrkamp, 1997). Here we find the following studies, which have not received proper attention from the perspective of a critical sociology of religion: *The Stars Down to Earth, The Psychological Technique of Martin Luther Thomas' Radio Addresses*, and *Studies in the Authoritarian Personality*. These are extremely important works as they provided the empirical background against which Adorno went on to develop some key philosophical insights about religion, insights that then went on to be incorporate into his more theoretical writings. Thus, from the study of the astrology columns in the *Los Angeles Times*, Adorno went on to extract those paragraphs that in *Minima Moralia* were called "Theses against occultism," see *Minima Moralia* (New York: Verso, 1974), 238–44.

18. This is unquestionably true of the work by Walter Benjamin, and Theodor W. Adorno, but it is less know that this is true of both Horkheimer and Habermas. On Horkheimer see Rudolf J. Siebert, *Horkheimer's Critical Sociology of Religion: The Relative and Transcendent* (Washington, DC: University Press of America, 1979), Guzelin Schmid Noerr, "Wahrheit, Macht und die Sprache der Philosophie. Zu Horkheimers sprachphilosophischen Reflexionen in seinem nachgelassenen Schriften zwischen 1939–1946), in Alfred Schmidt and Norbert Altwicker, eds., *Max Horkheimer heute: Werk und Wirkung* (Frankfurt am Main: Suhrkamp, 1986). For Habermas, see Eduardo Mendieta, "Introduction" to Jürgen Habermas, *Religion and Rationality: Essays on Reason, God, and Modernity* (Cambridge: Polity, 2002). For a general discussion of the centrality of religious language for the early Frankfurt School, see Martin Jay, "The Politics of Translation: Siegfried Kracauer and Walter Benjamin on the Buber-Rosenzweig Bible" in Martin Jay, *Permanent Exiles: Essays on the Intellectual Migration from Germany to America* (New York: Columbia University Press, 1986), 198–216.

19. This ("non-secular") is a circumlocution of an expression used by Gershom Scholem to characterize his type of critique of Jewish thinking. See "With Gershom Scholem: An Interview" in Gershom Scholem, *On Jews & Judaism in Crisis: Selected Essays*, ed. Werner J. Bannhauser (New York: Schocken Books, 1976), 46, where Scholem says that his "secularism is not secular."

20. See Karl Marx, "Critique of Hegel's Philosophy of Right: Introduction" in Karl Marx, *Early Writings*, introduced by Lucio Colleti, trans. Rodney Livingstone and Gregory Benton (New York: Vintage Books, 1975), 244. The full passage that I am paraphrasing reads: "Criticism has plucked the imaginary flowers on the chain not in order that man shall continue to bear that chain without fantasy or consolation but so that he shall throw of the chain and pluck the living flower. The criticism of religion disillusions man, so that he will think, act and fashion his reality like a man who has discarded his illusions and regained his senses, so that

he will move around himself as his true sun. Religion is only the illusory sun which revolves around man as long as he does not revolve around himself."

21. David Kaufmann, "Beyond Use, Within Reason: Adorno, Benjamin and the Question of Theology" in *New German Critique*, No. 83 (Spring/Summer 2001), 151–73 (at 171)..

22. See chapter 3 of Martin Jay's new book *Songs of Experience* (Berkeley: University of California Press, forthcoming), "The Consolation of Religious Experience," which traces magisterially the way in which religion was assimilated into "experience" by the philosophers of the Enlightenment and modernity.

23. Max Horkheimer and Theodor W. Adorno, *Dialectic of Enlightenment: Philosophical Fragments*, edited by Gunzelin Schmid Noerr, trans. Edmund Jephcott (Stanford: Stanford University Press, 2002), 1.

24. The first place where this thought is given explicit expression is in Ernst Bloch, *The Spirit of Utopia*, trans. Anthony A. Nassar (Stanford: Standford University Press, 2000), 201, where Bloch writes: "And God within must not just become visible in us in order to be, so that entire world-process is elastically reduced to the coordination between two "separate" realities: rather even God—as the problem of the radically new, absolutely redemptive, as the phenomenal of our freedom, of our true meaning—possesses himself within us only as a shadowy occurrence, something objectively not yet occurred, only as the coincidence of the darkness of the lived moment with the unconcluded self-symbol of the absolute question."

25. Theodor W. Adorno, "Sacred Fragment: Schoenberg's Moses und Aron," *Quasi Una Fantasia*, trans. Rodney Livingston (London: Verso, 1992), 226.

26. I am playing off of Adorno's analysis in *Studies in the Authoritarian Personality*, in *Soziologische Schriften* II.1, *Gesammelte Schriften* 9.1 (Frankfurt am Main: Suhrkamp, 1997), 440.

27. Ernst Bloch, *Atheism in Christianity: The Religion of the Exodus and the Kingdom*, trans. J. T. Swann (New York: Herder and Herder, 1972), 9.

28. See David Kaufmann, "Adorno and the Name of God" in *Flashpoint* 1.1 (1996): 65–70. This essay is available on line at: http:/www.flashpointmag.com/adorno.htm.

29. Max Horkheimer, *Dawn and Decline. Notes 1926–1931 & 1950–1969*, trans. Michael Shaw (New York: Seabury Press, 1978), 239.

30. See Jürgen Habermas, "Israel or Athens: Where does Anamnestic Reason Belong? Johannes Baptist Metz on Unity amidst Multicultural Plurality" and "A Conversation about God and the World: Interview with Eduardo Mendieta" both in Jürgen Habermas, *Religion and Rationality*, 129–138, 147–167, respectively.

31. I think that it is this kind of attitude that Jürgen Habermas sought to give expression in his speech for the acceptance of the Peace Prize, included in this volume as "Faith and Knowledge." Susan Buck-Morss has also developed this Cosmopolitan line, see *Thinking Past Terror: Islamism and Critical Theory on the Left* (London: Verso, 2003).

32. See Wayne Hudson's indispensable *The Marxist Philosophy of Ernst Bloch* (New York: St. Martin's Press, 1982), 4–19.

33. David Drew, "Introduction: From the other side: reflections on the Bloch centenary" in Ernst Bloch, *Essays on the Philosophy of Music*, trans. Peter Palmer (Cambridge: Cambridge University Press, 1985), xi–xlviii (citation at xli).

34. Theodor W. Adorno, *Minima Moralia*, 247.

35. David Kaufmann, "Correlations, Constellations and the Truth", see also David Kaufmann, "Thanks for the Memory: Bloch, Benjamin, and the Philosophy of History" in Jamie Owen Daniel and Tom Moylan, eds., *Not Yet: Reconsidering Ernst Bloch* (London: Verso, 1997), 15–32.

36. Jürgen Habermas, "Ernst Bloch: A Marxist Schelling (1960)" in *Philosophical-Political Profiles*, trans. Frederick Lawrence (Cambridge, MA: The MIT Press, 1983), 61–77. See also Joseph J. Godfrey, *A Philosophy of Human Hope* (Dordrecht/Boston/Lancaster: Martinus Nijhoff Publishers, 1987).

37. "Something's Missing: A Discussion between Ernst Bloch and Theodor W. Adorno on the Contradictions of Utopian Longing (1964)" in Ernst Bloch, *The Utopian Function of Art and Literature*, translated by Jack Zipes and Frank Mecklenburg (Cambridge, MA: The MIT Press, 1988), 1–17.

38. See Gerard Raulet, "Critique of Religion and Religion as Critique: The Secularized Hope of Ernst Bloch" in *New German Critique*, no. 9 (Autumn, 1976), 71–85.

39. On the break with Fromm, see Wiggershaus, *The Frankfurt School*, 265–273. See also the Editor's Afterword to Horkheimer and Adorno's *Dialectic of Enlightenment*, 229–231.
40. See Robert Hullot-Kentor, "Foreword: Critique of the Organic" in Theodor W. Adorno, *Kierkegaard: Construction of the Aesthetic*, trans. Robert Hullot-Kentor (Minneapolis: University of Minnesota Press, 1989), xi–xii.
41. In addition to Rudolf Seibert's already cited work, see the excellent introduction to a selection of Horkheimer's religious writings, Juan José Sanchez, "Religión como resistencia y solidaridad en el pensamiento tardio de Max Horkheimer" Max Horkheimer, *Anhelo de Justicia: Teoría crítica y religión*, ed. Juan José Sánchez (Madrid: Editorial Trotta, 2000), 11–48.
42. See the recent collection that makes evident the ways in which the Frankfurt School's analysis of religion has impacted German theology: Johann-Baptist Metz and Jürgen Moltmann, *Faith and the Future: Essays on Theology, Solidarity, and Modernity* (Maryknoll, NY: Orbis Books, 1995).
43. Helmut Peukert, *Science, Action, and Fundamental Theology: Toward a Theology of Communicative Action*, trans. James Bohman (Cambridge, MA: The MIT Press, 1984).
44. Prof. Habermas generously provided me with a manuscript that he had hoped to contribute, but he was unable to return to it for the time being. This manuscript takes the philosophical question of what religion can still say to us in an age of post-secularism. It many ways, it takes up where his "Faith and Knowledge" leave off.
45. See Giovanna Borradori, *Philosophy in a Time of Terror: Dialogues with Jürgen Habermas and Jacques Derrida* (Chicago: University of Chicago Press, 2003). See also the essays written during the early part of 2003 now collected in Max Pensky, ed. *Globalizing Critical Theory* (forthcoming).

I

Ernst Bloch

1
On the Original History
of the Third Reich

Ernst Bloch
Translated by Neville and Stephen Plaice

Nothing must bar this glance or make it blind itself. In the following there is mention of various old and peculiar elements.[1] There have been crooks at work, and how, but one must keep a close eye not only on the crook's fingers but also on that which he holds in them. Particularly if he has stolen it, if the soiled object was once in better hands. Hence there is no getting out of examining the concepts which the Nazi has both employed and purloined for the purpose of deception, but one to be ended. Führer, and above all Reich thus crop up, and if their meaning originally to be ended is investigated, they crop up in a different, more thoughtful way than has been customary of late. The material is still largely fresh, but that which blindness and crime have done with it is and had to become precisely all the more rotten. The somewhat dreamy essence of the matter was moreover often open to abuse. But even something beautiful and noble shines across from forgotten, unforgotten days, it is important to recall this.

After all, the Nazi did not even invent the song with which he seduces. Nor even the gunpowder with which he makes his fireworks, nor even the firm in whose name he deceives. The very term Third Reich has a long history, a genuinely revolutionary one. The Nazi was creative, so to speak, only in the embezzlement at all prices with which he employed revolutionary slogans to the opposite effect. With which—alongside the shabby nonsense of the backmost tables reserved for regulars—he used the dark lustre of old phrases and patinated the revolution which he claimed to be making. Such an old phrase is the Third Reich, sonorous through the very triple character alone ("as in a fairytale"), sonorous as the third coronation of Germany (after the Medieval Reich and

Bismarck's Reich). But in order that the revolutionary appearance did not come off badly, Moeller van den Bruck, the actual reviver of the term, added mystical traditions from very different "realms."[2] For in its original form the Third Reich had denoted the *social-revolutionary ideal dream of Christian heresy*: the dream of a Third Gospel and the world corresponding to it. The class struggles arising in the early Middle Ages found their first expression in hatred of the secularization of the Church. The more the situation of the peasants and ordinary urban citizens worsened, and the more visibly on the other hand mercantile capital and territorial princedom succeeded and the purely feudal empire, founded on economic modes of the past, disintegrated, the more powerfully the prophecy of a new, an "evangelical" age necessarily struck home; in the case of Münzer as a peasant—proletarian—petit-bourgeois battle-cry against increased exploitation, in the case of Luther, of course, as the ideology of the princes against central power and the Church. There were thus opposing interests which met in the mist of heresy; and yet alongside the cloud the left lacked the pillar of fire least of all; it was in the impetus and ideal of the revolutionary cause. The contents of modern socialism, of that in the process of being implemented, are no longer the theological ones, in class terms not even any longer the theologically disguised ones of those days. Nevertheless, socialism may pay respect to the dreams of its youth, it sheds their illusion but it fulfils their promises. Germany still heeds, as has been shown, the old dreams of saviour and Reich, even when they are advanced by deceivers, and it heeded them all the more seducibly when socialist propaganda was in many ways cold, schoolmasterish, and merely economistic. Two shining motifs aroused revolutionary consciousness from the twelfth to the sixteenth century: the motifs of saviour and simply of the Third, finally even of the Thousand-Year Reich, into which the saviour-liberator (mostly conceived as "emperor of the people") leads the way.

The Future Liberator

The poor help themselves only slowly and late. The wish for a *Führer* must be the oldest of all. It exists in the relationship between child and father and in the search of the young person if their father was a simpleton. Group animals have the strongest male at their head, hunting peoples who as yet know no division of labour whatsoever choose a chief. Moses represents the first image of the leader in the humanly splendid sense; he is at once a leader of the oppressed and one into the Promised Land. But even under very different circumstances the glances were directed forward and upward, often embellished what could be seen at the top. Alexander was already supposed to be a saviour, the lord of all-assembling peace. Augustus in particular was fêted as an emperor of peace, as the restorer of the Golden Age prophesied by the sibyl. The passage by Virgil, in the Fourth Eclogue, is well known, about the wonder boy who will shortly appear, who will lead up the happiness of primeval times after all the confusion in society and state. The Aeneid passed on this role of saviour to Augustus; later it was transferred to Trajan, Antoninus and other "good emperors." Social expectations of the fluctuating, landless masses of late Rome and the wishes of the upper strata for undisturbed tranquillity were almost indistinguishably muddled up in all this. Besides, the expectation of the wonder boy saviour is also very old and was inserted into dynastic dreams of salvation very early on; it captivated with its touching, gentle manner, moving in general human terms so to speak. The Egypt of the Middle Kingdom first augmented the oriental prophecy of a redeemer king with the image of smallness, indeed of the crib, with the idea of the divinely miraculous birth of the beneficent child Horus (cf. Eduard Norden, Die Geburt des Kindes (1924), p. 73f.). It was the same legend which was afterwards transferred to Jesus, this time with a distinctly proletarian and by no means patrician expectation of salvation; the image of Christ which was precisely supposed to keep the slaves up to scratch, although intimated in the Sermon on the Mount, was only formed in the Roman Imperial Church. On the whole, Jesus the saviour was merely supposed to redeem inwardly of course, only as the Paraclete, at the end of time, did he serve up his visible kingdom.[3] Thus earthly misery and real disorder were preserved, and thus the expectation of salvation of an earthly kind was also naturally prolonged, the prospect not of a distant Paraclete but of a near incarnate saviour, as invoked by Virgil; and the sibylline imperial legend continued in Byzantium. The more rotten the internal situation was there (burden of debt on the populace, palace revolutions), and the more menacing the external one (Arabs, Bulgars, Turks), the more promising the painted prospects seemed of earthly glad tidings alongside the heavenly ones. Such a book of consolation emerged towards the end of the seventh century in the prophecies of Methodius; at the same time the imperial legend here assumed a strange shape. For a death motif was mixed in with it in secular terms for the first time, and Methodius prophesies: a great powerful emperor will arise, "like a man awakening from sleep, people have looked upon him as a corpse." Alexander is probably meant here, who is introduced as the grandson of an Ethiopian king and rises from the dead from the direction of Ethiopia; before the end of the world (conceived to be near) he returns as emperor of the Greeks and Romans in power and glory. The ancient motif of the dying god of vegetation who rises from the dead in the spring, which had already been adapted to the death of Jesus, on Good Friday and Ascension Day, sees itself secularized here, is needed once again in this world. This change had a powerful influence on the later Kyffhäuser legend,[4] but besides this Byzantium transmitted another, totally magical saviour motif into the German imagination. It is contained in the legend of the so-called Prester John, and India is the setting, the magic land with its garden of paradise, its miraculous stones, its prophesying trees and the like. In deepest India lives the entranced priestly king (now Daniel, now John the Baptist, the Evangelist, the Divine all in one), the ten lost tribes of Israel are with him awaiting their hour, he possesses miracle-working stones which make him invisible, and other supernatural powers of his own. Undoubtedly the image of a yogi or mahatma is discernible here; but the Novum of the legend is the fact that his magical powers, which are indeed in a remote trance beyond the world, are supposed to stand in the service of Christian justice. Prester John, as a saviour from the East, was later even suspected to be in the army of the Turks by German peasants; as the most secret governor of Christ so to speak, as the messianic emperor abroad. The authentic dream of the leader now became more historical of course, namely referring to people who really existed or had really existed, the *imperial legend of the Middle Ages* which had become dynastic again, the Charlemagne legend of France, the German one about Friedrich II and his return. The Byzantine prophecy of Methodius is recalled (it was circulating in numerous copies) and its strange corpse-motif. It was precisely this which presented itself when the demonic Staufer[5] had died: Friedrich II, the dreamed-of and feared scourge of the Church, the rationalistic-imperialistic originator of the phrase about the "three deceivers" (Moses, Mohammed, Jesus), the Antichrist towards whom so many apocalyptic thoughts were directed precisely for this reason, Friedrich II was not able or allowed to remain dead, his work was undone, his sign unfulfilled, and only in his name—according to the prophecies of the Methodius-prophets of the time—could it be fulfilled. Such a new (very much higher) Methodius shortly before Friedrich was in fact the abbot Joachim of Fiore: his school as well as other widespread prophecies saw in the emperor the sign of social-chiliastic change. The emperor was not allowed to remain dead for the excited imagination, he admittedly had not gone to heaven, certainly not, but no more had he gone to hell, to no (transcendental) place whatsoever from where there is no return. But the legend transported the emperor into a mountain, first into Etna (perhaps Sicilian memories of the Empedocles legend continued to have a haunting effect here), then, proceeding northwards, into the Kyffhäuser. Ancient, chthonic images were associated with this figurative grave: in pre-Christian times a mountain cult was at home on the Kyffhäuser, and the mountain god was a subterranean one, lived in the caves of the interior among mysterious treasures. Friedrich II took his place and only much later did the heretical emperor change places with Friedrich I Barbarossa, the pious, insignificant ruler, the romantic epitome of banal imperial glory in the style of Wilhelm "the Great"[6] (whose monument now stands there). Meanwhile even the perverted legend has preserved its original social-chiliastic trend in the fact that the emperor always only appears to simple people of the populace. Just as it is associated with the old motif that the messianic emperor, when he has humbled the powers of social and religious deprivation, humbles himself, abdicates, marches to Golgotha and lays down his crown, sceptre and sword there (cf.

Kampers, *Die deutsche Kaiseridee in Prophetie und Sage* (1895), p. 104). Like Friedrich II, the Emperor Charlemagne is also dreaming, in the Untersberg;[7] indeed wherever the work of a supposed saviour appears not to be done or not to be completely done, popular belief has made of the dead saviour a merely vanished one, one of the Seven Sleepers[8] who is waiting for his day. Even today the motif of disappointment itself is so little extinct that the death of no vitality is willingly believed which has gripped the imagination. The content of the old sibylline saying, "vivit, non vivit," is revived afresh again and again in folklore. Even the death of such modern figures as Napoleon and also Ludwig II has not been willingly admitted by an unsatiated Fama:[9] for Fama, Napoleon lived on in the mask of a Turkish general around 1822 who attacked the English with amazing success, and a Bavarian peasant legend claims that Ludwig II fled to America and will return with a beautiful woman when his Bavarian nation is worst off. The motif of the Seven Sleepers is admittedly replaced in the case of Napoleon by the enlightened ruse of an apparent death and an escape, the Kyffhäuser has become St. Helena (as previously, with more justification, it had become Elba), but the pathos of return is not lacking and in the case of Ludwig II not even the pathos of the pupated saviour. All this indicates how extraordinarily firmly rooted the prototype of a saviour is, a revival of radiant figures of the past, or at least a revival of radiant times of the past by a new restorer. Here we also find those mounted messengers of the king who in the *Threepenny Opera*[10] are made to appear at the last moment and to change everything; whereby it by no means merely satirizes the cheap solutions of the old opera or of colportage. The fact that the mounted messengers very seldom arrive and the *deus ex machina* even more seldom, such a failure, as the Hitler effect in particular has just proved, does not cancel out the old outlook. Indeed even the actual archaic myth of resurrection lives on, even though in a very weakened, analogous, historically misrepresentative form. None other than Napoleon decorated himself as a returned Charlemagne, while Hitler (if it is at all possible to mention him in the same breath) marches to the grave of Henry the Lion[11] and thereby awakens associations for a future "incarnation." There is no doubt at least that in the case of the Nazi it was intended from the beginning to replace the embarrassed title of Führer with the title of emperor of the people on a tolerably triumphant occasion; though such an occasion will not arise any more. But the old vision of the saviour, which had gone to the dogs, was nevertheless a great help to the Nazi, and even more so the decisive vision in whose service it stood: precisely that of the *Third Reich*.

The Gospel of this World

People have mostly seen happiness in the place where they are not. Eating, living, loving are the simplest places, this is little changed. Since classes arose, two different kinds of people, this happiness has atrophied or even disappeared for the exploited kind. Where much is lacking, there are many wishes, there is much intoxication in wishful images, particularly in religious ones. But here there is intoxication in a double form: one consoling over the misery, one all the more roused against it. Thus we find defusing religions, which console with the other world or even with the flight into inwardness; Christianity has accomplished much with both. But if the other world seeks to plunge to earth and inwardness into outwardness, instead of opium an unparalleled explosive then of course arises in the subjective factor, a will towards heaven on earth. This volition also existed in Christianity, existed in the medieval prophecies of the above-mentioned abbot Joachim of Fiore, who proclaimed a third Testament or the due cash payment of the second one towards the end of the twelfth century. The point does not need to be laboured here that the thus produced revolutionary intoxication was abstract and mythological; that it had no eye to reality and was incapable of doing so; that it set in motion merely the subjective will to change the world, but not any concrete method for this change. However, the will itself was thorough enough, the dream of the Third Reich ardent and stimulating right down to the Hussite movement, right down to the Peasant Wars. It is not unimportant to descend into the cellar of this so infernally abused term; it is, after all, originally anything but a torture chamber (it contains rather too many charges of love than too few). In fact the foundations of this dream stretch down to *Origen*, to his doctrine of the three possible ways of interpreting the Christian records; a physical one, a mental one, a spiritual one. The physical interpretation is the literal one, the mental interpretation the moral-allegorical one, but the spiritual interpretation reveals from the veils of the Scriptures the "eternal gospel" intended within them. In purely contemplative form the doctrine of the three cognitive levels recurs in the twelfth century with *Richard and Hugh of St. Victor*, the contemporaries of Joachim, the great psychologists of inner meaning. Here the carnal interpretation appears as *cogitatio* or grasping of the bodily world, the mental one as *meditatio* or grasping of inwardness, the spiritual one as *contemplatio* or elevation to the *visio beatifica Dei*, indeed to the deification of man. The Victorines thus provided a salvation-based view of history through and through, a mystical novel of development[12] of stages and realms—it could almost be said, a first Phenomenology of Mind;[13] but the sequence of stages remained one of the mere individual. And the final stage did not lie ahead, for instance, the final realm was not in the process of utopian birth, but was present at all times in finished form together with its object. *Joachim of Fiore* himself probably knew the Victorines and used both them and Origen as his starting-point; but he splendidly abandoned the mere inwardness of both. He was the first to transform the trinity of standpoints from an individual-pedagogical sequence into one of progressive, unfinished humanity. What was in mysticism a graduated development of the soul, a coherent passing from one mental condition into the other, is projected by Joachim on to the whole process of humanity; there thus appears a graduated development of *history* through the degrees of spiritual perfection; and these degrees are not attainable by individual human beings, but only by whole ages in each case (cf. Grundmann, *Studien über Joachim von Floris* (1927), p. 131f.). Joachim was the first to voice this assertion, although later supporters of his doctrine also cite as a witness one of his contemporaries, the great pantheistic materialist Amalrich of Bena (*c.* 1200). Amalrich too is supposed to have specified the degrees of illumination not as individually attainable, but as historical: the Father became man through Abraham, and revealed himself in the Old Testament, the Son became man through Christ, and revealed himself through the New Testament, but now the age of the spirit was imminent, and the Christian sacrament had to disappear just as the Jewish law had disappeared. But whether Amalrich really taught this historical sequence cannot be determined from the surviving sources. The doctrine does not tally with Amalrich's anti-Christian pathos either, which must have seen in law and sacrament no preliminary stages of itself, but only lies. Thus the doctrine of deadlines authentically emanates only from Joachim, and with his name, above all from his work, it has influenced the future. Hence the light glows up three times, and it burns ever more precisely. Whereby Joachim's doctrine of the third status, the third kingdom is this: the first age was that of the servitude of the law, that of the Father and his Old Testament, of the laity and the married. The second age is an intermediate condition between flesh and spirit, it is initiated by the Son and his New Testament, is governed by the Church and its clerics. But the third age, which precedes the end of the world, is now in the process of being born; it is inhabited by monks, that is, by the viri spirituales, by the "freedom of the spirit." The letter of the gospel of Christ with its Church and its clerics will pass away, the early Christian community descends from heaven to earth, a communist brotherhood and realm of peace begin. The first age was that of "fear and narration," the second that of "research and wisdom," but the third will be that of "love and illumination," of the total Pentecost, of the "pouring out of the Holy Spirit." The first age lay in the night of the stars, the second in the red dawn, the third will be the full daylight, with the Holy Spirit not from the viewpoint of God the Father but that of the Son of Man (Joachim, *Concordia 5*, chapter 77). Strange as these categories may sound to the modern revolutionary (even more surprising than the recollected imperial birthday celebrations of the previous section), we equally must not allow ourselves to be thereby deterred from noticing and honouring the hunger for happiness and freedom, the images of freedom on the part of people deprived of their rights, in these dreams. Socialism has a fantastically splendid tradition; if at such early stages, as goes without saying, it lacks any kind of economic view, it certainly does not lack one of its other essential features; humaneness and the Advent view connected with it. The

sentence, "They deck the altars, and the poor man walks in bitter hunger," is
Joachite; the rejection of the "fear of the Lord" is Joachite. Even the coming
"age of the monks" is conceived less as an ascetic one than as a propertyless and
brotherly one, as general monastic and consumer communism. Indeed, the
monastic prophecies were so tinged with the this-worldly lustre of a "Thousand-
Year Kingdom" in Joachim's school (he had founded an order of his own) that
precisely the spiritual strictness became one of the zest for life and seized the
whole body. In this spirit Telesphorus of Cosenza proclaimed at the end of the
fourteenth century that God had become man so that the whole man should
become happy in himself, and not just the inner one, but "all the eyes, ears,
mouths, hands, feet, livers, kidneys," in short, the age of perfection was also to
give birth to all earthly happiness along with the sacred kind. The Joachite hymn
in Telesphorus thus sounds much more earthly than the Franciscan prayer to
brother sun: "O vita vitalis, dulcis et amabilis, semper memorabilis," "O lively
life, sweet and lovable, always memorable." If this song prophetically graced
the cradle[14] of the Joachite movement only latently so to speak, then at least the
nearness to a new earthly-sacred intertwining and career of happiness is already
completely manifest in Joachim: the path from the *servitus legis* to the *libertas
amicorum* occurs in this world. This is the actual boldness of Joachim: he directed the glances fixed on the other world towards a future period on earth,
and expected his ideal not in heaven but on earth. He proclaimed the freedom
of the new *viri spirituales* not as freedom from the world but for a new world,
and if he placed the earth under strict Christlike demands, if he broke through
the lax two-worlds doctrine of an even more lax Catholicism, if he did not
know religious-indifferent culture in the Third Kingdom and already did not
acknowledge it in the second, then it was only so that the other world should be
consumed and the word of love should already become flesh here below: the
kingdom of Christ is of this world, *as soon as this world has become a new one.*
This is the continuingly influential boldness of Joachim, continuingly influential in revolutionary terms down to the Peasant Wars, and the substance of his
world of ideas. Whereby it should be mentioned that Joachim satisfied even
the highest poetic judge of his age: Dante promotes him, the "prophetic spirit,"
to the solar sphere of paradise, to join the saints of knowledge (*Paradiso*, XII,
140f.). But Joachim restructured not only the mystical graduated doctrine of
knowledge but also its final content in such a way that the latter is stored in an
immanent image of history with a this-worldly, or at least descending heaven,
instead of in the relationship between this world and the other world. The "spiritualism" deriving from Joachim had just as revolutionizing an effect in its day,
i.e., the interpretation of the Bible (of the letter) in accordance with the "inwardly driving spirit." *Nemo audit verbum nisi spiritu intus docente*[15]—this
orthodox principle was already so overdone by the Joachites, as the first "enthusiasts," that the Scriptures, indeed everything outward and traditional in

general, were consigned to the interpretative arbitrariness of the "inner word." Whereas the arbitrariness of the inner word was in reality no such thing at all, but the spirit which illuminated, just like the spirit which drove, was *exclusively orientated towards the impetus and the wishful content of revolution* for the spiritualists of the time. Just as the *viri spirituales* were conceived as citizens of a communist age, so the inner word was "David's key" to unlock "the revelation of the freedom of the children of God" in the Bible and to bar all hindrances to this revelation. After all, from an economic standpoint, Christianity differs from all other religions in the fact that it began as an ideology of the oppressed; this rebellious beginning, despite its immediate deflection (into the inner world), and despite its later concealment and inversion by the Church, never completely vanished from the world. So that even Joachim's idea of the third age and realm lived on unperverted among the heretics, indeed could even be cited by *Lessing* with direct recollection of the enthusiasts of the thirteenth century. Lessing's "Education of the Human Race" introduced precisely the Joachite doctrine of stages into the Enlightenment and its tolerance; the study of the "primer" of Christianity begins to be complete, a kind of meta-religion composed of reason begins. "Beware," Lessing thus warns, "you more capable individual stamping and glowing over the last page of this primer, beware of allowing your weaker schoolfellows to notice what you can scent or are already beginning to see . . . It will certainly come, the age of a new eternal gospel, which is promised to us even in the primers of the New Testament. Perhaps even certain enthusiasts of the thirteenth and fourteenth century had caught a ray of this new eternal gospel and were only mistaken in the fact that they proclaimed its outbreak to be so near. Perhaps their three ages of the world was not such an empty whim, and certainly they had no bad intentions when they taught that the New Testament would have to become just as antiquated as the Old one had become . . . It was only that they . . . were over-hasty, it was only that they thought they could make their contemporaries, who had still hardly outgrown their childhood, without enlightenment, without preparation, at once into men who would be worthy of their third age." We can see from these astonishing words that even the German Enlightenment, in its boldest and clearest mind, knew how to use the old threefold division, the "resolution" of Christianity in an almost Hegelian double meaning of the word: as a destruction and preservation at one and the same time. The patriarchal age was the caterpillar, the ecclesiastical age the chrysalis of reason, and now the bourgeois revolution hails itself as the butterfly. The graduated division of history in accordance with the Old and New Testament is certainly itself the most antiquated, it is the remotest one from the real historical sequence, as one of class societies; but the end itself, the third age, proposed the same humane condition in the mist and in generality, towards which the socialist revolution seeks to steer in sunshine and precision. Hence it is not surprising that the idea of the Third Kingdom—still so powerful in

Lessing—expires with the victory of the bourgeoisie or usually occurs only sporadically and without being understood. As in the case of Schelling in his late work, the often reactionary lectures on the "Philosophy of Revelation"; the Joachite tradition, still alive in Lessing, was here already so threadbare that merely the pattern but not the content of the sequence remains in the memory. Solely epochs of ecclesiastical history (and further of "potencies in God"), but not of overall human history, are divided into the three realms by Schelling. St. Peter or Catholicism are regarded as the realm of the Father, St. Paul or Protestantism as the subsequent realm of the Son, and St. John wrote his gospel for the spiritual church of the future (Schelling himself maintains in the lectures that he discovered the "harmony" of this purely theological, indeed gnostically interpreted sequence with Joachim of Fiore only later). It is thus amazing that the Third Reich appears in *Ibsen* again, in the youthful drama *Emperor and Galilean*, though this time connected afresh with a kind of humaneness, with a premonitory echo of the late-bourgeois "emancipation" in the Art Nouveau period. The symbolism of the "three cornerstones of necessity" is enacted here palely and yet whisperingly: the first is admittedly classical antiquity rather than the Old Testament, the second Christianity, the third the synthesis of both, the fusion of "beauty and truth." Emperor Julian is to bring it about, the Third Kingdom of "joyful noblemen" is to appear—a particularly troubling hope in view of contemporary Germany. In view of Streicher, the nobleman, Hitler, Göring, Goebbels or the synthesis of truth and beauty. But it should not be forgotten that the Nazis also received the term Third Reich from literature; not from Ibsen, but rather from Dostoevsky. Or rather from the racy masculine perfume which Moeller van den Bruck, the editor of the German Dostoevsky, bottled from the latter in a half tsarist, half prophetic way. Moeller calls his book simply "The Third Reich," it became a "major work" of Nazism and gripped the "elite of the movement" much more powerfully than Hitler's stylistic exercise and Rosenberg's compilation did. "Africa is darkening up"—this is Moeller's alleged fear; he plays off Prussia-Germany against this, and also the well-known "socialism in the Prussian style." The peculiar connection which Dostoevsky had established between his neo-Byzantine speculations and the "presence of the Holy Spirit" (both united in the "God-bearing Russian people")—this unparalleled anti-Voltaire world was transferred by Moeller to Germany, to the Germany of monopoly capitalism, of incipient crisis, of impending revolution. So the "Third Reich" came in time anew, but what a different one from that of Joachim and Lessing; blazing darkness fell on the land, a night full of blood and nothing but Satan. So this is what has become of the "reality" of the old dreams of love and spirit; Lessing's "rational gospel" on the one hand, Hitler's *Mein Kampf* on the other. Nazism has uniquely mobilized for itself both economic ignorance and the still active image of hope, chiliastic image in earlier revolutions. *Chiliasm* of course, this is the last catchword to be dealt with; the doctrine of the *Thousand-Year Reich* was, as Luther said, "the conjurer's hat of all troop-leaders." In Luther's time, of course, chiliasm was a battle song of the rebellious peasants, in the "Third Reich" which has arrived today it stupefies or stupefied—in totally polluted, perverted, betrayed form—the victims of reaction.

Chiliasm or the Earth as Paradise

The wish for happiness was never painted into an empty and completely new future. A better past was always to be restored too, though not a recent past, but that of a dreamed-after, more beautiful earlier age. And this golden age was not only to be renewed but also surpassed by an as yet nameless happiness. It seems reasonable to discern in these dreams of the golden age memories of the early commune, especially when remnants of it (like common land) or that which had not yet been lost for too long (like freedom of hunting and fishing) supported the revolutionary praise of primeval times. This was clearly the case during the Peasant Wars: the demand for the return of the old "communal freedom" counteracted the wishes of some groups to parcel out the land, and strengthened Münzer's slogan, *Omnia sint communia*. The image of the golden age naturally does not reproduce any real beginning of history, any prehistoric reality at all; if only because the early commune, with its undeveloped forces of production, could not have been that paradisal. But hope had its first portent, and also content, in the freedom, equality and fraternity of the original gentes. It overdid this with a backward-looking utopia, but it caused it to approach again from the future all the more, from the future of the restored paradise. It is precisely here that the myth of the *Thousand-Year Reich* begins, of a happy final age towards which history is striving, or rather; which history has in store for the "just." The myth itself stems from the interaction between economic and political misery and shining memories from a past which in fact—with utopian, and not merely romantic longing for happiness—was bent over into a final age that lay as near as possible. The ideas of prophetic Judaism based on an eschatology of salvation, before and particularly after the period of exile, must have first given birth to these historical utopias; from the Orient they travelled, long before the victory of Christianity, to imperial Rome and spread the hope of the returning golden aeon. As far as the more specific case of the Thousand-Year Reich is concerned, this *ancient background* of the Third one, its entire content stems from the prophecy of Isaiah, chapters 30, 55, and 60, its chronology from the book of Daniel, chapter 7, and the battle between night and light at its inception from the Revelation of St. John, chapters 20 and 21. Wild Persian dualisms let off steam in the description of the last days; the dragon, the old snake, is bound for a thousand years and sealed in the abyss, but the just will return from the dead and rule with Christ for a thousand years; this is the first resurrection. But when a thousand years are completed, Satan is unbound again, he lures the pagans, the peoples of Gog and Magog into the final dispute, a time of final suffering and confusion reigns until the fire of God falls from heaven on his enemies, Doomsday and the Last Judgement begin, hell is prepared for sinners and a new heaven and a new earth for the chosen; this is the second resurrection. The furious pedantry of these prophecies preoccupied all the revolutionary movements of Christendom, right up until the Enlightenment; even today it still circulates among the socalled Jehovah's Witnesses, among those banned by Hitler. If such nightmares of salvation are essentially noteworthy only in historical terms, this is not the case with the *content* of the final realm, particularly in the form imagined for it by Isaiah. For this content surprises, for all its extravagance, not only by its rational purity, but even more by its hedonism, not to say by its humane materialism. Compare the following sentences from the cited chapters of *Isaiah*, concerning the happy last days: "Then shall he give the rain of thy seed, that thou shalt sow the ground withal; and bread of the increase of the earth, and it shall be fat and plenteous: in that day shall thy cattle feed in large pastures (30, 23) . . . Ho, every one that thirsteth, come ye to the waters, and he that hath no money; come ye, buy, and eat; yea, come, *buy wine and milk without money and without price* (55, 1) . . . For brass I will bring gold, and for iron I will bring silver, and for wood brass, and for stones iron: I will also *make thy officers peace, and thine exactors righteousness* (60, 17) . . . A little one shall become a thousand, and a small one a strong nation" (60, 22). Thus far Isaiah, thus far the primitive-socialist content of the imagined covenant between God, man, beast and all existence. All later depictions of the millennium[16] in sectarian theology follow Isaiah. Long life is prophesied, sin and death are weakened, the body attains undreamt-of strength, the soil bears thousand-fold fruit, the desert is transformed into orchards, the whole of nature into a human house, godlike existence begins in innocence, peace and pervasive joy. Thus though the empty promises and passive fantasies are conspicuous here, the class-hostile heresy is also just as conspicuous in these constructs, or rather the standard it caused to be applied to the Christian Church, and even to the Christian state. Consequently the chiliastic hopes in this world were soon rejected by the official doctrine of the Church, most vigorously by *Augustine*: the fire was deadened, the standard desocialized. For according to Augustine the millennium already begins with Jesus; if a person professes faith in his Redeemer, this is already the first resurrection. The kingdom in which the just who have been resurrected reign with Christ is solely the ecclesiastical community of the faithful, the earthly City of God, the *civitas Dei terrena*. The second resurrection and the Last Judgement accordingly have no significance for the history of humanity, but only for the individual soul—the kingdom of God on earth is and remains the expanding Church. Augustine certainly put the state itself on trial, both as a Church thinker and as a philosopher of Christian inwardness; in the historical state structures, including Rome, Augustine perceives only a community of the damned, one divided by discord. Here alone is world history (namely gradually increasing separation between the realm of sinners and that of grace). Salvation history is not world history, however, but merely that of individuals, just as the future is solely the individual other world. Augustine had every reason for this dismissal of the millennium, for chiliasm certainly had not expired in the early Church. Even in the second century AD a "prophet" had appeared against the "secularized Church," the dervish *Montanus* had founded an early Christian community which, secluded from the world, was to prepare itself for the descent of the higher Jerusalem. In the third century restlessly strict Montanism began a triumphal march through the world; only towards the end of the fourth century was chiliasm ruled out; from then on it was universally regarded as heresy.

But precisely for this reason the dream banned by the Church particularly appealed to the rabble-rousers. It lured forward with double affinity, and the rejection by the masters attested it. But the fact that the fantasies of the millennium on earth, of the new Jerusalem, could not be eradicated despite the victory of the Church, and that they continually had an inflammatory effect in league with social deprivation, was proved much later, in social revolutionary epochs, by the Münster of the Anabaptists, and above all the Tabor of the Hussites. The Hussite movement marks the first heroic age of a communist (communist-spirited) revolution; at its ideological centre, however, stood chiliasm itself, as the teacher of a possible this-worldly character of the other world. Its Taborite preachers proclaimed, wholly in the style of Isaiah, the Zionist kingdom of freedom and equality for the "just," for those returning to the paradisal state of innocence. Only in this hope was Tabor founded—a New Jerusalem in which the Christian communism of love of the early Christian community was to be renewed: no castes, no domination, no private property, no taxes; a democratic community under God as the mystical king. The fact that the sectarian politics of these times brought absolutely no paradisal innocence but intergrated itself into manufacture, indeed supplied the ideology for the purest forms of capitalism (England, America), is well known. The materialistic logic of the forces of production at the time was stronger than the early Christian moral will and the apocalyptic-revolutionary melting-point in false consciousness. Nevertheless, the Hussite and Baptist movement would not have got off the ground at all if chiliasm had not kindled it ideologically; if it had not added to the revolution the apparently objective certainty on top of the subjective one. Chiliasm (as incidentally also the astrological prophecies at the end of the Middle Ages of a "necessary" change of times) represented at that time the science of revolution so to speak, namely its objectivity and inevitability; the times were experienced as not just subjectively but also objectively ripe for revolution, the revolution stood "at the hearing," the heavenly court-clock seemed to be striking its hour. It is impossible to overestimate the fostering of the will to rebellion by such reflections and anchorings of it, and this too is certain: it was not chiliasm which prevented the economic consciousness, and the concrete control of reality at that time. It certainly did not stand in the way of this consciousness (as a quack stands in the way of a doctor, for instance, and prevents his timely intervention), but rather, no economic consciousness existed at the time purely for economic reasons, and if chiliasm had not existed, no revolutionary consciousness would have existed either, and therefore no revolution whatsoever. And it was not because of chiliasm that this revolution perished or expired in the period of manufacture, and especially in Puritan captialism. But just the reverse: up to the French Revolution, if not longer, chiliasm—in rationalized form—incited broad masses not to put up with their current "fate," and to commit revolutionary acts for the "breakthrough of the kingdom." The slim or wholly lacking correspondence of these acts, and even goal-definitions, to reality is obvious of course, indeed it occasionally gives late chiliasms like those of Weitling,[17] and especially Fourier,[18] a curious aspect from the Marxist standpoint. Precisely because, in times for which economic consciousness had become possible, they treated both the present and the near future as blank areas or undiscovered tracts of land; because, instead of the lions with which the old cartographers had decorated their blank areas, they sketched in exuberant palm leaves or other abstractions of mere wishful imagination. Nevertheless, fantasy must not be allowed to conceal either the power of ancient dreams or the explosive force which—both for evil and for good— is still inherent in them. The explosive force existed wherever the promise did not have a quiescent effect, did not seem like internal-spiritual tinsel or even like contemplative fibbing, but provocative like a withheld good and illuminating like the Land of Cockaigne. Until, of course, a Pied Piper[19] appeared here as well, "at the twelfth hour," and is leading towards just as glorious times as his predecessor did, namely towards war. No swords are beaten by Hitler into pruning-hooks, no spears into ploughshares;[20] rather the reverse; instead, the new Thousand-Year Reich will last several hundred thousand years from the outset, allegedly without a Last Judgement. An enormous mouth, a mouth like a bowl of blood, drains the container of the entire future. Thus the Thousand-Year Reich is also realized in Germany just as splendidly as the messianic emperor, and the Third Reich. There is German socialism, practised by *viri spirituales* beyond compare; there are Reichsbank bills of exchange drawn on the third gospel, payable in the currency of the Kingdom of God.[21] "I will also make thy officers peace, and thine exactors righteousness"—but these words do not yet seem to have been completely fulfilled by the German super-race. And in other respects as well, Hitler's Third Reich has about as much similarity with that imagined by Joachim of Fiore as his socialism has with the realm of freedom.

Result for a Part of Concrete-Utopian Practice

Everything flows, but the river comes from a source every time. It takes matter with it from the regions through which it has run, this colours its waters for a long time. Equally for that new form there are remnants of an older one, there is no absolute cut between today and yesterday. There is no totally new work, least of all the revolutionary kind; the old work is merely continued more clearly, brought to success. The older paths and forms are not neglected with impunity, as has been shown. Dreams in particular, even the most wakeful ones, have a past history, and they carry it with them. Among backward strata these remnants are particularly strong and often totally musty, but even the revolutionary class honours its precursors and still heeds them. The old forms partly help, if correctly deployed, with the new.

The fact that they are extremely effective has been better noted by the enemy than by our friends. Some old material is due to be made our own again, the needs of the moment insist upon it. The soft arrogance with which a Kautsky[22] smiled and did nothing but smile at "heroes" or "little samples of apocalyptic mysticism" is at an end in theoretical and practical terms. Even such an apparently absurd and undemocratic structure as the old dream of the Führer (leaving the "revolutionary" imperial dream out of account) does not appear in practice—*mutatis mutandis*—to be quite so stupid. The revolutionary class and quite certainly those who are still undecided in revolutionary terms wish for a face at the top which will captivate them. A helmsman they trust and whose course they trust; the work on board ship is then made easier. The voyage is safer if everyone does not find it necessary to check the direction all the time. All this has been proven in practice, with the best democratic conscience; there must be a vanguard and a spearhead on the march. As long as the march is still theoretical, this does not become so apparent, but as soon as it is realized it does so at once. The *Communist Manifesto* still contains no mention of leaders, or only between the lines, in the given existence of its authors as it were, of those who issued it. But as soon as the *Manifesto* began to be realized, the name of Lenin flashed up alongside the founding fathers of Marxism, and the appearance of Dimitrov[23] in Leipzig was of greater help to the revolution than a thousand blatherers or speakers at meetings. Such human matters as revolution can hardly be implemented without visible human beings, without the image of real individuals (not idols). In the classless society this may and will be superfluous, indeed totally different.

The further dreams of olden times, those that are still misty, are not also the safest ones. After all, precisely the total opposite has set in in their name, the opposite not of the mist, but of the dream. But must the seed therefore be sacrificed with the husk, or is it not the case that even the seed of the dream, properly extricated, refutes the monstrous forgery which the Nazis have perpetrated by means of the misty husk? The question is practical and it arrives in time precisely under the banner of the incipient German popular front or, more specifically, of Christian anti-fascism within the popular front. Shortly before Hitler, a public discussion took place in Berlin, between the half- and high-class Nazi Hielscher, the Jesuit father Przywara,[24] and the Protestant theologian Dehn,[25] on the topic "Reich and Cross." Dehn (already persecuted by the Nazis at that time) declared on the basis of his Christian premises that the imperialist Nazi Reich "nowhere took into account the ideas of peace and justice"; indeed he played off the Communist doctrine against the barrenness of this concept of the Reich, in so far as in the former there were at least still echoes of expectations derived from salvation history. But the Nazi Reich was devoid of any human content, it came from the darkness of mere drives, from the cunning of mere capitalist interests which were making use of these drives, and would return into the darkness. Unlike the Communist idea of the Reich, it could not be substantiated by the "idea" of the classless society, which involved not least a topical transformation of early Christian and theologically heretical specifications. Thus far Dehn; thus far the neutralization, indeed possible sympathy of these men for Communism. However, his "early Christian definition" may be corrected and reprimanded, this is the most important point of contact between Christian and Communist anti-fascism. It is the function of Communist propaganda (or more precisely, of the traditional revolutionary company which it has to carry along with it) to look after things at this point and to correct the superstitious fear among the devout of the "movement of the godless." Without the problems of atheism even having to be touched upon, without the slightest embarrassment, let alone dishonesty, such propaganda has a place among members of the Confessional Church and humane Catholics. Many precursors of socialism were so from the standpoint of Christianity; this unites both, this is a common stretch of road at this time. And later times, in which previous religion will be stale, will more easily do justice to the source of power which flowed in the "freedom of the children of God" alongside all empty promises and ideologies of exploitation.

We have already touched on the question whether precisely the mist did not make the old dreams so useful to the Brownshirts. Economic ignorance has undoubtedly made their deception easier for the Nazis, and they have undoubtedly exploited the old dark words in a highly demagogic way. But much more important is the question whether this use, this abuse, did not succeed so easily precisely because the genuine revolutionaries did not keep a look-out here. Economic vagueness, petit-bourgeois mustiness and mystical mist certainly go splendidly together; one assists the other. But economic clarity and the critique of metaphysical appearance do not yet therefore need to disavow *a priori* the entire extent and content of the constituents described as irrational. This had a revolutionary point in Voltaire's times, but today, as the German effect has shown, it almost exclusively serves the forces of counter-revolution. There is also no realism at all in this mechanism of refusal; on the contrary, large strata of social, and indeed physical, reality are cordoned off by such mechanical banality. The times of this narrow-mindedness are over, the understanding and the application of Marxism are attaining ever more complete objectivity, ever greater width and depth. At the same time, however—and it is important to stress this here, on the very threshold—at the same time, however, the attained width and depth directs irrational overblownness much more thoroughly and knowledgeably than the pseudo-Enlightenment was ever able to do. Indeed, in the improbable event that mysticism should make up further ground as a result of this anti-banality, then the very knowledge of width and depth itself, as such, will move to the head of the opposition, the opposition against mysticism. For mystical banality is not a hair's breadth better, but rather a whole kitschy mane more objectionable, than the rationalist kind; mysticism is the ignorant caricature of depth, just as the pseudo-Enlightenment was the quarter-educated caricature of clarity. Reason is and remains the instrument of reality, though concrete-materialist reason of course, which *does justice to the whole of reality; consequently, also to its complicated and imaginative components.* Accordingly the right-minded therefore know that the difficult voyage of the world, that the many unresolved features of its past, that the horizons of its future which have not yet appeared—that all these constituent factors towards dialectical-real tendency represent no objectives of secondary modern school enlightenment any more than they do those of Martin Buber or Keyserling[26] mysticism. Thorough philosophical, i.e., truly Marxist, reason directs and corrects itself in the same act as its opposite: irresponsible windbaggery, mysticism. The Nazis thrived on the latter, but they were only able to deceive with it so undisturbed precisely because an all too abstract (namely backward) left undernourished the imagination of the masses. Because it almost surrendered the world of imagination, without regard to its highly different characters, methods and objects or, more pointedly, without proper differentiation between the mystic Eckhart and the "mystic" Hanussen[27] or Weissenberg.[28] But there is a lasting distinction between prophecy from tea-leaves and that other prophecy of Meister Eckhart, in the "Sermon on Birth," about the hidden glory of man: "I become aware of something in myself which shines in my reason; I certainly feel that it is something, but what it is I cannot grasp; only this much strikes me: if I could grasp it, I would know all of the truth." This is the same *human feeling of glory* which subsequently made Thomas Münzer, the disciple of Eckhart, Tauler,[29] and Suso,[30] into the ideologist of the Peasant Wars; which, beyond hunger and scurvy, aroused protest against the conditions in which man, in Marx's words, had become an oppressed, contemptible, lost being.[31] German mysticism of the Middle Ages, with its lay preaching, its practical Christianity, its thirst for the "revelation of the freedom of the children of God," stems from early revolutionary movements of the bourgeoisie. And the existing mist was not one of the *entire content*; this rather comprised goal-setting light, the same light which caused Münzer to state quite reciprocally, with a mutual functional harmony of his rebellion and his Christianity, in his "Highly Provoked Rebellion": "Just as Christendom has to be put straight in a quite different way, the profiteering villains must be removed." Thus the mist is certainly not everything in the old dreams (whether they be the political-chiliastic ones, or whether they be the only seemingly individual ones of mystical slave-smashing, Son-becoming, of charging with immanent glory). Hence, paradoxical as it may sound, a large part of revolutionary pride came into the world only through German mysticism, and Christian-humane utopia acted it out before it.

We must repeatedly distinguish between mist and light, of course, and the light also corrects itself. This is particularly true of the further sequence of utopian dreams, of the narrowing they underwent in the so-called fairytales of an ideal state of modern times. They extend from Thomas More to Weitling, only to expire seriously after Marx; science superseded them. Over half of this constructive form of utopia was subjective intellectual arrogance, undialectical postulation, mythological transference of an unconscious class-interest into the "last days" or into a "distant land" in general. But the impetus and the background of these constructs is here likewise something different from the husk in which they are cloaked. Hence as certainly as the defects of this abstract system exist, and as economically as socialism has progressed from this kind of utopia into a science, just as little must the core be confused with the husk here either, and just as little is it destroyed with it. Lenin even extricated a good core in the concept of *ideology*, a core without mist and deception, and he emphasized it when he called socialism the ideology of the working class. The rescue of the good core of *utopia* is equally overdue (as a concept which at the most lay in mist, never in deception); the *concrete-dialectical utopia of Marxism, that grasped and alive in real tendency*, is such a rescue. The undialectically attached dreaming was the mist of the matter, and in the mist lay—although with distinctions—all the wishful times and wishful spaces of the old utopia. The phantasmagorias which the longing for a better world projected into future times or distant islands or inaccessible valleys also mainly contained only the respective class-contents of the respectively oppressed class (even though transparent for classless premonitions in general). Most old utopias also stagnated in the reality given to them, they condensed only the torpor out of it as it were and distilled out the spirit, they recognized no *process* and no *totality* of renewal. The *concrete utopia of Marxism*, on the other hand, runs with the process of the forces of production towards the classless society per se in tendency. Thus Marxism, on most careful mediation with the material tendency, ventures forward into the not yet arrived, not yet realized. Even the happiness which has its career in Marxist terms is not that of an already existing and simply more plentifully allocated kind: like the "bliss" in the religious utopias, like the boredom of a permanent Sunday in the bourgeois ones. On the contrary, the Marxist hope is so productive even here that it does not embark on mere mythological transpositions of something already given, although something relatively better given. Marxism teaches that all previous happiness stands in the mere prehistory, or at best in the suggestion of the right thing; it keeps its this-world, its corporeal this-world, as one which is both open and still unfathomed. But precisely this is genuine utopia, and only this extracts lasting velleity and humane imagination from the fairytales of an ideal state, and particularly from the dreams of the Reich. Stands in the closest connection with everything which was contained in the old utopia in the way of genuineness, in the way of dreams which continue to fire with enthusiasm. Stands beyond the subjective postulate, beyond the mythological distant transposition of finished wishful contents. But the sphere itself is not absolutely different from that of Joachim of Fiore, nor is it absolutely deserted. In other words, the Marxist-directed work criticizes the *ideology* of uncomprehended *necessity* by comprehending and *destroying* it, but the *utopias* of uncomprehended *freedom* by comprehending and *fulfilling* them. The socialist revolution is distinguished from its predecessors by its scientific character and concreteness, by its proletarian mandate and classless goal, yet it is just as fundamentally connected with them through the fire and the humane content of the revolutionary impetus and intended realm of freedom. The so little realized dreams of this realm still intervene in the present so that they are concretely corrected and fulfilled.

Notes

1. In this section it must be borne in mind that Reich also has religious and mystical connotations of "kingdom" and "realm," as well as the political dynastic sense so familiar from the Nazi collocation "Third Reich." The thousand-year "Reich" that Hitler promised was also semantically the traditional "millennium" prophesied for Christ's reign on earth in Revelations by St. John the Divine, and anticipated by many utopian movements and spiritual leaders in the Middle Ages.
2. "Reichen": see preceding note.
3. Reich: see preceding note.
4. See "Amusement Co., horror, Third Reich," n. 33 in E. Block, *Heritage of Our Times* (Cambridge, Polity Press, 1991) 56–63.
5. Member of the Hohenstaufen dynasty, named after the family seat at Hohenstaufen castle.
6. Bloch is alluding here to Kaiser Wilhelm I.
7. Untersberg: a mountain in the Berchtesgaden Alps near Salzburg. Hitler of course also built a retreat, Berghof, in these mountains.
8. Seven legendary Christians of Ephesus, who slept for two centuries after being incarcerated by a Roman Emperor.
9. "Fama": an allusion to the allegorical figure of Fame or Rumour.
10. Brecht's *Dreigroschenoper*, 1928.
11. Heinrich der Löwe, 1142–1180, Duke of Saxony and Bavaria, early champion of German expansion and founder of the cities of Lübeck and Munich.
12. "Entwicklungsroman": Bloch uses a German literary term here, a reference to a genre of novels tracing one person's central spiritual development.

13. Bloch has Hegel's famous work in mind here.
14. Bloch is using the phrase "an der Wiege gesungen," "sung at the cradle," literally and figuratively here. Its figurative meaning is "foreseen of somebody or something."
15. "Nobody hears the word unless with an inwardly teaching spirit."
16. "Des tausendjährigen Reiches"; "Millennium" and "Thousand-Year Reich" are the same in German. In certain, specifically non-Nazi contexts as here, we have chosen to translate it with the more usual "millennium."
17. Wilhelm Weitling, 1808–1871, early German socialist.
18. Charles Fourier, 1772–1837, French utopian socialist.
19. "Rattenfänger," literally "rat-catcher," can also mean "rabble-rouser" in a figurative sense. Both meanings are implied here.
20. cf.. Isaiah 2,4: "And they shall beat their swords into ploughshares, and their spears into pruning-hooks."
21. Bloch is punning here on the political and religious connotations of "Reichsbank" and "Reich Gottes."
22. Karl Kautsky, 1854–1938, socialist politician and theorist.
23. Georgi Dimitrov, 1882–1949, Bulgarian Communist, acquitted on the charge of arson (burning of the Reichstag in Berlin) in Leipzig in 1933; 1933–1943, General Secretary of the Comintern in Moscow; 1946–1949 Bulgarian Prime Minister.
24. Erich Przywara, 1889–1972, philosopher of religion, sought a synthesis of Thomism and modern philosophy.
25. Günther Karl Dehn, 1882–1970, Protestant theologian and early critic of the Nazis, and consequently relieved of his chair at Halle university in 1933.
26. Hermann Graf Keyserling, 1880–1946, mystical philosopher.
27. Jan Erik Hanussen, 1889–1933, notorious clairvoyant and charlatan in the twenties, whose prophecies were later exploited by the Nazis.
28. Joseph Weissenberg, 1855–1941, occultist and mystic healer, founder of various minor religious sects.
29. Johann Tauler, c. 1300–1361, Dominican monk and mystic.
30. Heinrich Suso, 1295–1366, mystic, pupil of Meister Eckhart.
31. An allusion to a favourite quotation of Bloch's from Marx's *Einleitung zur Kritik der Hegelschen Rechtsphilosophie*.

2
Not Hades,
But Heaven on Earth

Ernst Bloch
Translated by Neville and Stephen Plaice

Every Now is already differently there tomorrow. It is even possible that misery subsides a little. Then a lot of ordinary people stop running with the pack. They return to that centre which can be one for them anew. The mere shallow yesterday which they are and have intended begins again.

But this calm, if it comes, hardly lasts for a long time. The recuperation is likely to be short, and certainly no longer as unquestionable as the earlier ones. A sting is left behind, both of insecurity and of former baiting and degeneration. What is now already clearly changing is also less the misery than the trust in Hitler. His enormous credit is slowly crumbling away, creditors and the credulous are grumbling, the payday has been missed too often. Perhaps "disillusioned" SA proletarians and also younger sections of a proletarianized and utopianized petite bourgeoisie are becoming ripe for Communism. But the non-contemporaneous contents of this stratum, which have been indicated here, have thereby not yet become inoperative themselves, of course.

Against these the red remedy is only halfway effective, or mostly not at all as yet. Nazis speak deceitfully, but to people, the Communists quite truly, but only of things. The Communists often also flog slogans to death, but many from which the alcohol has long since disappeared and which are merely schematic. Or they bring their most correct figures, examinations and registered entries to those who are stultified with nothing but figures, registered entries, office and dry work all day long, and are thus subjectively weary of the entire "business world." Here linguistic and propagandist reform are the needs of the moment:

41

of the head which must not be allowed to become stuffed with nonsense or fossilized, of the limbs by means of which the revolt also progresses among employees and the non-contemporaneous. Even an expectable turning towards Communism will long be a negative one, a mere disillusionment with Hitler; this alone does not yet secure the new loyalty. For will slogans which were *too weak* to penetrate the National Socialist front be *sufficient to embrace* the *deserters?* In the country there are as yet no grain factories, in the town the middle classes are admittedly proletarianized but far from being proletarian. They are proletarian neither in their economic being nor even in their consciousness, do not speak the language of the proletarians, have non-contemporaneous memories or seek them, and not totally empty ones. But freethinking vulgar Marxism seems to lie under a curse of virtually confirming the hatred of reason among those who are proletarianized (as if all reason resembled the halved capitalist kind of today). In a time and a country where capitalism, with its poor rationalization, has also discredited the Ratio for "broad circles," the separate emotional values of Communism are hardly sufficiently stressed, and nobody points towards the genuine and full, the concrete Ratio; as the liberation from the economic system, as the means precisely towards the humanization and totalization of existence. Dialectical materialism is not separated comprehensibly enough from the miserable "materialism" of the industrialists; the fact is hardly sufficiently stressed that Communist materialism is not an attitude but a doctrine, that it is not a total economy over again, but precisely the lever to place the controlled economy at the periphery and human beings at the centre for the first time. Instead, much vulgar Marxism almost supports the caricature which irrational minds have drawn of "mechanical" reason. But the times are so strange that the revolution cannot directly intervene in impoverishment, but—among the proletarianized—only in emotional and irrational contents, not just in claptrap and ignorance but also in intoxications and "ideals" which contradict misery in a non-contemporaneous way. If some of these contents have already been meddled with in an imitative fashion (which, with regard to nationalism for instance, Hitler the original can do better), the next step is none other than dialectical mobilization, as a grasping of the dialectical hook which all these ambiguously contradictory resources contain. There will be no successful attack on the irrational front without dialectical intervention, no rationalization and conquest of these areas without its own "theology," adjusted to the always still irrational revolutionary content. It is necessary that Marxism should no longer be misunderstood as the other side of "empty mechanics," that it should irradiate those depths of revolutionary content within it which it abandons to its enemies for deception, to non-contemporaneous elements for exploitation, although it has its origin in them itself and alone. This situation even has its "Teutonic" parallel or, in the face of the Nazis, the following comparison: when the Teutons once migrated south and west, the Slavs streamed into the vacated, originally German regions; laboriously, say the Nazis, knights of various orders reconquered East Elbia. When scientific socialism incorporated France and England, i.e., the French Enlightenment, the English economy, but vulgar Marxism had forgotten the inheritance of the German Peasant Wars and of German philosophy, the Nazis streamed into the vacated, originally Münzerian regions; laboriously, peasant propaganda and deepened theory are reconquering the profusion. Expelling all mist, all "irratio" of merely false consciousness, all mythology; but the peasant is alive, even the pauperized petit bourgeois of today is to be taken very seriously, and most seriously of all the voice of the human What For (still beyond the next step). Marx writes at one point in "The Eighteenth *Brumaire*": "Through the discontented peasants starving to death on their parcel of land the proletarian revolution receives the chorus without which its solo in all peasant nations becomes a song of death"; this statement is of decisive importance even among petit bourgeois nations, especially among "irrationally" accustomed, "irrationally" starved ones. The primacy of the proletariat or of controlled contemporaneous contradictions also proves to be a critical-dialectical handling of non-contemporaneous ones.

Enlightenment and Dialectical Wisdom Together

The dust of what is old does not settle differently. It is repeatedly blown up where the New does not have the whole person. It therefore will not do to speak only ironically with often very cheap understanding where the dearest kind should at least be ready to be surprised. It will not do to write thick books about National Socialism, if after reading them the question as to what it is that is thus influencing many millions of people is even more obscure than before. The problem becomes all the greater the *more simply* the water-bright author has managed the water-clear solution; namely for his vulgar Marxist needs, which simplify everything for him just as their stupid enthusiasm does for the National Socialists. Even a critique which solely notes "barren clichés" in the "self-integration into the ancestral peasant blood kinship," in the "fanatical religious bond with the soil," abstractly cordons off dangerous depths of older ideology instead of dialectically analysing and practically grasping them. The creative form of Communism is instead, precisely with regard to such inequalities, *wisdom*, that dialectical wisdom which Russia displays in many respects. Which not without reason provokes such precise questions of larger dialectics as this: can the house which has become musty be dismantled in order to be used in a socially new way in individual components, that of the mother for instance? Or can the bond with the soil which has become mouldy be converted from an element of family egoism into solidarity and thereby into a new mainstay of the village commune? In order to lead contents through the great crisis to which circumstances have subjected them, their previous vehicles, applications and manifestations must of course have become alien; but what then appears is no Not-only-but-also of the social-democratic type (which almost consists of nothing but Not-only), but rather that centre of which Brecht says that it belongs to Communism, because it is the middle course: "Communism is not radical, it is capitalism that is radical." It is above all that centre which abandons convictions in the face of wisdom, in short, which recognizes no abstract principles when new contents press forward, but which recognizes only one *content* as the sole "principle" itself, namely the production of conditions for the victory of the proletariat, for bringing about the classless society. But until then the unrest cannot be observed separately enough which both causes to darken and itself darkens today. The "diversion" had only fished in shining troubled waters, but the "intoxication" fishes in chaotic ones, which are much more ambiguous and more charged at the same time. Or as far as the dust is concerned, Lützow's[1] hunt disturbs it all the more, but not in fact as the sparkling, interrupting dust of diversion, but as veiling and excessive outburst at the same time, as *dust to the power of three* as it were. But at the same time that kind of enlightenment is thereby called into question anew which once had its revolutionary locus, whereas today, with its principles, it misses the new locus. In the second half of the nineteenth century mechanical materialism, at least in Germany, still had a certain revolutionary role against the nobility, against the Church allied with it, and even against the great bourgeois and his ledger "with God"; thus Marx could leave the broad "metaphysical" legacies of the dialectical method—not that they were lacking—*implicit*. Whereas today, when precisely the main upper middle-class opponents of revolution are "materialistic," when no financial backer of the National Socialists can be surpassed in any way in cynical freethinking or even fears it as a weapon, it is precisely the "irrational" which not least grounds their contradiction for susceptible peasants and petit bourgeois—and ideologically prevents their contact with Marxism. The proletarian-Marxist avant-garde has a "faith" which was never more real, but the petit bourgeois, however impoverished he is does not heed it. Instead, just as they have stolen the red flag, the first of May, and finally even the hammer and sickle, stolen and perverted them for the purpose of forgery, the Nazis have also particularly known how to make use of the less manifest symbols of revolution for their own ends. It is not as if philosophy "missed" something in socialism or wished to "improve" it with contents which did not grow in the soil of the historically decisive class; as a Marburgizing[2] of the irrational so to speak. But rather this is the basic question recurring from all sides: whether the less manifest symbols and contents of revolution with which the Nazi goes crabbing among the petite bourgeoisie were not simply able to serve to deceive so easily because they were still too little highlighted by propaganda, because the *well-exposed* backgrounds of Marxism have been still too little *developed* and made into prints. It thus becomes a concrete task to *show* the *mediated* transcending (repeat: transcending) in Marxism *urbi et orbi* as well; it becomes a duty also to make public and explicit its ultraviolet, the future "transcendence," mediated in dialectical materialism, which Marxism implicitly contains, for the purpose of occupying and rationalizing the irrational movements and contents. For the Marxist world in which it is possible to think and act concretely is least of all mechanistic, in the sense of bourgeois bigotry, least of all fact- and law-based in the sense of mechanical materialism. But rather it is a movement in which human work can be deposited, and then a process of helpful contradictions, towards a dawning, arch-human goal: it is working, dialectical, hoping, inheriting per se. To forget nothing, to transform everything, both powers fall due here. Charon, of course, does not ferry whole figures but merely *shades* across the river; but it is Charon. *Socialism does not want Hades, however, but heaven on earth*; it thus ferries across the entire substance of history, in its both corrected and transfigured body. All the bourgeois-feudal share in ideologies is unmasked by *dialectical* materialism, but the undischarged and "cultural" remnant, as substance with reluctance, is inherited by it.

Examples of Transformation

If we look back, three trends[3] ran crosswise in the Now. They bear *early*, or at least earlier banners and symbols, those which contradict. *Youth* longs for discipline and a leader, the *peasantry* takes root in soil and homeland more strongly than ever, and the impoverished *urban centre* seeks to spare itself the class struggle through the corporate state, installs Germany—a blood-based, aryanized one, not the present one—as a gospel. These three discontented groups bear all the non-contemporaneous contents of today; and they bear them towards the right. For capital, of course, it is ultimately extrinsic whether parliaments or generals "rule," whether the Republic or the Third Reich provides the backdrop of true power. There is no doubt here that from a contemporaneous-material viewpoint there is nothing in National "Socialism" but "anti-capitalist" demagogy of total mendacity and insubstantiality; the sole *contemporaneous* content of Hitlerism is control of big business through increased pressure and romantic illusions. But the *seducibility* through these very illusions, the *material* of this seducibility still lies in a different region; here class contents of non-contemporaneous impoverishment are in mere service and predominant abuse by big business. It is thus only partly correct when Lukács writes: "Fascism as the collective ideology of the bourgeoisie of the post-war period inherits all tendencies of the imperialistic epoch in so far as decadent-parasitic features are expressed in them; yet all mock-revolutionary and sham opposition elements also belong here. Admittedly this inheriting is a restructuring, a rebuilding at the same time: that which was merely shaky or confused in earlier imperialistic ideologies is transformed into the openly reactionary.

But whoever gives his little finger to the devil of imperialistic parasitism—and everyone does this who falls in with the pseudo-critical, abstractly distorting, mythicizing character of the imperialistic sham oppositions—will find he takes his whole hand" ("Greatness and Decline of Expressionism," 1934[1]). This turning away, this *a priori* ready-made analysis of an otherwise so significant thinker admittedly has the advantage of decidedly circling above its subjects and not proffering the littlest finger to them, but it brings nothing home either; it does not blur the difference between petit-bourgeois romantic and proletarian concrete opposition by means of any gangplank, but it does not construct any boarding-plank either. A *non-contemporaneously revolutionary* opposition nevertheless exists, that genuine stock of "irrational" contents as well, which, if it currently hinders contact with the revolution, indeed will remain a restorational danger zone for a long time to come, may still equally remain unfavourable to capitalism in the long run. Much ignorance will disappear when the fascist deception has come to light cash down; many class-based and more genuine non-contemporaneities will balance themselves out in the *process* of revolution. And just as it is not up to theory to make demands instead of seeing the concrete possibilities of the tendency, it would be foolish to set an invariably idealistic programme *in extenso* for the dialecticization of non-contemporaneous contradictions. In this respect even the entire orientation attempted here had to appear "abstract," so to speak, precisely because it is not so, because it avoided rashly concretizing from abstractions. However, it would be just as wrong to prevent the existing possibilities of the "auxiliary troop" artificially; even more wrong to find merely blind alleys in the "Irratio," instead of those explosive aspects of hope which were never alien to the economic revolutionary impetus and ought not to be artificially strangulated. How differently young student fraternity members[4] embarked on their early enthusiasm, how similarly others push forward to poor peasants and their ancient language. How differently Lenin's Russia already fitted in *homeland* and *folklore* (the early communist gentes shine through); not just in bourgeois conformist or affixed terms, the organic forces of the *family* and the organic-historically remaining ones of the *nation* appear here refunctioned and placed in the service of a *national community*, but a genuine one. How concretely even the fight against "religion" wrenches from the latter its *longings* and *symbolic powers*, not just, as the Russians still have to agitate, "in order to abolish heaven" (capitalism managed this both here and there), but in order finally to "establish it as the truth of this world." The path of inheritance continues, for there are—as not only fascism shows—many ruins of Rome which are or remain none. After all, the geometry of the non-contemporaneous is so strange that even the Third Reich of the National Socialists is equally smaller and larger than itself; by both and only by both together, by the analysis of deception and by the extrication of the appearance of substance, it will be destroyed in the long run, without new masks, without pseudomorphoses. History is not merely spectres and a rubbish heap, nor merely chaff, and all the corn is already removed at the last stage, on the last threshing floor in each case: but precisely because so much of the past has not yet come to an end, the latter also clatters through the early dawnings of newness. The German Walpurgis Night will disappear and come in no new year only when the first of May makes it completely light; and "Museums of the religious past" will really arise only when the genuine relics are removed from them. When they have to serve "heaven on earth" and keep alive the will towards it. In another space than that of opium fumes and not in no religion, but in a religion without lies.

Notes

1. See "Rough night in town and country," n. 28, see E. Block, *Heritage of Our Times* (Cambridge, Polity Press, 1991), 48–55.
2. A reference to the neo-Kantian school of philosophy in Marburg in the late nineteenth century.
3. "Zug" also has the sense of "procession" here.
4. Reference to the progressive political dimension of original German student fraternities in the early nineteenth century.

3
Hunger, "Something in a Dream," "God of Hope," Thing-For-Us

Ernst Bloch
Translated by J. T. Swann

> Just as an elastic body contains its greater dimension only by striving after it, so a monad contains its future state . . . One can say that in the soul, as in everything else, the present is pregnant with the future.
>
> *Leibnitz, Letter to Bayle* (1702)

Man's whole *raison d'être*, the What-for of all life's work and, ultimately, of the life-force itself, can easily fall prey to fierce questioning when, despite a plentiful supply of daily bread, the other bread of life, the concrete "What" of What-for and Where-to, begins to dwindle.

These questions will not, of course, be raised in the slums and hovels of stifling poverty, nor, at the other end of the scale, in those quarters where the profit race (still largely based on a more or less exotic poverty) provides its own ready-made answers, and where life is led by the bourgeoisie who cannot in any case (according to Marx) see beyond the end of their corporate nose. Money makes for sensuality; cash can laugh.

The other hunger, the unassuaged, explosive hunger of the life-force, presents itself as the continual Not-yet of true human possession. It is an aspect of the quest for meaning, and, far from drugging the hunger for meaning (and with it the non-meaning of death) with any opium of the people in the form of dreamed-up compensation in another world, it fills it with the food of restless labor, working away, unswerving and incorrupt, to gain a true awareness and

49

genuine satisfaction of man's Utopian needs. Only in this way—not in the ideological apologias of any ruling class, nor in the remorseless morality and finality of the Utopia of missing expectations which echoes through the pages of a homeless, twisted history—only in this way can that other dream come into being: the radical, subversive dream of the Bible which, far from being rooted in a haze of opium, stems from a profound wakefulness to the future, to the great dimension of light with which the world is pregnant. This dream can make the future present even in the past. It harbors no crippling historicism and no over-abrupt Jacobinism, but simply the irrepressible sense of the awakening of meaning. In Marx's words: "It will then become evident that the world possesses something in a dream of which it need only become aware to possess it in truth" (*Letter to Ruge*, 1843).

The "something" in this dream, and the awareness which brings it to reality are, even in Marx, neither more nor less than the anticipated presence of the Kingdom of Freedom, kept alive in the hope of those who walk with the laborers and heavy-laden, the degraded and despised, and available only to those who can stand up on their own two feet. The "something in a dream" was, and is in its avowed utopianism, nothing to do with the acquisition of profits and the mis-appropriation of values which only laugh on one side of their face, nor with the subjectively lonely world of illusion, so alien to all ideas of tendency. The ultimate concrete awareness of all true hunger, and its concrete activity, is directed towards possession of this "something" in its Not-yet-being. But the really paradoxical element in all this is that Utopia does not end with its final, concrete realization—it begins there. That is the meaning of Marx's words. For the "something in a dream" is, after all, *rebus fluentibus*, in some way an *objective, concrete "something"*; it is something in a state of process, something *still pending in latent hope*, drawn on to its vanishing point in the perspective of meaning, drawn to the gravitational center of an as yet unrealized At-all, which men used to call God; but which a-theism sees as the Utopian Omega of the fulfilled Moment, the Eschaton of our immanence, the illumination of our incognito.

The forward-look has replaced the upward-look. Feelings of humility and obeisance vis-à-vis the prince and lord are no more than a memory, as are prayers of supplication and all the rest of the baptized beggary. Even the Bible's ownmost emotion of hope is unworthy of us whenever it makes man a servile retainer, waiting only for manna from on high. Hope cannot at the same time raise itself from the ground in a transcending sweep and bow down humbly to take alms, conscious only of the so-called Fall behind it as the symbol of human nullity, and of the imperious, unmerited (if you follow Luther) realm of grace above it. Where there is hope there is religion, but where there is religion there is not always hope: not the hope built up from beneath, undisturbed by ideology.

What then is the goal of this hope? It is not only the theocratic sections of the Bible that give the ever-open reply to those whose nature is pure enough to receive it: "and everlasting joy will dwell upon them"—the unveiled light of Utopian joy, the light of man, welling up *de profundis*, from his depths, not his lowliness. It is the final apocalyptic result of the "dream," the utmost limit of Utopia where that "dream" would pass over from its proper dimension of hope (at the worst a dimension full of fantasy) into the most alien and heteronomous of hope-dimensions—the point where the real newness of the Bible, with its Exodus and Kingdom, would give way to the On-high, where there is no room for man.

This being so, hope is able to inherit those features of religion which do not perish with the death of God. There are such features—for, contrary to all pure facticity, the *Futurum* of hope was thought of as property of God's being, and one which distinguished him from all other gods. The Thing-for-us, the world-for-us in the "dream" of something-without-God but with the hope that is his essence. This world has one perspective only; it is the perspective of the front . . . openness . . . *Novum* . . . the ultimate matter for being . . . to be . . . Utopia. And no secret is at the same time so remote and so near as that of *homo absconditus* in the midst of this world which has its own mystery and its own problem to bear, in the how and the why and the wherefore of its being. These questions remain at their deepest level unsolved, waiting for the answer that will bring identity; and they do so not only where we men are concerned, not only where our knowledge of the world is concerned, but also with respect to the world itself in its ownmost process.

4

Marx and the End of Alienation

Ernst Bloch

"Come to your senses!" An appeal at once very old and very new. Give up being used—misused—for other men's gain. Give up being a beast for other men's burden. Give up being made to fight your own flesh and blood, and dying for those who are not your flesh and blood at all—while our Sunday-men, one moment worldly, the next moment spiritual, but always loyal to their lord, stand by and give their blessing.

The pastors paid willing homage to the power which had crucified the first Christian heretic—it was, after all, often their own power. But to the poor and the exploited and the deprived they preached patient tolerance, not force. They were not, of course, disturbed when the oppressors used force, whether it was the constant intimidation of daily life or the unmasked brutality which countered all outbreaks of impatience down below. In those circumstances gas and pistol were called means of defense, and rebellion, however justified, was terror. The power of the On-high was draped in ideology, and songs of praise were ready even for the loaded revolver. "They deck out the altars, and the poor suffer bitter hunger"—Amos's words have always been relevant, and generally in vain. Even the "decking out" of art and philosophy, apart from "giving expression to their age in thought," has often in fact put up an apologetic mask in front of it, gilding the fog of false conscience, spinning a thick web of words.

But prescinding now from all this whitewashing, the ideology of late capitalism contains a special element of the class-conditioned alienation of man from himself, an element first brought to the light of day by Marx. This ever-intensified form of alienation can be seen most clearly in the society governed

53

by monopoly capitalism, where both man and material things are reduced to the status of goods, and where a thoroughly misguided consciousness has brought with it the most astonishing self-alienation and wasteful self-sacrifice to empty, false and alien interests. Not without reason has the anthropological and religious critique of gods and goddery come down to earth from heaven. Not without reason did Marx speak of the "fetishistic" character of commodities, and of the "illusions" of ideology, until in the end, thanks to economics, these somewhat less transcendent scales also fell from men's eyes. Significantly enough, in fact, the whole analysis of alienation and the attempt to restore the alienated factors to the human subject began with the critique of religion: with the young Hegel's statement about the "treasures squandered on heaven," and the anthropological insights added forcefully—if not very profoundly—by Feuerbach. It was again from books that the fire broke out when Marx publicized the fact that a mythical heaven had stolen and alienated the ultra-earthly phenomenon of goods, along with their producer, whom it had reduced to a personified work-force, a mere commodity. One must never forget here that Marx's critique of alienation and goods would hardly have arisen at all if it had not been for his previous involvement in, and critique of, religion. Unlike Feuerbach, however, he was not content to see man's treasures squandered on heaven simply in order to bring them back from alienation to some abstract species man. Instead of that, he put the whole ideology of the On-high on a par with heaven, and denounced not the condition of abstract man but the actual, given ensemble of capitalist relations and, above all, its victims, the laborers and the heavy-laden. For they are the most alienated of all (whether they know it or not); and they are at one and the same time a possible lever towards the downfall of those relations which hold man in abandoned slavery, and the immediate their to that fall.

This detective glance at history, seeing through it and its ideologies, undoubtedly belongs to the cold current in Marxist thought. But the What-for, the distant goal of this penetrating glance, belongs to the warm current evident in the beginnings of Marxism, for it is unquestionably rooted in the originally Christian ground-plan for the "Kingdom of Freedom" itself. It is the *cold current*, however, that brings the statement, relevant to most of our past history, that "when ideas and interests meet it is always the ideas that capitulate." And it is the cold current that says of the revolution, which at long last is objective and not a mere figment of abstract Utopia, that "the working class does not have to implement ideals, but [has] to liberate the tendencies towards those ideals which are already present in society." In the same way, too, Engels (quite rightly) gave one of his books the very cooling title: "The progress of socialism from Utopia to science"; though sometimes, as the *warm current*, and the results of its absence, proclaim, this particular progress can be overdone. And then the warm current needs science, not as somehow non-Utopian, but as the concrete realization, at last, of Utopia.

Far from being a contradiction in terms, concrete Utopia is the firmest of handholds, and by no means only where the propaganda and implementation of socialism is concerned. The whole *surplus force* of culture finds its salvation there, and these forces are becoming more and more relevant to us all the time—above all, the wealth of artistic allegories and religious symbols, whose day is not yet done when the ideology which bore them disappears. An old sage once said that man is easier to save than to feed. The coming age of socialism will find, when everyone has sat down to the meal, that the conventional reversal of this paradox is very indigestible indeed: that man is easier to feed than to save. Taking everything into consideration, that is—ourselves and socialism and death, and the crucial secret that there is in fact a world at all to be set straight. For the really enduring sort of self-alienation is not so dependent on the false society that it will go when that society goes: its sources lie deeper than that. Marx said: "To be radical is to grasp things at their roots. But the root of all (viz. social) things is man." The first letter of John (3.2) also takes man as the root, but rather as being on the way to something than as being a real cause: "It does not yet appear what we shall be, but we know that when he appears we shall be like him, for we shall see him as he is. And every one who thus hopes in him purifies himself as he is pure." The "he" admittedly refers to the so-called Father in heaven, but it is the Son of Man, of one essence with the Father, that is really meant: he is our own, true, radical identity, appearing at the end of history. If these two tests had ever come face to face, the encounter would have shed a searching Utopian light on the problem of universal alienation and its possible cure. From the Christian point of view, "that which men call God" would have become man at last; from the philosophical point of view, Hegelian phenomenology would have been left high and dry by the idea that substance is now subject.

It would be a strange meeting—but then, why not? The meeting is strange even when it occurs at far less remote places than the root-point of man, the root which has not yet flowered. Or, if it has flowered, then only in such a way that the bloom always has to bear an alien blight. Only at its deepest moments (and they were not deep) did the nineteenth century see the end of all metaphysics as the consequence of such strange atheistic systems as those concerned with the dissolution of alienation (*Dieu et létat*). The vulgar Marxists can be left out of the reckoning here, let alone the transcendence conservationists. *Hic rhodus, hic salta*—daring to dance, to leap, to explore the new, without any sort of catechism.

There is a passage in the *Economic and Philosophic Manuscripts of 1844* in which Marx reaches out in an astounding piece of speculation, constructing a chiasmus that in recent years has become so well known as to be almost un-known again. He goes so far as to speak of the "resurrection of nature," and to do so with a certain humor, a mysterious lightness of touch, which makes the break with the past all the easier, and even more so the break with the oppres-sion of the moment, in which this supremely Utopian chiasmus must seem both scandal and folly. His words are well known: "Naturalization of man, hu-manization of nature"—an ultimate, teleological solution of a sort very rare in Marx. The warm current is at work here in the complete reversal of alienation. But it would be banal to see the naturalization as no more than *mens sana in corpore sano*, and the humanization as a mere domestication of nature in an improved late-Arcadian key. This is, in fact, a really penetrating phrase; there are a lot of them latent in Marxism, but too few ever get actually said. It is a phrase whose two halves could have come from Jacob Böhme and Franz Baader respectively, with on the one hand their well-springs of fresh water and on the other their Sun-man or Man-sun.

Marx himself did not need such an encounter, but Marxism in its reduced form certainly does. And, so far as Christianity is concerned, how else, apart from the chiasmic interchange of man and nature with its real, crucial secret, can it hope to get away from the transcendence it has just seen through? Natu-ralization of man—that would mean his incorporation into the community, his final this-wordly awakening, so that, free from all alienation, we could really control our *hic et nunc*. Humanization of nature—that would mean the opening-up of the cosmos, still closed to itself, to be our Home: the Home once expressed in the mystical fantasy of new heaven and new earth, and echoing on through the beauty and quality of nature as these have found expression in painting and poetry, with the great leap out of the realm of necessity drawing ever closer to man. Not to mention that out-and-out qualitative, all-shattering horizon of *apocalypsis cum figuris* kept open not in antiquity but in the Chris-tianity of Dürer's day, at least in the realm of fantasy.

The effort to turn such far-flung images as these into a more concrete form of Utopia is, of course, only thinkable in terms of a leap of memory; at the foreshadowing-point of imminent earthly liberation and freedom there is more than enough for man to do if he is to make anything more solid. The only thing is that no humanism would be tolerable if it did not implicitly possess these far-flung but profoundly happy images of the Where-to, the What-for and the At-all to complement its morality. And the freedom of these images lies in the extension of the as yet unextended *homo absconditus* in the world—in the experiment of the world. In that experiment the human dimension is quite open enough to utter destruction, and there is more than enough disparate universe surrounding a now-dead world. If that were all there was, the whole Prometheus-dimension, and the realm of the freedom-seeker would provide at the very most an element of beauty, but with no sign of a movement towards meaning. However, the whole world to date, the world of mere facts with their openness to annihilation, is untrue. The only true things are the process found in the world, and the voice of that rebel who said to Pilate, with a very different party-allegiance in mind, allegiance to the *Novum:* "Every one who is of the truth hears my voice." And then their place is the struggle, the point of resolution, the warm current, with the cry of mankind in their ears, and the memory of that cry, out on the front of world-process.

Non omnis confundar: I shall not altogether be confounded; that holds good for our humanized nature even in its extra-territoriality. It is, of course, not a proximate goal; one cannot live from it, and our human history is a far more day-to-day affair than this distant aim at a final goal. All the more reason, then, why the ideologies and illusions, the mythologies and theocracies of ecclesiastical Christianity should by now have run their day, along with the fixed, transcendent, stationary In-the-highest of a world beyond all cares. True Marxism has no time for all that, but takes true Christianity seriously—too seriously for just another grey and compromising dialog. When Christians are really concerned with the emancipation of those who labor and are heavy-laden, and when Marxists retain the depths of the Kingdom of Freedom as the real content of revolutionary consciousness on the road to becoming true substance, the alliance between revolution and Christianity founded in the Peasant Wars may live again—this time with success. Florian Geyer, the great fighter of those wars, is reputed to have had the words "*Nulla crux, nulla corona*" scratched on the blade of his sword. That could be the motto of a Christianity free, at last, from alienation. And the far-reaching, inexhaustible depths of emancipation in those words could also serve as a motto for a Marxism aware of its depths.

Vivant sequentes. Marxism, and the dream of the unconditioned, follow the same path and the same plan of campaign. A *Humanum* free from alienation, and a World into which it could fit—a world as yet still undiscovered, but already somehow sensed: both these things are definitively present in the experiment of the Future, the experiment of the World.

II

Erich Fromm

5
The Dogma of Christ

Erich Fromm
Translated by James Luther Adams

Social psychology wishes to investigate how certain psychic attitudes common to members of a group are related to their common life experiences. It is no more an accident in the case of an individual whether this or that libido direction dominates, whether the Oedipus complex finds this or that outlet, than it is an accident if changes in psychic characteristics occur in the psychic situation of a group, either in the same class of people over a period of time or simultaneously among different classes. It is the task of social psychology to indicate why such changes occur and how they are to be understood on the basis of the experience common to the members of the group.

The present investigation is concerned with a narrowly limited problem of social psychology, namely, the question concerning the motives conditioning the evolution of concepts about the relation of God the Father to Jesus from the beginning of Christianity to the formulation of the Nicene Creed in the fourth century. In accordance with the theoretical principles just set forth, this investigation aims to determine the extent to which the change in certain religious ideas is an expression of the psychic change of the people involved and the extent to which these changes are conditioned by their conditions of life. It will attempt to understand the ideas in terms of men and their life patterns, and to show that the evolution of dogma can be understood only through knowledge of the unconscious, upon which external reality works and which determines the content of consciousness.

The method of this work necessitates that relatively large space be devoted to the presentation of the life situation of the people investigated, to their spiritual, economic, social, and political situation—in short, to their "psychic surfaces." If this seems to involve a disproportionate emphasis, the reader should bear in mind that even in the psychoanalytic case study of an ill person, great space is given to the presentation of the external circumstances surrounding the person. In the present work the description of the total cultural situation of the masses of people being investigated and the presentation of their external environment are more decisive than the description of the actual situation in a case study. The reason for this is that in the nature of things the historical reconstruction, even though it is supposed to be offered only to a certain extent in detail, is incomparably more complicated and more extensive than the report of simple facts as they occur in the life of an individual. We believe, however, that this disadvantage must be tolerated, because only in this way can an analytical understanding of historical phenomena be achieved.

The present study is concerned with a subject that has been treated by one of the most prominent representatives of the analytic study of religion, Theodor Reik.[1] The difference in content, which necessarily results from the different methodology, will, like the methodological differences themselves, be considered briefly at the end of this essay.

Our purpose here is to understand the change in certain contents of consciousness as expressed in theological ideas as the result of a change in unconscious processes. Accordingly, just as we have done with regard to the methodological problem, we propose to deal briefly with the most important findings of psychoanalysis as they touch upon our question.

The Social-Psychological Function of Religion

Psychoanalysis is a psychology of drives or impulses. It sees human behavior as conditioned and defined by emotional drives, which it interprets as an outflow of certain physiologically rooted impulses, themselves not subject to immediate observation. Consistent with the popular classifications of hunger drives and love drives, from the beginning, Freud distinguished between the ego, or self-preservation, drives and the sexual drives. Because of the libidinous character of the ego drives of self-preservation, and because of the special significance of destructive tendencies in the psychic apparatus of man, Freud suggested a different grouping, taking into account a contrast between life-maintaining and destructive drives. This classification needs no further discussion here. What is important is the recognition of certain qualities of the sex drives that distinguish them from the ego drives. The sex drives are not imperative; that is, it is possible to leave their demands ungratified without menacing life itself, which would not be the case with continued failure to satisfy hunger, thirst, and the need for sleep. Furthermore, the sex drives, up to a certain and not insignificant point, permit a gratification in fantasies and with one's own body. They are, therefore, much more independent of external reality than are the ego drives. Closely connected with this are the easy transference and capacity for interchange among the component impulses of sexuality. The frustration of one libidinal impulse can be relatively easily offset by the substitution of another impulse that can be gratified. This flexibility and versatility within the sexual drives are the basis for the extraordinary variability of the psychic structure and therein lies also the basis for the possibility that individual experiences can so definitely and markedly affect the libido structure. Freud sees the pleasure principle modified by the reality principle as the regulator of the psychic apparatus. He says:

> We will therefore turn to the less ambitious question of what men them-selves show by their behavior to be the purpose and intention of their lives. What do they demand of life and wish to achieve in it? The answer to this can hardly be in doubt. They strive after happiness; they want to become happy and remain so. This endeavor has two sides, a positive and a negative aim. It aims, on the one hand, at an absence of pain and unpleasure, and on the other, at the experiencing of strong feelings of pleasure. In its narrower sense the word "happiness" only relates to the last. In conformity with this dichotomy in his aims, man's activity devel-ops in two directions, according as it seeks to realize—in the main, or even exclusively—the one or the other of these aims.[2]

The individual strives to experience—under given circumstances—a maxi-mum of libido gratification and a minimum of pain; in order to avoid pain, changes or even frustrations of the different component sex impulses can be accepted. A corresponding renunciation of the ego impulses, however, is im-possible.

The peculiarity of an individual's emotional structure depends upon his psychic constitution and primarily upon his experiences in infancy. External reality, which guarantees him the satisfaction of certain impulses, but which compels the renunciation of certain others, is defined by the existing social situ-ation in which he lives. This social reality includes the wider reality which em-braces all members of society and the narrower reality of distinct social classes.

Society has a double function for the psychic situation of the individual, both frustrating and satisfying. A person seldom renounces impulses because he sees the danger resulting from their satisfaction. Generally, society dictates such renunciations: first, those prohibitions established on the basis of social recognition of a real danger *for the individual himself,* a danger not readily sensed by him and connected with the gratification of impulse; second, repres-sion and frustration of impulses whose satisfaction would involve harm not to the individual but to the group; and, finally, renunciations made not in the interest of the group but only in the interest of a controlling class.

The "gratifying" function of society is no less clear than its frustrating role. The individual accepts it only because through its help he can to a certain degree count on gaining pleasure and avoiding pain, primarily with regard to the satisfaction of the elementary needs of self-preservation and, secondarily, in relation to the satisfaction of libidinous needs.

What has been said has not taken into account a specific feature of all historically known societies. The members of a society do not indeed consult one another to determine what the society can permit and what it must prohibit. Rather, the situation is that so long as the productive forces of the economy do not suffice to afford to all an adequate satisfaction of their material and cultural needs (that is, beyond protection against external danger and the satisfaction of elementary ego needs), the most powerful social class will aspire to the maximum satisfaction of their own needs first. The degree of satisfaction they provide for those who are ruled by them depends on the level of economic possibilities available, and also on the fact that a minimum satisfaction must be granted to those who are ruled so that they may be able to continue to function as cooperating members of the society. Social stability depends relatively little upon the use of external force. It depends for the most part upon the fact that men find themselves in a psychic condition that roots them inwardly in an existing social situation. For that purpose, as we have noted, a minimum of satisfaction of the natural and cultural instinctual needs is necessary. But at this point we must observe that for the psychic submission of the masses, something else is important, something connected with the peculiar structural stratification of the society into classes.

In this connection, Freud has pointed out that man's helplessness in the face of nature is a repetition of the situation in which the adult found himself as a child, when he could not do without help against unfamiliar superior forces, and when his life impulses, following their narcissistic inclinations, attached themselves first to the objects that afforded him protection and satisfaction, namely, his mother and his father. To the extent that society is helpless with respect to nature, the psychic situation of childhood must be repeated for the individual member of the society as an adult. He transfers from father or mother some of his childish love and fear and also some of his hostility to a fantasy figure, to God.

In addition, there is a hostility to certain real figures, in particular to representatives of the elite. In the social stratification, the infantile situation is repeated for the individual. He sees in the rulers the powerful ones, the strong, and the wise—persons to be revered. He believes that they wish him well; he also knows that resistance to them is always punished; he is content when by docility he can win their praise. These are the identical feelings which, as a child, he had for his father, and it is understandable that he is as disposed to believe uncritically what is presented to him by the rulers as just and true, as in childhood he used to believe without criticism every statement made by his father. The figure of God forms a supplement to this situation; God is always the ally of the rulers. When the latter, who are always real personalities, are exposed to criticism, they can rely on God, who, by virtue of his unreality, only scorns criticism and, by his authority, confirms the authority of the ruling class.

In this psychological situation of infantile bondage resides one of the principal guarantees of social stability. Many find themselves in the same situation they experienced as children, standing helplessly before their father; the same mechanisms operate now as then. This psychic situation becomes established through a great many significant and complicated measures taken by the elite, whose function it is to maintain and strengthen in the masses their infantile psychic dependence and to impose itself on their unconscious as a father figure.

One of the principal means of achieving this purpose is religion. It has the task of preventing any psychic independence on the part of the people, of intimidating them intellectually, of bringing them into the socially necessary infantile docility toward the authorities. At the same time it has another essential function: it offers the masses a certain measure of satisfaction that makes life sufficiently tolerable for them to prevent them from attempting to change their position from that of obedient son to that of rebellious son.

Of what sort are these satisfactions? Certainly not satisfactions of the ego drives of self-preservation, nor better food, nor other material pleasures. Such pleasures are to be obtained only in reality, and for that purpose one needs no religion; religion serves merely to make it easier for the masses to resign themselves to the many frustrations that reality presents. The satisfactions religion offers are of a libidinous nature; they are satisfactions that occur essentially in fantasy because, as we have pointed out before, libidinous impulses, in contrast to ego impulses, permit satisfaction in fantasies.

Here we confront a question concerning one of the psychic functions of religion, and we shall now indicate briefly the most important results of Freud's investigations in this area. In *Totem and Taboo*, Freud has shown that the animal god of totemism is the elevated father, that in the prohibition to kill and eat the totem animal and in the contrary festive custom of nevertheless violating the prohibition once a year, man repeats the ambivalent attitude which he had acquired as a child toward the father who is simultaneously a helping protector and an oppressive rival.

It has been shown, especially by Reik, that this transfer to God of the infantile attitude toward the father is found also in the great religions. The question posed by Freud and his students concerned the psychic quality of the religious attitude toward God; and the answer is that in the adult's attitude toward God, one sees repeated the infantile attitude of the child toward his father. This infantile psychic situation represents the pattern of the religious situation. In his *The Future of an Illusion*, Freud passes beyond this question to a broader one. He no longer asks only how religion is psychologically possible; he asks also why religion exists at all or why it has been necessary. To this question he gives an answer that takes into consideration psychic and social facts simultaneously. He attributes to religion the effect of a narcotic capable of bringing some consolation to man in his impotence and helplessness before the forces of nature:

> For this situation is nothing new. It has an infantile prototype, of which it is in fact only the continuation. For once before one has found oneself in a similar state of helplessness: as a small child, in relation to one's parents. One had reason to fear them, and especially one's father; and yet one was sure of his protection against the dangers one knew. Thus it was natural to assimilate the two situations. Here, too, wishing played its part, as it does in dream-life. The sleeper may be seized in a presentiment of death, which threatens to place him in the grave. But the dream-work knows how to select a condition that will turn even that dreaded event into a wish-fulfillment: the dreamer sees himself in an ancient Etruscan grave which he has climbed down into, happy to find his archaeological interests satisfied. In the same way, a man makes the forces of nature not simply into persons with whom he can associate as he would with his equals—that would not do justice to the overpowering impression which those forces make on him—but he gives them the character of a father. He turns them into gods, following in this, as I have tried to show, not only an infantile prototype but a phylogenetic one.
>
> In the course of time the first observations were made of regularity and conformity to law in natural phenomena, and with this the forces of nature lost their human traits. But man's helplessness remains and along with it his longing for his father, and the gods. The gods retain their threefold task: they must exorcize the terrors of nature, they must reconcile men to the cruelty of fate, particularly as it is shown in death, and they must compensate them for the sufferings and privations which a civilized life in common has imposed on them.[3]

Freud thus answers the question, "What constitutes the inner power of religious doctrines and to what circumstances do these doctrines owe their effectiveness independently of rational approval?"

> These [religious ideas], which are given out as teachings, are not precipitates of experience or end results of thinking: they are illusions, fulfillments of the oldest, strangest, and most urgent wishes of mankind. The secret of their strength lies in the strength of those wishes. As we already know, the terrifying impression of helplessness in childhood aroused the need for protection—protection through love—which was provided by the father, and the recognition that this helplessness would last throughout life made it necessary to cling to the existence of a father, but this time a more powerful one. Thus the benevolent rule of divine Providence allays

our fear of the dangers of life; the establishment of a moral world-order ensures the fulfillment of the demands of justice, which have so often remained unfulfilled in human civilization; and the prolongation of earthly existence in a future life provides the local and temporal framework in which these wish-fulfillments shall take place. Answers to the riddles that tempt the curiosity of man, such as how the universe began or what the relation is between the body and mind, are developed in conformity with the underlying assumptions of this system. It is an enormous relief to the individual psyche if the conflicts of its childhood arising from the father—complex-conflicts which it has never wholly overcome—are removed from it and brought to a solution that is universally accepted.[4]

Freud therefore sees the possibility of the religious attitude in the infantile situation; he sees its relative necessity in man's impotence and helplessness with respect to nature, and he draws the conclusion that with man's increasing control over nature, religion is to be viewed an an illusion that is becoming superfluous.

Let us summarize what has been said thus far. Man strives for a maximum of pleasure; social reality compels him to many renunciations of impulse, and society seeks to compensate the individual for these renunciations by other satisfactions harmless for the society—that is, for the dominant classes.

These satisfactions are such that in essence they can be realized in fantasies, especially in collective fantasies. They perform an important function in social reality. Insofar as society does not permit real satisfactions, fantasy satisfactions serve as a substitute and become a powerful support of social stability. The greater the renunciations men endure in reality, the stronger must be the concern for compensation. Fantasy satisfactions have the double function which is characteristic of every narcotic: they act both as an anodyne and as a deterrent to active change of reality. The common fantasy satisfactions have an essential advantage over individual daydreams: by virtue of their universality, the fantasies are perceived by the conscious mind as if they were real. An illusion shared by everyone becomes a reality. The oldest of these collective fantasy satisfactions is religion. With the progressive development of society, fantasies become more complicated and more rationalized. Religion itself becomes more differentiated, and beside it appear poetry, art, and philosophy as the expressions of collective fantasies.

To sum up, religion has a threefold function: for all mankind, consolation for the privations exacted by life; for the great majority of men, encouragement to accept emotionally their class situation; and for the dominant minority, relief from guilt feelings caused by the suffering of those whom they oppress.

The following investigation aims to test in detail what has been said, by examining a small segment of religious development. We shall attempt to show what influence social reality had in a specific situation upon a specific group of men, and how emotional trends found expression in certain dogmas, in collective fantasies, and to show further what psychic change was brought about by a change in the social situation. We shall try to see how this psychic change found expression in new religious fantasies that satisfied certain unconscious impulses. It will thereby become clear how closely a change in religious concepts is connected, on the one hand, with the experiencing of various possible infantile relationships to the father or mother, and on the other hand, with changes in the social and economic situation.

The course of the investigation is determined by the methodological presuppositions mentioned earlier. The aim will be *to understand dogma on the basis of a study of people, not people on the basis of a study of dogma.* We shall attempt, therefore, first to describe the total situation of the social class from which the early Christian faith originated, and to understand the psychological meaning of this faith in terms of the total psychic situation of these people. We shall then show how different the mentality of the people was at a later period. Eventually, we shall try to understand the unconscious meaning of the Christology which crystallized as the end product of a three-hundred-year development. We shall treat mainly the early Christian faith and the Nicene dogma.

Early Christianity and Its Idea of Jesus

Every attempt to understand the origin of Christianity must begin with an investigation of the economic, social, cultural, and psychic situation of its earliest believers.[5]

Palestine was a part of the Roman Empire and succumbed to the conditions of its economic and social development. The Augustan principate had meant the end of domination by a feudal oligarchy, and helped bring about the triumph of urban citizenry. Increasing international commerce meant no improvement for the great masses, no greater satisfaction of their everyday needs; only the thin stratum of the owning class was interested in it. An unemployed and hungry proletariat of unprecedented size filled the cities. Next to Rome, Jerusalem was the city with relatively the largest proletariat of this kind. The artisans, who usually worked only at home and belonged largely to the proletariat, easily made common cause with beggars, unskilled workers, and peasants. Indeed, the Jerusalem proletariat was in a worse situation than the Roman. It did not enjoy Roman civil rights, nor were its urgent needs of stomach and heart provided for by the emperors through great distributions of grain and elaborate games and spectacles.

The rural population was exhausted by an extraordinarily heavy tax burden, and either fell into debt slavery, or, among the small farmers, the means of production or the small landholdings were all taken away. Some of these farmers swelled the ranks of the large-city proletariat of Jerusalem; others resorted to desperate remedies, such as violent political uprising and plundering. Above this impoverished and despairing proletariat, there arose in Jerusalem, as throughout the Roman Empire, a middle economic class which, though suffering under Roman pressure, was nevertheless economically stable. Above this group was the small but powerful and influential class of the feudal, priestly, and moneyed aristocracy. Corresponding to the severe economic cleavage within the Palestinian population, there was social differentiation. Pharisees, Sadducees, and Am Ha-aretz were the political and religious groups representing these differences. The Sadducees represented the rich upper class: "[their] doctrine is received but by a few, yet by those of the greatest dignity."[6] Although they have the rich on their side, Josephus does not find their manners aristocratic: "The behavior of the Sadducees one towards another is in some degree wild, and their conversation is as barbarous as if they were strangers to them."[7]

Below this small feudal upper class were the Pharisees, representing the middle and smaller urban citizenry, "who are friendly to one another, and are for the exercise of concord and regard for the public."[8]

> Now, for the Pharisees, they live meanly, and despise delicacies in diet; and they follow the conduct of reason, and what that prescribes to them as good for them, they do; and they think they ought earnestly to strive to observe reason's dictates for practice. They also pay respect to such as are in years; nor are they so bold as to contradict them in anything they have introduced; and, when they determine that all things are done by fate, they do not take away from men the freedom of acting as they think fit; since their notion is, that it hath pleased God that events should be decided in part by the council of fate, in part by such men as will accede thereunto acting therein virtuously or viciously. They also believe that souls have an immortal vigour in them, and that under the earth there will be rewards or punishments, according as they have lived virtuously or viciously in this life; and the latter are to be detained in an everlasting prison, but that the former shall have power to revive and live again; on account of which doctrines, they are able greatly to persuade the body of the people, and whatsoever they do about divine worship, prayers, and sacrifices, they perform them according to their direction.[9]

Josephus' description of the middle class of the Pharisees makes it appear more unified than it was in reality. Among the following of the Pharisees were elements that stemmed from the lowest proletarian strata that continued their relationship with them in their way of life (for example, Rabbi Akiba). At the same time, however, there were members of the well-to-do urban citizenry. This social difference found expression in different ways, most clearly in the political contradictions within Pharisaism, with regard to their attitude toward Roman rule and revolutionary movements.

The lowest stratum of the urban *Lumpenproletariat* and of the oppressed peasants, the so-called "Am Ha-aretz" (literally, land folk), stood in sharp opposition to the Pharisees and their wider following. In fact, they were a class that had been completely uprooted by the economic development; they had nothing to lose and perhaps something to gain. They stood economically and socially outside the Jewish society integrated into the whole of the Roman Empire. They did not follow the Pharisees and did not revere them; they hated them and in turn were despised by them. Entirely characteristic of this attitude is the statement of Akiba, one of the most important Pharisees, who himself stemmed from the proletariat: "When I was still a common [ignorant] man of the Am Ha-aretz, I used to say: 'If I could lay my hands on a scholar I would bite him like an ass.'"[10] The Talmud goes on: "Rabbi, say 'like a dog,' an ass does not bite," and he replied: "When an ass bites he generally breaks the bones of his victim, while a dog bites only the flesh." We find in the same passage in the Talmud a series of statements describing the relations between the Pharisees and the Am Ha-aretz.

> A man should sell all his possessions and secure the daughter of a scholar for a wife, and if he cannot secure the daughter of a scholar, he should try to obtain a daughter of a prominent man. If he cannot succeed in that, he should endeavor to obtain a daughter of a synagogue director, and if he cannot succeed in that, he should try to obtain a daughter of an alms collector, and if he cannot succeed even in this, he should try and obtain the daughter of an elementary-school teacher. He should avoid wedding the daughter of a common person [a member of the Am Ha-aretz], for she is an abomination, their women are an abhorrence, and concerning their daughters it is said, "Accursed be any who sleepeth with a cow." (Deut. 27)

Or, again, R. Jochanan says:

> One may tear a common person to pieces like a fish. . . . One who gives his daughter to a common person in marriage virtually shackles her before a lion, for just as a lion tears and devours his victim without shame, so does a common person who sleeps brutally and shamelessly with her.

R. Eliezer says:

> If the common people did not need us for economic reasons, they would long ago have slain us. . . . The enmity of a common person toward a scholar is even more intense than that of the heathens toward the Israelites. . . . Six things are true of the common person: One may depend upon no common person as a witness and may accept no evidence from him, one may not let him share a secret, nor be a ward for an orphan, nor

a trustee of funds for charitable funds, one may not go on a journey in his company and one should not tell him if he has lost something.[11]

The views here cited (which could be multiplied considerably) stem from Pharisaic circles and show with what hatred they opposed the Am Ha-aretz, but also with what bitterness the common man may have hated the scholars and their following.[12]

It has been necessary to describe the opposition within Palestinian Judaism between the aristocracy, the middle classes and their intellectual leaders on the one hand, and the urban and rural proletariat on the other, in order to make clear the underlying causes of such political and religious revolutionary movements as early Christianity. A more extensive presentation of the differentiation among the extraordinarily variegated Pharisees is not necessary for the purpose of the present study and would lead us too far afield. The conflict between the middle class and the proletariat within the Pharisaic group increased, as Roman oppression became heavier and the lowest classes more economically crushed and uprooted. To the same extent the lowest classes of society became the supporters of the national, social, and religious revolutionary movements.

These revolutionary aspirations of the masses found expression in two directions: *political* attempts at revolt and emancipation directed against their own aristocracy and the Romans, and in all sorts of *religious-messianic* movements. But there is by no means a sharp separation between these two streams moving toward liberation and salvation; often they flow into each other. The messianic movements themselves assumed partly practical and partly merely literary forms.

The most important movements of this sort may be briefly mentioned here.

Shortly before Herod's death, that is, at a time when, in addition to Roman domination, the people suffered oppression at the hands of Jewish deputies serving under the Romans, there took place in Jerusalem, under the leadership of two Pharisaic scholars, a popular revolt, during which the Roman eagle at the entrance to the Temple was destroyed. The instigators were executed, and the chief plotters were burned alive. After Herod's death a mob demonstrated before his successor, Archelaus, demanding the release of the political prisoners, the abolition of the market tax, and a reduction in the annual tribute. These demands were not satisfied. A great popular demonstration in connection with these events in the year 4 B.C. was suppressed with bloodshed, thousands of demonstrators being killed by the soldiers. Nevertheless, the movement became stronger. Popular revolt progressed. Seven weeks later, in Jerusalem, it mounted to new bloody revolts against Rome. In addition, the rural population was aroused. In the old revolutionary center, Galilee, there were many struggles with the Romans, and in Trans-Jordan there was rioting. A former shepherd assembled volunteer troops and led a guerrilla war against the Romans.

This was the situation in the year 4 B.C. The Romans did not find it altogether easy to cope with the revolting masses. They crowned their victory by crucifying two thousand revolutionary prisoners.

For some years the country remained quiet. But shortly after the introduction in 6 A.D. of a direct Roman administration in the country, which began its activity with a popular census for tax purposes, there was a new revolutionary movement. Now began a separation between the lower and the middle classes. Although ten years earlier the Pharisees had joined the revolt, there developed now a new split between the urban and the rural revolutionary groups on the one side and the Pharisees on the other. The urban and rural lower classes united in a new party, namely, the Zealots, while the middle class, under the leadership of the Pharisees, was prepared for reconciliation with the Romans. The more oppressive the Roman and the aristocratic Jewish yoke became, the greater the despair of the masses, and Zealotism won new followers. Up to the outbreak of the great revolt against the Romans there were constant clashes between the people and the administration. The occasions for revolutionary outbreaks were the frequent attempts of the Romans to put up a statue of Caesar or the Roman eagle in the Temple of Jerusalem. The indignation against these measures, which were rationalized on religious grounds, stemmed in reality from the hatred of the masses for the emperor as leader and head of the ruling class oppressing them. The peculiar character of this hatred for the emperor becomes clearer if we remember that this was an epoch in which reverence for the Roman emperor was spreading widely throughout the empire and in which the emperor cult was about to become the dominant religion.

The more hopeless the struggle against Rome became on the political level, and the more the middle class withdrew and became disposed to compromise with Rome, the more radical the lower classes became; but the more revolutionary tendencies lost their political character and were transferred to the level of religious fantasies and messianic ideas. Thus a pseudo-messiah, Theudas, promised the people he would lead them to the Jordan and repeat the miracle of Moses. The Jews would pass through the river with dry feet, but the pursuing Romans would drown. The Romans saw in these fantasies the expression of a dangerous revolutionary ferment; they killed the followers of this messiah and beheaded Theudas. Theudas had successors. Josephus provides an account of an uprising under the provincial governor Felix (52–60). Its leaders

> . . . deceived and deluded the people under pretense of divine inspiration, but were for procuring innovations and changes of the government; and these prevailed with the multitude to act like madmen, and went before them into the wilderness, as pretending that God would there show them the signals of liberty; but Felix thought this procedure was to be the be-

ginning of a revolt; so he sent some horsemen, and footmen both armed, who destroyed a great number of them.

But there was an Egyptian false prophet that did the Jews more mischief than the former; for he was a cheat, and pretended to be a prophet also, and got together thirty thousand men that were deluded by him: these he led round about from the wilderness to the mount which was called the Mount of Olives, and was ready to break into Jerusalem by force from that place.[13]

The Roman military made short shrift of the revolutionary hordes. Most of them were killed or put in prison, the rest destroyed themselves; all tried to remain in hiding at home. Nevertheless, the uprisings continued:

Now, when these were quieted, it happened, as it does in a diseased body, that another part was subject to an inflammation; for a company of deceivers and robbers [that is, the messianists and more politically-minded revolutionaries] got together, and persuaded the Jews to revolt, and exhorted them to assert their liberty, inflicting death on those that continued in obedience to the Roman government, and saying, that such as willingly chose slavery, ought to be forced from their desired inclinations; for they parted themselves into different bodies, and lay in wait up and down the country, and plundered the houses of the great men, and slew the men themselves, and set the villages on fire; and this till all Judea was filled with the effects of their madness. And thus the flame was every day more and more blown up, till it came to a direct war.[14]

The growing oppression of the lower classes of the nation brought about a sharpening of the conflict between them and the less oppressed middle class, and in this process the masses became more and more radical. The left wing of the Zealots formed a secret faction of the "Sicarii" (dagger carriers), who began, through attacks and plots, to exert a terroristic pressure on the well-to-do citizens. Without mercy they persecuted the moderates in the higher and middle classes of Jerusalem; at the same time they invaded, plundered, and reduced to ashes the villages whose inhabitants refused to join their revolutionary bands. The prophets and the pseudo-messiahs, similarly, did not cease their agitation among the common folk.

Finally, in the year 66 the great popular revolt against Rome broke out. It was supported first by the middle and lower classes of the nation, who, in bitter struggles, overcame the Roman troops. At first the war was led by the property owners and the educated, but they acted with little energy and with the tendency to arrive at a compromise. The first year, therefore, ended in failure despite several victories, and the masses attributed the unhappy outcome to the weak and indifferent early direction of the war. Their leaders attempted by every means to seize power and to put themselves in the place of the existing leaders. Since the latter did not leave their positions voluntarily, in the winter of 67–68 there developed "a bloody civil war and abominable scenes, such as only the French Revolution may boast."[15] The more hopeless the war became, the more the middle classes tried their luck in a compromise with the Romans; as a result, the civil war grew more fierce, together with the struggle against the foreign enemy.[16]

While Rabbi Jochanan ben Sakkai, one of the leading Pharisees, went over to the enemy and made peace with him, the small tradesmen, artisans, and peasants defended the city against the Romans with great heroism for five months. They had nothing to lose, but also nothing more to gain, for the struggle against the Roman power was hopeless and had to end in collapse. Many of the well-to-do were able to save themselves by going over to the Romans, and although Titus was extremely embittered against the remaining Jews, he nevertheless admitted those who were in flight. At the same time the embattled masses of Jerusalem stormed the king's palace, into which many of the well-to-do Jews had brought their treasures, took the money, and killed the owners. The Roman war and the civil war ended with victory for the Romans. This was accompanied by the victory of the ruling Jewish group and the collapse of a hundred thousand Jewish peasants and the urban lower classes.[17]

Alongside the political and social struggles and the messianically colored revolutionary attempts are the popular writings originating at that time and inspired by the same tendencies: namely, the apocalyptic literature. Despite its variety, the vision of the future in this apocalyptic literature is comparatively uniform. First there are the "Woes of the Messiah" (Macc. 13:7,8), which refer to events that will not trouble "the elect"—famine, earthquakes, epidemics, and wars. Then comes the "great affliction" prophesied in Daniel 12:1, such as had not occurred since the creation of the world, a frightening time of suffering and distress. Throughout apocalyptic literature in general there runs the belief that the elect will also be protected from this affliction. The horror of desolation prophesied in Daniel 9:27, 11:31, and 12:11 represents the final sign of the end. The picture of the end bears old prophetic features. The climax will be the appearance of the Son of Man on the clouds in great splendor and glory.[18]

Just as in the struggle against the Romans the different classes of people participated in different ways, so apocalyptic literature, too, originated in different classes. Despite a certain uniformity, this is clearly expressed by the difference in emphasis on individual elements within the various apocalyptic writings. Despite the impossibility of detailed analysis here, we may cite as an expression of the same revolutionary tendencies that inspired the left wing of the defenders of Jerusalem, the concluding exhortation of the Book of Enoch:

Woe to those that build their homes with sand; for they will be over-thrown from their foundation and will fall by the sword. But those who acquire gold and silver will perish in the judgment suddenly. Woe to you ye rich, for ye have trusted in your riches and from your riches ye shall be torn away, because you have not remembered the most High in the days of judgment. . . . Woe to you who requite your neighbor with evil, for you will be requited according to your works. Woe to you lying witnesses. . . . Fear not, ye that suffer, for healing will be your portion: A bright light will shine and you will hear the voice of rest from heaven. (Enoch 94–96).

Besides these religious-messianic, sociopolitical, and literary movements characteristic of the time of the rise of Christianity, another movement must be mentioned, in which political goals played no role and which led directly to Christianity, namely, the movement of John the Baptist. He enkindled a popular movement. The upper class, regardless of its persuasion, would have nothing to do with him. His most attentive listeners came from the ranks of the despised masses.[19] He preached that the kingdom of heaven and judgment day were at hand, bringing deliverance for the good, destruction for the evil. "Repent ye, for the kingdom of heaven is at hand" was the burden of his preaching.

To understand the psychological meaning of the first Christians' faith in Christ—and this is the primary purpose of the present study—it was necessary for us to visualize what kind of people supported early Christianity. They were the masses of the uneducated poor, the proletariat of Jerusalem, and the peasants in the country who, because of the increasing political and economic oppression and because of social restriction and contempt, increasingly felt the urge to change existing conditions. They longed for a happy time for themselves, and also harbored hate and revenge against both their own rulers and the Romans. We have observed how varied were the forms of these tendencies, ranging from the political struggle against Rome to the class struggle in Jerusalem, from Theudas' unrealistic revolutionary attempts to John the Baptist's movement and the apocalyptic literature. From political activity to messianic dreams there were all sorts of different phenomena; yet behind all these different forms was the same motivating force: the hatred and the hope of the suffering masses, caused by their distress and the inescapability of their socioeconomic situation. Whether the eschatological expectation had more social, more political, or more religious content, it became stronger with the increasing oppression, and more active "the deeper we descend into the illiterate masses, to the so-called Am Ha-aretz, the circle of those who experienced the present as oppression and therefore had to look to the future for the fulfillment of all their wishes."[20]

The bleaker the hope for real improvement became, the more this hope had to find expression in fantasies. The Zealots' desperate final struggle against the

Romans and John the Baptist's movement were the two extremes, and were rooted in the same soil: the despair of the lowest classes. This stratum was psychologically characterized by the presence of hope for a change in their condition (analytically interpreted, for a good father who would help them), and, at the same time, a fierce hatred of oppressors, which found expression in feelings directed against the Roman emperor, the Pharisees, the rich in general, and in the fantasies of punishment of the Day of Judgment. We see here an ambivalent attitude: these people loved in fantasy a good father who would help and deliver them, and they hated the evil father who oppressed, tormented, and despised them.

From this stratum of the poor, uneducated, revolutionary masses, Christianity arose as a significant historical messianic-revolutionary movement. Like John the Baptist, early Christian doctrine addressed itself not to the educated and the property owners, but to the poor, the oppressed, and the suffering.[21] Celsus, an opponent of the Christians, gives a good picture of the social composition of the Christian community as he saw it almost two centuries later:

He asserts:

> In private houses also we see wool-workers, cobblers, laundry-workers, and the most illiterate and bucolic yokels, who would not dare to say anything at all in front of their elders and more intelligent masters. But whenever they get hold of children in private and some stupid women with them, they let out some astounding statements as, for example, that they must not pay any attention to their father and school-teachers, but must obey them; they say that these talk nonsense and have no understanding, and that in reality they neither know nor are able to do anything good, but are taken up with mere empty chatter. But they alone, they say, know the right way to live, and if the children would believe them, they would become happy and make their home happy as well. And if just as they are speaking they see one of the school-teachers coming, or some intelligent person, or even the father himself, the more cautious of them flee in all directions; but the more reckless urge the children on to rebel. They whisper to them that in the presence of their father and their schoolmasters they do not feel able to explain anything to the children, since they do not want to have anything to do with the silly and obtuse teachers who are totally corrupted and far gone in wickedness and who inflict punishment on the children. But, if they like, they should leave father and their schoolmasters, and go along with the women and little children who are their playfellows to the wooldresser's shop, or to the cobbler's or the washerwoman's shop, that they may learn perfection. And by saying this they persuade them.[22]

The picture Celsus gives here of the supporters of Christianity is characteristic not only of their social but also of their psychic situation, their struggle and hatred against paternal authority.

What was the content of the primitive Christian message?[23]

In the foreground stands the eschatological expectation. Jesus preached the nearness of the kingdom of God. He taught the people to see in his activities the beginning of this new kingdom. Nevertheless,

> The completion of the kingdom will only appear when he returns in glory in the clouds of heaven to judgment. Jesus seems to have announced this speedy return a short time before his death, and to have comforted his disciples at his departure with the assurance that he would immediately enter into a supermundane position with God.
>
> The instructions of Jesus to his disciples are accordingly dominated by the thought that the end—the day and hour of which, however, no one knows—is at hand. In consequence of this, also, the exhortation to renounce all earthly goods takes a prominent place.[24]

> The conditions of entrance to the kingdom are, in the first place, a complete change of mind, in which a man renounces the pleasures of this world, denies himself, and is ready to surrender all that he has in order to save his soul; then, a believing trust in God's grace which he grants to the humble and the poor, and therefore hearty confidence in Jesus as the Messiah chosen and called by God to realize his kingdom on the earth. The announcement is therefore directed to the poor, the suffering, those hungering and thirsting for righteousness . . . to those who wish to be healed and redeemed, and finds them prepared for entrance into . . . the kingdom of God, while it brings down upon the self-satisfied, the rich and those proud of their righteousness, the judgment of obduracy and the damnation of Hell.[25]

The proclamation that the kingdom of heaven was at hand (Matt. 10:7) was the germ of the oldest preaching. It was this that aroused in the suffering and oppressed masses an enthusiastic hope. The feeling of the people was that everything was coming to an end. They believed that there would not be time to spread Christianity among all the heathen before the new era arrived. If the hopes of the other groups of the same oppressed masses were directed to bringing about political and social revolution by their own energy and effort, the eyes of the early Christian community were focused solely on the great event, the miraculous beginning of a new age. The content of the primitive Christian message was not an economic nor a social-reform program but the blessed promise of a not-distant future in which the poor would be rich, the hungry would be satisfied, and the oppressed would attain authority.[26]

The mood of these first enthusiastic Christians is clearly seen in Luke 6:20 ff.:

> Blessed are you poor, for yours is the kingdom of God. Blessed are you that hunger now, for you shall be satisfied. Blessed are you that weep now, for you shall laugh. Blessed are you when men hate you, and when they exclude you and revile you, and cast out your name as evil, on account of the Son of man! Rejoice in that day, and leap for joy, for behold, your reward is great in heaven; for so their fathers did to the prophets. But woe to you that are rich, for you have received your consolation. Woe to you that are full now, for you shall hunger. Woe to you that laugh now, for you shall mourn and weep.

These statements express not only the longing and expectation of the poor and oppressed for a new and better world, but also their complete hatred of the authorities—the rich, the learned, and the powerful. The same mood is found in the story of the poor man Lazarus, "who desired to be fed with what fell from the rich man's table" (Luke 16: 21), and in the famous words of Jesus: "How hard it is for those who have riches to enter the kingdom of God! For it is easier for a camel to go through the eye of a needle than for a rich man to enter the kingdom of God." (Luke 18: 24) The hatred of the Pharisees and the tax collectors runs like a red thread through the gospels, with the result that for almost two thousand years, opinion of the Pharisees throughout Christendom has been determined by this hatred.

We hear this hatred of the rich again in the Epistle of James, in the middle of the second century:

> Come now, you rich, weep and howl for the miseries that are coming upon you. Your riches have rotted and your garments are moth-eaten. Your gold and silver have rusted, and their rust will be evidence against you and will eat your flesh like fire. You have laid up treasure for the last days. Behold, the wages of the laborers who mowed your fields, which you kept back by fraud, cry out; and the cries of the harvesters have reached the ears of the Lord of hosts. You have lived on the earth in luxury and in pleasure; you have fattened your hearts in a day of slaughter. You have condemned, you have killed the righteous man; he does not resist you. Be patient, therefore, brethren, until the coming of the Lord. . . . behold, the Judge is standing at the doors. (James 5:1 ff.)

Speaking of this hatred, Kautsky rightly says: "Rarely has the class hatred of the modern proletariat attained such forms as that of the Christian proletariat."[27] It is the hatred of the Am Ha-aretz for the Pharisees, of the Zealots and the

Sicarii for the well to do and the middle class, of the suffering and harassed people of town and country for those in authority and in high places, as it had been expressed in the pre-Christian political rebellions and in messianic fantasies.

Intimately connected with this hatred for the spiritual and social authorities is an essential feature of the social and psychic structure of early Christianity, namely, its democratic, brotherly character. If the Jewish society of the time was characterized by an extreme caste spirit pervading all social relationships, the early Christian community was a free brotherhood of the poor, unconcerned with institutions and formulas.

We find ourselves confronted by an impossible task if we wish to sketch a picture of the organization during the first hundred years. . . . The whole community is held together only by the common bond of faith and hope and love. The office does not support the person, but always the person the office. . . . Since the first Christians felt they were pilgrims and strangers on the earth, what need was there for permanent institutions?[28]

In this early Christian brotherhood, mutual economic assistance and support, "love-communism," as Harnack calls it, played a special role.

We see, therefore, that the early Christians were men and women, the poor, uneducated, oppressed masses of the Jewish people, and later, of other peoples. In place of the increasing impossibility of altering their hopeless situation through realistic means, there developed the expectation that a change would occur in a very short time, at a moment's notice, and that these people would then find the happiness previously missed, but that the rich and the nobility would be punished, in accordance with justice and the desires of the Christian masses. The first Christians were a brotherhood of socially and economically oppressed enthusiasts held together by hope and hatred.

What distinguished the early Christians from the peasants and proletarians struggling against Rome was not their basic psychic attitude. The first Christians were no more "humble" and resigned to the will of God, no more convinced of the necessity and immutability of their lot, no more inspired by the wish to be loved by their rulers than were the political and military fighters. The two groups hated the ruling fathers in the same way, hoping with equal vigor to see the latter's downfall and the beginning of their own rule and of a satisfactory future. The difference between them lay neither in the presuppositions nor in the goal and direction of their wishes, but only in the sphere in which they tried to fulfill them. While the Zealots and Sicarii endeavored to realize their wishes in the sphere of political reality, the complete hopelessness of realization led the early Christians to formulate the same wishes in fantasy. The expression of this was the early Christian faith, especially the early Christian idea concerning Jesus and his relationship to the Father-God.

What were the ideas of these first Christians?

The contents of the faith of the disciples, and the common proclamation which united them, may be comprised in the following propositions. Jesus of Nazareth is the Messiah promised by the prophets. Jesus after his death is by the Divine awakening raised to the right hand of God, and will soon return to set up his kingdom visibly upon the earth. He who believes in Jesus, and has been received into the community of the disciples of Jesus, who, in virtue of a sincere change of mind, calls on God as Father, and lives according to the commandments of Jesus, is a saint of God, and as such can be certain of the sin-forgiving grace of God, and of a share in the future glory, that is, of redemption.[29]

"God has made him both Lord and Christ" (Acts 2:36). This is the oldest doctrine of Christ that we have, and is therefore of great interest, especially since it was later supplanted by other, more extensive, doctrines. It is called the "adoptionist" theory because here an act of adoption is assumed. Adoption is here used in contrast to the natural sonship which exists from birth. Accordingly, the thought present here is that Jesus was not messiah from the beginning; in other words, he was not from the beginning the Son of God, but became so only by a definite, very distinct act of God's will. This is expressed particularly in the fact that the statement in Psalms 2:7, "You are my son, today I have begotten you," is interpreted as referring to the moment of the exaltation of Jesus (Acts 13:33).

According to an ancient Semitic idea, the king is a son of God, whether by descent or, as here, by adoption, on the day he mounts the throne. It is therefore in keeping with the oriental spirit to say that Jesus, as he was exalted to the right hand of God, became the Son of God. This idea is echoed even by Paul, although for him the concept "Son of God" had already acquired another meaning. Romans 1:4 says of the Son of God that he was "designated Son of God in power . . . by his resurrection from the dead." Here two different forms of the concept conflict: the Son of God who was Son from the very beginning (Paul's idea); and Jesus, who, after the resurrection, was exalted to Son of God in power, that is, to kingly ruler of the world (the concept of the early community). The difficult combination of the two ideas shows very clearly that here two different thought patterns encountered each other. The older, stemming from the early Christian community, is consistent, in that the early community characterizes Jesus, before the exaltation, as a man: "a man attested to you by God with mighty works and wonders and signs which God did through him in your midst" (Acts 2:22). One should observe here that Jesus has not performed the miracle, but God through him. Jesus was the voice of God. This idea prevails to some extent in the Gospel tradition, where, for example, after the healing of the lame, the people praise God (Mark 2:12). In particular, Jesus is characterized as the prophet whom Moses promised: "The Lord God will raise up for you a prophet from your brethren" (Acts 3:22; 7:37; Deut. 18:15).[30]

We see thus that the concept of Jesus held by the early community was that he was a man chosen by God and elevated by him as a "messiah," and later as "Son of God." This Christology of the early community resembles in many respects the concept of the messiah chosen by God to introduce a kingdom of righteousness and love, a concept which had been familiar among the Jewish masses for a long time. In only two ideas of the new faith do we find elements that signify something specifically new: in the fact of his exaltation as Son of God to sit at the right hand of the Almighty, and in the fact that this messiah is no longer the powerful, victorious hero, but his significance and dignity reside just in his suffering, in his death on the cross. To be sure, the idea of a dying messiah or even of a dying god was not entirely new in the popular consciousness. Isaiah 53 speaks of this suffering servant of God. The Fourth Book of Ezra also mentions a dying messiah, although of course in an essentially different form, for he dies after four hundred years and after his victory.[31] The idea of a dying god may have become familiar to the people from an entirely different source, namely, the Near Eastern cults and myths (Osiris, Attis, and Adonis).

> The fate of man finds its prototype in the passion of a god who suffers on earth, dies, and rises again. This god will permit all those to share in that blessed immortality who join him in the mysteries or even identify themselves with him.[32]

Perhaps there were also Jewish esoteric traditions of a dying god or a dying messiah, but all these precursors cannot explain the enormous influence which the teaching about the crucified and suffering savior immediately had upon the Jewish masses, and soon upon the pagan masses as well.

In the early community of enthusiasts, Jesus was thus a man exalted after his death into a god who would soon return in order to execute judgment, to make happy those who suffer, and to punish the rulers.

We have now gained insight into the psychic surfaces of the followers of early Christianity sufficiently to attempt our interpretation of these first christological statements. Those intoxicated by this idea were people who were tormented and despairing, full of hatred for their Jewish and pagan oppressors, with no prospect of effecting a better future. A message which would allow them to project into fantasy all that reality had denied them must have been extremely fascinating.

If there was nothing left for the Zealots but to die in hopeless battle, the followers of Christ could dream of their goal without reality immediately showing them the hopelessness of their wishes. By substituting fantasy for reality, the Christian message satisfied the longings for hope and revenge, and although it failed to relieve hunger, it brought a fantasy satisfaction of no little significance for the oppressed.[33]

The psychoanalytic investigation of the christological faith of the early Christian community must now raise the following questions: What was the significance for the first Christians of the fantasy of the dying man elevated to a god? Why did this fantasy win the hearts of so many thousands in a short time? What were its unconscious sources, and what emotional needs were satisfied by it?

First, the most important question: A man is raised to a god; he is adopted by God. As Reik has correctly observed, we have here the old myth of the rebellion of the son, an expression of hostile impulses toward the father-god. We now understand what significance this myth must have had for the followers of early Christianity. These people hated intensely the authorities that confronted them with "fatherly" power. The priests, scholars, aristocrats, in short, all the rulers who excluded them from the enjoyment of life and who in their emotional world played the role of the severe, forbidding, threatening, tormenting father— they also had to hate this God who was an ally of their oppressors, who permitted them to suffer and be oppressed. They themselves wanted to rule, even to be the masters, but it seemed to them hopeless to try to achieve this in reality and to overthrow and destroy their present masters by force. So they satisfied their wishes in a fantasy. Consciously they did not date to slander the fatherly God. Conscious hatred was reserved for the authorities, not for the elevated father figure, the divine being himself. But the unconscious hostility to the divine father found expression in the Christ fantasy. They put a man at God's side and made him a co-regent with God the father. This man who became a god, and with whom as humans they could identify, represented their Oedipus wishes; he was a symbol of their unconscious hostility to God the father, for if a man could become God, the latter was deprived of his privileged fatherly position of being unique and unreachable. The belief in the elevation of a man to god was thus the expression of an unconscious wish for the removal of the divine father.

Here lies the significance of the fact that the early Christian community held the adoptionist doctrine, the theory of the elevation of man to God. In this doctrine the hostility to God found its expression, while in the doctrine that later increased in popularity and became dominant—the doctrine about the Jesus who was always a god—was expressed the elimination of these hostile wishes toward God (to be discussed in greater detail later). The faithful identified with this son; they could identify with him because he was a suffering human like themselves. This is the basis of the fascinating power and effect upon the masses of the idea of the suffering man elevated to a god; only with a suffering being could they identify. Thousands of men before him had been crucified, tormented, and humiliated. If they thought of this crucified one as elevated to god, this meant that in their unconscious, this crucified god was themselves.

The pre-Christian apocalypse mentioned a victorious, strong messiah. He was the representative of the wishes and fantasies of a class of people who were oppressed, but who in many ways suffered less, and still harbored the hope of victory. The class from which the early Christian community grew, and in which the Christianity of the first one hundred to one hundred fifty years had great success, could not identify with such a strong, powerful messiah; their messiah could only be a suffering, crucified one. The figure of the suffering savior was determined in a threefold way: First in the sense just mentioned; secondly by the fact that some of the death wishes against the father-god were shifted to the son. In the myth of the dying god (Adonis, Attis, Osiris), god himself was the one whose death was fantasied. In the early Christian myth the father is killed in the son.

But, finally, the fantasy of the crucified son had still a third function: Since the believing enthusiasts were imbued with hatred and death wishes—consciously against their rulers, unconsciously against God the father—they identified with the crucified; they themselves suffered death on the cross and atoned in this way for their death wishes against the father. Through his death, Jesus expiated the guilt of all, and the first Christians greatly needed such an atonement. Because of their total situation, aggression and death wishes against the father were particularly active in them.

The focus of the early Christian fantasy, however—in contrast to the later Catholic faith, to be dealt with presently—seems to lie, not in a masochistic expiation through self-annihilation, but in the displacement of the father by identification with the suffering Jesus.

For a full understanding of the psychic background of the belief in Christ, we must consider the fact that at that time the Roman Empire was increasingly devoted to the emperor cult, which transcended all national boundaries. Psychologically it was closely related to monotheism, the belief in a righteous, good father. If the pagans often referred to Christianity as atheism, in a deeper psychological sense they were right, for this faith in the suffering man elevated to a god was the fantasy of a suffering, oppressed class that wanted to displace the ruling powers—god, emperor, and father—and put themselves in their places. If the main accusations of the pagans against the Christians included the charge that they committed Oedipus crimes, this accusation was actually senseless slander; but the unconscious of the slanderers had understood well the unconscious meaning of the Christ myth, its Oedipus wishes, and its concealed hostility to God the father, the emperor, and authority.[34]

To sum up: In order to understand the later development of dogma, one must understand first the distinctive feature of early Christology, its adoptionist character. The belief that a man is elevated to a god was an expression of the unconscious impulse of hostility to the father that was present in these masses. It presented the possibility of an identification and the corresponding expectation that the new age would soon begin when those who were suffering and oppressed would be rulers and thus become happy. Since one could, and did, identify with Jesus because he was the suffering man, the possibility was offered of a community organization without authorities, statutes, and bureaucracy, united by the common identification with the suffering Jesus raised to a god. The early Christian adoptionist belief was born of the masses; it was an expression of their revolutionary tendencies, and offered a satisfaction for their strongest longing. This explains why in such an extraordinarily rapid time it became the religion also of the oppressed pagan masses (although soon not theirs exclusively).

The Transformation of Christianity and the Homoousian Dogma

The early beliefs concerning Jesus underwent a change. The man raised to God became the Son of Man who was always God and existed before all creation, one with God and yet to be distinguished from Him. Has this change of ideas about Jesus also a sociopsychological meaning such as we were able to demonstrate for the early adoptionist belief? We shall find an answer to this question by studying the people who, two to three hundred years later, created this dogma and believed in it. In this way we may be able to understand their real life situation and its psychic aspects.

The most important questions are these: Who were the Christians in the early centuries after Christ? Does Christianity remain the religion of the suffering Jewish enthusiasts of Palestine, or who takes their place and joins them?

The first great change in the composition of believers occurred when Christian propaganda turned toward the pagans, and, in a great victorious campaign, won followers among them in almost the entire Roman Empire. The significance of change of nationality among the followers of Christianity should not be underestimated, but it played no decisive role as long as the social composition of the Christian community did not change essentially, as long, that is, as it was made up of poor, oppressed, uneducated people feeling common suffering, common hatred, and common hope.

The familiar judgment of Paul concerning the Corinthian community holds without doubt for the second and third generations of most of the Christian communities as well as for the apostolic period:

"For consider your call, brethren; not many of you were wise according to worldly standards, not many were powerful, not many were of noble birth; but God chose what is foolish in the world to shame the wise, God chose what is weak in the world to shame the strong, God chose what is low and despised in the world, even things that are not, to bring to nothing things that are." (I Cor. 1:26–28)[35]

But although the great majority of the followers Paul won for Christianity in the first century were still people of the lowest classes—lowly artisans, slaves, and emancipated slaves—gradually another social element, the educated and the well-to-do, began to infiltrate the communities. Paul was indeed one of the first Christian leaders that did not stem from the lower classes. He was the son of a well-to-do Roman citizen, had been a Pharisee and therefore one of the intellectuals that scorned the Christians and was hated by them.

He was not a proletarian unfamiliar with and hatefully opposed to the political order, not one who had no interest in its continuance and who hoped for its destruction. He had from the beginning been too close to the powers of government, had had too much experience of the blessings of the sacred order not to be of a quite different mind concerning the ethical worth of the state, than, say, a member of the native Zealot party, or even than his Pharisaic colleagues who saw in the Roman domination at most the lesser evil compared with the half-Jewish Herodians.[36]

With his propaganda, Paul appealed primarily to the lowest social strata, but certainly also to some of the well-to-do and of the educated people, espe- cially merchants who through their wanderings and travels became decidedly significant in the spread of Christianity.[37] But until well into the second cen- tury, a substantial element in the communities belonged to the lower classes. This is shown by certain passages from the original literature, which, like the Epistle of James or the Book of Revelation, breathe flaming hatred for the power- ful and the rich. The artless form of such pieces of literature and the general tenor of eschatology show that "the members of the [Christian] communions of the post-apostolic period were still drawn mainly from the ranks of the poor and the unfree.[48]

About the middle of the second century, Christianity began to win followers among the middle and higher classes of the Roman Empire. Above all, it was women of prominent position, and merchants, who took charge of the propa- ganda; Christianity spread in their circles and then gradually penetrated the circles of the ruling aristocracy. By the end of the second century, Christianity had already ceased to be the religion of the poor artisans and slaves. And when under Constantine it became the state religion, it had already become the religion of larger circles of the ruling class in the Roman Empire.[39]

Two hundred and fifty to three hundred years after the birth of Christianity, the adherents of this faith were quite different from the first Christians. They were no longer Jews with the belief, held more passionately than by any other people, in a messianic time soon to come. They were, rather, Greeks, Romans, Syrians, and Gauls—in short, members of all the nations of the Roman Empire. More important than this shift in nationality was the social difference. Indeed, slaves, artisans, and the "shabby *proletariat*," that is, the masses of the lower classes, still constituted the bulk of the Christian communion, but Christianity had simultaneously become the religion also of the prominent and ruling classes of the Roman Empire.

In connection with this change in the social structure of the Christian churches we must glance at the general economic and political situation of the Roman Empire, which had undergone a fundamental change during the same period. The national differences within the world empire had been steadily disappearing. Even an alien could become a Roman citizen (Edict of Caracalla, 212). At the same time, the emperor cult functioned as a unifying bond, leveling national differences. The economic development was characterized by a process of gradual but progressive feudalization:

> The new relationships, as they were consolidated after the end of the third
> century, no longer knew any free work, but only compulsory work in the
> status groups (or estates) that had become hereditary, in the rural popula-
> tion and the colonies, as well as with the artisans and the guilds, and also
> (as is well known) with the patricians who had become the principal
> bearers of the tax burden. Thus the circle was completed. The development
> comes back to the point from which it has started. The medieval order is
> being established.[40]

The political expression of this declining economy, which was regressing into a new estate-bound "natural economy," was the absolute monarchy as it was shaped by Diocletian and Constantine. A hierarchical system was developed with infinite dependencies, at the apex of which was the person of the divine emperor, to whom the masses were to render reverence and love. In a relatively short time the Roman Empire became a feudal class state with a rigidly established order in which the lowest ranks could not expect to rise because the stagnation due to the recession of productive powers made a progressive development impossible. The social system was stabilized and was regulated from the top, and it was imperative to make it easier for the individual who stood at the bottom to be content with his situation.

In the main this was the social situation in the Roman Empire from the beginning of the third century on. The transformation which Christianity, especially the concept of Christ and of his relation to God the Father, underwent from its early days down to this era, must be understood primarily in the light of this social change and of the psychic change conditioned by it, and of the new sociological function which Christianity had to assume. The vital element in the situation is simply not understood if we think that "the" Christian religion spread and won over to its thinking the great majority of the population of the Roman Empire. The truth is, rather, that the original religion was transformed into another one, but the new Catholic religion had good reason for concealing this transformation.

We shall now point out what transformation Christianity underwent during the first three centuries, and show how the new religion contrasted with the old.

The most important point is that the eschatological expectations which had constituted the center of the faith and hope of the early community gradually disappeared. The core of the missionary preaching of the early communion was, "The kingdom of God is at hand." People had prepared for the kingdom, they had even expected to experience it themselves, and they doubted whether in the short time available before the coming of the new kingdom, it would be possible to proclaim the Christian message to the majority of the heathen world. Paul's faith is still imbued with eschatological hopes, but with him the expected time of the kingdom's coming already began to be postponed further into the future. For him the final consummation was assured by the elevation of the messiah, and the last struggle, which was still to come, lost its significance in view of what had already happened. But in the subsequent development, belief in the immediate establishment of the kingdom tended more and more to disappear: "What we perceive is, rather, the gradual disappearance of an original element, the Enthusiastic and Apocalyptic, that is, of the sure consciousness of an immediate possession of the Divine Spirit, and the hope of the future conquering the present."[41]

If the two conceptions, the eschatological and the spiritual, were closely bound together at the beginning, with the main stress on the eschatological conception, they slowly became separated. The eschatological hope gradually receded, the nucleus of the Christian faith drew away from the second advent of Christ, and "it would then necessarily be found in the first advent, in virtue of which salvation was already prepared for man and man for salvation."[42]

The process of propagating the early Christian enthusiasm quickly died out. To be sure, throughout the later history of Christianity (from the Montanists to the Anabaptists), there were continual attempts to revive the old Christian enthusiasm with its eschatological expectation—attempts that emanated from those groups who, in their economic, social, and psychic situation, because they were oppressed and striving for freedom, resembled the first Christians. But the Church was through with these revolutionary attempts, ever since she had, in the course of the second century, won the first decisive victory. From that time on, the burden of the message was not in the cry, "The kingdom is at hand," in the expectation that judgment day and the return of Jesus would come soon; the Christians no longer looked to the future or to history, but, rather, they looked backward. The decisive event had already taken place. The appearance of Jesus had already represented the miracle.

The real, historical world no longer needed to change; outwardly everything could remain as it was—state, society, law, economy—for salvation had become an inward, spiritual, unhistorical, individual matter guaranteed by faith in Jesus. The hope for real, historical deliverance was replaced by faith in the already complete spiritual deliverance. The historical interest was supplanted by the cosmological interest. Hand in hand with it, ethical demands faded away. The first century of Christianity was characterized by rigorous ethical postulates, in the belief that the Christian community was primarily a fellowship of holy living. This practical, ethical rigorism is replaced by the means of grace dispensed by the Church. Very closely connected with the renunciation of the original rigorous ethical practice was the growing reconciliation of Christians with the state. "The second century of the existence of the Christian church already exhibits along all lines a development which moves toward a reconciliation with the state and society."[43] Even the occasional persecutions of the Christians by the state did not affect in the least this development. Although there were attempts here and there to maintain the old rigorist ethic hostile to the state and middle-class life,

> . . . the great majority of Christians, especially the leading bishops, decided differently. It now sufficed to have God in one's heart and to confess faith in Him when a public confession before the authorities was unavoidable. It was enough to flee the actual worship of idols, otherwise the Christian could remain in every honorable calling; there he was allowed to come into external contact with the worship of idols, and he should conduct himself prudently and cautiously so that he neither contaminated himself nor even ran the risk of contaminating himself and others. The church adopted this attitude everywhere after the beginning of the third century. The state thereby gained numerous quiet, dutiful, and conscientious citizens who, far from causing it any difficulty, supported order and peace in society. . . . Since the church had abandoned her rigid, negative attitude toward the world, she developed into a state-supporting and state-reforming power. If we may introduce a modern phenomenon for comparison, we may say that the world-fleeing fanatics who awaited the heavenly state of the future became revisionists of the existing order of life.[44]

This fundamental transformation of Christianity from the religion of the oppressed to the religion of the rulers and of the masses manipulated by them, from the expectation of the imminent approach of judgment day and the new age to a faith in the already consummated redemption; from the postulate of a pure, moral life to satisfaction of conscience through ecclesiastical means of grace; from hostility to the state to cordial agreement with it—all this is closely connected with the final great change about to be described. Christianity, which had been the religion of a community of equal brothers, without hierarchy or bureaucracy, became "the Church," the reflected image of the absolute monarchy of the Roman Empire.

In the first century there was not even a clearly defined external authority in the Christian communities, which were accordingly built upon the independence and freedom of the individual Christian with respect to matters of faith. The second century was characterized by the gradual development of an ecclesiastical union with authoritative leaders and thus, also, by the establishment of a systematic doctrine of faith to which the individual Christian had to submit. Originally it was not the Church but God alone who could forgive sins. Later, *Extra ecclesiam nulla salus;* the Church alone offers protection against any loss of grace. As an institution, the Church became holy by virtue of her endowment, the moral establishment that educates for salvation. This function is restricted to the priests, especially to the episcopate, "which in its unity guarantees the legitimacy of the church and has received the jurisdiction of forgiveness of sins."[45] This transformation of the free brotherly fellowship into a hierarchical organization clearly indicates the psychic change that had occurred.[46] As the first Christians were imbued with hatred and contempt for the educated rich and the rulers, in short, for all authority, so the Christians from the third century on were imbued with reverence, love, and fidelity to the new clerical authorities.

Just as Christianity was transformed in every respect in the first three centuries of its existence and became a new religion as compared with the original one, this was true also with respect to the concept of Jesus. In early Christianity the adoptionist doctrine prevailed, that is, the belief that the man Jesus had been elevated to a god. With the continued development of the Church, the concept of the nature of Jesus leaned more and more toward the pneumatic viewpoint: A man was not elevated to a god, but a god descended to become man. This was the basis of the new concept of Christ, until it culminated in the doctrine of Athanasius, which was adopted by the Nicene Council: Jesus, the Son of God, begotten of the Father before all time, of one nature with the Father. The Arian view that Jesus and God the Father were indeed of similar but not identical nature is rejected in favor of the logically contradictory thesis that two natures, God and his Son, are only one nature; this is the assertion of a duality that is simultaneously a unity. What is the meaning of this change in the concept of Jesus and his relation to God the Father, and what relation does the change in dogma bear to the change in the whole religion?

Early Christianity was hostile to authority and to the state. It satisfied in fantasy the revolutionary wishes of the lower classes, hostile to the father. The Christianity that was elevated to the official religion of the Roman Empire three hundred years later had a completely different social function. It was intended to be, at the same time, a religion for both the leaders and the led; the rulers and the ruled. Christianity fulfilled the function which the emperor and the Mithras cult could not nearly as well fulfill, namely, the integration of the masses into the absolutist system of the Roman Empire. The revolutionary situation which had prevailed until the second century had disappeared. Economic regression had supervened; the Middle Ages began to develop. The economic situation led to a system of social ties and dependencies that came to their peak politically in the Roman-Byzantine absolutism. The new Christianity came under the leadership of the ruling class. The new dogma of Jesus was created and formulated by this ruling group and its intellectual representatives, not by the masses. *The decisive element was the change from the idea of man becoming God to that of God becoming man.*

Since the new concept of the Son, who was indeed a second person beside God yet one with him, changed the tension between God and his Son into harmony, and since it avoided the concept that a man could become God, it eliminated from the formula the revolutionary character of the older doctrine, namely, hostility to the father. The Oedipus crime contained in the old formula, the displacement of the father by the son, was eliminated in the new Christianity. The father remained untouched in his position. Now, however, it was not a man, but his only begotten Son, existing before all creation, who was beside him. Jesus himself became God without dethroning God because he had always been a component of God.

Thus far we have understood only the negative point: why Jesus could no longer be the man raised to a god, the man set at the right hand of the father. The need for recognition of the father, for passive subordination to him, could have been satisfied by the great competitor of Christianity, the emperor cult. Why did Christianity and not the emperor cult succeed in becoming the established state religion of the Roman Empire? Because Christianity had a quality that made it superior for the social function it was intended to fulfill, namely, faith in the crucified Son of God. The suffering and oppressed masses could identify with him to a greater degree. But the fantasy satisfaction changed. The masses no longed identified with the crucified man in order to dethrone the father in fantasy, but, rather, in order to enjoy his love and grace. The idea that a man became a god was a symbol of aggressive, active, hostile-to-the-father tendencies. The idea that God became a man was transformed into a symbol of the tender, passive tie to the father. The masses found their satisfaction in the fact that their representative, the crucified Jesus, was elevated in status, becoming himself a pre-existent God. People no longer expected an imminent historical change but believed, rather, that deliverance had already taken place, that what they hoped for had already happened. They rejected the fantasy which represented hostility to the father, and accepted another in its place, the harmonizing one of the son placed beside the father by the latter's free will.

The theological change is the expression of a sociological one, that is, the change in the social function of Christianity. Far from being a religion of rebels and revolutionaries, this religion of the ruling class was now determined to keep the masses in obedience and lead them. Since the old revolutionary representative was retained, however, the emotional need of the masses was satisfied in a new way. The formula of passive submission replaced the active hostility to the father. It was not necessary to displace the father, since the son had indeed been equal to God from the beginning, precisely because God himself had "emitted" him. The actual possibility of identifying with a god who had suffered yet had from the beginning been in heaven, and at the same time of eliminating tendencies hostile to the father, is the basis for the victory of Christianity over the emperor cult. Moreover, the change in the attitude toward the real, existing father figures—the priests, the emperor, and especially the rulers—corresponded to this changed attitude toward the father-god.

The psychic situation of the Catholic masses of the fourth century was unlike that of the early Christians in that the hatred for the authorities, including the father-god, was no longer conscious, or was only relatively so; the people had given up their revolutionary attitude. The reason for this lies in the change of the social reality. Every hope for the overthrow of the rulers and for the victory of their own class was so hopeless that, from the psychic viewpoint, it would have been futile and uneconomical to persist in the attitude of hatred. If it was hopeless to overthrow the father, then the better psychic escape was to submit to him, to love him, and to receive love from him. This change of psychic attitude was the inevitable result of the final defeat of the oppressed class.

But the aggressive impulses could not have disappeared. Nor could they even have diminished, for their real cause, the oppression by the rulers, was neither removed nor reduced. Where were the aggressive impulses now? They were turned away from the earlier objects—the fathers, the authorities—and directed back toward the individual self. The identification with the suffering, crucified Jesus offered a magnificent opportunity for this. In Catholic dogma the stress was no longer, as in the early Christian doctrine, on the overthrow of the father but on the self-annihilation of the son. The original aggression directed against the father was turned against the self, and it thereby provided an outlet that was harmless for social stability.

But this was possible only in connection with another change. For the first Christians, the authorities and the rich were the evil people who would reap the deserved reward for their wickedness. Certainly the early Christians were not without guilt feelings on account of their hostility to the father; and the identification with the suffering Jesus had also served to expiate their aggression;

but without doubt the emphasis for them was not in the guilt feelings and the masochistic, atoning reaction. For the Catholic masses later on the situation had changed. For them no longer were the rulers to blame for wretchedness and suffering; rather, the sufferers themselves were guilty. They must reproach themselves if they are unhappy. Only through constant expiation, only through personal suffering could they atone for their guilt and win the love and pardon of God and of his earthly representatives. By suffering and castrating oneself, one finds an escape from the oppressive guilt feeling and has a chance to receive pardon and love.[47]

The Catholic Church understood how to accelerate and strengthen in a masterful way this process of changing the reproach against God and the rulers into reproach of the self. It increased the guilt feeling of the masses to a point where it was almost unbearable; and in doing so it achieved a double purpose: first, it helped turn reproaches and aggression away from the authorities and toward the suffering masses; and, second, it offered itself to these suffering masses as a good and loving father, since the priests granted pardon and expiation for the guilt feeling which they themselves had engendered. It ingeniously cultivated the psychic condition from which it, and the upper class, derived a double advantage: the diversion of the aggression of the masses and the assurance of their dependency, gratitude, and love.

For the rulers, however, the fantasy of the suffering Jesus not only had this social function but also an important psychic function. It relieved them of the guilt feelings they experienced because of the distress and suffering of the masses whom they had oppressed and exploited. By identifying with the suffering Jesus, the exploiting groups could themselves do penance. They could comfort themselves with the idea that, since even God's only-begotten Son had suffered voluntarily, suffering, for the masses, was a grace of God, and therefore they had no reason to reproach themselves for causing such suffering.

The transformation of christological dogma, as well as that of the whole Christian religion, merely corresponded to the sociological function of religion in general, the maintenance of social stability by preserving the interests of the governing classes. For the first Christians it was a blessed and satisfying dream to create the fantasy that the hated authorities would soon be overthrown and that they themselves, now poor and suffering, would achieve mastery and happiness. After their final defeat, and after all their expectations had proved futile, the masses became satisfied with a fantasy in which they accepted responsibility for all suffering; they could, however, atone for their sins through their own suffering and then hope to be loved by a good father. He had proved himself a loving father when, in the form of the son, he became a suffering man. Their other wishes for happiness, and not merely forgiveness, were satisfied in the fantasy of a blissful hereafter, a hereafter which was supposed to replace the historically happy condition in this world for which the early Christians had hoped.

In our interpretation of the Homoousian formula, however, we have not yet found its unique and ultimate unconscious meaning. Analytic experience leads us to expect that behind the logical contradiction of the formula, namely, that two are equal to one, must be hidden a specific unconscious meaning to which the dogma owes its significance and its fascination. This deepest, unconscious meaning of the Homoousian doctrine becomes clear when we recall a simple fact: There is one actual situation in which this formula makes sense, the situation of the child in its mother's womb. Mother and child are then two beings and at the same time are one.

We have now arrived at the central problem of the change in the idea of the relation of Jesus to God the Father. Not only the son has changed but the father as well. The strong, powerful father has become the sheltering and protecting mother; the once rebellious, then suffering and passive son has become the small child. Under the guise of the fatherly God of the Jews, who in the struggle with the Near Eastern motherly divinities had gained dominance, the divine figure of the Great Mother emerges again, and becomes the dominating figure of medieval Christianity.

The significance that the motherly divinity had for Catholic Christianity, from the fourth century on, becomes clear, first, in the role that the Church, as such, begins to play; and second, in the cult of Mary.[48] It has been shown that for early Christianity the idea of a *church* was still quite alien. Only in the course of historical development does the Church gradually assume a hierarchical organization; the Church itself becomes a holy institution and more than merely the sum of its members. The Church mediates salvation, the believers are her children, she is the Great Mother through whom alone man can achieve security and blessedness.

Equally revealing is the revival of the figure of the motherly divinity in the cult of Mary. Mary represents that motherly divinity grown independent by separating itself from the father-god. In her, the motherly qualities, which had always unconsciously been a part of God the Father, were now consciously and clearly experienced and symbolically represented.

In the New Testament account, Mary was in no way elevated beyond the sphere of ordinary men. With the development of Christology, ideas about Mary assumed an ever increasing prominence. The more the figure of the historical human Jesus receded in favor of the pre-existent Son of God, the more Mary was deified. Although, according to the New Testament, Mary in her marriage with Joseph continued to bear children, Epiphanius disputed that view as heretical and frivolous. In the Nestorian controversy a decision against Nestorius was reached in 431 that Mary was not only the mother of Christ but also the mother of God, and at the end of the fourth century there arose a cult of Mary, and men addressed prayers to her. About the same time the representation of Mary in the plastic arts also began to play a great and ever increasing role. The succeeding centuries attached more and more significance to the mother of God, and her worship became more exuberant and more general. Altars were erected to her, and her pictures were shown everywhere. From a recipient of grace she became the dispenser of grace.[49] Mary with the infant Jesus became the symbol of the Catholic Middle Ages.

The full significance of the collective fantasy of the nursing Madonna becomes clear only through the results of psychoanalytic clinical investigations. Sándor Radó has pointed out the extraordinary significance which the fear of starvation, on the one hand, and the happiness of oral satisfaction, on the other, play in the psychic life of the individual:

> The torments of hunger become a psychic foretaste of later "punishments," and through the school of punishment they become the primitive mechanism of a self-punishment which finally in melancholia achieves so fateful a significance. Behind the boundless fear of pauperization felt by the melancholy is hidden nothing other than the fear of starvation; this fear is the reaction of the vitality of the normal ego-residue to the life-threatening, melancholic act of expiation or penance imposed by the church. Drinking from the breast, however, remains the shining example of the unfailing, pardoning proffer of love. It is certainly no accident that the nursing Madonna with the child has become the symbol of a powerful religion and through her mediation the symbol of a whole epoch of our Western culture. In my opinion, the derivation of the meaning-complex of guilt atonement and pardon from the early infantile experience of rage, hunger, and drinking from the breast solves our riddle as to why the hope for absolution and love is perhaps the most powerful configuration we encounter in the higher levels of human psychic life.[50]

Radó's study makes entirely intelligible the connection between the fantasy of the suffering Jesus and that of the child Jesus on the mother's breast. Both fantasies are an expression of the wish for pardon and expiation. In the fantasy of the crucified Jesus, pardon is obtained by a passive, self-castrating submission to the father. In the fantasy of the child Jesus on the breast of the Madonna, the masochistic element is lacking; in place of the father one finds the mother who, while she pacifies the child, grants pardon and expiation. The same happy feeling constitutes the unconscious meaning of the Homoousian dogma, the fantasy of the child sheltered in the womb.

This fantasy of the great pardoning mother is the optimal gratification which Catholic Christianity had to offer. The more the masses suffered, the more their real situation resembled that of the suffering Jesus, and the more the figure of the happy, suckling babe could, and must, appear alongside the figure of the suffering Jesus. But this meant also that men had to regress to a passive, infantile attitude. This position precluded active revolt; it was the psychic attitude corresponding to the man of hierarchically structured medieval society, a human being who found himself dependent on the rulers, who expected to secure from them his minimum sustenance, and for whom hunger was proof of his sins.

Notes

1. "Dogma und Zwangsidee," *Imago, XII* (1927). cf., *Dogma and Compulsion* (New York: International Universities Press, Inc., 1951), and other works on psychology of religion by Reik; E. Jones, *Zur Psychoanalyse der christlichen Religion*; and A. J. Storfer, *Marias jungfraüliche Mutterschaft.*
2. Sigmund Freud, *Civilization and Its Discontents* (Standard edition), XXI, 76.
3. Sigmund Freud, *The Future of an Illusion* (Standard edition), XXI, 17–18.
4. Ibid., p. 30
5. For the economic development, see especially M. Rostovtzeff, Social and Economic History of the Roman Empire (Oxford: 1926); Max Weber, "Die sozialen Gründe des Untergangs der antiken Kultur," in *Gesammelte Aufsätze zur Sozial- und Wirtschaftsgeschichte,* 1924; E. Meyer, "Sklaverei im Altertum," *Kleine Schriften,* 2d ed., Vol. I; K. Kautsky, *Foundations of Christianity* (Russell, 1953).
6. *The Life and Works of Flavius Josephus, The Antiquities of the Jews,* XVIII, 1, 4, translated by William Whiston (New York: Holt, Rinehart and Winston, Inc., 1957).
7. *The Life and Works of Flavius Josephus, The Wars of the Jews,* II, 8, 14.
8. Ibid.
9. Josephus, *The Wars of the Jews,* XVIII, 1, 3.
10. Talmud, Pesachim 49b.
11. The three passages just cited are in the Talmud, Pesachim 48b.
12. cf.. Friedlander, *Die religiösen Bewegungen innerhalb des Judentums im Zeitalter Jesu* (Berlin, 1905).
13. Josephus, *The Wars of the Jews,* II, 13, 4, 5.
14. Ibid., II, 13, 6. It is important to note that Josephus, who himself belonged to the aristocratic elite, is describing the revolutionaries in terms of his own bias.
15. E. Schürer, *Geschichte des jüdischen Volkes im Zeitalter Jesu Christi* (3d ed.; 1901), I, 617.
16. cf.. T. Mommsen, *History of Rome,* Vol. V.
17. Josephus, *The Wars of the Jews,* Vol. VI.
18. cf.. Johannes Weiss, *Das Urchristentum* (Gottingen, 1917).
19. cf.. M. Dibelius, *Die urchristliche Ueberlieferung von Johannes dew Taufer* (Stuttgart, 1911).
20. Ibid., p. 130.
21. cf.. for the social structure of primitive Christianity, R. Knopf, Das nachapostolische Zeitalter (Tübingen, 1905); Adolph Harnack, *Die Mission und Ausbreitung des Christentums* (4th ed.; 1923), Vol. 1; Adolph Harnack, "Kirche und Staat bis zur Gründung der Staatskirche," *Kultur der Gegenwart,* 2d ed.; Adolph Harnack, "Das Urchristentum und die soziale Frage," *Preussische Jahrbücher,* 1908, Vol. 131; K. Kautsky, *Foundations of Christianity* (Russell, 1953).
22. Origen, *Contra Celsum,* translated by Henry Chadwick (London: Cambridge University Press, 1953), III, 55.
23. The problem of the historical Jesus need not concern us in this connection. The social effect of the primitive Christian message is to be understood only on the basis of the classes to which it was directed and by which it was accepted; and only the understanding of their psychic situation is important for us here.
24. Adolf Harnack, *History of Dogma* (New York: Dover Publications, Inc., 1961), I, 66–67.
25. Ibid., pp. 62–63.

26. cf.. Weiss, *Das Urchristentum*, p. 55.
27. K. Kautsky, *Der Ursprung des Christentums*, p. 345.
28. H. von Schubert, *Grundzüge der Kirchengeschichte* (Tübingen, 1904).
29. Adolph Harnack, *History of Dogma*, I, 78.
30. Weiss, op.cit., p. 85.
31. cf.. Psalm 22 and Hosea 6.
32. F. Cumont, "Die orientalischen Religionen in ihrem Einfluss auf die europäischen Religionen des Altertums," *Kultur der Gegenwart* (2d ed.; 1923), Vol. I, Pt. III, p. 1; cf. also Weiss, op. cit., p. 70.
33. A remark must be inserted here about one problem which has been the object of severe polemies, the question as to how far Christianity can be understood as a revolutionary class movement. Kautsky, in *Vorläufer des neuen Sozialismus* (Stuttgart, 1895), and later in *Foundations of Christianity*, has set forth the view that Christianity is a proletarian class movement, that in essence, however, its significance lay in its practical activity, that is, in its charitable work and not in its "pious fanaticisms." Kautsky overlooks the fact that a movement may have a class origin without the existence of social and economic motives in the consciousness of its instigators. His contempt for the historical significance of religious ideas demonstrates only his complete lack of understanding of the meaning of fantasy satisfaction within the social process. His interpretation of historical materialism is so banal that it is easy for Troeltsch and Harnack to give an appearance of refuting historical materialism. They, like Kautsky, do not put at the center of the inquiry the problem of the class relationship that conditioned Christianity, but rather the problem as to how much of a role these class relationships played in the consciousness and ideology of the first Christians. Although Kautsky misses the real problem, the class foundations of early Christianity are nevertheless so clear that the tortuous attempt, especially of Troeltsch (in his *Social Teaching of the Christian Churches*), to explain them away, betrays all too plainly the political tendencies of the author.
34. The accusations of ritual murder and of sexual licentiousness can be understood in a similar way.
35. Knopf, *Das nachapostolische Zeitalter*, p. 64.
36. Weiss, op. cit., p. 132.
37. cf.. Knopf, op. cit., p. 70.
38. Knopf, op. cit., pp. 69 ff. The admonitions of St. Hippolytus still reveal the ethical rigorism and the hostility to middle-class life, as is seen in chapter 41 (cited by Harnack, *Die Mission und Ausbreitung des Christentums*, I, 300): "Inquiry shall likewise be made about the professions and trades of those who are brought to be admitted to the faith. If a man is a pander, he must desist or be rejected. If a man is a sculptor or painter, he must be charged not to make idols; if he does not desist, he must be rejected. If a man is an actor or pantomimist, he must desist or be rejected. A teacher of young children had best desist, but if he has no other occupation, he may be permitted to continue. A charioteer, likewise, who races or frequents races, must desist or be rejected. A gladiator or a trainer of gladiators, or a huntsman (in the wild-beast shows), or anyone connected with these shows, or a public official in charge of gladiatorial exhibitions must desist or be rejected. A soldier of the civil authority must be taught not to kill men and to refuse to do so if he is commanded, and to refuse to take an oath; if he is unwilling to comply, he must be rejected. A military commander or civic magistrate that wears the purple must resign or be rejected. If a catechumen or a believer seeks to become a soldier, they must be rejected, for they have despised God. A harlot or licentious man or one who has emasculated himself, or any other who does things not to be named must be rejected, for they are defiled. An enchanter, a diviner, a soothsayer, a user of magic verses, a juggler, a mountebank, an amulet-maker must desist or be rejected. A concubine, who is a slave and has reared her children and has been faithful to her master alone, may become a hearer; but if she has failed in these matters she must be rejected. If a man has a concubine, he must desist and marry legally; if he is unwilling, he must be rejected. If, now, we have omitted anything, the facts will instruct your mind; for we all have the Spirit of God."
39. As an example of the character of the community in Rome, Knopf gives a picture of the development of the social composition of the Christian church in the first three centuries. Paul, in the Epistle to the Philippians (4:22), asks that his greeting be conveyed "especially

to those of Caesar's household." The fact that the death sentences imposed by Nero upon the Christians (mentioned by Tacitus, *Annales*, xv, 44), such as being sewed up in hides, dog-baiting, crucifixion, being made into living torches, might be used against only *humiliores* and not against *honestiores* (the more prominent), shows that the Christians of this period belonged mainly to the lower ranks, even though some rich and prominent people may already have joined them. How greatly the composition of the post-apostolic church had changed is shown by a passage cited by Knopf from *I Clement*, 38:2: "The rich should offer help to the poor and the poor man should thank God that He has given him someone through whom his need can be helped." One does not observe here any trace of that animosity against the rich which pervades other documents. This is the way in which one can speak in a church where richer and more prominent people are not so very rare and also where they perform their duties to the poor (Knopf, op. cit., p. 65). From the fact that in A.D. 96, eight months before his death, Domitian had his cousin, Consul Titus Flavius, executed, and sent the cousin's first wife into exile (punishing him probably and the woman certainly on account of their adherence to Christianity), shows that already at the end of the first century, Christians in Rome had penetrated into the emperor's household. The growing number of rich and prominent Christians naturally created tensions and differences in the churches. One of these differences arose early, as to whether Christian masters should free their Christian slaves. This is shown by Paul's exhortation that slaves should not seek emancipation. But since in the course of its development, Christianity became more and more the faith of the ruling groups, these tensions were bound to grow. "The rich did not fraternize any too well with the slaves, the emancipated and the proletarians, especially in public. The poor for their part see the rich as belonging half to the devil" (Knopf, op. cit., p. 81). Kermas gives a good picture of the changed social composition: "Those who do much business also sin much, being engrossed in their business, and serving their Lord in nothing" (*Sim*. VIII, 9). "These are they who were faithful, but became rich and in honor among the heathen; then they put on great haughtiness and became high-minded, and abandoned the truth, and did cleave to the righteous, but lived together with the heathen, and this way pleased them better" (*Sim*. IX, 1). "The rich cleave with difficulty to the servants of God, fearing that they will be asked for something by them" (*Sim.*, XX, 2). It would appear that only in the times after the Antonines did the rich and prominent, the people of blood and means, join the Christian church, as is rightly understood by Eusebius in a familiar passage where he says that "during the reign of Commodus the affairs [of the Christians] took an easier turn, and, thanks to the divine grace, peace embraced the churches throughout the whole world . . . insomuch that already large numbers even of those at Rome, highly distinguished for wealth and birth, were advancing towards their own salvation with all their households and kindred" (Eusebius, *Ecclesiastical History,* Book V, 21, 1). Thus in the main metropolis of the world, Christianity had ceased to be a religion primarily of poor people and slaves. From then on its power of attraction appeared in the different ranks of property and education.

40. Eduard Meyer, "Sklaverei im Altertum," *Kleine Schriften* (2d ed.; 1924), I, 81.
41. Harnack, *History of Dogma*, I, 49. Harnack emphasizes that originally, two interrelated views prevailed regarding the purpose of the coming of Christ or the nature and means of salvation: Salvation was conceived, on the one hand, as sharing in the glorious kingdom of Christ soon to appear, and everything else was regarded as preparatory to this sure prospect; on the other hand, however, attention was turned to the conditions and to the provisions of God wrought by Christ, which first made men capable of becoming sure of it. Forgiveness of sin, righteousness, faith, knowledge, etc., are the things which come into consideration here, and these blessings themselves, so far as they have as their sure result life in the kingdom of Christ, or, more accurately, eternal life, may be regarded as salvation. (Ibid., pp. 129–130).
42. Ibid., p. 130.
43. Harnack, "Kirche und Staat bis zur Gründung der Staatskirche," *Kultur der Gegenwart*, Vol. I, Pt. 4, p. 1; 2d ed., p. 239.
44. Harnack, op. cit., p. 143.
45. Cyprian, *Epistle* 69, 11.
46. cf.. Harnack, *History of Dogma*, II, 67–94.
47. cf.. Freud's remarks in *Civilization and Its Discontents* (Standard edition), XXI, 123 ff.

48. cf.. A. J. Storfer, *Marias fungfräuliche Mutterschaft* (Berlin, 1913).
49. The connection of the worship of Mary with the worship of the pagan mother divinities has been dealt with a number of times. A particularly clear example is found in the Collyridians, who, as priestesses of Mary, carry cakes about in a solemn procession on a day consecrated to her, similar to the cult of the Canaanite queen of heaven mentioned by Jeremiah. cf.. Rösch (Th. St. K., 1888, pp. 278 f.), who interprets the cake as a phallic symbol and views the Mary worshiped by the Collyridians as identical with the Oriental-Phoenician Astarte [see *Realenzy-klopädie für protestantische Theologie und Kirche*, Vol. XII (Leipzig: 1915)].
50. *Internationale Zeitschrift für Psychoanalyse*, XIII, 445.

III

Leo Löwenthal

6
The Demonic
Project for a Negative Philosophy of Religion

Leo Löwenthal
Translated by Mathias Fritsch

I. The Goal

> In the year that king Uzziah died I saw also the Lord sitting upon a throne,
> high and lifted up, and his train filled the temple. Above it stood the
> seraphims: each one had six wings; with twain he covered his face, and
> with twain he covered his feet, and with twain he did fly. And one cried
> unto another, and said, Holy, holy, holy, is the LORD of hosts: the whole
> earth is full of his glory. And the posts of the door moved at the voice of
> him that cried, and the house was filled with smoke. Then said I, Woe is
> me! for I am undone; because I am a man of unclean lips, and I dwell in
> the midst of a people of unclean lips: for mine eyes have seen the King,
> the LORD of hosts. Then flew one of the seraphims unto me, having a
> live coal in his hand, which he had taken with the tongs from off the
> altar: And he laid it upon my mouth, and said, Lo, this hath touched thy
> lips; and thine iniquity is taken away, and thy sin purged. Also I heard the
> voice of the Lord, saying, Whom shall I send, and who will go for us?
> Then said I, Here am I; send me.
>
> Isaiah 6: 1–8

Did Isaiah really see the Lord before the angel flew to him? Was Isaiah's sanctifica-
tion as a prophet accomplished only when the angel burned the brink of his
lips with glowing coal?

Isaiah saw nothing before the angel left the Lord; he intimated the Lord, he
sensed the shudder and mysteries of the eternal, which was still covered by

angels' wings. It is the situation of the believer that Scripture describes: he who senses the great mystery, to him a solution is presented, but his Father conceals himself in the cover of a cloud. The believer becomes a prophet only when an angel leaves the Lord: "when a tip of the mystery is lifted," as the people pronounce it in profound symbolic words. For the soaking in divine breath does not occur in the consecration of the lips, but in viewing the unconcealed divine being; and the great end, the utopian rays of the star, will rise when all angels withdraw from God, and He reveals Himself, without cover or mediator, in "mystic democracy" as the most intrepid certainty and figure.

Thus, the shivering view turns to the last revelations of the mystery, and wishes, in unbearable longing, to rise above the viewing of the formations granted to us. But here, with us, only one or the other is given grace, and the merciless master keeps himself secret for the many. That is why the whole hocus pocus of pagan, biblical, and Christian demonology and hierarchy does its work, and separates us in good and evil intention from Him. Thus, the problem of the demonic begins with the unfortunate enchantment of this world, whose utter state of abandonment passes into our hands the desperation of a negative proof of God. In baroque rapture, the realm of the figures of the intermediate world—the angels, the devil, the amourettes—becomes visible, all of which are the monstrous product and curse of the "present" God that, however "is not." And this is what remains of the task of a new "negative theology": to pursue this bizarre whole through the process that wishes to unfold itself from the mythical, from what is bound to nature, to the last state of differentiation of that which is only psychical, in order to find sublimation, tranquility, and form in the messianic goal.

He who thinks he may approach this as a psychologist reveals himself as a "negative" metaphysician in disguise whose claim to approach objective formations in purely theoretical interest would turn into an analysis of his own self, from now on merely "functional." Or he who believes himself to be able to render the phenomena "intelligible" in a sociological and immanent analysis of meaning, in truth functions as the witness of a "negative" philosophy of history whose conferral of meaning, however, again remains restricted to the "mobility" of the spirit [*Geist*] which organizes the temporal formations. No, what is crucial is to truly pass through the realm of absolute negation, in which the devil's grotesque faces and grinning figures have found their sedate abode. For it is here, in this isolated wilderness that expands without paths, that modern thought, out of anguish and anxiety, out of defiance and ignorance, created for itself the quarrel of "is" and "ought." It is here that from the ego the unknown self fled as the enthroned new God who, already *ab ovo*, had to remain unattainable and unknown. Here, only here, could the terrible blasphemy of the syncretism of all parts of the earth and all times occur. Only here could frantic delusion take the merging of Buddha and Christ for the great motherly redemption and purification that has finally been granted.

But this should not be the end, and the defiance against God shall give an account of the beginning of the new faith and of the new inwardness. For our speech needs a new meaning, a new responsibility. This new meaning communicates itself as soon as it becomes aware of its own sin: its loss of connectedness [*Zusammenhang*]. The striving of modern thought for system, the expression of the longing for this connectedness, is still merely indicated, unconscious, and impure. It is strongest precisely where—in Marx—the incorruptible view of the non-existence of meaning, and of the fact that the cosmos is saturated with economic law, falls upon the totality of godlessness and lack of redemption. Here, the "realistic" thinker meets Husserl who appears so distant from the light of day. His phenomenology admits the banishment of value from our so terribly frozen times, and, in ultimate honesty, tears down all veils to reveal the naked, bloody body as the plea and cry of anger. For it is precisely this absolutely critical and most negative of attitudes that signifies the only possible theodicy, and that wishes to present all things, this helpless "*hic et nunc*," so that it may receive its blessing anew.

Thus, from a unified basic attitude, Marx's world-historical, dialectical economics has to merge with the phenomenological tendency in a "negative philosophy of religion." It is to recognize the whole of this unilluminated mash of things, to transform it into a temporally ordered cosmos, and to present this cosmos in childish longing, so that the miracle may be permitted to occur.

Admittedly, this must be understood in the right way. It is not the labor and vocation of a single human being to return to us, to our time, the lost divine meaning from a messianically distant sphere. Rather, it is frivolity of the most worrisome sort when awaiting the "figure," which has become solace for some people today in the solitude and breadth of their spirit, is reinterpreted as awaiting the One, the human being whose laying of hands purifies the world of sin, overflows it anew with his blessing, and now accomplishes, for a last and final time, the miracle of the purely human.

Rather: the path leads us through the abysses and flashiness of the end of the world. The valuelessness but lawfulness of the economic and of the chaos of drives of the phenomena must present the whole nakedness of the world of things in final clarity and evidence. And it is to be refrained from pronouncements about results.

But this much remains certain: only then, in this dissolved, shaken up, and woken world of figures, do the conditions obtain for the occurrence of the miracle of "transformation," so that the heavenly blessed water and bread takes form in essential "transcendence," which, however, will then be at the same time "immanence": the proper blood of the proper body, womb, conception, and fruit.

II. The Path

1.

The study forces its way into the God-cursed and God-seeking realm between paradise and Messiah, between the answers without questions and the total negation of all those questions that have ever been posed in heresy and despair. It places itself into this yawning abyss in order to, temporally and in principle, search in it the structure of those formations that, in each case, represent the questionable and unsettling: the in-finite in the bad sense that Hegel already condemned.

Yet the ascent remains simple and plainly unambiguous. Only in the more differentiated sphere of the psychical does the dangerous inferno release the entire brew of its forms and grotesque faces. But the man of myth, still caught up in his dream and barely weaned from paradise, begins his confrontation with the most naïve object: with nature, with the exterior. For the total unfolding of all possibilities may only be accomplished by the ego that confronts the subject as object. The animal and the grove, the plant and the river, sun and lightning— everything that passes beyond the merely animalistic functions, and yet claims meaningfulness in its immediate reality—becomes the mysterious bearer (rather: the intermediary bearer) of the ultimate forces. Here, the demonic finds its first abode. It becomes the final explanation in order to interpret what, to the anxious soul, appears to require interpretation. The necessity of finding one's way in the uncanny and enigmatic character of living and dying thus engenders the "daimon" as the true "dispenser," according to the Greek meaning of the word.

When conceptual analysis approaches the "daimon" it admits the impossibility of grasping its content. That the latter is secondary and impossible is revealed by the meaning of all of the fore-going considerations. Nonetheless, three constitutive determinations of *form* prove to be valid throughout:

1. Concrete interpenetration. Nature defies its dissolution in systematically lined up causal chains; it forces an enchantment of the laws of cause and effect. If at all, it becomes approximately accessible to the analogues of human life. A kind of "magic causality"—according to a phrase Wilhelm Wundt once coined for this primitive demonology—sets up a relation between "subject" and "object" from the side of the subject.

2. This is connected to an emphasis on value. For the transfer of the human to the natural transfers above all the properties of good and evil. This becomes understandable if we remember that a vital need wished to interpret nature in its meaning for human beings, that is, in the effects of its powers. Thus, death and hail had to be evil demons, birth and the sun of the harvest good demons.

3. For the sake of completion, we should add the moment in which the phenomenon reveals its proper secret, but which we have already shown to a sufficient degree: the demonic is *not an ultimate*. Admittedly, in the primitive stage this does not mean very much. But the possibility of there being good *and* evil demons already indicates the peculiarity of a succession of stages, namely, that no threshold is permitted to become an absolute "principle." The demonic means going through stages. It is not the devil, it is not God, and not even the demiurge, working from beyond and above all evaluation; it is the expression of the dynamic which is condemned to go through the antinomies of values in a certain order.

2.

This becomes clearer in a second stage whose place shall be fixed by reference to Homeric Greece. Here, the natural thing that requires interpretation for the most primitive needs no longer, according to an illustrious expression of Jaspers, tells its story. The view has turned to its own interior, and has discovered the world of gods in its own psychical powers in a religious experience, an experience that is estranged from the last sense, and thus formed anthropomorphically. This view projects the world of gods in an Olympus whose geographical and transcendent melting-together, however, is far removed from the evidence of Sinaitic revelation. And yet, the "principle," that which has final validity, is here posited in the form of Jupiter Maximus. Now that which does not subject itself to this "principle" (and, according to its genesis, this must already be an immense manifold); that which escapes the absolute and yet does not make itself felt as the ownmost psychical substrate; all this of the intermediary world, the "space of air under the moon," as both Xenocrates and Philo put it; the enigmatic remainder—all this becomes the ruling domain of the demonic. He who points out that, in this way, we are merely giving a name to that which is really ungraspable, raises a nonsensical objection: it is the necessity of those human beings who live in the half-emptied and half-dreaming world, a world already split into claiming "subject" and defiant "object," to interpret throughout and to still grasp that which is no longer graspable in the timid robe of a word, hardly a concept.

3.

But now, we are carried further, beyond this primitive state. The air becomes thinner, and the veils are falling off of the images of the old gods, images that have already become empty and that are merely staring as masks. The primitive-metaphysical worldview dissolves and makes room for the "en-lightenment" of a starless sky. The magic causality of the demonic is robbed of its robe, its vivacity dwindles, and it becomes subject to the immensely broad view of theoretical study as the "*problem*" in general. The insolubility of existing things is no longer a danger to this attitude, for it operates with the concept of an infinite task and an infinite solution, of the in-principle possible and continuously progressing analysis and explanation of that which has not yet been absorbed without remainder. Here, we rediscover ourselves, in this terrifying desert of the emptied self and the formless world. The rhythm of the path is revealed in Hegelian dialectic: the thesis of the world of gods and demons, full of meaning, is opposed by a godless world that is, in addition, without relation to the ego. However, it gains its justification. For it blasts open the framework of a naïve totality and overcomes myth when the latter, in its forms, had become the rigid formality of a cult alienated from reality. To be sure, the world becomes disenchanted, the illustriousness of the grotesque faces of the demon turns into the abstractness of the question. But the continuity of the demonic is preserved in its "negative" reception as questionability in general. The impossibility of giving the answer— and in this lies the peculiarity of this stage—becomes the as-yet impossibility of giving it, and thus the consolation of finding it in the future.

4.

Here, the temporal process ends, and what remains is to grasp, from the end, the further types in the necessity of their insertion in the series.

Language is pulled along into the empty space; only through the form of the paradox does it win, by fighting, the possibility of escaping the gloomy hold of unknown goallessnesses. And by throwing back the willful lie at the claimed truth, by sneeringly showing that which is indestructibly "non-genuine" to that which claims to be genuine, language succeeds in developing the process further. However, he who sinks deeper and deeper in empty space without sensing the substance of the level to which everything heads in slow and yet uncanny speed, does not become aware of the fact that the longing for the miraculous, the propensity for the horrific, is a sure sign of dynamic progress. What expresses itself here is the feeling that, in whatever abstraction, the connectedness of the whole, which was either believed to have been reached already or which is at least in principle accessible to being reached, may not be able to withstand the "manifold of faces." Shaftesbury once said that man had no greater amusement than the pleasure "of hearing and telling strange and unbelievable things." But in the end, this amusement proves to spring from a righteousness that is not satisfied with the "harmonious" interpretation and "systematic" inclusion of the totality, and the constant experience of shrill disharmonies which mock every violation by "systems." Thus, "personal experience," which is supposed to be irrelevant for this objectified, abstract view, a view so distant from the subject, mixes itself into this view. (Here is the place, but also the tomb, of the theosophical worldview.) The so-called subject recognizes again the necessity of internal relations with the so-called object. And then, the differentiation brought along with it the tearing apart of the connectedness: the intrusion of the unexplained then demands, at the least, the honest admission that the connectedness has been torn apart and thus opens the rift, the abyss, for the workings of the demon.

However, the strongest impulse toward this honesty derives from the psychical. Here, a hitherto restrained scream first wrests itself from an anxious heart (I am thinking of a painting by Edvard Munch, which insightfully allows the deep psychological secret of modern agony to reveal itself). The scream endows the feeling of emptiness with sound, a feeling brought along by the abstraction of formal imperatives. "Biological and sociological life has a deep propensity to remain within its own immanence: human beings merely want to live and the formations wish to remain untouched; and the distance and absence of the active God would grant sole domination to the sluggishness and self-sufficiency of this quietly rotting life if human beings were not at times possessed by the power of the demon, passing beyond themselves in a manner without reason and justification, canceling all psychological and sociological basic states of their existence." And in truly illuminated words, Georg Lukács continues: "Then, suddenly, the God-forsakenness of the world reveals itself as a lack of substance, as an irrational mixture of density and permeability. What previously seemed to be very solid crumbles like dry clay at the first contact with a man possessed by a demon, and the empty appearance behind which attractive landscapes were previously to be seen is suddenly transformed into a glass wall against which men beat in vain, like bees against a window, incapable of breaking through, incapable of understanding that the way is barred."[1]

Thus, doctrine and life are leaving their abodes and find themselves halfway along: in the semi-darkness of baroque disquiet. The quiet of the immeasurably spreading expanse of form of the abstract laws is left behind: to the theoretician, the expanse of form appears untrue (and even more, aesthetically it appears boring and yawning); to the ethicist, it appears evil and immoral because it is empty. So the demonic is sought by one, and demanded by the other as the driving force, as the in principle unprincipled, as the horrific, as that which is on our heels. However, this demonology keeps its distance from the miracle. The miracle is at home in God's womb who releases it as greeting and mission of his absolute power, as that which is without relation, that which is to be taken as it is. But the unclear breakthrough of the demonic transcendence is in impure league with human beings and proves to belong to the sphere of the stages that mediates and presents the antinomy of the divine and the devilish in its passage through human beings.

But this stage too is granted its good justification. It reveals a courage for which the continuous explanation by reference to the abstract law is no longer sufficient. At the same time, this courage sees the impossibility of an explanation of that which is inexplicable according to its essence and its origin; it does not rest content with the weakness and the lack of conscience of the expectation that one day we will be able to explain it, one day we will be able to get ahead. This attitude, according to Georg Lukács' explication, comes to a head in irony: "The writer's irony is a negative mysticism to be found in times without a god. It is an attitude of *docta ignorantia* towards meaning, a portrayal of the kindly and malicious workings of demons, a refusal to comprehend more than the mere fact of these workings; and in it there is the deep certainty, expressible only by form-giving, that through not-desiring-to-know and not-being-able-to-know he has truly encountered, glimpsed and grasped the ultimate, true substance, the present, non-existent God."[2]

However, the demonic does not find its rightful place with the mystic of divine times or the one who alone is inspired, the one who steps in front of God without mediator in "democratic" blessing. It is only the temptation of the devil to desecrate the absence of mystery in the realm beyond the split and, in destruction, to give away the "*unio mystica.*" That which is restlessly wandering about [*das Ahasverische*], and eternally homeless, may not intrude into this static world itself, in which, according to the unchangeable saying, everything occupies its secure abode, beyond the antinomy of the "ego" and the "It," which demands dynamism.

But here, it may, as graspable ungraspability, show its emptiness to the abstraction, and capture the vanity and contentedness of the formal, subjectless interpretation vis-à-vis *du rien*, in order to throw it back into the antinomies of reality.

However, we have not yet discussed our three constitutive determinations of form. Without doubt, the proof of the intermittent, unstable character is coming to the light of day: for the graphic clarity, the "experience" with its ever graspable content, tears apart the abstraction, without regard for the latter's proud claim, or even its certainty, to have it all in secure possession. And that which has the character of value, which showed itself clearly in the ethical realm, can be detected equally well in the hellish horror of the theoretical attitude.

The question, as pure question, was the product of the third stage. But since the product turned its meaning against its origin, it at the same time left the mother and wandered about in "non-genuine" form. However, it matures and celebrates its feast in the perfection of wisdom.

Here, the path of "natural" demonology has reached its goal. From here on, it passes into the highs and lows of the psychical manifold. But now—only provisionally, to be sure—everything is clarified in order to let that which, according to its essence, is the least clarified, stand out most in its form.

5.

It is Goethe who shall here illuminate the entire sphere. He escapes the afore-mentioned non-genuineness. The demonic is no longer sought; it cannot be conjured up by any of the rites or by the conjurations, from the coarsest cultic customs to the most inventive deceptions of theosophical pseudo-science.

> "Geheimnisvoll am lichten Tag
> Läßð sich Natur des Schleiers nicht berauben,
> Und was sie deinem Geist nicht offenbaren mag,
> Das zwingst du ihr nicht ab mit Hebeln und mit
> Schrauben."

> ["Mysterious in the light of day,
> Nature, in veils, will not let us perceive her,
> And what she is willing to betray,
> You cannot wrest from her without thumbscrews,
> Wheel, or lever."[3]]

However: very soon it shows itself to the observant view. For Faust, who has become more than sick of abstraction, and who awakens to self-reflection, ex-periences the irresolvability of the world into conceptual systems, experiences the defiance of the "It" which parades as "ego." The "It" ultimately resists being squeezed into connections [*Zusammenhänge*] after all, and shows its scornfully grinning grotesque face to all harmony and order. For, in the end, something ambiguous always remains as an unabsorbed remainder after all, and this some-thing scorns every principled insertion into an order. It is the Goethean phenom-enon of the "situation," namely the relations between given naturalness and human beings, in which the aforementioned mystery manifests itself: every success and every effect is enigmatic and "demonic" as soon as the psychical goes along with it. Once again, the empty formula "the demonic" would be pale and meaningless if it did not gain its meaning by passing through the bipolarity of good and evil. To cite the famous words, the demonic ". . . was not godlike, for it seemed unreasonable; not human, for it had no understanding; nor devilish, for it was beneficent; nor angelic, for it often betrayed a malicious pleasure. It resembled chance, for it evolved no consequences: it was like Provi-dence, for it hinted at connection. All that limits us it seemed to penetrate; it seemed to sport at will with the necessary elements of our existence; it contracted time and expanded space. In the impossible alone did it appear to find pleasure, while it rejected the possible with contempt."[4] It is precisely that which seems to issue the command "stop!" to the observer in the face of what can be explained;

it appears as that which upsets all meaning in the end. However, it is not a constitutive category of the world's architecture; to the God who "pushed from the outside" it would be dissolved in a synthesis of meaning that transcends our view, and that overlooks the cosmos in encompassing totality. But it is that which breaks again and again what we demand as the constituting factor, which then has to retreat into the darkness of insufficiency.

6.

The process advances with necessity: he who is wise points beyond himself [*der Weise weist über sich hinaus*]. For he recognizes the contemplative peace of observing everything, understanding everything, charitably interpreting everything, despite its theoretical superiority, as ultimately inferior to the meaningful actor who, to be sure, does not know everything, or even knows very little, but who subjects everything to the realm of his demands and his activity.

Thus the path turns more and more inward and finally ends in the center of the soul.

In part, and only with resistance, one grants to psychology a role here which inserts the demonic in a field beyond good and evil, and which quite neutrally presents, in very determined peculiarity, the human being in whom the demon is at work and formative as one possible type among others. The human being, in whom the demon thus holds sway as the eternal wanderer and electrifier, is far removed from the frivolity and incomprehensibility of a chaotic scatter-brain who indeed has nothing by which he could be grasped. This human being is equally removed from the life form of a consistently stubborn person, a life form that is abstract, at times even empty, fanatical, and that has lost its goal. To the demonic person, every situation becomes questionable in its being what it is; every situation demands its own answer. At the same time, from the psychological viewpoint, he himself turns into a "demonic" phenomenon through the problem and peculiarity of the given answer, through, once again, that which has the character of stages which so well escapes the chaotic person's state of being emptied of antinomies as well as the consistent person's violation of antinomies. For here, his own law of life is, quite easily and consolingly, revealed to even the most impartial observer: how human beings manifest the consciousness of the right path in the products of their actions in a dark force that is concealed to them. This rendering-vivid, this abrupt illumination of an almost forgotten but operative power that is ignited in the ego, appears fascinating, and all categories of good and evil, of the meaningful and the nonsensical, are extinguished in their validity as torches and pointers of the way that have become too weak. And the soldiers follow Caesar as the children follow the Pied Piper...

Yet all of a sudden a voice resounds in this bustle without value, in this inferno of incessantly pushing restless infinities: the voice of warning, then the voice of the one who calls for new values. For the demonic person can never reach perfection. The driving force becomes mere driving; that which originally promised to overcome the content-drained realm of the consistent person of the "enlightened" stage, now itself loses form and content and becomes the merely unruly calling for content. Should this be the end?

No: for the dialectical rhythm which, by means of "non-genuineness," granted a new abode to the demonic—deprived of its home in the realm of abstractions—expels it a second time from the home which it had won. For the returning value domineeringly casts it out to the land of evil, because in its sphere morality must proscribe and banish all unfreedom. In the border province, the figure of Socrates becomes visible, with whom the "daimonion" is suspended from its activity, its immediate ability to intervene, and with whom it may only raise its finger as a warning of the evil, and thus as the gate opener to the abode of the noble.

7.

Now the end comes in sight: for the remark that the good, springing from the idea of freedom, drives out the demonic, does not hold for the already castigated formal imperatives. Rather, the morality of this last and final stage resides in the re-inspired realm and draws its power and pathos from the "transcendence" it experienced. He who gives indications here already sins or chatters. The forms may only be outlined in brevity.

According to Kierkegaard, the danger of sin consists in the human proclivity for fear. But the most immoral and devilish thing is fear of the good. This flight from the divine into the empty space of the ego is the demonic. "The only thing which may truly arm us against the sophistry of fear is faith." The inability to have faith, the fear of salvation, wishes to gain a foothold in the demonic by distorting and violently turning this *inability* to have faith into the *unwillingness* to have it. Similarly, in his "Spirit of Utopia" Ernst Bloch castigates the demonic as the immoral, as that which must be overcome and rejected: "What holds us in its inept and then vengeful hand: blocking, tormenting, deluding us, the spider, the kill or be killed, the poisonous scorpion, the angel of death, the demon of chance, of disaster, of death, the homelessness of everything meaningful, the dense, banal, almost impassable mountain range separating us from all Providence, the wizard of a 'pious' panlogism—all that *can not* be the same principle that will one day pronounce judgment, and then claim always to have been watching over us by inscrutable, supra-rational means, and, in spite of the 'Fall' cause by our overweening pride, to have kept us close to its heart."[5] This is precisely what is rejected: the claim of the demonic to be a principle and to preserve us and give us a home by "super-rational" means. For the pathos of a morality that has been intuited in transcendence, and that is known in immanence by passing through all eternities, through all heavens and hells, banishes of itself all heteronomy of ambiguous, illegitimate demonology. "For we are mighty: only the unjust exist through their God, but the just—God exists through them, and into their hands is given the consecration of the Name."[6] Here, towards the end, the view again penetrates toward us in our anguish and promises, in blasphemous piety, transformation, and miracle.

8.

However, at the end lies the ruin of all demonology, for the bright messianic light signifies the principled negation and destruction of all that is tenebrous. And the useful role of the demonic as that which interrogates without remainder is over in a final, all-comprehensive "*unio mystica*" which finds its peace in God the Lord.

Notes

1. Georg Lukács, *The Theory of the Novel*, translated by Anna Bostock (Cambridge, Masachussetts, 1971), 90. All notes henceforth are the Translator's notes.
2. Ibid., 90.
3. Goethe's *Faust*, The Original German and a New Translation and Introduction by Walter Kaufmann (Garden City, New York: Doubleday & Company, Inc., 1961), lines 673–76.
4. *The works of J. W. von Goethe in Forteen Volumes*, edited by Nathan Haskell Dole, translations by Sir Walter Scott, Sir Theodore Martin John Oxenford, Thomas Carlyle, and others (London and Boston: Francis A. Niccols & Co. No Date), Volume 5. *Truth and Fiction*, book twenty, 423. For the German, see Johann Wolfgang Goethe, *Sämtliche Werke*, vol. 16, *Dichtung und Wahrheit*, 820, lines 19–27.
5. Ernst Bloch, *The Spirit of Utopia*, trans. Anthony A. Nassar (Stanford: Standford University Press, 2000), 274.
6. Ibid., 278.

IV
Herbert Marcuse

7

A Study on Authority

Luther, Calvin, Kant

Herbert Marcuse
Translated by Jorisdes Bres

The authority relationship, as understood in these analyses, assumes two essential elements in the mental attitude of he who is subject to authority: a certain measure of freedom (voluntariness: recognition and affirmation of the bearer of authority, which is not based purely on coercion) and conversely, submission, the tying of will (indeed of thought and reason) to the authoritative will of an Other. Thus in the authority relationship freedom and unfreedom, autonomy and heteronomy, are yoked in the same concept and united in the single person of he who is subject. The recognition of authority as a basic force of social praxis attacks the very roots of human freedom: it means (in a different sense in each case) the surrender of autonomy (of thought, will, action), the tying of the subject's reason and will to pre-established contents, in such a way that these contents do not form the "material" to be changed by the will of the individual but are taken over as they stand as the obligatory norms for his reason and will. Yet bourgeois philosophy put the autonomy of the person right at the centre of its theory: Kant's teachings on freedom are only the clearest and highest expression of a tendency which has been in operation since Luther's essay on the freedom of the Christian man.

The concept of authority thus leads back to the concept of freedom: it is the practical freedom of the individual, his social freedom and its absence, which is at stake. The union of internal autonomy and external heteronomy, the disintegration of freedom in the direction of its opposite is the decisive characteristic of the concept of freedom which has dominated bourgeois theory since the

115

Reformation. Bourgeois theory has taken very great pains to justify these contradictions and antagonisms.

The individual cannot be simultaneously free and unfree, autonomous and heteronomous, unless the being of the person is conceived as divisible and belonging to various spheres. This is quite possible once one ceases to hypostatize the I as the "substance." But the decisive factor is the mode of this division. If it is undertaken dualistically, the world is split in half: two relatively self-enclosed spheres are set up and freedom and unfreedom as totalities divided between them in such a way that one sphere is wholly a realm of freedom and the other wholly a realm of unfreedom. Second, what is internal to the person is claimed as the realm of freedom: the person as member of the realm of Reason or of God (as "Christian," as "thing in itself," as intelligible being) is free. Meanwhile, the whole "external world," the person as member of a natural realm or, as the case may be, of a world of concupiscence which has fallen away from God (as "man," as "appearance"), becomes a place of unfreedom. The Christian conception of man as "created being" "between" natura naturata and natura naturans, with the unalterable inheritance of the Fall, still remains the unshaken basis of the bourgeois concept of freedom in German Idealism.

But the realm of freedom and the realm of unfreedom are not simply contiguous with or superimposed on each other. They are founded together in a specific relation. For freedom—and we must hold fast to this astonishing phrase despite its paradoxical nature—is the condition of unfreedom. Only because and in so far as man is free can he be unfree; precisely because he is "actually" (as a Christian, as a rational person) completely free must he "unactually" (as a member of the "external" world) be unfree. For the full freedom of man in the "external" world as well would indeed simultaneously denote his complete liberation from God, his enslavement to the Devil. This thought reappears in a secularized form in Kant: man's freedom as a rational being can only be "saved" if as a sensual being he is entirely abandoned to natural necessity. The Christian doctrine of freedom pushes the liberation of man back until it pre-dates his actual history, which then, as the history of his unfreedom, becomes an "eternal" consequence of this liberation. In fact, strictly speaking there is no liberation of man in history according to this doctrine or, to put it more precisely, Christian doctrine has good reasons for viewing such a liberation as primarily something negative and evil, namely the partial liberation from God, the achievement of freedom to sin (as symbolized in the Fall).

As an "internally" free being man is born into a social order which, while it may have been posited or permitted by God, by no means represents the realm in which the existence or non-existence of man is decided upon. Whatever the nature of this order may be, the inner freedom of man (his pure belief and his pure will, provided they remain pure) cannot be broken in it. "The power of the temporal authority, whether it does right or wrong, cannot harm the soul."[1]

This absolute inwardness of the person, the transcendent nature of Christian freedom *vis-à-vis* all worldly authority, must at the same time mean an "internal" weakening and breaking of the authority relationship, however completely the individual may submit externally to the earthly power. For the free Christian knows that he is "actually" raised above worldly law, that his essence and his being cannot be assailed by it and that his subordination to the worldly authorities is a "free" act, which he does not "owe" them. "Here we see that all works and all things are free to a Christian through his faith. And yet because the others do not yet believe, the Christian bears and holds with them, *although he is not obliged to do these things. He does this freely . . ."*[2] This simultaneous recognition and transcendence of the whole system of earthly authorities announces a very important element in the Christian-bourgeois doctrine of freedom—its *anti-authoritarian tendency.* The social meaning of this doctrine of freedom is not simply that the individual should submit *in toto* to any earthly authority and thus affirm *in toto* the given system of authorities at any time. The Protestantism of Luther and Calvin which gave the Christian doctrine of freedom its decisive form for bourgeois society, is bound up with the emergence of a new, "young" society which had first to conquer its right to exist in a bitter struggle against existing authorities. Faced with the universal bonds of traditionalist feudalism it absolutely required the liberation of the individual within the earthly order as well (the individual free subject of the economic sphere later essentially became the model of its concept of the individual)—it required the liberation of the territorial sovereign from the authority of an internationally centralized Church and a central imperial power. It further required the liberation of the "conscience" from numerous religious and ethical norms in order to clear the way for the rise of the bourgeoisie. In all these directions an *anti-authoritarian attitude* was necessary: and this will find its expression in the writers we shall discuss.

However, this anti-authoritarian tendency is only the complement of an order which is directly tied to the functioning of as yet opaque relationships of authority. From the very outset the bourgeois concept of freedom left the way open for the recognition of certain metaphysical authorities and this recognition permits external unfreedom to be perpetuated within the human soul.

This point announced a fresh duality in the Protestant-bourgeois concept of freedom: an opposition between Reason and Faith, rational and irrational (in fact anti-rational) factors. As opposed to the rational, "calculating" character of the Protestant-capitalist "spirit" which is often all too strongly emphasized, its irrational features must be particularly pointed out. There lies an ultimate lack of order at the very root of this whole way of life, rationalized and calculated down to the last detail as an "ideal type," this whole "business" of private life, family and firm: the accounts do not, after all, add up—neither in the particular, nor in the general "business." The everyday self-torture of "inner-worldly asceticism" for the sake of success and profit still ultimately has to experience these things, if they really occur, as unforeseeable good fortune. The individual is confronted again and again with the fear of loss: the reproduction of the whole society is only possible at the price of continual crises. The fact that the production and reproduction of life cannot be rationally mastered by this society constantly breaks through in the theological and philosophical reflections on its existence. The terrible hidden God of Calvinism is only one of the most severe forms of such a breakthrough: Luther's strong defence of the "unfree will" is a similar case, as is the yawning gulf between the pure form of the universal law and the material for its fulfilment in Kant's ethic. The bourgeoisie fought its greatest battles under the banner of "Reason" but it is precisely bourgeois society which totally deprives reason of its realization. The sector of nature controlled by man through rational methods is infinitely larger than in the Middle Ages; society's material process of production has in many instances been rationalized down to the last detail—but as a *whole* it remains "irrational." These antagonisms appear in the most varied forms in the ambivalence of bourgeois relationships of authority: they are rational, yet fortuitous, objective, yet anarchic, necessary, yet bad.

I. Luther and Calvin

Luther's pamphlet *The Freedom of a Christian* brought together for the first time the elements which constitute the specifically bourgeois concept of freedom and which became the ideological basis for the specifically bourgeois articulation of authority: freedom was assigned to the "inner" sphere of the person, to the "inner" man, and at the same time the "outer" person was subjected to the system of worldly powers; this system of earthly authorities was transcended through private autonomy and reason; person and work were separated (person and office) with the resultant "double morality"; actual unfreedom and inequality were justified as a consequence of "inner" freedom and equality. Right at the start of the work[3] are those two theses which, following on from St Paul, express the internally contradictory nature of the Christian concept of freedom with a conscious emphasis on this paradoxical antinomy: "A Christian is free and independent in every respect, a bondservant to none. A Christian is a dutiful servant in every respect, owing a duty to everyone" (p. 357). And the dissolution of the contradiction: the first sentence deals with "the spiritual man, his freedom and his supreme righteousness," the second sentence refers to "the outer man": "In as far as he is free, he requires to do nothing. In as far as he is a servant he must do everything" (p. 369). That expresses clearly and sharply the dualistic doctrine of the two realms, with freedom entirely assigned to the one, and unfreedom entirely assigned to the other.

The more specific determinations of internal freedom are all given in a counter-attack on external freedom, as negations of a merely external state of freedom: "No outer thing . . ." can make the free Christian "free or religious," for his freedom and his "servitude" are "neither bodily nor outward"; none of the external things "touches the soul, either to make it free or captive" (pp. 357–358). Nothing which is in the world and stems from the world can attack the "soul" and its freedom; this terrible utterance, which already makes it possible entirely to deprecate "outer" misery and to justify it "transcendentally," persists as the basis of the Kantian doctrine of freedom; through it, actual unfreedom is subsumed into the concept of freedom. As a result, a peculiar (positive and negative) ambiguity enters into this concept of freedom: the man who is enclosed in his inner freedom has so much freedom over all outer things that he becomes free *from* them—he doesn't even *have* them any more, he has no control over them (p. 367). Man no longer *needs* things and "works"—not because he already has them, or has control over them, but because in his self-sufficient inner freedom he doesn't need them at all. "If such works are no longer a prerequisite, then assuredly all commandments and laws are like broken chains; and if his chains are broken, he is assuredly free" (p. 362). Internal freedom. But the realm of external freedom which opens up is, from the standpoint of "spiritual" salvation as a whole, a realm of "things indifferent": what man is free to do here, what can be done or not done, is in itself irrelevant to the salvation of his soul. "But 'free' is that in which I have choice, and may use or not, yet in such a way that it profit my brother and not me."[4] The "free" things in this realm can also be called the "unnecessary" things: "Things which are not necessary, but are left to our free choice by God, and which we keep or not."[5] Freedom is a total release and independence, but a release and independence which can never be freely fulfilled or realized through a deed or work. For this freedom so far precedes every deed and every work that it is always already realized when man begins to act. His freedom can never be the result of an action; the action can neither add to nor diminish his freedom. Earthly "works" are not done to fulfil the person who requires this; the fulfilment must have occurred "through faith before all works . . . works follow, once the commandments have been met" (p. 364).

But what sense is left in the earthly work of man if it always lags behind fulfilment? For the "internal" man there is in fact no sense at all. Luther is quite clear on this point: "Works are lifeless things, they can neither honour nor praise God . . ." (loc. cit). A sentence pregnant with consequences: it stands at the beginning of a development which ends with the total "reification" and "alienation" of the capitalist world. Luther here hit on the nodal points of the new bourgeois *Weltanschauung* with great accuracy: it is one of the origins of the modern concept of the subject as person. Straight after he has proclaimed that works are "lifeless things" he continues: "But here we seek him who is not done, as works are, but is an initiator and a master of work" (loc. cit). What is sought is the person (or that aspect of the person) who (or which) is not done (by another) but who is and stays the real subject of activity, the real master over his works: the autonomously acting person. And at the same time—this is the decisive point—this person is sought in contradistinction to his ("lifeless") works: as the negation and negativity of the works. Doer and deed, person and work are torn asunder: the person as such essentially never enters into the work, can never be fulfilled in the work, eternally precedes any and every work. The true human subject is never the subject of *praxis*. Thereby the person is relieved to a previously unknown degree from the responsibility for his praxis, while at the same time he has become free for all types of praxis: the person secure in his inner freedom and fullness can only now really throw himself into outer praxis, for he knows that in so doing nothing can basically happen to him. And the separation of deed and doer, person and praxis, already posits the "double morality" which, in the form of the separation of "office" and "person" forms one of the foundation stones of Luther's ethics:[6] later we shall have to return to the significance of this divorce.

But we have not yet answered the question. What meaning can the praxis of a person thus separated from his works still possess? His praxis is at first completely "in vain": it is obvious that man as a person "is free from all commandments, and quite voluntarily does all that he does without recompense, and apart from seeking his own advantage or salvation. He already has sufficient, and he is already saved through his faith and God's grace. What he does is done just to please God" (p. 372). The person does not need the works, but they must nevertheless be done, so that "man may not go idle and may discipline and care for his body" (p. 371). The praxis which has been separated from the being of the person serves the sinful body, which is struggling against inner freedom, as a discipline, an incentive and a divine service. Here we cannot elaborate any further on this conception of inner-worldly asceticism, or its suitability for rationalizing life and its various modifications in Lutheranism and Calvinism; we need only point out that it is implanted in the Protestant concept of freedom, to which we now return.

Man is embedded in a system of earthly order which by no means corresponds to the fundamental teachings of Christianity. This contradiction provides a function for the "double morality" as combined with the sharp distinction between the "Christian" and the worldly human existence, between "Christian" morality and "external morality, which is the motive force in offices and works." The former refers only to the "inner" man: his "inner" freedom and equality,[7] his "inner" poverty, love and happiness (at its clearest in Luther's interpretation of the Sermon on the Mount, 1530).[8] The "external" order, on the other hand, is measured completely by the rules to which praxis and works are subjected when taken in isolation from the person. It is very characteristic that here—in accordance with the idea of praxis as the discipline and service performed by an utterly sinful existence—the earthly order appears essentially as a system of "authorities" and "offices," as an order of universal subordination, and that these authorities and offices in turn essentially appear under the sign of the "sword." (In one of his fiercest passages about worldly authority, still in anti-authoritarian idiom, Luther calls the Princes of God "jailers," "hangmen" and "bailiffs.")[9] This whole system of subordination to authorities and offices can admittedly be justified as a whole by referring to the ordinances of God: it has been set up to punish the bad, to protect the faithful and to preserve the peace— but this justification is by no means sufficient to sanction the system of subordination that exists at any one time, the particular office or the particular authority and the way it uses the "sword." Can an un-Christian authority be ordained by God and lay claim to unconditional subordination? Here the separation of office and person opens up a path which has far reaching consequences: it holds fast to the unconditional authority of the office, while it surrenders the officiating person to the fate of possible rejection. "First a distinction must be made: office and person, work and doer, are different things. For an office or a deed may well be good and right in itself which is yet evil and wrong if the person or doer is not good or right or does not do his work properly."[10] There was already a separation of this kind before Luther, in Catholicism, but in the context of the doctrine of the inner freedom of the Christian man and of the rejection of any justification by "works" it paves the way for the theoretical justification of the coming, specifically bourgeois, structure of authority.

The dignity of the office and the worthiness of the officiating person no longer coincide in principle. The office retains its unconditional authority, even if the officiating person does not deserve this authority. From the other side, as seen by those subject to authority, in principle every "under-person" is equal as a person to every "over-person": with regard to "inner" worthiness he can be vastly superior to the authority. Despite this he must give it his complete obedience. There is a positive and a negative justification for this. Negatively: because after all the power of the wordly authority only extends over "life and property, and external affairs on earth,"[11] and thus can never affect the being of the person, which is all that matters. Positively: because without the unconditional recognition of the ruling authorities the whole system of earthly order would fall apart, otherwise "everyone would become a judge against the other, no power or authority, no law or order would remain in the world; there would be nothing but murder and bloodshed."[12] For in this order there is no way in which one person can measure the worthiness of another or measure right and wrong at all. The system of authority proclaimed here is only tenable if earthly justice is taken out of the power of the people or if the existing injustice is included in the concept of earthly justice. God alone is judge over earthly injustice, and "what is the justice of the world other than that everyone does what he owes in his estate, which is the law of his own estate: the law of man or woman, child, servant or maid in the house, the law of the citizen or of the city in the land . . ."[13] There is no tribunal that could pass judgement on the existing earthly order—except its own existing tribunal: "the fact that the authority is wicked and unjust does not excuse tumult and rebellion. For it is not everyone who is competent to punish wickedness, but only the worldly authority which wields the sword . . ."[14] And just as the system of worldly authorities is its own judge in matters of justice, so also in matters of mercy: the man who appeals to God's mercy in the face of the blood and terror of this system is turned away. "Mercy is neither here nor there; we are now speaking of the word of God, whose will is that the King be honoured and rebels ruined, and who is yet surely as merciful as we are. If you desire mercy, do not become mixed up with rebels, but fear authority and do good."[15]

We are looking here only at those consequences which arise from this conception for the new social structure of authority. A rational justification of the existing system of worldly authorities becomes impossible, given the absolutely transcendental character of "actual" justice in relation to the worldly order on the one hand, and the separation of office and person and the essential immanence of injustice in earthly justice on the other. In the Middle Ages authority was tied to the particular bearer of authority at the time; it is the "characteristic of him who communicates the cognition of a judgement"[16] and as a "characteristic" it is inseparable from him; he always "has" it for particular reasons (which again can be rational or irrational). Now the two are torn apart: the particular authority of a particular worldly bearer of authority can now only be justified if we have recourse to authority in general. Authority must exist, for otherwise the worldly order would collapse. The separation of office and person is only an expression for the autonomization (*Verselbständigung*) and reification of authority freed from its bearer. The authority-system of the existing order assumes the form of a set of relationships freed from the actual social relationships of which it is a function; it becomes eternal, ordained by God, a second "nature" against which there is no appeal. "When we are born God dresses and adorns us as another person, he makes you a child, me a father, the one a lord, the other a servant, this one a prince, that one a citizen and so on."[17] And Luther accuses the peasants who protested against serfdom of turning Christian freedom into "something completely of the flesh": "Did not Abraham and other patriarchs and prophets also have slaves?"[18]

It is no coincidence that it is the essence of "Christian freedom" which is held up to the rebellious peasants, and that this does not make them free but actually confirms their slavery. The recognition of actual unfreedom (particularly the unfreedom caused by property relations) is in fact part of the sense of this concept of freedom. For if "outer" unfreedom can attack the actual being of the person, then the freedom or unfreedom of man is decided on earth itself, in social praxis, and man is, in the most dangerous sense of the word, free from God and can freely become himself. The "inner," *a priori* freedom makes man completely helpless, while seeming to elevate him to the highest honour: it logically precedes all his action and thought, but he can never catch his freedom up and take possession of it.

In the young Marx's formulation, this unfreedom conditioned by the internalization of freedom, this dialectic between the release from old authorities and the establishment of new ones is a decisive characteristic of Protestantism: "Luther, without question, defeated servitude through devotion, but only by substituting servitude through conviction. He shattered the faith in authority, by restoring the authority of faith. . . . He freed man from external religiosity by making religiosity the innermost essence of man."[19]

One of the most characteristic passages for the unconditional acceptance of actual unfreedom is Luther's admonition to the Christian slaves who had fallen into the hands of the Turks, telling them not to run away from their new lords or to harm them in any other way: "You must bear in mind that you have lost your freedom and become someone's property, and that without the will and knowledge of your master you cannot get out of this without sin and disobedience." And then the interesting justification: "For thus you would rob and steal your body from your master, which he has bought or otherwise acquired, after which it is not your property but his, like a beast or other goods in his possession."[20] Here, therefore, certain worldly property and power relationships are made the justification of a state of unfreedom in which even the total abandonment of the Christian to the unbeliever is of subordinate importance to the preservation of these property relationships.[21]

With the emergence of the independence of worldly authority, and its reifications, the breach of this authority, rebellion and disobedience, becomes the social sin pure and simple, a "greater sin than murder, unchastity, theft, dishonesty and all that goes with them."[22] "No evil deed on earth" is equal to rebellion; it is a "flood of all wickedness."[23] The justification which Luther gives for such a hysterical condemnation of rebellion reveals one of the central features of the social mechanism. While all other evil deeds only attack individual "pieces" of the whole, rebellion attacks "the head itself." The robber and murderer leave the head that can punish them intact and thus give punishment its chance; but rebellion "attacks punishment itself" and thereby not just disparate portions of the existing order, but this order itself (op. cit., pp. 380–381), which basically rests on the credibility of its power of punishment and on the recognition of its authority. "The donkey needs to feel the whip and the people need to be ruled with force; God knew that well. Hence he put a sword in the hands of the authorities and not a featherduster" (op. cit., p. 376). The condition of absolute isolation and atomization into which the individual is thrown after the dissolution of the medieval universe appears here, at the inception of the new bourgeois order, in the terribly truthful image of the isolation of the prisoner in his cell: "For God has fully ordained that the under-person shall be alone unto himself and has taken the sword from him and put him into prison. If he rebels against this and combines with others and breaks out and takes the sword, then before God he deserves condemnation and death."[24]

Every metaphysical interpretation of the earthly order embodies a very significant tendency: a tendency towards *formalization*. When the existing order, in the particular manner of its materiality, the material production and reproduction of life, becomes ultimately valueless with regard to its "actual" fulfilment, then it is no more than the form of a social organization as such, which is central to the organization of this life. This form of a social order ordained by God for the sinful world was for Luther basically a system of "over-persons" and "under-persons." Its formalization expressed itself in the separation of dignity and worthiness, of office and person, without this contradiction giving any rightful basis for criticism or even for the reform of this order. It was thus that the encompassing system of worldly authorities was safeguarded: it required unconditional obedience (or, if it intruded on "Christian freedom," it was to be countered with spiritual weapons or evaded).

But danger threatened from another quarter. Initially, the unconditional freedom of the "person," proclaimed by Luther, encouraged an anti-authoritarian tendency, and, indeed, precisely on account of the reification of authority. The dignity of the office was independent of the worthiness of its incumbent; the bourgeois individual was "privately" independent of authority. The assertion of Christian freedom and the allied conception of a "natural realm" of love, equality and justice was even more destructive. Although it was separated from the existing social order by an abyss of meaning, it must still have threatened the completely formalized social order simply by its claims and its full materiality. The ideas of love, equality and justice, which were still effective enough even in their suppressed Lutheran form, were a recurrent source of anxiety to the rising bourgeois society owing to their revolutionary application in peasant revolts, Anabaptism and other religious sects. The smoothing-out of the contradictions appearing here, and the incorporation of these destructive tendencies into the bourgeois order, was one of the major achievements of Calvin. It is significant that this synthesis was possible only because the contradictions were simultaneously breaking out anew in a different dimension—although now in a sphere no longer transcending the bourgeois order as a whole but immanent in it. The most important marks of this tendency are Calvin's "legalism" and his doctrine of the "right to resist."

It has often been pointed out in the relevant literature that in Calvin the Lutheran "natural law" disappears. The dualism of the two "realms" is removed:[25] admittedly Calvin too had sharply to emphasize that (precisely because of his increased interest in the bourgeois order) "the spiritual kingdom of Christ and civil government are things very widely separated,"[26] but the Christian realm of freedom is no longer effective as the material antithesis of the earthly order. In the face of the completely sinful and evil world there is ultimately only the person of God who, through the sole mediation of Christ, has chosen individuals for redemption by a completely irrational system of predestination. Luther had been greatly disturbed by the tensions between his teaching and the teachings of the "Sermon on the Mount," where the transcendence of the existing order is most clearly expressed and a devastating critique of this order made, which no degree of "internalization" could ever completely suppress: in Calvin these tensions no longer exist. The more inexorably Calvin elaborates the doctrine of eternal damnation, the more the positive biblical promises lose their radical impulse.[27] The way is made clear for a view of the wordly order which does not recognize its dubious antithesis. This does not mean that the world is somehow "sanctified" in the Christian sense: it is and remains an order of evil men for evil men, an order of concupiscence. But in it, as the absolutely prescribed and sole field for their probation, Christians must live their life to the honour and glory of the divine majesty, and in it the success of their praxis is the *ratio cognoscendi* (reason of knowing) of their selection. The *ratio essendi* (reason of existence) of this selection belongs to God and is eternally hidden from men. Not love and justice, but the terrible majesty of God was at work in the creation of this world, and the desires and drives, the hopes and laments of men are correspondingly directed not towards love and justice but towards unconditional obedience and humble adoration. Very characteristically, Calvin conceived original sin, i.e., the act which once and for all determined the being and essence of historical man, as disobedience, *inoboedientia*,[28] or as the crime of lese-majesty (while in St. Augustine's interpretation of original sin as *superbia* [overwhelming pride]—which Calvin aimed to follow here—there is still an element of the defiant freedom of the self-affirming man). And obedience is also the mechanism which holds the wordly order together: a system, emanating from the family, of *subjectio* and *superioritas*, to which God has given his name for protection: "The titles of Father, God and Lord, all meet in him alone, and hence, whenever any one of them is mentioned our mind should be impressed with the same feeling of reverence" (*Institutes*, Book II, ch. VIII, para. 35).

By freeing the worldly order from the counter-image of a Christian realm of love, equality and justice and making it as a whole a means for the glorification of God, the formalization operative in Luther is withdrawn; the sanction granted it now also affects its materiality: ". . . in all our cares, toils, annoyances, and other burdens, it will be no small alleviation to know that all these are under the superintendence of God. The magistrate will more willingly perform his office, and the father of the family confine himself to his proper sphere. Every one in his particular mode of life will, without refining, suffer its inconveniences, cares, uneasiness, and anxiety, persuaded that God has laid on the burden" (op. cit., Book III, ch. X, para. 6). The new direction manifests itself in the often described activism and realism of Calvin's disciples: in the concept of an occupation as a vocation, in Calvin's "state rationalism," in his extensive and intensive practico-social organization. With the abolition of Luther's formalization, the separation of office and person and the "double morality" linked with it also disappear in Calvin (although it will be shown that this does not remove the reification of authority, i.e., the understanding of it as an element of a natural or divine feature of an institution or a person instead of as a function of social relationships): the religious moral law—and essentially in the form represented in the decalogue, which it is claimed is also a "natural" law—is regarded as the obligatory norm for the practical social organization of the Christian "community." This was a step of great significance. It is true that the decalogue complied to a much greater degree with the demands of the existing social order than with the radical transcendental Christianity of the New Testament, and that it provided a considerably greater amount of latitude. Nevertheless, the new form of the law stabilized a norm, against which the officiating authorities could be "critically" measured. "But now the whole doctrine is pervaded by a spirit which desires to see society shaped and moulded for a definite purpose, and a spirit which can criticize law and authority according to the eternal standards of divine and natural law."[29] Luther's irrationalist doctrine of authority as "power for power's sake," as Troeltsch characterized it in a much disputed phrase, has been abandoned. In so far as obedience to the officiating authority leads to a transgression of the law, this authority loses its right to obedience.[30] It is a straight line from here to the struggle of the *Monarchomachi* against absolutism. From a source very close to Calvin, from his pupil, Théodore de Beza, comes the famous work *De jure magistratum in subditos* which presents the opinion that "even armed revolution is permissible, if no other means remain . . ."[31]

Yet these tendencies already belong to the later development of the bourgeoisie; in Calvin the right to resist in the face of worldly authorities is in principle limited from the start. Immediately after his warning to unworthy princes ("May the princes hear, and be afraid") Calvin continues: "But let us at the same time guard most carefully against spurning or violating the venerable and majestic authority of rulers, an authority which God has sanctioned by the surest edicts, although those invested with it should be most unworthy of it, and, as far as in them lies, pollute it with their iniquity. Although the lord takes vengeance on unbridled domination, let us not therefore suppose that that vengeance is committed to us, to whom no command has been given but to obey and suffer. I speak only of private men" (*Institutes*, Book IV, ch. XX, para. 31). Worldly authority retains its independence and its reification. And in a characteristic modification of the Lutheran concept of the *homo privatus* as a free person, this *homo privatus* is now primarily unfree: he is the man who obeys and suffers. In no case is the *homo privatus* entitled to change the system of officiating authorities:[32] "The subject as a private person has no independent political rights, rather he has the ethical-religious duty to bear patiently even the extremities of oppression and persecution."[33] Even in the case of the most blatant transgression of the Law, when obedience to the worldly authority must lead to disobedience to God, Calvin allows only a "right of passive resistance." Where the Christian organization of society is actually already under attack the right of veto is allowed only to the lower magistrates themselves, never to the "people" or to any postulated representatives of the people. And so in Calvin too we encounter the Lutheran idea of the immanence of the law within the existing system of worldly authorities: decisions regarding their rightness or wrongness are made exclusively within their own order, among themselves.

The direct ordination of the system of worldly authorities by God, when combined with the Calvinist concept of God as the absolute "sovereign," means both a strengthening and a weakening of worldly authorities—one of the many contradictions which arose when the Christian idea of transcendence ceased to be effective. Direct divine sanction increases the power of the earthly authorities: "The lord has not only declared that he approves of and is pleased with the function of magistrates, but also strongly recommended it to us by the very honourable titles which he has conferred upon it"[34]—although at the same time it should not thereby under any circumstances be allowed to lead to a diminution or a division of the sovereignty of God. All worldly power can only be a "derivative right": authority is a "jurisdiction as it were delegated by God." But for the people this delegacy is irremovable and irrevocable.[35] The relation-ship of God to the world appears essentially as the relationship of an unlimited sovereign to his subjects. Beyerhans has pointed out, with due caution, although clearly enough, that Calvin's concept of God "betrays the influence of worldly conceptions of law and power."[36]

A good index for the status of Protestant-bourgeois man in relation to the system of worldly order is the contemporary version of the concept of freedom. On the road from Luther to Calvin the concept of *libertas christiana* becomes a "negative" concept. "Christian freedom … is not understood positively as mastery over the world but in a purely negative manner as the freedom from the damning effect of the law."[37] Calvin's interpretation of *libertas christiana* was essentially based on the polemic interpretation of Christian freedom. Luther's concept of freedom had not been positive in Lobstein's sense either. But in the establishment of an unconditional "inner" freedom of the person there was none the less an element which pointed forward towards the real autonomy of the individual. In Calvin this moment is forced into the back-ground. The threefold definition of *libertas christiana* in the *Institutes* (Book III, ch. XIX, paras 2, 4, 7) is primarily negative in all its three elements: (a) freedom of the conscience from the necessity of the law—not indeed as a higher authority to be relied on against the validity of the law, but (b) as "voluntary" subordination to the law as to the will of God: "they voluntarily obey the will of God, being free from the yoke of the law itself,"[38] and (in the sense already indicated in Luther) (c) freedom from external things "which in themselves are but matters indifferent," and which "we are now at full liberty either to use or omit."[39] We should stress, precisely in view of this last definition that, combined with Calvin's idea of vocation and of probation in the vocation, the adiaphorous character of the external things has become a strong ideological support for Protestant economic praxis under capitalism. The negativity of this concept of freedom is revealed here by its inner connection with a social order which despite all external rationalization is basically anti-rational and anarchic, and which, in view of its final goal, is itself negative.

What remains as a positive definition of freedom is freedom in the sense of freedom to obey. For Calvin it is no longer a problem that "spiritual freedom can very well coexist with political servitude" (*Institutes*, Book IV, ch. XIX, para 1). But the difficulty of uniting freedom and unfreedom reappears in the derivative form of the union of freedom and the unfree will. Calvin agrees with Luther that Christian freedom not only does not require free will, but that it excludes it. Both Luther and Calvin base the unfree will on a power which man simply cannot eradicate: on the depravity of human nature which arose from the Fall and the absolute omnipotence of the divine will. The unfree will is an expression of the eternal earthly servitude of men:[40] it cannot and may not be removed without exploding the whole Christian-Protestant conception of man and the world. For Calvin, not only man's sensuality but also his reason is ultimately corrupt. This provides the theological justification for an anti-rationalism which strongly contrasts with Catholic teaching. In the Catholic doctrine there was still an awareness that reason and freedom are correlative concepts, that man's rationality will be destroyed if it is separated from the free possibility of rational acting and thinking. For Thomas Aquinas, man, as a rational animal, is necessarily also free and equipped with free will: "And forasmuch as man is rational is it necessary that man have a free will."[41] In Luther reason itself attests to the fact "that there is no free will either in man or in any other creature."[42] Reason is here characteristically appraised as the index of human unfreedom and heteronomy: thus we read in Luther's *Treatise on Good Works*, after the interpretation of the first four commandments: "These four preceding commandments do their work in the mind, that is, they take man prisoner, rule him and bring him into subjection so that he does not rule himself, does not think himself good, but rather acknowledges his humility and lets himself be led, so that his pride is restrained."[43] To this should be added the loud warnings which Luther gives against an overestimation of human reason and its realm ("We must not start something by trusting in the great power of human reason . . . for God cannot and will not suffer that a good work begin by relying upon one's own power and reason"),[44] and the rejection of a rational reform of the social order in Calvin. This is all a necessary support for the demand for unconditional subordination to independent and reified wordly authorities, for which any rational justification is rejected.

But this doctrine of the "unfree will" contains a new contradiction which must be resolved. How can man conceivably still be responsible for himself if the human will is fully determined? Man's responsibility must be salvaged: the Christian doctrine of sin and guilt, the punishment and redemption of man requires it, but the existing system of worldly order requires it too, for—as we have indicated—this system for both Luther and Calvin is essentially tied to the mechanism of guilt and punishment. Here the concept of "psychological freedom" offers a way out: Calvin expounds the concept of a necessity (*necessitas*) which is not coercion (*coactio*) but a "spontaneous necessity." The human will is necessarily corrupt and necessarily chooses evil. This does not mean, however, that man is forced, "against his will" to choose evil; his enslavement in sin is a "voluntary enslavement" (*servitus voluntaria*). "For we did not consider it necessary to sin, other than through weakness of the will; whence it follows that this was voluntary."[45] Thus despite the *necessitas* of the will, responsibility can be ascribed for human deeds. The concept of enslavement or voluntary necessity signifies one of the most important steps forward in the effort to perpetuate unfreedom in the essence of human freedom: it remains operative right up until German Idealism. Necessity loses its character both as affliction and as the removal of affliction; it is taken from the field of man's social praxis and transferred back into his "nature." In fact necessity is restored to nature in general and thus all possibility of overcoming it is removed. Man is directed not towards increasingly overcoming necessity but towards voluntarily accepting it.

As is well known, a programmatic reorganization of the family and a notable strengthening of the authority of the *pater familias* took place in the context of the bourgeois-Protestant teachings of the Reformation. It was firstly a necessary consequence of the toppling of the Catholic hierarchy; with the collapse of the (personal and instrumental) mediations it had set up between the individual and God, the responsibility for the salvation of the souls of those not yet responsible for themselves, and for their preparation for the Christian life, fell back on the family and on its head, who was given an almost priestly consecration. On the other hand, since the authority of the temporal rulers was tied directly to the authority of the *pater familias* (all temporal rulers, all "lords" become "fathers"), their authority was consolidated in a very particular direction. The subordination of the individual to the temporal ruler appears just as "natural," obvious, and "eternal" as subordination to the authority of the father is meant to be, both deriving from the same divinely ordained source. Max

Weber emphasizes the entry of "calculation into traditional organizations brotherhood" as a decisive feature of the transformation of the family through the
penetration of the "capitalist spirit": the old relationships of piety decay as soon
as things are no longer shared communally within the family but "settled" along
business lines.[46] But the obverse side of this development is that the primitive,
"naïve" authority of the *pater familias* becomes more and more a planned authority, which is artificially generated and maintained.

The key passages for the doctrine of the authority of the *pater familias* and
of the "derivation" of worldly authorities from it are Luther's exegeses of the
Fourth Commandment in the *Sermon on Good Works* and in the *Large Catechism,* and Calvin's interpretation in the *Institutes,* Book II, ch. VIII. Luther
directly includes within the Fourth Commandment "obedience to over-persons,
who have to give orders and rule," although there is no explicit mention of
these. His justification, thus, characteristically, runs as follows: "For all authority
has its root and source in parental authority. For where a father is unable to
bring up his child alone, he takes a teacher to teach him; if he is too weak, he
takes his friend or neighbour to help him; when he departs this life, he gives
authority to others who are chosen for the purpose. So he must also have servants, men and maids, under him for the household, so that all who are called
master stand in the place of parents, and must obtain from them authority and
power to command. Wherefore in the bible they are all called fathers."[47] Luther
saw clearly that the system of temporal authorities constantly depends on the
effectiveness of authority within the family. Where obedience to father and
mother are not in force "there are no good ways and no good governance. For
where obedience is not maintained in houses, one will never achieve good governance, in a whole city, province, principality or kingdom."[48] Luther saw that
the system of society which he envisaged depended for its survival as such on
the continued functioning of parental authority; "where the rule of the parents
is absent, this would mean the end of the whole world, for without governance
it cannot survive."[49] For the maintenance of this world "there is no greater dominion on earth than the dominion of the parents,"[50] for there is "nothing more
essential than that we should raise people who will come after us and govern."[51]
The wordly order always remains in view as a system of rulers and ruled to be
maintained unquestioningly.

On the other hand, however, parental authority (which is always paternal
authority in Luther) is also dependent on worldly authority: the *pater familias*
is not in a position to carry out the upbringing and education of the child on
his own. Alongside the parents, there is the school, and the task of educating
the future rulers in all spheres of social life is impressed on it too. Luther sees
the reason for divinely sanctioned parental authority in the breaking and humiliation of the child's will: "The commandment gives parents a position of honour
so that the self-will of the children can be broken, and they are made humble

and meek":[52] "for everyone must be ruled, and subject to other men."[53] Once again it is the image of the wordly order as universal subordination and servitude which is envisaged by Luther, a servitude whose simple "must" is no longer even questioned. The freedom of the Christian is darkened by the shadow of the coming bourgeois society; the dependence and exploitation of the greatest part of humanity appears implanted in the "natural" and divine soil of the family; the reality of class antagonisms is turned into the appearance of a natural-divine hierarchy, exploitation becomes the grateful return of gifts already received. For that is the second ground for unconditional obedience: "God gives to us and preserves to us through them [the authorities] as through our parents, our food, our homes, protection and security";[54] "we owe it to the world to be grateful for the kindness and benefits that we have received from our parents."[55] And servants and maids ought even to "give up wages" out of pure gratefulness and joy at being able to fulfil God's commandment in servitude.[56]

The personal characteristics which the coming social order wishes to produce require a change in all human values from earliest childhood. Honour (*Ehrung*) and fear (*Furcht*) or, taken together, reverence (*Ehrfurcht*) take the place of love as the determining factor in the relationship between the child and its parents.[57] "For it is a far higher thing to honour than to love, since honouring does not simply comprise love [but] obedience, humility and reverence, as though towards some sovereign hidden there."[58] The terrible majesty of Calvin's God comes to the surface in the authority of the *pater familias*. It is precisely discipline and fear which raises honouring one's parents above love: "honour is higher than mere love, for it includes within it a kind of fear which, combined with love, has such an effect on a man that he is more afraid of injuring them than of the ensuing punishment."[59] Just as disobedience is the greatest sin, obedience is the highest "work" after those commanded in Moses's first tablet; "so that to give alms and all other work for one's neighbour is not equal to this."[60]

There are also passages in Luther in which parental and governmental authority are explicitly contrasted. Thus in the *Table Talks*: "Parents look after their children much more and are more diligent in their care of them than the government is with its subjects . . . The power of the father and mother is a natural and voluntary power and a dominion over children which has grown of itself. But the rule of the government is forced, an artificial rule."[61] There is also some wavering on the question of the extension of the "double morality" of office and person to parental authority. In the *Sermon on Good Works* (1520) Luther says: "Where the parents are foolish and raise their children in a wordly manner, the children should in no way be obedient to them. For according to the first three Commandments God is to be held in higher esteem than parents."[62] Nine years later, in the *Large Catechism*, he writes: "Their [the parents'] condition or defect does not deprive them of their due honour. We must not regard their persons as they are, but the will of God, who ordered and arranged things thus."[63]

In the passages quoted above one can see the tendency towards a separation of natural and social authority. Luther did not advance any further along the road from the "natural" unity of the family to the "artificial" and "forced" unity of society; he was satisfied with establishing that the family is the "first rule, in which all other types of rule and domination have their origins."[64] Calvin went a little further in this direction; he presents an exceptionally interesting psychological interpretation: "But as this command to submit is very repugnant to the preversity of the human mind (which, puffed up with ambitious longings, will scarcely allow itself to be subjected) that superiority which is most attractive and least invidious is set forth as an example calculated to soften and bend our minds to the habits of submission. From that subjection which is most tolerable, the lord gradually accustoms us to every kind of legitimate subjection, the same principle regulating all."[65]

Calvin agrees with Luther on the close association between subjection to authority in general and parental authority;[66] we saw how for him too the titles *Dominus* and *Pater* are interchangeable. But Calvin ascribes to the authority relationship of the family a quite definite function within the mechanism of subjection to social authorities. This function is psychological. Since subjection is actually repugnant to human nature, man should, through a type of subordination which by its nature is pleasant and will arouse the minimum of ill will, be gradually prepared for types of subordination which are harder to bear. This preparation occurs in the manner of a softening, bowing and bending; it is a continual habituation, through which man becomes accustomed to subjection. Nothing need be added to these words: the social function of the family in the bourgeois authority-system has rarely been more clearly expressed.

II. Kant

There are two ways of coming to an appreciation of the level reached by Kant in dealing with the problem of authority: the impact and the transformation of the "Protestant ethic" could be traced in the Kantian doctrine of freedom, or the problem of authority and freedom could be developed immanently from the centre of Kant's ethics. The inner connections between Lutheran and Kantian ethics are plainly apparent. We shall point only to the parallels given by Delekat:[67] the conception of "inner" freedom as the freedom of the autonomous person: the transfer of ethical "value" from the legality of the "works" to the morality of the person; the "formalization" of ethics; the centring of morality on reverential obedience to duty as the secularization of "Christian obedience"; the doctrine of the actual unconditional authority of worldly government. But with this method those levels of Kantian ethics which cannot be comprehended under the heading of the "Protestant ethic" would be given too short a shrift and appear in a false light. The second way would indeed be a genuine approach, but would require an extensive elaboration of the whole conceptual apparatus of Kantian ethics, which we cannot provide within the framework of this investigation. We will necessarily have to choose a less adequate route: there are as it were two central points around which the problematic of authority and freedom in Kant's philosophy is concentrated: firstly, the philosophical foundation itself, under the heading of the autonomy of the free person under the law of duty, and secondly the sphere of the "application" of ethics, under the heading of the "right of resistance." In this second section Kant deals with the problem in the context of a comprehensive philosophical interpretation of the legal framework of bourgeois society.[68] The level of concreteness of the present treatment admittedly cannot compensate for its vast distance from the actual philosophical foundation, but it offers a good starting point.

In the small treatise, *Reply to the Question: What is Enlightenment?* (1784), Kant explicitly poses the question of the relation between social authority and freedom. To think and to act according to an authority is for Kant characteristic of "immaturity," a "self-inflicted immaturity," for which the person is himself to blame. This self-enslavement of man to authority has in turn a particular social purpose, in that civil society "requires a certain mechanism, for some affairs which are in the interests of the community, whereby some members of the community must behave purely passively, so that they may, by means of an artificial consensus, be employed by the government for public ends (or at least deterred from vitiating them)."[69] Bourgeois society has an "interest" in "disciplining" men by handling them in an authoritarian manner, for here its whole survival is at stake. In the closing note of his *Anthropology*, Kant described religion as a means of introducing such a discipline and as a "requirement" of the constituted bourgeois order "so that what cannot be achieved through external compulsion can be effected through the inner compulsion of the conscience. Man's moral disposition is utilized for political ends by the legislators . . ."[70]

How can one square man's "natural" freedom with society's interest in discipline? For Kant firmly believes that the free autonomy of man is the supreme law. It presupposes the exit of man from the state of immaturity which is his own fault; this process is, precisely, "enlightenment." Nothing is needed for this except freedom, the freedom "to make *public* use of one's reason in all matters."[71] The freedom which confronts authority thus has a public character; it is only through this that it enters the concrete dimension of social existence; authority and freedom meet within *bourgeois society* and are posed as problems of bourgeois society. The contradiction is no longer between the "inner" freedom of the Christian man and divinely ordained authority, but between the "public" freedom of the citizen and bourgeois society's interest in discipline. Kant's solution remains dualistic; his problematic is in parallel with Luther's:

"the *public* use of man's reason must always be free, and this alone can bring about enlightenment among men; the *private* use of the same may often be very strictly limited, yet without there by particularly hindering the progress of enlightenment."[72] That seems to be the exact opposite of Luther's solution, which, while unconditionally preserving the "inner" freedom of the private person, had also unconditionally subordinated public freedom to the worldly authority. But let us see what Kant means by the "public" and "private" use of freedom. "But by the public use of one's own reason I mean that use which anyone may make of it *as a man of learning* addressing the entire *reading public*. What I term the private use of reason is that which a person may make of it in a particular *civil* post or office with which he is entrusted."[73] What is "private" is now the bourgeois "office," and its bearer has to subordinate his freedom to society's interest in discipline. Freedom in its unrestricted, public nature, on the other hand, is shunted off into the dimension of pure scholarship and the "world of readers." Social organization is privatized (the civil "office" becomes a private possession) and in its privatized form appears as a world of disciplined, controlled freedom, a world of authority. Meanwhile the "intellectual world" is given the appearance of being actually public and free but is separated from public and free *action*, from real social praxis.

Kant places the problem of authority and freedom on the foundation of the actual social order, as a problem of "bourgeois society." Even if this concept is by no means historically defined in Kant, but signifies the overall "idea" of a social order (as a "legal order"), the actual features of bourgeois society are so much a part of it that the above formulation is justified. We must examine Kant's explication of bourgeois society more closely in order to describe adequately his attitude to the problem of authority. It is to be found in the first part of the *Metaphysics of Morals*, in the *Metaphysical Elements of the Theory of Law*.

Bourgeois society is, for Kant, the society which "safeguards Mine and Thine by means of public laws."[74] Only in a bourgeois context can there be an external Mine and Thine, for only in this context do public laws "accompanied by power" guarantee "to everyone his own";[75] only in bourgeois society does all "provisional" acquisition and possession become "peremptory."[76] Bourgeois society essentially achieves this legally secure position for the Mine and the Thine in its capacity as "legal order," indeed, it is regarded as the "ultimate purpose of all public right" to ensure the peremptory security of the Mine and Thine.

What then is "right," this highest principle of the bourgeois order? Right is "the sum total of those conditions under which the will of one person can be united with the will of another in accordance with a universal law of freedom."[77] All formulations of Kant's concept of right signify a synthesis of opposites: the unity of arbitrary will and right, freedom and compulsion, the individual and the general community. This synthesis must not be thought of as a union which is the sum of individual "parts"; instead, one should "see the concept of right as consisting immediately of the possibility of combining universal reciprocal coercion with the freedom of everyone."[78]

"Only the external aspect of an action"[79] is subject to right in Kant's view. The person as a "moral" subject, as the locus of transcendental freedom, stands entirely outside the dimension of right. But the meaning of right here is the order of bourgeois society. Transcendental freedom only enters into the legal order in a very indirect way, in so far as the universal law of rights is meant to counteract certain hindrances to the "manifestations" of transcendental freedom.[80] With this relegation of law to the sphere of "externality," both law and the society ordered by law are relieved of the responsibility for "actual" freedom and opened up for the first time to unfreedom. In the synthesis of law we thus have the concerns of the "externally" acting man before us; what do they look like?

We see a society of individuals, each one of whom appears with the natural claim to the "free exercise of his will," and confronts everyone else with this claim (since the field of possible claims is limited); a society of individuals, for each one of whom it is a "postulate of practical reason" to have as his own very external object of his will[81] and who all, with equal rights, confront each other with the natural striving after "appropriation" and "acquisition."[82] Such a society is a society of universal insecurity, general disruption and all-round vulnerability. It can only exist under a similarly universal, general and all-round order of coercion and subordination, the essence of which consists in securing what is insecure, stabilizing what is tottering and preventing "lesions." It is highly significant that almost all the basic concepts of Kant's theory of right are defined by negative characteristics like securing, lesion, restriction, prevention and coercion. The subordination of individual freedom to the general authority of coercion is no longer "irrationally" grounded in the concupiscence of the "created being" and in the divinely ordained nature of government, but grows immanently out of the requirements of bourgeois society—as the condition of its existence.

But Kant still feels the contradiction between a society of universal coercion and the conception of the "naturally" free individual. The synthesis of freedom and coercion must not occur in such a way that the original freedom of the individual is sacrificed to social heteronomy. Coercion must not be brought to the individual from without, the limitation of freedom must be a self-limitation, the unfreedom must be voluntary. The possibility of a synthesis is found in the idea of an original "collective-general" will to which all individuals agree in a resolution of generally binding self-limitation under laws backed by power. That this "original contract" is only an "Idea"[83] needs no further discussion, but before we examine its content we must note the significance of its "ideal" character for the development of the problem under discussion.

First it transforms the historical facticity of bourgeois society into an *a priori* ideal. This transformation, which is demonstrable in Kant's theory of right at the very moment of its occurrence, does not simply mean the justification of a particular social order for all eternity; there is also at work in it that tendency towards the transcendence of the bourgeois authority-system which had already emerged in the Reformers of the sixteenth century. These destructive moments appear in the replacement of a (believed and accepted) fact by a (postulated) "as if." For Luther, divinely ordained authority was a given fact; in Kant the statement "All authority is from God" only means we must conceive of authority "*as if*" it did not come from men, "but none the less must have come from a supreme and infallible legislator."[84] Correspondingly, the idea of a "general will" only requires that every citizen be regarded "as if he had consented within the general will."[85] Certainly the "transcendental As If" signifies a marked shift in the weight of authority towards its free recognition by the autonomous individual, and this means that the structure of authority has become rational— but the guarantees which are set up within the legal order itself against the destruction of the authority relationship are correspondingly stronger.

The "original contract" is, so to speak, a treaty framework into which the most varied social contents are inserted. But this multiplicity of elements is centred on one point; on the universal, mutual effort to make possible and secure "peremptory" property, the "external Mine and Thine," on the "necessary unification of everyone's private property."[86] In this way the mere "fortuitousness" and arbitrariness of "empirical" property is transformed into the legal validity and regularity of "intelligible" property in accordance with the postulate of practical reason.[87] We must briefly follow this road through its most important stages, for it is at the same time the route towards the foundation of (social) authority.

Our starting-point is the peculiar (and defining) character of private property as something external, with which "I am so connected that the use which another would like to make of it without my permission would injure me."[88] The fact that someone else can use something possessed by me at all presupposes a very definite divorce between the possession and its possessor, presupposes that property does not merely consist in physical possession. The actual "technical explanation" of the concept of "private property" must therefore include this feature of "property with physical possession": "that which is externally mine is that which, if I am hindered in its use, would injure me, *even if I am not then in possession of it* (if the object is not in my hands)."[89] What type of property is this property "even without possession," which is the real subject dealt with by the legal order?

The separation of empirical and intelligible property lies at the basis of one of Kant's most profound insights into the actual structure of bourgeois society: the insight that all empirical property is essentially "fortuitous" and is based on acquisition by "unilateral will" ("appropriation") and thus can never present a universally binding legal title; "for the unilateral will cannot impose on everyone an obligation which is in itself fortuitous. . . ."[90] This empirical property is not therefore sufficient to justify its all-round and lasting security at the centre of the bourgeois legal order; instead of this, the possibility of an external Mine and Thine as a "legal relationship" is "completely based on the axiom that a purely rational form of property without possession is possible."[91]

The way in which Kant constructs this axiom and in which he effects the return from empirical property to a "purely rational form of property" in many ways corresponds to bourgeois sociology's handling of the problem. Kant says: "In order to be able to extend the concept of property beyond the empirical and to be able to say that every external entity subjected to my will can be counted as mine by right if it is . . . in my power without being in possession of it, all conditions of the attitude which justifies empirical property must be eliminated [ignored] . . ."[92] The "removal of all empirical conditions in space and time," abstraction from the "sensuous conditions of property"[93] leads to the concept of "intellectual appropriation." By this route Kant arrives at the idea of an original joint ownership of the land and on the basis of this collectivity a collective general will can be established which legally empowers every individual to have private property. "The owner bases himself on the innate *communal ownership* of the land and a general will which corresponds *a priori* to this and allows *private ownership* on the land. . . ."[94] Thus in a highly paradoxical manner communal property becomes the "legal basis" for private property; total ownership "is the only condition under which it is possible for me to exclude every other owner from the private use of the object in question. . . ."[95] No one can oblige anyone else through unilateral will to refrain from the use of an object: the private appropriation of what is universal is only possible as a legal state of affairs through the "united will of all in total ownership." And this "united will" is then also the foundation of that general community which puts every individual under a universal coercive order backed by force and which takes over the defence, regulation and "peremptory" securing of the society based on private property.

Thus in the origins of bourgeois society the private and general interest, will and coercion, freedom and subordination, are meant to be united. The bourgeois individual's lack of freedom under the legal authority of the rulers of his society is meant to be reconciled with the basic conception of the essentially free person by being thought of as the mutual self-limitation of all individuals which is of equally primitive origin. The formal purpose of this self-limitation is the establishment of a general community which, in uniting all individuals, becomes the real subject of social existence.

"The general community" is society viewed as the totality of associated individuals. This in turn has two connotations:

1. A *total communality* of the kind that reconciles the interests of every individual with the interests of the other individuals—so that there is really a general interest which supersedes private interests.
2. A *universal validity* of such a kind that the general interest represents a *norm equally binding* on all individuals (a law). In so far as the interests of the individuals do not prevail "on their own," and do not become reconciled with each other "on their own" (in a natural manner), but rather require social planning, the general community confronts the individuals as *a priority* and as a *demand*: in virtue of its general "validity" it must demand recognition and achieve and safeguard this by coercion if necessary.

But now everything depends on whether the general community as the particular form of social organization does in fact represent a supersession of private interests by the general interest, and whether the people's interests are really guarded and administered in it in the best possible way. When Kant deals with social problems in the context of the "general community," this already signifies a decisive step in the history of social theory: it is no longer God but man himself who gives man freedom and unfreedom. The unchaining of the conscious bourgeois individual is completed in theory: this individual is so free that he alone can abrogate his freedom. And he can only be free if at the same time freedom is taken away from all others: through all-round, mutual subordination to the authority of the law. The bearer of authority (in the sense of being the source of authority) is not God, or a person or a multiplicity of persons, but the general community of all (free) persons in which every individual is both the person delegated and the person delegating.

But not every general community, i.e., every actually constituted society, is truly universal. German Idealism uses bourgeois society as a model for its exposition of the concept of universality: in this sense, its theory signifies a new justification of social unfreedom. The characteristics of real universality are not fulfilled in this society. The interests of the ruling strata stand in contradiction with the interests of the vast majority of the other groups. The universally obligatory authority of the law is thus finally based not on a "genuine" universality (in which the interests of all the individuals are common to all) but on an appearance of universality; there is an apparent universality because the particular interests of certain strata assume the character of general interests by making themselves apparently independent within the state apparatus. The true constituents of this universality are property relationships as they existed at the "beginning" of bourgeois society and these can only be peremptorily guaranteed through the creation of a universally binding organization of social coercion.

This universality retains its "private" character; in it the opposing interests of individuals are not transcended by the interests of the community but cancelled out by the executive authority of the law. The "fortuitousness" of property is not eliminated by the "elimination" of the empirical conditions under which it was appropriated: right rather perpetuates this fortuitous character while driving it out of human consciousness. The universality which comes from the combination of private possessions can only produce a universal order of injustice. Kant knew that he had constituted his theory of right for a society whose very foundations had this inbuilt injustice. He knew that "given man's present condition . . . the good fortune of states grows commensurably with the misery of men,"[96] and that it must be a "principle of the art of education" that "children should be educated not towards the present, but towards the future, possibly better, conditions of the human race."[97] He has said that in this order justice itself must become injustice and that "the legislation itself (hence also the civil constitution), so long as it remains barbarous and undeveloped, is to blame for the fact that the motives of honour obeyed by the people are subjectively incompatible with those measures which are objectively suited to their realization, so that public justice as dispensed by the state is *injustice* in the eyes of the people."[98]

None the less Kant stuck to the view that the universality of the "united will" was the basis of society and the foundation of authority. He drew all the resultant consequences from the unconditional recognition of the government ruling at any particular time to the exclusion of economically dependent individuals from civil rights.[99] Like Luther he maintained that right was immanent in the civil order and described rebellion against this order as the "overthrow of all right,"[100] and as "the road to an abyss which irrevocably swallows everything,"[101] the road to the destruction of social existence altogether. "There can thus be no legitimate resistance of the people to the legislative head of state; for a state of right is only possible through submission to his universal legislative will. . . ."[102] His justification is in the first place purely formal: since every existing system of domination rests only on the basis of the presupposed general will in its favour, the destruction of the system of domination would mean the "self-destruction" of the general will. The legal justification is of the same formal kind: in a conflict between people and sovereign there can be no tribunal which makes decisions having the force of law apart from the sovereign himself, because any such tribunal would contravene the "original contract"; the sovereign is and remains, says Kant in a characteristic phrase, in sole "possession of the ultimate enforcement of the public law."[103] This is the consequence of the immanence of the law in the ruling system of authority already observed in Luther: the sovereign is his own judge and only the judge himself can be the plaintiff: "Any alteration to a defective political constitution, which may certainly be necessary at times, can thus be carried out only by the sovereign himself through *reform*, but not by the people, and, consequently, not by *revolution*. . . ."[104]

It has been pointed out in connection with Kant's strict rejection of the right of resistance that although he does not acknowledge a (positive) "right" of resistance as a component of any conceivable legal order, the idea of possible resistance or even of the overthrow by force of a "defective" social order, is fully in line with his practical philosophy. The main support for this interpretation (which can be reconciled with the wording of the quoted passages of his theory of right) is Kant's apotheosis of the French Revolution in the *Contest of the Faculties*,[105] and the unconditional demand for the recognition of every new order arising from a revolution.[106] Such an interpretation strikes us as correct, as long as it does not attempt to resolve the contradiction present in Kant's position in favour of one side or the other. The transcendental freedom of man, the unconditional autonomy of the rational person, remains the highest principle in all dimensions of Kant's philosophy; here there is no haggling and calculating and no compromise. This freedom does not become a practical social force, and freedom to think does not include the "freedom to *act*";[107] this is a feature of precisely that social order in the context of which Kant brought his philosophy to concreteness.

The internal antinomy between freedom and coercion is not resolved in the "external" sphere of social action. Here all freedom remains a state of merely free existence under "coercive laws," and each individual has an absolutely *equal* inborn right "to coerce others to use their freedom in a way which harmonizes with his freedom."[108] But mere self-subordination to general coercion does not yet provide the foundation for a generality in which the freedom of individuals is superseded. On the road from empirical to intelligible property, from the existent social universality to the Idea of an original universality, the solution of the antinomy is transferred to the transcendental dimension of Kant's philosophy. Here too the problem appears under the heading of a universality in which the freedom of the individual is realized within a general system of legislation.

In the "external" sphere the relationship between freedom and coercion was defined in such a way that coercion was made the basis of freedom, and freedom the basis of coercion. This notion is most pregnantly expressed in the formula which Kant uses in his discussion of a "purely republican" constitution: it is the only state form "which makes *freedom* into the principle, indeed the *condition*, of all coercion."[109] Just as "legitimate" coercion is only possible on the basis of freedom, so "legitimate" freedom itself demands coercion in order to survive. This has its rationale within the "external" sphere: "bourgeois" freedom (this is what is at stake here), is only possible though all-round coercion. But the result is not a supersession but a reinforcement of actual unfreedom: how then can this be reconciled with transcendental freedom?

The concept of transcendental freedom (the following discussion will be limited to this, unless otherwise indicated) appears in Kant as a concept of causality. This concept stands in opposition to that of causality in nature: it refers to causality resulting from free actions as opposed to causality resulting from necessity and its causal factors, which are of "external" origin (i.e. causality in the sequence of temporal phenomena). People have seen in this definition of freedom as a type of causality an early derivation of the problem of freedom—a dubious transference of the categories of natural science into the dimension of human existence, and a failure to understand the "existential" character of human freedom. But we believe that what shows the superiority of Kant's ethics over all later existential ontology is precisely this understanding of freedom as, from the start, a particular type of actual effectiveness in the world; freedom is not relegated to a static mode of existence. And since the definition of causation resulting from freedom has to meet from the outset the demand for "universal validity" and since the individual is placed in a universal, a general rational realm of free persons which exists "before" and "over" all natural aspects of the community, all later misinterpretations of the organicist theory of society are refuted from the start. However, freedom is now set up as unconditional autonomy and pure self-determination of the personal will, and the required universal validity is posited as *a priori* and formal: here we see the impact of the inner limits of Kant's theory of freedom (and these limits are by no means overcome by proposing a "material ethic of value" as against "formal" ethics).

Freedom for Kant is a transcendental "actuality," a "fact"; it is something which man always already has if he wants to become free. As in Luther, freedom always "precedes" any free act, as its eternal *a priori*; it is never the result of a liberation and it does not first require liberation. Admittedly freedom "exists" for Kant only in activity in accordance with the moral law, but this activity is, in principle, free to everyone everywhere. By the ultimate reference of freedom to the moral law as its only "reality," freedom becomes compatible with every type of unfreedom; owing to its transcendental nature it cannot be affected by any kind of restriction imposed on actual freedom. Admittedly freedom is also a liberation—man making himself free from all "empirical" determinants of the will, the liberation of the person from the domination of sensuality which enters into the constitution of the human animal as a "created being"—but this liberation leaves all types of actual servitude untouched.

The self-imposed and self-observed moral law of the free person possesses "universal validity" in itself as the reason of knowing of its truth, but this means that it contains reference to a "world" of universality consisting of the mutual coexistence of individuals. Nevertheless, this universality is formal and aprioristic; it may not carry over anything of the material quality of this mutual coexistence into the law of action. Yet another "form" is concealed in the bare "form" of the moral law; namely the bare form of the coexistence of individuals, the form of a "society as such." This means that in all his actual decisions about action the individual only has the form of social existence in view: he must disregard or, so to speak, leap over the social materiality before him. Precisely to the extent that the individual acts under the law of freedom can no element of this materiality be permitted to become a determinant of his will. The fact that it is entirely excluded from the determinants of free praxis means that the individual comes up against it as a brute fact. Transcendental freedom is by its nature accompanied by social unfreedom.

The criterion for decisions concerning action under the moral law is, as already in the sphere of the theory of right, the internal coherence of maxims as a universal law: a bad maxim, if it were made into a "universal system of legislation," would abolish the order of human coexistence; it would signify the self-destruction of social existence. It has already been shown elsewhere that this criterion cannot operate in the intended sense in a single one of the applications which Kant himself adduces.[110] It would not be the form of a social order as such which would be destroyed by "false" maxims but always only a particular social order (Kant's ethics are by no means as formal as is claimed by the material ethics of value). Between the formal universality of the moral law and its possible universal material validity, there yawns a contradiction which cannot be overcome within the Kantian ethic. The existing order, in which the moral law is meant to become a practical reality, is not a field of real universal validity. And the alteration of this order cannot in principle serve as a maxim of free praxis, for it would in actual fact, judged according to Kant's criterion, transcend social existence as such (a universal law for the alteration of the existing order would be an absurdity).

The reversion from personal and institutional authority to the authority of the law corresponds to the justificatory reversion from the subject-matter of praxis to the form of the "law." This "formalization" is something quite different from Luther's "formal" recognition of the existing wordly authorities, without reference to their individual and social basis. For Kant, every personal and institutional authority has to justify itself in face of the idea of a universal law, which the united individuals have given themselves and which they themselves observe. In the "external" sphere of social existence this law—as we have seen in the theory of right—justifies not only the authority of the actual system of "governments" but also authority in general as a social necessity; universal voluntary self-limitation of individual freedom in a general system of the subordination of some and the domination of others is necessary for the peremptory securing of bourgeois society, which is built up on relations of private property. This is the highest rationalization of social authority within bourgeois philosophy.

But just as, with the application of the law, rationalization is brought to a standstill in face of the internal contradictions of bourgeois society, in face of its immanent "injustice," so it is with the origin of legislation itself: "the possibility of an intelligible property, and thus also of the external Mine and Thine, is not self-evident, but must be deduced from the postulate of practical reason."[111]

The law remains an authority which right back to its origins cannot be rationally justified without going beyond the limits of precisely that society for whose existence it is necessary.

Notes

1. Luther, *Treatise on Good Works* (1520), in *Selected Writings of Martin Luther*, vol. I, Philadelphia, 1967, p. 174.
2. Op. cit., p. 118 (my italics).
3. Luther, *The Freedom of a Christian* (1520), in *Reformation Writings of Martin Luther*, vol. I, London, 1952, pp. 357ff.
4. Luther, *The First Lent Sermon at Wittenberg* (9 March 1522), *in Selected Writings*, vol. II, p. 238.
5. Luther, *The Third Lent Sermon at Wittenberg* (11 March 1522), in op. ci vol. II, p. 243.
6. Luther, *Sermon on the Ban* (1520), in *Luther's Works*, vol. 39, ed. H. Lehmann, Philadelphia, 1970, p. 8; and *Whether Soldiers, Too, Can Be Saved* (1526), in *Selected Writings*, vol. III, p. 434.
7. Luther, *Temporal Authority: To What Extent It Should be Obeyed* (1523), *Selected Writings*, vol. II, p. 307: emphasizing the exclusively "inner" equality of men.
8. Translated into English in *Luther's Works*, vol. 21, ed. J. Pelikan, Philadelphia, 1956, pp. 3ff.
9. *Selected Writings*, vol. II, p. 303.
10. *Selected Writings*, vol. III, p. 434, and cf. *Werke*, ed. Buchwald, Berlin 1905, vol. III, pt 2, p. 393.
11. *Temporal Authority* (1523), in *Selected Writings*, vol. II, p. 295.
12. *Admonition to Peace: A Reply to the Twelve Articles of the Peasants in Swabia* (1525), in *Selected Writings*, vol. III, p. 327.
13. *Werke*, ed. Buchwald, Berlin, 1905, vol. III, pt 2, p. 300.
14. *Admonition to Peace,* in *Selected Writings*, vol. III, p. 325.
15. *An Open Letter on the Harsh Book against the Peasants* (1525), in *Selected Writings*, vol. III, p. 371.
16. Grimmich, Lehrbuch der theoretischen Philosophie auf themistischer Grundlage, Freiburg, 1893, p. 177.
17. *Werke*, ed. Buchwald, Berlin, 1905, vol. II, pt. 2, p. 296.
18. *Admonition to Peace,* in *Selected Writings*, vol. III, p. 339.
19. Marx, *Introduction to a Contribution to the Critique of Hegel's Philosophy of Right, in Karl Marx: Early Writings*, trans. T. B. Bottomore, London, 1963, p. 53.
    The contradiction between anti-authoritarian and authoritarian tendencies which pervades the whole of Luther's work has been clearly elaborated by R. Pascal, *The Social Basis of the German Reformation*, London, 1933. Pascal shows that this contradiction is determined by the social and economic situation of the urban petty bourgeoisie, to whose interests Luther's Reformation corresponds. Pascal further strongly emphasizes the basically authoritarian character of Lutheranism, into which the anti-authoritarian streams are ultimately also fitted, so that after the achievement of the socially necessary economic and psychological liberations they work completely in the interests of the stabilization and strengthening of the existing world order. Even on the rare occasions when Luther breaks his doctrine of unconditional obedience to the worldly authority (as in 1531 with regard to the question of armed resistance to the Emperor by the Princes, after Luther had finally had to abandon his hope of winning the Emperor for the Protestant cause), the position he takes is by no means revolutionary but conservative: the Emperor appears as the wanton destroyer of an order which must be preserved under all circumstances.
20. *On War Against the Turk* (1529), in *Selected Writings*, vol. IV, p. 42.
21. Thomas Münzer's attack on Luther deals precisely with this connection between Luther's concept of authority and a particular property order: "The poor flatterer wants to cover himself with Christ in apparent goodness. . . . But he says in his book on trading that one can with certainty count the princes among the thieves and robbers. But at the same time he conceals the real origin of all robbery. . . . For see, our lords and princes are the basis of

all profiteering, theft and robbery; they make all creatures their property. The fish in the water, the birds of the air, the plants on the earth must all be theirs (Isaiah 5). Concerning this they spread God's commandment among the poor and say that God has commanded that you shall not steal, but it does them no good. So they turn the poor peasant, the artisan and all living things into exploiters and evil-doers" (*Hoch verursachte Schutzrede* (1525), in *Flugschriften aus der Reformationszeit*, vol. X, Halle, 1893, p. 25).

22. *Treatise on Good Works*, in *Selected Writings*, vol. I, p. 163.
23. An Open Letter, in *Selected Writings*, vol. III, p. 381.
24. *Selected Writings*, vol. III, p. 466.
25. Beyerhaus, *Studien zur Staatsanschauung Calvins*, Berlin, 1910, points out that although "theoretically" a distinction is made between the two spheres, 'practically' they become a unity precisely in the realization of Calvin's idea of the state (p. 50).
26. Calvin, *Institutes of the Christian Religion*, trans. F. L. Battles, London, 1961, Book IV, ch. XX, para. 1.
27. H. Engelland, *Gott und Mensch bei Calvin*, Munich, 1934, pp. 113ff.
28. cf. Barnikel, *Die Lehre Calvins vom unfreien Willen* . . . , Bonn dissertation, 1927, pp. 104ff; Beyerhaus, op. cit., p. 79.
29. Troeltsch, *The Social Teaching of the Christian Churches*, trans. O. Wyon, vol. II, London, 1931, p. 616.
30. Ibid., p. 618.
31. Ibid., p. 629.
32. Troeltsch, op. cit., p. 616; Lobstein, *Die Ethik Calvins*, Strasburg, 1877, p. 116.
33. Beyerhaus, op. cit., p. 97.
34. *Institutes*, Book IV, ch. XX, para. 4.
35. Beyerhaus, op. cit., p. 87.
36. Beyerhaus, op. cit., p. 79.
37. Lobstein, op. cit., p. 148.
38. Op. cit., Book III, ch. XIX, para. 4. cf.. in I Peter, ch. 2, verse 16: "The purpose of our liberty is this, that we should obey more readily and more easily" (Lobstein, op. cit., p. 37).
39. Op. cit., Book III, ch. XIX, para. 7.
40. "For where there is servitude, there is also necessity." cf. Barnikel, op. cit., p. 113.
41. *Summa Theol.* I, quaestio 83, art. 1.
42. Martin Luther *on the Bondage of the Will*, translation of *De Servo Arbitrio*, (1525) by J. I. Packer and O. R. Johnston, London, 1957, p. 317; cf. Barnikel, op. cit., p. 46.
43. Treatise on Good Works, in *Selected Writings*, vol. I, p. 182.
44. *To the Christian Nobility of the German Nation Concerning the Reform of the Christian Estate* (1520), in *Selected Writings*, vol. I, p. 261.
45. Calvin, *Opera*, vol. VI, p. 280.
46. Max Weber, *General Economic History*, trans. F. H. Knight, Glencoe, 1930, p. 356.
47. *The Large Catechism* (1529), in *Luther's Primary Works*, trans. H. Wace and C. A. Buchheim, London, 1896, p. 58.
48. Quoted from *Luther als Pädagog*, ed. E. Wagner (Klassiker der Pädagogik, Vol. II), Langensalza, 1892, p. 70.
49. Ibid., p. 73.
50. Ibid., p. 64.
51. Ibid., p. 119.
52. *Selected Writings*, vol. I, p. 168.
53. Op. cit., p. 164.
54. Luther's Primary Works, p. 60.
55. Op. cit., p. 56.
56. Op. cit., p. 59.
57. For a contrary passage, cf. *Luther als Pädagog*, p. 64.
58. *Luther's Primary Works*, p. 52.
59. *Selected Writings*, vol. 1, p. 163.
60. *Luther's Primary Works*, p. 56.
61. *Luther als Pädagog*, p. 53.
62. *Selected Writings*, vol. 1, p. 166.
63. Luther's Primary Works, p. 52.

64. *Luther als Pädagog*, p. 70. cf.. Levin Schücking, *Die Familie im Puritanismus*, Leipzig, 1929, p. 89.
65. *Institutes*, Book II, ch. VIII, para. 35.
66. Troeltsch, op. cit., p. 603.
67. *Handbuch der Pädagogik*, ed. Nohl-Pallat, vol. 1, Langensalza, 1928, pp. 221ff.
68. *Translator's note*: "Bourgeois society" is here a translation of "bürgerliche Gesellschaft," more usually rendered as "civil society." While Kant and Hegel certainly used the term in the sense of "civil society," Marcuse used it in 1936 in the sense of "bourgeois society," since, as he states in relation to Kant's concept of "civil society," the "actual features of bourgeois society are so much a part of it that this formulation is justified" (*infra*, p. 82).
69. *Kant's Political Writings*, trans. H. B. Nisbet, ed. H. Reiss, Cambridge, 1970, p. 56.
70. *Werke*, ed. Cassirer, Berlin, 1912, vol. VIII, p. 227.
71. *Kant's Political Writings*, p. 55.
72. Loc. cit.
73. Loc. cit.
74. *Werke*, vol. VII, p. 44.
75. Op. cit., p. 59.
76. Op. cit., p. 68, and *Kant's Political Writings*, p. 163.
77. *Kant's Political Writings*, p. 133.
78. *Kant's Political Writings*, p. 134.
79. Loc. cit.
80. Op. cit., p. 133. cf.. Haensel, *Kants Lehre vom Widerstandsrecht*, Berlin, 1926, pp. 10ff.
81. *Werke*, vol. VII, p. 48.
82. Op. cit., p. 70.
83. *Translator's note:* "Idea" is used here in the Kantian sense of a regulative principle of reason not found in experience but required to give experience an order and unity it would otherwise (according to Kant) lack.
84. *Kant's Political Writings*, p. 143 (Marcuse's emphasis).
85. Op. cit., p. 79.
86. *Werke*, vol. VI, p. 130.
87. Ibid., vol. VII, paras 6, 7 and 11.
88. Ibid., p. 47.
89. Ibid., p. 51.
90. Ibid., pp. 66ff.
91. Ibid., p. 57.
92. Ibid., p. 54.
93. Ibid., pp. 67 and 72.
94. Ibid., p. 52.
95. Ibid., p. 64.
96. Ibid., vol. VIII, pp. 465ff.
97. Ibid., vol. VIII, pp. 462ff.
98. *Kant's Political Writings*, p. 159.
99. Op. cit., pp. 139ff.; p. 78.
100. Op. cit., p. 162.
101. Op. cit., p. 146 (Kant's footnote to paragraph 49).
102. Op. cit., pp. 144ff.; other important passages are in op. cit., p. 143, pp. 81–82, pp. 126–7, and in *Werke*, vol. VII, pp. 179ff.
103. *Kant's Political Writings*, p. 82.
104. Op. cit., p. 146.
105. Op. cit., pp. 182–5.
106. Op. cit., p. 147.
107. Op. cit., p. 59.
108. Op. cit., p. 76.
109. Op. cit., p. 163.
110. *Zeitschrift für Sozialforschung*, II (1933), pp. 169ff.
111. Op. cit., vol. VII, pp. 57f.

V

Theodor W. Adorno

8
Reason and Sacrifice

Theodor W. Adorno
Translated by Robert Huilot-Kentor

Self-Destruction of Idealism

Of those modern philosophies in which the self-imprisoned consciousness of idealism is aware of its own imprisonment and attempts to escape from its immanence, each develops an exclusive category, an undeviating intention, a distinguishing trait that, under the rule of the idea of totality acknowledged by all these philosophies, is intended to mollify the rigidity of this imprisonment. Ultimately, however, this category dissolves the idealist construction itself, which then disintegrates into its antinomies. Thus Hegel, the most extreme exponent of the idea of totality and to all appearances anything but a critic of idealism, developed a dialectical process that employed the claim to totality so dynamically that particular phenomena never result from the systematic subordinating concept; instead the system—from which reality truly results—is to be synonymous with the quintessence of fulfilled actuality. Kierkegaard tirelessly ridiculed Hegel for deferring every statement that would be binding for real existence until some imaginary completion of the system. But precisely in this regard Kierkegaard is more similar to Hegel than he would have cared to recognize. For through such deferment of the whole, the particular present—and even more the past—gains a concrete fullness that Kierkegaard's repetitions seek in vain to procure.—Similarly, Feuerbach moved his enlightenment concept of humanity, as a corrective, to the center of his philosophy; a concept that can no longer be contained by autonomous spirit. Similarly, again, Marx ultimately subordinated all his thought to the category of exchange-value, of the commodity. Indeed even this category, as the quintessence of the phenomena of capitalist society, maintains allegiance to the concept of totality. However, it shifts the emphasis of explanation from the side of consciousness to that of the "material" in such a fashion that the unity of the "idea" of capitalist society is destroyed by contents that do not arise continuously from any idea because they place the reality of the idea itself in question. Although all these categories originate in the self-enclosing infinity of the system, they draw the systematic structures into themselves like whirlpools in which they disappear. Kierkegaard's case is no different. He becomes a critic of the system because consciousness, as consciousness of an existence that is not deducible from itself, establishes itself as the ultimate contradiction of his idealism. From the totality of consciousness, which is extensive yet produced in a single point, his thought returns to this one point in order to gain the single category that will break the power of the system and restore ontology. The point that he seizes, his own fulcrum, is the archimedean point of systematic idealism itself: the prerogative of thought, as its own law, to found reality. The category that dialectically unfolds here, however, is that of paradoxical sacrifice. Nowhere is the prerogative of consciousness pushed further, nowhere more completely denied, than in the sacrifice of consciousness as in the fulfillment of ontological reconciliation. With a truly Pascalian expanse, Kierkegaard's dialectic swings between the negation of consciousness and its unchallenged authority. His spiritualism, the historical figure of objectless inwardness, is to be understood according to the immanent logic of the crisis of idealism. For Kierkegaard, consciousness must have pulled itself free from all external being by a movement of "infinite resignation"; through choice and decisiveness, it must have freely posited every content in order finally, in the face of the semblance of its own omnipotence, to surrender its omnipotence and, foundering, to purify itself of the guilt it acquired in having supposed itself autonomous. The sacrifice of consciousness, however, is the innermost model of every sacrifice that occurs in his philosophy. It constitutes the nexus of the mythical and the intrahistorical in his categorical structure. For sacrifice indeed wants to absolve nature, and nature has its determining power at Kierkegaard's historical moment and even for his knowledge in the spirit of the isolated individual. Just as, for Kierkegaard, the spirit of the individual stands as the archetype not only of all spirit, but of nature itself, which does not appear except as "spirit," so sacrifice, the final category of nature to which he raises himself and at the same time the final category of the destruction of the natural, is in his terms a sacrifice of spirit. With the greatest tension of which system-building idealism was still capable, he carried out this sacrifice both for the system as a whole and in all phenomena that fall within the system. The category of sacrifice, by means of which the system transcends itself, at the same time and fully contrary to expectation, holds Kierkegaard's philosophy systematically together as its encompassing unity through the sacrificial abstraction of all encountered phenomena. In intellectual sacrifice the mythical origin of sacrifice appears most unalloyed; its historical function appears most spontaneously.

The two meet on the stage of spirit and carry out the dialogue of idealism as mythical thought's own play of lamentation. Idealism, however, is ultimately revealed as mythical in that although it indeed transcends itself, it is unable to immanently fulfill the claim to reconciliation that it announces. Nature, withdrawn into human spirit, hardens itself in idealism and usurps the power of creation. While the ruin that idealism brings upon itself is therefore able to free it from the semblance of autonomy, reconciliation as catharsis cannot be vouchsafed for a fully collapsing idealism.

Mythical Sacrifice

Of the many commentators, only Monrad gives any insight into the relation between Kierkegaard's sacrifice and the mythical. As part of a sketch of Kierkegaard's character, he quotes a passage from the *Havamal* of nordic mythology: "Odin speaks: I know that I hung from a wind-blown tree nine nights long, wounded by a spear, consecrated to Odin: I myself, consecrated to myself."[1] Monrad emphasizes the phrase "consecrated to Odin: I myself, consecrated to myself"; it could in fact serve as the motto of a theology of sacrifice in which the individual must "perish" to become "himself." Nothing is added here by the observation of more recent Danish authors of Kierkegaard's "genuinely nordic character."[2] The relation is evident in the material. The god sacrifices himself, that is, autonomously; for himself, that is, remaining in the natural domain of his own domination. Ultimately the sacrifice transpires, as the continuation of Monrad's passage makes evident, because the god wanted "to procure a higher knowledge through the transcendence of runes"[3]; even Kierkegaard's philosophical intention of "transparentness," including the model of the cipher, is contained in the passage from the *Edda*. Kierkegaard himself compares the concept of philosophy with mythology: "No philosophy . . . no mythology . . . has ever had this idea."[4] The idea, however, that should overcome philosophy and the context of mere nature is that of the paradox.—Kierkegaard himself perceived in the aesthetic sphere that sacrifice is mythical. He wrote of Euripides' "Iphigenia in Aulis": "Agamemnon is about to sacrifice Iphigenia. Aesthetics demands silence of Agamemnon, inasmuch as it would be unworthy of the hero to seek comfort from any other person, just as out of solicitude for the women he ought to hide it from them as long as possible. On the other hand, in order to be a hero, the hero also has to be tried in the dreadful spiritual trial that the tears of Clytemnestra and Iphigenia will cause. What does aesthetics do? It has a way out; it has the old servant in readiness to disclose everything to Clytemnestra. Now everything is in order."[5] What is specified here as the aesthetic character of sacrifice is in truth mythical: it is the silence of speechless submission to fate; the mute struggle that the hero puts up against fate as he submits and by submitting inserts a caesura in the fateful circle. The servant's speech, however, is no aesthetic "way out"; rather, his disembodied voice is the echo of fate itself that announces its consummation to the taciturn hero. The paradox also offers up a sacrifice, one comparable to the silent hero, and therefore falls prey to that mythology that Kierkegaard imagines never to have "had this idea." For just as the hero, deprived of all hope, is handed over as absolution to blind natural forces, paradox sacrifices hope, the favorite child of spirit, to spirit itself as expiation. In this fashion Kierkegaard himself "aesthetically" bans the paradoxical, to which he "religiously" succumbs specifically in the mythical figure of memory. As mere imageless spirit, memory destroys the pictorial configuration of hope: "I can describe hope so vividly that every hoping individual will acknowledge my description; and yet it is a deception, for while I picture hope, I think of memory."[6] This already points the way, by means of a "transcendence of spheres," to Kierkegaard's Christology: while hope here falls to the mercy of memory that is as mythical as the recollection of what has always been, in the Christology all worldly existence is ultimately consecrated to the simply different that cancels the "deception" of existence but without reconciling it. The mythical figure of pure spirit ascends out of the hell of memory: "No power in the play, no power on earth, has been able to coerce Don Juan, only a spirit, an apparition from another world, can do that. If this be understood correctly, then this will again throw light upon the interpretation of Don Juan. A spirit, a ghost, is a replication; this is the mystery which lies in its apparition; Don Juan can do everything, can withstand everything, except the replication of life, precisely because he is immediate sensuous life, whose negation the spirit is."[7] Thus power over natural life remains dedicated to its annihilation in spirit rather than to reconciliation. The annihilation of natural life, originating in the statue of the commander, is correctly understood as ghostly. For here it is not merely natural life that is destroyed by spirit; spirit itself is annihilated natural life and bound to mythology. For this reason, spirit is without hope, and, even in Kierkegaard's doctrine of faith, paradoxy distorts hope as the simple annihilation of nature by spirit: "And next the spirit brings hope, hope in the strictest Christian sense, this hope which is hope against hope. For in every man there is a spontaneous hope, in one man it may be more vitally strong than in another, but in death (i.e. when thou dost die from) every such hope dies and transforms itself into hopelessness. Into this night of hopelessness (it is in fact death we are describing) comes then the life-giving spirit and brings hope, the hope of eternity. It is against hope, for according to that merely natural hope there was no hope left, and so this is hope against hope."[8] In spite of its forcefulness, this image of hope is false. Hope does not unfold in this image in the absurdity of a life that is natural, fallen to nature, and yet at the same time created. Rather the absurdity turns against hope itself. By annihilating nature, hope enters the vicious circle of nature; originating in nature itself, hope is only able to truly overcome it by maintaining the trace of nature. The twilight of Kierkegaardian hope is the sallow light of the twilight of the gods that proclaims the vain end of an age or the aimless beginning of a new one, but not salvation. Thus, in the dialectic of hope, Kierkegaard's paradox proves to be caught up in nature by virtue of its antinatural spiritualism. His polemic against mythical hope becomes mythical hopelessness just as the movement of "existence" changes into the despair that initiated its flight into the labyrinth. According to its stated intention, his interpretation of Christianity is directly opposed to any mythological interpretation. He would like to exclude every mythical content that propagates itself in images; with the greatest severity, he criticizes "childish religiosity"[9] for its "immediacy"; and he equally repudiates infant baptism and anabaptism as "external" because of their theological symbolic form, which he attribute to myth. Blinded, however, it escapes him that the image of sacrifice is itself mythical and occupies the innermost cell of his thought, accessible equally by way of his philosophy as by his theology. The sacrifice of Christ and the "disciple" of reason cannot be finally distinguished. The claim "that Christ came into the world to suffer,"[10] paradoxical and yet all too laconic, transforms the Christian doctrine of reconciliation itself into the mythical. However unrelentingly he undertook to extirpate the mythical origin of sacrifice through dialectics and however effectively the ambiguity of this mythical origin supported him in this, he nevertheless unintentionally betrays the mythical essence of his theology in otherwise unimposing sentences: "If Christianity once changed the face of the world by overcoming the crude passions of immediacy and ennobling the state, it will find in culture a resistance just as great."[11] Thus the dialectical refraction of subordination to nature, of the "crude passions of immediacy," is to become a danger for Christianity itself, is to break Christianity—with the result that Christianity reverts to subordination to nature. The fact that Kierkegaard, to mollify nature, polemically substituted the reified and questionable concept of culture for a reconciling dialectic that issues from nature changes nothing in this situation.

"Gnosis"

There is thus a mythologization of Christianity in the last instance, although in all preceding instances, nature had been driven out of Christianity. Christ's death itself is for Kierkegaard not so much an act of reconciliation as a propitiating sacrifice. However the *Training in Christianity* may employ the phrase "reconciling death,"[12] the "doctrine of reconciliation" is still explicitly defined as atonement: "It is taught that Christ has made satisfaction for hereditary sin."[13] In vain, Kierkegaard denies that which to him marks Christ and likewise man as an "exception": "It was not in order to appease the angry gods that Abraham transgressed the universal"[14]—but why else? For all authentic existence is atonement for Kierkegaard: in *The Instant* he demands that Christians "live as sacrificed men in this world of falsehood and evil."[15] All thereby violate "the universal." Moral requirements are properly promulgated only in a life for which reconciliation is a continuous possibility; if life is sacrificed, ethos disappears with it in the abyss of the natural. The distinction of good and evil no longer holds under the domination of death. For this reason, ethics constitutes for Kierkegaard a "transitional stage"; since no life is begrudged it, it cannot prove itself. Sacrifice is that point in the system where the tangent of an abstract and unreachable "meaning" touches the closed circle of life, and his doctrine insists on this "point" without progressing along the circumference; if, according to the paradox, it is only here that he can participate in "meaning," he must pay for it according to a graceless mythical calculus with the loss of the living person. In his ethics human life sets itself, powerlessly, against sacrificial annihilation— Through sacrifice, the difference between Christ and man is abolished. If Christ, as sacrifice, falls to the mercy of the natural, in sacrifice the individual raises himself up, sacrificially, as a follower. Of Christ, it is said: "This story, the story of constant maltreatment which finally ended in death, or shall I say the story of this suffering, is the story of his whole life. It can be told in several ways. It can be told briefly in two words, nay even in one: it was the story of the passion."[16] Thus the story is mythically reduced to a sacrifice, systematically reduced to a single point, as in the morose thesis that "indeed every day of His life was a day of burial for Him who was appointed to be a sacrifice."[17] The life of the individual is "relegated"—through sacrifice—to nothing else: "Now if for any individual an eternal happiness is his highest good, this will mean that all finite satisfactions are volitionally relegated to the status of what must be renounced in favor of an eternal happiness."[18] Renounced by the strength of the "follower": the Christian is to "make 'the pattern' so vividly present that" he experiences "such suffering as if in contemporaneousness you had recognized Him for what he is. All ado made afterwards, all ado about building his tomb etc., etc., etc., etc., etc., etc., is, according to the judgment of Jesus Christ, hypocrisy and the same blood-guilt as that of those who put him to death. This is the Christian requirement. The mildest, mildest form for it after all is surely that which I have used in *Training in Christianity*: that you must admit that this is the requirement, and then have recourse to grace"[19]—a grace for which Kierkegaard knows no other criterion than suffering. The mythical content of suffering is hardly mastered by Christology and by being a follower; occasionally this mythical content breaks through, autonomously, and sacrifice is presented in its true natural form: as expiation, performed for the sinful corps of the present "generation." "The thought goes very far back in my recollection that in every generation there are two or three who are sacrificed for the others, are led by frightful sufferings to discover what redounds to the good of others. So it was that in my melancholy I understood myself as singled out for such a fate."[20] The emancipation from the Christian prototype, the separation of the sacrifice from the name and fulfillment of Christ, the fetishistic autonomization of the sacrifice are—in this passage—no accident of expression. In fact his philosophy develops the cult of sacrifice with such tenacity that it finally becomes a gnosis, which Kierkegaard as a Protestant would have otherwise passionately opposed. Gnosis erupts in late idealism when—through spiritualism—mythical thought gains power over Christian thought and, in spite of all talk of grace, draws Christianity into the graceless immanence of the course of nature. Kierkegaard's gnostic doctrines are presented as "literary works" and fantasies. This is perhaps not simply on formal grounds the result of the requirements of the material, as set out in the *Concluding Unscientific Postscript*, but also in order to mask the heterodox character of these doctrines—a requirement that Kierkegaard must have been aware of. Yet these gnostic doctrines return so relentlessly; they present such a tight nexus of motives; they pursue so strictly the course of transcendence defined by the system of spheres; that the critic of the mythical content of Kierkegaard's philosophy finds its real basis in them. The mythical character of sacrifice becomes evident in the fateful necessity of the "offense," over which God is supposed to have no control: "This precisely is the sorrow in Christ: 'He can do no other.' He can humble himself, take the form of a servant, suffer and die for man, invite all to come unto him, sacrifice every day of his life and every hour of the day, and sacrifice his life—but the possibility of the offense he cannot take away. Oh, unique work of love! Oh, unfathomable sorrow of love! that God himself cannot, as in another sense he does not will, cannot will it, but, even if he would, he could not make it impossible that this work of love might not turn out to be for a person exactly the opposite, to be the extremest misery! For the greatest possible human misery, greater even than sin, is to be offended in Christ and remain offended. And Christ cannot, 'love' cannot render this impossible. Lo, for this reason He says, 'Blessed is he who shall not be offended in me.' More he cannot do."[21] Indeed, it is not the sacrifice itself, but its acceptance by the creature that is withdrawn from the control of the deity; just as in the astrology of the spheres, so in the demonic "offense," necessity rules. God's sadness over the unreachable, the "lost" person, responds gnostically to this necessity as the final word of Kierkegaard's theology. In ambiguous reconciliation divine love itself laments: "Behold, he therefore brought to completion this work of love, he offered the sacrifice (in which for his part he exulted), but not without tears. Over this—what shall I call it?—historical painting of inwardness there hovered that dark possibility. And yet, if this had not hovered over it, his work would not have been that of true love."[22] Thus the "historical painting of inwardness" as the theological prototype of all melancholy: God's mournfulness over humanity is itself mythical. In the image of this mournfulness, the creator founders and falls helpless; in sacrifice he is devoured by nature. This is the self-evident and gnostic heresy posited by Kierkegaard's doctrine of the imprisonment of God in his own "incognito," just as this imprisonment follows rationally for Kierkegaard from the paradox of the immediate unity of divine and human nature: "And now in the case of the God-Man! He is God, but chooses to become the individual man. This, as we have seen, is the profoundest incognito, or the most impenetrable unrecognizableness that is possible; for the contradiction between being God and being an individual man is the greatest possible, the infinitely qualitative contradiction. But this is His will, His free determination, therefore an almightily maintained incognito. Indeed, he has in a certain sense, by suffering himself to be born, bound himself once and for all; his incognito is so almightily maintained that in a way he is subjected to it, and the reality of his suffering consists in the fact that it is not merely apparent, but that in a sense the assumed incognito has power over him."[23] If a theology of the "strictly different" were prohibited from any pronouncement over "God's mournfulness," it must be fully confounded since it denies God's freedom and subsumes the incarnate God to a necessity that he cannot "revoke." Kierkegaard's theology cannot escape this entanglement because the conception of the paradoxy and absolute difference of God is itself bound to the autonomous spirit as God's systematic negation, an autonomous spirit that ultimately cancels divine transcendence by construing God dialectically out of itself and its own necessity. Just as in the depths of perdition the dialectic of pure spirit turns toward deliverance, it plummets from the heights of sacrifice into mythology, which subjects its god to abstract fate: "But the unrecognizableness of the God-Man is an incognito almightily maintained, and the divine seriousness consists precisely in the fact that it is so almightily maintained that He Himself suffers under His unrecognizableness in a purely human way."[24] Haecker criticizes Kierkegaard's spiritualism: "The Individual is to become spirit, as he is intended to be, pure spirit if possible; this is an almost gnostic error on Kierkegaard's part"[25]; and this gnosis proceeds from the definition of man as purely spiritual to a theology that classifies god in the categories of pure spirit, as which man appears to god. The result is that god disappears into that nature that is in truth precisely man's spirituality. Mythical dialectic consumes Kierkegaard's god, as did Kronos his children.

Paradox Sacrifice of Mere Spirit

The mythical sacrifice itself is carried out in Kierkegaard by spiritualism, the historical figure that nature takes on in his thought. It is the sacrifice of mere spirit into which all reality has been transformed. The model of this sacrifice is paradoxy: a movement of thought, completed in pure thought, and negated as totality in this movement of thought, in order, sacrificed, to draw toward itself the "strictly different," its absolute contrary. What, according to Kierkegaard, characterizes demonic nature and despair in *The Sickness unto Death*, namely

the impulse toward self-destruction and annihilation, returns in "consciousness at its apex"—in absolute spirituality. "However, one should not think slight-
ingly of the paradoxical; for the paradox is the source of the thinker's passion,
and the thinker without a paradox is like a lover without feeling: a paltry medi-
ocrity. But the highest pitch of every passion is always to will its own downfall;
and so it is also the supreme passion of reason to seek a collision, though this
collision must in one way or another prove its undoing. The supreme paradox
of all thought is the attempt to discover something that thought cannot think."[26]
The paradoxical character of sacrifice is already marked by the determinant of
hereditary sin, which, itself exclusively spiritual, is to be absolved through sacrifice: "Sin is: before God in despair not to will to be oneself, or before God in
despair to will to be oneself. But is not this definition, even though in other
aspects it may be conceded to have advantages (and among them this which is
the weightiest of all, that it is the only scriptural definition, for the scripture
always defines sin as disobedience), is it not after all too spiritual? To this one
must first of all make answer that a definition of sin can never be too spiritual
(unless it becomes so spiritual that it does away with sin); for sin is precisely a
determinant of spirit."[27] If, however, the creature's sin is defined by spirit, its
atonement appears just as much posited by spirit as it is contrary to spirit and
therefore paradoxically: "But the religious consists precisely in being religiously
concerned about oneself infinitely, and not about visions; in being concerned
about oneself infinitely, and not about a positive aim, which is negative and
finite, because the infinitely negative is the only adequate form for the infinite."[28] The sacrifice of consciousness is carried out according to its own categories, rationally. It is no accident that Kierkegaard is fond of using
mathematical metaphors in his doctrine of the Christian paradox: "Like the
straight line that is tangent to the circle at only one point—so was He, in the
world and yet outside the world, only serving one master."[29] Thus Kierkegaard's
paradoxy is here compared to the mathematical-rational paradox of a point
that "has no extension," just as, in fact, the point serves as the model of every
Kierkegaardian paradox from the *Journal of a Seducer* on. The idea of the point,
however, which cannot be purely represented visually, refers to the autonomous *ratio* as its origin. The "spontaneous center" of idealism, the abstract
transcendental unity of apperception, the Kantian "principle," is itself a point.
That Kierkegaard's paradox is to be understood as precisely this point of spontaneous production may be extracted literally from the *Philosophical Fragments*: "The conclusion of belief is not so much a conclusion as a resolution,
and it is for this reason that belief excludes doubt."[30] The category of "resolution," which Kierkegaard expressly terms "ethical," subsuming it thereby to "freedom" and autonomy, is to be, paradoxically, the "religious starting point": "The
resolution is not man's strength, it is not man's courage, it is not man's talent
(these are only immediate analogies which do not furnish an objective measure

for the immediacy of love, since they belong to the same sphere and are not a new immediacy), but it is a religious starting-point."[31] Thus Kierkegaard legitimates "religious" paradoxy by a spontaneous act of consciousness. This has the consequence that all sacrifice in the domain of consciousness assumes the form of the paradoxical. It is not the symbolic, objective completion of sacrifice that is decisive for Kierkegaard, but rather, that with each sacrifice the autonomy of thought be destroyed by determinations of thought. Opposed to this analysis is the common objection to any "intellectualization" of Kierkegaard, who—it is said—had whatever fundamental religious experiences that he represented in the form of rational paradoxes as the tribute of his thought to "his age." This objection arbitrarily tears apart time and thought, which are interwoven in him in such a fashion that the modern is the site of the archaic, while the archaic becomes incorporeal vapor as soon as any inquiry into it is made. Kierkegaard did not present fundamental religious experiences as rational paradoxes; the locus of mythical sacrifice in his work is the historical figure of consciousness; objectless inwardness. This objectless interiority did not carry on a timeless discussion with God; by breaking free from the outer world through the strength of its historical position and inserting itself into an indissoluble dialectic as the quintessence of creation and equally as the guarantor of the meaningfulness of this dialectic, the alleged dialogue in fear and trembling can be nothing other than the deceptive echo that answers back out of nothingness to a self-confined spirituality. Rational sacrifice is not the mere copy of an ontic sacrifice; absolute spirit is incapable of any other sacrifice than itself. Kierkegaard's "profundity"— if one insists on the misused concept—is by no means located in his recreation of an absolute, fundamental religious meaning in the guise of idealism. He presented mythical content as concomitantly historical, as the "fundamental meaning" of idealism, in the moment of its historical collapse.—The primacy of rational paradoxy in Kierkegaard's sacrificial realm can be verified immanently by the fact that paradoxy is not limited to the spiritual Christology; it does not converge with the traditional paradoxy of theological symbols. If sacrifice is the dialectical structure of his oeuvre, and if the leap and negation in every case complete the surrender of the "sphere" from which they derive, every sacrifice is alloted paradoxy as the sign of its systematic seal of authenticity. The astonishing catalog of paradoxes listed in one passage of the *Concluding Unscientific Postscript* can be explained in no other way: "The reader will remember: A revelation is signalized by mystery, happiness by suffering, the certainty of faith by uncertainty, the ease of the paradoxical-religious life by its difficulty, the truth by absurdity."[32] What would be blasphemous in the face of the once inspiring symbol fits passively into the form of a universally rational legality according to its "applications," as if this legality were one that stamped the "cases" as content of whatever paradox and turned it materially against the *ratio*. The paradox is Kierkegaard's fundamental, categorial form; he undertakes the synthesis of multiplicity paradoxically, and in the categorial unity and totality the rational origin persists that the determinate paradoxies respectively disavow. Such paradoxies therefore occur in every "sphere." The oneness of time and eternity is already conceived "aesthetically"; this is evident not only in the parody of seduction but in a positive form in the doctrine of art: "Through Don Juan [Mozart] is introduced into that eternity that does not lie outside of time but in the midst of it, which is not veiled from the eyes of men, where the immortals are introduced, not once for all, but constantly, again and again, as the generations pass and turn their gaze upon them, find happiness in beholding them, and go to the grave, and the following generation passes them again in review, and is transfigured in beholding them."[33] The "ethical" stage is constituted by paradoxy in precisely the same way: "The highest expression of immediate love is that the lover feels himself as nothing in the presence of the beloved, and this feeling is mutual, for to feel oneself as something conflicts with love."[34] Love is defined, therefore, by the simple negation of that self to which, according to Kierkegaard's doctrine, the full content of the doctrine depends. Corresponding to the paradoxy of emotion is that of the moral commandment itself: "This shows that the individual is at once the universal and the particular. Duty is the universal which is required of me; so if I am not the universal, I am unable to perform duty. On the other hand, my duty is the particular, something for me alone, and yet it is duty and hence the universal."[35] Even the non-Christian "religiosity 'A'" is ultimately paradoxical, and in such a precise sense that its delimitation from the Christian becomes impossible. Paradoxy therefore furnishes the unifying subordinating concept of Kierkegaard's positive theology: "Was Job proved to be in the wrong? Yes, eternally, for there is no higher court than the one that judged him. Was Job proved to be in the right? Yes, eternally, by being proved to be in the wrong before God."[36] The all-inclusive function of paradoxy is made possible by its abstractness, by the inclusion of all specific contents in it as their categorial form. This abstractness, however, is again grounded in sacrifice, the essence of paradoxy, and is therefore not to be fulfilled or corrected through the multiplicitousness of the contents. The coherence of the living person, according to Kierkegaard the "reality" of the self, is sacrificed in the paradox: "The religiousness which is fetched directly from reality is a dubious religiousness; it may be that aesthetic categories are employed and worldly wisdom acquired; but when reality has not been able to crush an individual and he falls by himself, the religious factor is clearer."[37] The collapse of the individual is, however, concretely the annihilation of time and therefore the surrender of the immanent coherence of life itself. For Kierkegaard, time distinguishes the realm of human existence from the realm of merely fallen nature: "But the historical is the past (for the present pressing upon the confines of the future has not yet become historical). How then can it be said that nature, though immediately present, is historical, except in the sense of the said ingenious speculation? The difficulty comes from the fact that nature is too abstract to have a dialectic with respect to time in the stricter sense. This is nature's imperfection, that it has no history in any other sense."[38] But for Kierkegaard the historicity of Christ in the paradox remains precisely as abstract as he perceives the paradox to be in the processes of mere nature because the Kierkegaardian sacrifice is nothing other than that of mere nature: "If the contemporary generation had left nothing behind them but these words: 'We have believed that in such and such a year the God appeared among us in the humble figure of a servant, that he lived and taught in our community, and finally died,' it would be more than enough. The contemporary generation would have done all that was necessary; for this little advertisement, this *nota bene* on a page of universal history, would be sufficient to afford an occasion for a successor, and the most voluminous account can in all eternity do nothing more."[39] In such a construction of the paradoxy, the appearance of Jesus in time becomes arbitrarily interchangeable because, indeed, time occurs in the paradox exclusively as an abstract, contentless *nota bene*. This suffices to show how fundamentally Kierkegaard's doctrine of the paradox, as a unity of time and eternity, turns against its own fundamental thesis, according to which "the historical fact that the God has been in human form is the essence of the matter."[40] In fact Kierkegaard's paradox omits that concrete moment of time that it precisely should have maintained and that instead appears as simple temptation: "There is in the immediate contemporaneity," as in the experience of the temporally concrete life of Christ, "an unrest, which does not cease until the word goes forth that it is finished. But the succeeding tranquillity must not be such as to do away with the historical, for then everything will be Socratic"[41]; or the "contemporaneity" is called "an intermediate situation, having its significance indeed, and not eliminable without, as you would say, turning back to the Socratic order of things, but nevertheless without absolute significance for the contemporary."[42] Just as in the "point" concrete time is wiped out by sacrificial paradoxy, so the image of eternity also fades into the most extreme abstractness; natural life is sacrificed, and the sacrifice that occurs remains bound to natural (be it even spiritual) life, unable to posit determinate transcendence: "Nor is it true that the absolute telos becomes concrete in the relative ends, for the absolute distinction that was fixed between them in the moment of resignation will secure the absolute *telos* against fraternization at every moment."[43] In that the telos becomes incomparable, it also becomes indeterminate; in that it demolishes all pictorial mythology, it sinks into the imageless mythology of pure negation. What Kierkegaard was reluctant to state as Christ is expressed by Job in the doctrine of the paradox in "religiosity A": "It is a weak point in the structure of the Book of Job that God appears in the clouds and also appears as the most accomplished dialectician: for what makes God the terrible dialectician he is, is precisely the fact that one has him at very much closer quarters, and therewith the softest whisper is more blissful, and the softest whisper is more terrible, than seeing him enthroned upon the clouds and hearing him in the thunder. Hence one cannot argue dialectically with him, for God brings to bear all the dialectical power in the soul of the man concerned against this man."[44] If in such sentences Kierkegaard's dialectic meant to raise itself above mythology, it here falls entirely to its mercy. For although the mythical images of transcendence are destroyed in the instant of "faith," in the same instant human consciousness itself usurps the power of the absolute through the paradoxy that it posits. "Subjectivity is truth": the paradox reveals the horrible lineaments of the sacrificial mask. In the demonic sacrifice of consciousness, man is still the ruler of a sinful creation; through sacrifice he asserts his rule, and the name of the divinity succumbs to his demonic nature. Here the philosophical criticism of Kierkegaard converges with the psychological question that current research prefers to pose and that can indeed be answered rigorously only on the basis of knowledge of the philosophical content itself: was Kierkegaard a true believer? To ask this of the person is neither legitimate nor possible; the text of the last conversations with Boesen alone prevents its affirmation. Philosophically, in the face of the mythical essence of Kierkegaard's paradoxy, the question can be decided negatively, and indeed according to the evidence furnished by the concept of the "follower." This concept ultimately becomes the guarantor of theological substance itself, but in such a fashion that this substance is secularized in the paradox: "Just as the ascension shatters or defies natural law (such in fact is the objection doubt raises), so the pressing need of the follower shatters the purely human sources of comfort (how could these give comfort to men who must suffer because they have done well?), and presses for another sort of comfort, pressingly needs the ascension of their lord and master, and believingly presses through to the ascension. So it always is with human need, 'from the eater cometh forth meat': where the need is, it produces as it were that which it needs. And the followers verily had need of his ascension in order to hold out in such a life as they led—so therefore it was a certainty to them."[45] However carefully, perhaps even ambiguously, this is formulated, in that the sacrifice of the follower in the "uncertainty" of faith constitutes the single criterion of truth, this truth is turned over to a pragmatism that, although it is still concealed in the point, could have been grasped by its consequences if Kierkegaard had ever relinquished the "point." Kierkegaard's theology would have disintegrated had it ever established itself as such. In sacrifice immanence reaches out beyond itself only to plunge into the blind relentless context of nature in which the immanent follower is to procure assurance of the transcendent ascension, rather than the reverse. The theology quoted by the sacrifice is subordinate to intraworldly categories to the extent that the sacrifice again intervenes, occasionally if not continuously, as *deus ex machina*, and subjective immanence submerges in the void of abstract negation. Lukács's thesis that Kierkegaard's "leap" was simply a helpless flight from meaninglessness is justified by the same interpretation that makes Kierkegaard a "nihilist"; and although the methodology of Ludwig Marcuse's cultural-philosophical cogitations is questionable, his results are critically unchallengeable where he classifies Kierkegaard as a "romantic" and comes to the conclusion that "the ideal of faith, which he sketches, is indeed ultimately romantic fantasy, not an image of existence"[46] and where he says of the paradox that "this romantic credo *quia absurdum* is not inner certainty in the face of all sorts of cognitive aporia; the cognitive aporia themselves are to render certainty"[47]—in the mythical sacrifice of reason. Reason, which in Hegel as infinite reason produces actuality out of itself, is in Kierkegaard, again as infinite reason, the negation of all finite knowledge: if the former is mythical by its claim to universal sovereignty, the latter becomes mythical through universal annihilation. Kierkegaard's continuously repeated assurances that he was not one of the faithful are therefore not to be taken as an expression of Christian modesty but as the truth of the matter. Precisely the assurances—conjuring formulas like the words "scripture" and "paradox"—are too stereotypically repeated to ever confirm the revived sentiment of modesty; they do not sternly ward off imposture from religion, but rather the reconciling word from the mythical circle that it would burst. In the ideal of speaking "without authority," the profound knowledge of the heterodoxy of paradoxy—which Kierkegaard sets up as the standard of Christianity—becomes obdurately impenitent. This explains Kierkegaard's zealous concern for the "boundary," which fills his book against Adler: in priestly fashion, it would rather secure the ritual tradition of the cult of sacrifice than a Christianity that, if it were truly held, would know itself secure as revealed truth even in depravation and misrepresentation; it is instead threatened by demons because it is itself demonic. This is what gives the mythical tone to a passage in *For Self-Examination*: "In the case now anyone among us dares to step out ethically in the role here indicated, appealing moreover as an individual to a direct relationship with God [as does Adler] then I shall instantly (so it is I understand myself at this instant, but I cannot even know whether the next instant I may not be deprived even of the conditions for being able to do it, the next instant, perhaps while I am getting this published), I shall instantly be at his service, by undertaking what before God I shall understand as my task. This task of mine will be to follow him, the Reformer, step by step, never budging from his side, to see if step by step he is in the true character of his role, is actually the Extraordinary."[48] A border-guard mentality, unchallengeable discipline, the power of fascination—these the deluded Kierkegaard owes not, as he claims, to the purity of his Christian doctrine, but to its mythical reinterpretation in the paradox. Here the excessiveness of the created is revenged mercilessly on the manufactured system. As booty for the sacrifice of reason, reason receives whatever falls within its region. Sacrificed reason governs as a demigod.

Passio

The governance of sacrificed reason—in Kierkegaard's philosophy—traces the outlines of passion.[49] Along with melancholy, anxiety, and despair, *passio* is counted by him among the affects that, as ciphers, take the place of a blocked truth, yet at the same time give witness to the merely agitated subjectivity. *Passio* aims at the sacrifice of the self, whose passion is that of self-destruction: "If the individual is inwardly defined by self-annihilation before God, then we have *religiousness A*."[50] And *passio* is a subjective category: the natural urge of spirit, continually reconceived by Kierkegaard on the model of erotic inclination. Kierkegaard even intended to assure himself of the transcendental content of faith by the psychological content of passion. "But the highest passion in a person is faith"[51]; thus the double sense of his concept of *passio* encourages misinterpretations, which are condensed, most drastically, in the title of Vetter's book, *Piety as Passion*. This double sense is, however, dialectical. It is the old double sense of *passio* which, according to Benjamin's formulation, constitutes the "high pass of mythology": passion and sacrificial suffering. It is not accidental that Kierkegaard's "ethical" passion—from which he indeed thought he had "excised everything incommensurable," had banished nature—requires such an opaque and equivocal determination as that of sympathy: "sympathy is an essential quality of man, and every resolution in which sympathy is not given its due, in which it fails to gain adequate expression, is not in the largest sense an idealizing resolution."[52] The ambiguousness of sympathy is mythical. It is expressed, in Kierkegaard's "ethical sphere," through *passio*, which as the passion of the intellect preserves its natural instinctual character. This instinct is able to articulate itself vividly. Its dialectic appears bound to the totality of "existence," which the dialectic expiates altogether through annihilation. Its claim to totality, however, is bound to absolute spirit's claim to domination. If this claim disappears, passion receives another dialectical form than that of atonement and complete annihilation. Passion may then fulfill itself in its impulses according to the rhythm with which it encounters them individually, without submitting to the rigid subordinating concept; the steps of fulfillment are transformed by it into those of reconciliation. It is Kierkegaard's second plan of the dialectic, the dialectic of the mythical itself, which reawakens in the depth of his philosophy and turns against a sacrificial mythology that could have "isolated" the plan but indeed not subsumed it in its paradoxies. If passion, as an all-powerful, infinite, insatiable natural power knows only its own destruction wherever it finds any satisfaction in the finite, then despair, previously passion's demonic totality, loses its power over passion and the dialectical sickness unto death is transposed into the force of reconciled-historical life. It is not, as Kierkegaard's doctrine of total sin and total expiational sacrifice supposes, a "superficial understanding" that permits the assumption that "the doctrine of reconciliation is the qualitative difference between paganism and Christianity."[53] Reconciliation is the imperceptible gesture in which guilty nature renews itself historically as created nature; unreconciled, it remains obsessed with its greatest gesture, that of sacrifice. Christianity distinguishes itself from mere natural religion in the name of reconciliation and not in the nameless execution of the paradox. What Kierkegaard mythically neglects in Christianity, he recognizes, in truth with greater Christianity, in myth itself; in the nordic "Saga of Agnes and the Merman," which he recounts, transforms, and comments upon in *Fear and Trembling*. For here the dialectical transition from passion to reconciliation is understood, if not as already fulfilled, then indeed as without sacrifice: "The merman is a seducer who rises up from his hidden chasm and in wild lust seizes and breaks the innocent flower standing on the seashore in all her loveliness and with her head thoughtfully inclined to the soughing of the sea. This has been the poets' interpretation until now. Let us make a change. The merman was a seducer. He has called to Agnes and by his wheedling words has elicited what was hidden in her. In the merman she found what she was seeking, what she was searching for as she stared down to the bottom of the sea. Agnes is willing to go with him. The merman takes her in his arms. Agnes throws her arms around his neck; trusting with all her soul, she gives herself to the stronger one. He is already standing on the beach, crouching to dive out into the sea and plunge down with his booty/then Agnes looks at him once more, not fearfully, not despairingly, not proud of her good luck, not intoxicated with desire, but in absolute faith and in absolute humility, like the lowly flower she thought herself to be, and with this look she entrusts her whole destiny to him in absolute confidence./And look! The sea no longer roars, its wild voice is stilled; nature's passion, which is the merman's strength, forsakes him, and there is a deadly calm/and Agnes is still looking at him this way."[54] The "change" that Kierkegaard has undertaken is so small and perfect that it can be compared only with what the sagas once underwent at the hands of the attic tragedians: the enigmatic step that leads out of mere nature by remaining within it; the reconciling redemption of sacrifice. Sacrifice disappears, and in its place dialectic holds its breath for an instant; a caesura appears in its progress, as is represented, graphically, by the solidus before "And look!" Certainly, to the eyes of Kierkegaard the existentialist, reconciliation passes by overhead like a radiant meteor that never reaches the earth. Sacrifice, as renunciation, once more breaks into the fleetingly reconciled landscape: "Then the merman breaks down. He cannot withstand the power of innocence, his natural element is disloyal to him, and he cannot seduce Agnes. He takes her home again/he explains that he only wanted to show her how beautiful the sea is when it is calm, and Agnes believes him./Then he returns alone, and the sea is wild but not as wild as the merman's despair. He can seduce Agnes, he can seduce a hundred Agneses, he can make any girl infatuated/but Agnes has won, and the merman has lost her.

Only as booty can she be his; he cannot give himself faithfully to any girl, because he is indeed only a merman."[55] This he remains through renunciation: sacrifice throws him back again into the mythical element, into the "passion of nature," which "forsakes him" in the instant of reconciliation, dissolved by the fulfilling gesture of the girl who holds true to nature till the end. In sacrificial renunciation, however, the merman becomes "demonic": he falls silent. His silence binds him to mere nature. Thus Kierkegaard himself understood it: "We shall now give the merman a human consciousness and let his being a merman signify a human preexistence, in consequence of which his life was entrapped. There is nothing to hinder his becoming a hero, for the step he now takes is reconciling. He is saved by Agnes; the seducer is crushed, he has submitted to the power of innocence, he can never seduce again. But immediately, two forces struggle over him: repentance, Agnes and repentance. If repentance alone gets him, then he is hidden; if Agnes and repentance get him, then he is disclosed."[56] In scarcely another passage is Kierkegaard's idealism of objectless inwardness more self-evidently mythical than here where he holds up to himself the image of reconciliation. Objectless inwardness must silently endure, like the refractory natural demon. The sole organ of reconciliation, however, is the word. "Meanwhile, there is no doubt that the merman can speak"[57]; this speech, as "the disclosed," would draw him out of mythology, to which he is banned by his silence—the archaic silence of his unmediated natural existence as well as the dialectical silence of "repentance" shut within itself and sacrificially annihilating itself without ever finding the reconciling word. The "merman" is truly the "preexistence" of Kierkegaardian inwardness: in silence its dialectical sacrifice reveals itself as archaic. This confirms his idealism as the historical figure of the mythical. Where, however, nature—free of resignation—perseveres as desirous instinct and eloquent consciousness, it is able to survive, whereas in sacrifice nature succumbs to itself; nature, which truly cannot be driven out with a pitch-fork and returns until genius is reconciled with it.

Notes

1. O. P. Monrad, *Søren Kierkegaard. Sein Leben und seine Werke* (Jena, 1909), 3.
2. E. Geismar, *Søren Kierkegaard. Seine Entwicklung und seine Wirksamkeit als Schriftsteller* (Goettingen, 1929), 14ff.
3. Monrad, *Soren Kierkegaard*, 4.
4. *Philosophical Fragments*, originally trans. and introduced by D. Swenson; new introduction and commentary by N. Thulstrup; trans. rev. and commentary trans. H. V. Hong (Princeton, NJ: Princeton University Press, 1967), 137–38.
5. *Fear and Trembling and Repetition*, ed. and trans. H. V. Hong and E. H. Hong (Princeton, NJ: Princeton University Press, 1983), 87.
6. *Either/Or*, vol. 1, trans. D. F. Swenson and L. M. Swenson with revisions and a foreword by H. A. Johnson (Princeton, NJ: Princeton University Press, 1971), 35.
7. Ibid., 111–12.
8. *For Self-Examination and Judge for Yourselves!*, trans. W. Lowrie (Princeton, NJ: Princeton University Press), 101.

9. cf. *Concluding Unscientific Postscript*, trans. D. F. Swenson and W. Lowrie (Princeton, NJ: Princeton University Press, 1968), 523 ff.

10. Ibid., 529.

11. Ibid., 536.

12. *Training for Christianity and the Edifying Discourse Which 'Accompanied' It*, trans. with an introduction and notes by W. Lowrie (London: Oxford University Press, 1972), 181.

13. *The Concept of Anxiety*, ed. and trans. with introduction and notes by R. Thomte in collaboration with A. B. Anderson (Princeton, NJ: Princeton University Press, 1980), 28.

14. *Fear and Trembling and Repetition*, 58.

15. *Attack Upon "Christendom,"* trans. with an introduction and notes by W. Lowrie; new introduction by H. A. Johnson (Princeton, NJ: Princeton University Press, 1972), 205.

16. *Training in Christianity and the Edifying Discourse Which 'Accompanied' It*, 168.

17. Ibid., 169.

18. *Concluding Unscientific Postscript*, 350.

19. *Attack Upon "Christendom,"* 243,

20. *The Point of View, etc., including The Point of View for My Work as an Author*, trans. with an introduction and notes by W. Lowrie (London: Oxford University Press, 1972), 79.

21. *Fear and Trembling and The Sickness unto Death*, trans. with an introduction and notes by W. Lowrie (Princeton, NJ: Princeton University Press, 1974), 257.

22. Ibid., 258.

23. *Training in Christianity and the Edifying Discourse Which 'Accompanied' It*, 131.

24. Ibid., 131–32.

25. Theodor Haecker, *Søren Kierkegaard und die Philosophie der Innerlichkeit* (Munich, 1913), 13

26. *Philosophical Fragments*, 46.

27. *Fear and Trembling and The Sickness unto Death*, 212.

28. *Stages of Life's Way*, trans. W. Lowrie (Princeton, NJ: Princeton University Press, 1974), 438.

29. *For Self-Examination and Judge for Yourselves!*, 178.

30. *Philosophical Fragments*, 104.

31. *Stages of Life's Way*, 159.

32. *Concluding Unscientific Postscript*, 387.

33. *Either/Or*, vol.1, 49.

34. *Stages of Life's Way*, 119.

35. *Either/Or*, vol. 2, trans. W. A. Lowrie with rev. and a foreword by H. A. Johnson (Princeton, NJ: Princeton University Press, 1971), 268.

36. *Fear and Trembling and Repetition*, 212.

37. *Stages of Life's Way*, 406.

38. *Philosophical Fragments*, 94.

39. Ibid., 130–31.

40. Ibid., 130.

41. Ibid., 133–34.

9

Reason and Revelation

Theodor W. Adorno
Translated by Henry W. Pickford

1

The dispute regarding revelation was fought out in the eighteenth century. It ended in a negative resolution and during the nineteenth century actually fell into oblivion. Its revival today owes more than a little to that oblivion. Because of this revival, however, the critic of revelation at the outset finds himself in a difficult position, and he would do well to describe it lest he become its victim. If one repeats the rather comprehensive catalog of arguments made during the Enlightenment, then one opens oneself up to the reproach of being eclectic, of relying on old truisms that no longer interest anyone. If one finds reassurance in the thought that the religion of revelation at that time could not withstand critique, then one is suspected of old-fashioned rationalism. There is a widely accepted habit of thinking these days that, instead of objectively reflecting about truth and falsity, shifts the decision onto the age as such and even plays a more remote historical past against a more recent one. If one does not want either to fall under the sway of the notion that whatever has long been well known is for that reason false, or to accommodate oneself to the current religious mood that—as peculiar as it is understandable—coincides with the prevailing positivism, then one would do best to remember Benjamin's infinitely ironic description of theology, "which today, as we know, is wizened and has to keep out of sight."[1] Nothing of theological content will persist without being transformed; every content will have to put itself to the test of migrating into the realm of the secular, the profane. In contrast to the richly and concretely developed religious imagination of old, the currently prevailing opinion, which claims that the life and experience of people, their immanence, is a kind of glass case, through whose walls one can gaze upon the eternally immutable ontological stock of a *philosophia* or *religio perennis*, is itself an expression of a state of affairs in which the belief in revelation is no longer substantially present in people and in the organization of their relationships and can be maintained only through a desperate abstraction. What counts in the endeavors of ontology today, its attempt to leap without mediation out of the ongoing nominalistic situation into realism, the world of ideas in themselves, which then for its part is rendered into a product of mere subjectivity, of so-called decision, namely an arbitrary act—all this is also in large measure valid for the closely related turn toward positive religion.

2

Those in the eighteenth century who defended faith in revelation maintained a fundamentally different position than do those who defend it today, just as in general the same ideas can acquire extremely divergent meanings according to their respective historical moments. At that time a scholastic concept, which was inherited from the tradition and more or less supported by the authority of society, was being defended against the attack by an autonomous *ratio* that refuses to accept anything other than what stands up to examination on its own terms. Such a defense against *ratio* had to be carried out with rational means and was in this respect, as Hegel pronounced in the *Phenomenology*, hopeless from the very start: with the means of argumentation it used, the very defense already assumed the principle that belonged to its adversary. Today the turn toward faith in revelation is a desperate reaction to just these very means, to *ratio*. The irresistible progress of *ratio* is seen solely in negative terms, and revelation is invoked so as to halt what Hegel calls the "fury of destruction": because supposedly it would be a good thing to have revelation. Doubts about the possibility of such a restoration are muffled by appealing to the consensus of all the others who also would like it. "Today it is no longer at all unmodern to believe in God," a lady once told me whose family had returned to the religion of her childhood after a stormy enlightenment intermezzo. In the best case, that is, where it is not just a question of imitation and conformity, it is desire that produces such an attitude: it is not the truth and authenticity of the revelation that are decisive but rather the need for guidance, the confirmation of what is already firmly established, and also the hope that by means of a resolute decision alone one could breathe back that meaning into the disenchanted world under whose absence we have been suffering so long, as though we were mere spectators staring at something meaningless. It seems to me that the religious renaissances of today are philosophy of religion, not religion. In any case, here they concur with the apologetics of the eighteenth and early nineteenth centuries in that they strive through rational reflection to conjure up its opposite, but now they apply rational reflection to *ratio* itself with a mounting willingness to strike out at it and with a tendency toward obscurantism that is far more vicious than all the restrained orthodoxy of the earlier period, because it does not completely believe in itself. The new religious attitude is that of the convert, even among those who do not formally convert or who simply support emphatically whatever seems sanctioned as the "religion of the fathers" as well as what with fatherly authority since time immemorial—and even in Kierkegaard's understanding of the individual—helped to suppress through intimidation the rising doubt.

3

The sacrifice of the intellect that once, in Pascal or Kierkegaard, was made by the most progressive consciousness and at no less a cost than one's entire life has since then become socialized, and whoever makes this sacrifice no longer feels any burden of fear or trembling; no one would have reacted to it with more indignation than Kierkegaard himself. Because too much thinking, an unwavering autonomy, hinders the conformity to the administered world and causes suffering, countless people project this suffering imposed on them by society onto reason as such. According to them, it is reason that has brought suffering and disaster into the world. The dialectic of enlightenment, which in fact must also name the price of progress—all the ruin wrought by rationality in the form of the increasing domination of nature—is, as it were, broken off too early, following the model of a condition that is blindly self-enclosed and hence appears to block the exit. Convulsively, deliberately, one ignores the fact that the excess of rationality, about which the educated class especially complains and which it registers in concepts like mechanization, atomization, indeed even de-individualization, is a lack of rationality, namely, the increase of all apparatuses and means of quantifiable domination at the cost of the goal, the rational organization of mankind, which is left abandoned to the unreason of mere constellations of power, an unreason that consciousness, dulled by constantly having to consider the existing positive relations and conditions, no longer dares rise to engage at all. Certainly a *ratio* that does not wantonly absolutize itself as a rigid means of domination requires self-reflection, some of which is expressed in the need for religion today. But this self-reflection cannot stop at the mere negation of thought by thought itself, a kind of mythical sacrifice, and cannot realize itself through a "leap": that would all too closely resemble the politics of catastrophe. On the contrary, reason must attempt to define rationality itself, not as an absolute, regardless of whether it is then posited or negated, but rather as a moment within the totality, though admittedly even this moment has become independent in relation to the totality. Rationality must become cognizant of its own natural essence. Although not unknown to the great religions, precisely this theme requires "secularization" today if, isolated and inflated, it is not to further that very darkening of the world it wants to exorcise.

4

The renaissance of revealed religion particularly enjoys appealing to the concept of bonds that it claims are necessary: as it were, one relies on a precarious autonomy only then to choose the heteronomous. But these days, despite all the world's profanity, there are too many bonds rather than too few. The massive concentration of economic powers, and consequently of political and administrative ones as well, to a large extent reduces every individual into a mere functionary of the machinery. Individuals are probably much more connected today than in the era of high liberalism, when they had not yet called for bonds. Their need for bonds is therefore increasingly a need for a spiritual and intellectual reduplication and justification of an authority that is nonetheless already present. The talk of transcendental homelessness, which once expressed the distress of the individual within individualistic society, has become ideology, has become a pretext for bad collectivism that, as long as no authoritarian state is available, relies on other institutions with supra-individualist pretensions. The disparity between societal power and societal impotence, increasing beyond measure, extends into the weakening of the inner composition of the ego, so that finally the ego cannot endure without identifying itself with the very thing that condemns it to impotence. Only weakness seeks bonds; the urge for bonds, which exalts itself as though it had relinquished the restrictions of egoism, of mere individual interest, in truth is not oriented toward the humane; on the contrary, it capitulates before the inhumane. Certainly underlying this is the illusion society needs and reinforces with all its conceivable means: that the subject, that people are incapable of humanity—the desperate fetishization of presently existing relations. The religious theme of the corruption of the human species since Adam's fall appears in a new guise, radically secularized already in Hobbes, distorted in the service of evil itself. Because it is supposedly impossible for people to establish a just order, the existing unjust order is commended to them. What Thomas Mann in speaking against Spengler called the "defeatism of humanity" has expanded universally. The turn toward transcendence functions as a screen-image for immanent, societal hopelessness. Intrinsic to it is the willingness to leave the world as it is, because the world could not possibly be different. The real determining model of this behavior is the division of the world into two colossal blocs that rigidly oppose and reciprocally threaten one another, and every individual, with destruction. The extreme innerworldly fear of this situation, because there is nothing discernible that might lead beyond it, is hypostatized as an existential or indeed a transcendental anxiety. The victories that revealed religion gains in the name of such anxiety are Pyrrhic. If religion is accepted for the sake of something other than its own truth content, then it undermines itself. The fact that recently the positive religions have so willingly engaged in this and at times compete with other public institutions testifies only to the desperation that latently inheres in their own positivity.

5

The irrationalism of revealed religion today is expressed in the central status of the concept of religious paradox. It is enough here merely to recall dialectical theology. Even it is not a theological invariant but has its historical status. What the apostle in the age of the Hellenistic enlightenment called a folly for the Greeks and what now demands the abdication of reason was not always so. At its medieval height Christian revealed religion defended itself powerfully against the doctrine of the two types of truth by claiming that the doctrine was self-destructive. High Scholasticism, and especially the *Summa* of St. Thomas, have their force and dignity in the fact that, without absolutizing the concept of reason, they never condemned it: theology went so far only in the age of nominalism, particularly with Luther. The Thomistic doctrine reflected not merely the feudal order of its epoch, which indeed had already become problematical, but also accorded with the most advanced developments in science at the time. But once faith no longer accords with knowledge, or at least no longer exists in productive tension with it, it forfeits the quality of binding power, that character of "necessitation" Kant subsequently set out to save in the moral law as a secularization of the authority of faith. Why one should adopt *that* particular faith and not another: nowadays consciousness can find no other justification than simply its own need, which does not warrant truth. In order that I be able to adopt the revealed faith, it must acquire an authority in relation to my reason that would already presuppose that I have adopted the faith—an inescapable circle. If, as high Scholastic doctrine maintains, my will is added as an express condition of faith, then one does not escape the circle. Will itself would be possible only where the conviction about the contents of belief already exists, that is, precisely that which can be gained only by an act of will. If religion at last is no longer folk religion, no longer substantial in the Hegelian sense—if it ever was that at all—then it becomes something taken up contingently, an authoritarian view of the world, in which compulsion and caprice intertwine. It was insight into this situation that probably induced the theology of Judaism to stipulate virtually no dogmas and to demand nothing but that people live according to the law; what is called Tolstoy's primitive Christianity is presumably something very similar. Even if this allows the antinomy of knowledge and faith to be circumvented and the very alienation between the religious precept and the subject to be bridged, the contradiction continues to operate implicitly.

For the question of where the authority of doctrine comes from was not resolved but rather removed as soon as the Haggadah element had dissociated itself completely from the halachah element. The excision of the objective element from religion is no less harmful to it than the reification that aims to impose dogma—the objectivity of faith—inflexibly and antirationally upon the subject. The objective element, however, no longer can be asserted because it would have to submit itself to the criterion of objectivity, of knowledge, whose claim it arrogantly rejects.

6

In the wake of the general reductive neutralization of everything intellectual and spiritual to the level of mere culture during the last hundred and fifty years, the contradiction is hardly felt any more between traditional revealed religion and knowledge—rather both simply exist side by side as branches of the culture industry, something like the rubrics "Medicine," "Radio," "Television," "Religion" come one after another in magazines. However, the exorbitant demand that revealed religion has made upon consciousness since the Enlightenment has not diminished but, on the contrary, has increased immeasurably. The reason why no one speaks of it anymore can be explained by the fact that it is no longer possible to bring the two together at all. Attempts to transfer the critical results of modern science into religion, which, for example, particularly flourish on the borders of quantum physics, are rash. Here one should consider not only the geocentric and anthropocentric character of the great traditional religions—which stands in the starkest opposition to the present status of cosmology—whereby this crass incongruity, namely, the ridiculousness of a confrontation of religious doctrine with the findings of the natural sciences in general, is often used in order to ridicule the confrontation itself for being primitive and crude. There once was a time when religion, with good reason, was not so discriminating. It insisted upon its truth even in the cosmological sense, because it knew that its claim to that truth could not be separated from its material and concrete contents without incurring damage. As soon as religion abandons its factual content, it threatens to vanish into mere symbolism and that imperils the very existence of its truth claim. Perhaps more decisive, however, is the rupture between the social model of the great religions and the society of today. The great religions were modeled upon the transparent relations of the "*primary community*,"* or at most the simple economy of goods. A Jewish poet once wrote quite rightly that a village air suffuses Judaism and Christianity. This cannot be overlooked without violently reinterpreting the religious doctrinal content: Christianity is not equally close to all ages, and human beings are not affected timelessly by what they once perceived as good tidings. The concept of daily bread, born from the experience of deprivation under the conditions of uncertain and insufficient material production, cannot simply be translated into the world of bread factories and surplus production, in which famines are natural catastrophes wrought by society and precisely not by nature. Or, the concept of the neighbor refers to communities where people know each other face to face. Helping one's neighbors, no matter how urgent this remains in a world devastated by those natural catastrophes produced by society, is insignificant in comparison with a praxis that extends beyond every mere immediacy of human relationships, in comparison with a transformation of the world that one day would put an end to the natural catastrophes of society. Were one to remove phrases such as these from the Gospel as irrelevant, while presuming to preserve the revealed doctrines and yet express them as they supposedly should be understood *hic et nunc,* then one would fall into a dichotomy of bad alternatives. Either revealed doctrines must be adapted to contemporary circumstances: that would be incompatible with the authority of revelation. Or contemporary reality would be confronted with demands that are unrealizable or that fall short of their most essential concern, the real suffering of people. Yet if one were simply to disregard all these concrete socio-historically mediated conditions and to heed literally the Kierkegaardian dictum that holds that Christianity is nothing other than a nota bene—namely, the nota bene that God once became man without that moment entering consciousness as such, that is, as a concretely historical moment—then in the name of a paradoxical purity revealed religion would dissolve into something completely indeterminate, a nothingness that could hardly be distinguished from religion's liquidation. Anything more than this nothingness would lead immediately to the insoluble, and it would be a mere ruse of imprisoned consciousness to transfigure into a religious category this very insolubility itself, the failure of finite man, whereas it instead attests to the present impotence of religious categories. Therefore, I see no other possibility than an extreme ascesis toward any type of revealed faith, an extreme loyalty to the prohibition of images, far beyond what this once originally meant.

Note

1. Walter Benjamin, *Schriften,* ed. Theodor W. Adorno and Gretel Adorno with the assistance of Friedrich Podszus (Frankfurt: Suhrkamp, 1955), 1:494. [*Translator's note:* "Theses on the Philosophy of History," in *Illuminations,* trans. Harry Zohn, ed. Hannah Arendt (New York: Schocken Books, 1968), 253.]

10
Meditations on Metaphysics

Theodor W. Adorno
Translated by E. B. Ashton

1. After Auschwitz

We cannot say any more that the immutable is truth, and that the mobile, transitory is appearance. The mutual indifference of temporality and eternal ideas is no longer tenable even with the bold Hegelian explanation that temporal existence, by virtue of the destruction inherent in its concept, serves the eternal represented by the eternity of destruction. One of the mystical impulses secularized in dialectics was the doctrine that the intramundane and historic is relevant to what traditional metaphysics distinguished as transcendence—or at least, less gnostically and radically put, that it is relevant to the position taken by human consciousness on the questions which the canon of philosophy assigned to metaphysics. After Auschwitz, our feelings resist any claim of the positivity of existence as sanctimonious, as wronging the victims; they balk at squeezing any kind of sense, however bleached, out of the victims' fate. And these feelings do have an objective side after events that make a mockery of the construction of immanence as endowed with a meaning radiated by an affirmatively posited transcendence.

Such a construction would affirm absolute negativity and would assist its ideological survival—as in reality that negativity survives anyway, in the principle of society as it exists until its self-destruction. The earthquake of Lisbon sufficed to cure Voltaire of the theodicy of Leibniz, and the visible disaster of the first nature was insignificant in comparison with the second, social one, which defies human imagination as it distills a real hell from human evil. Our metaphysical faculty is paralyzed because actual events have shattered the basis on which speculative metaphysical thought could be reconciled with experience. Once again, the dialectical motif of quantity recoiling into quality scores an

175

unspeakable triumph. The administrative murder of millions made of death a thing one had never yet to fear in just this fashion. There is no chance any more for death to come into the individuals' empirical life as somehow conformable with the course of that life. The last, the poorest possession left to the individual is expropriated. That in the concentration camps it was no longer an individual who died, but a specimen—this is a fact bound to affect the dying of those who escaped the administrative measure.

Genocide is the absolute integration. It is on its way wherever men are leveled off—"polished off," as the German military called it—until one exterminates them literally, as deviations from the concept of their total nullity. Auschwitz confirmed the philosopheme of pure identity as death. The most far out dictum from Beckett's *End Game*, that there really is not so much to be feared any more, reacts to a practice whose first sample was given in the concentration camps, and in whose concept—venerable once upon a time—the destruction of nonidentity is ideologically lurking. Absolute negativity is in plain sight and has ceased to surprise anyone. Fear used to be tied to the *principium individuationis* of self-preservation, and that principle, by its own consistency, abolishes itself. What the sadists in the camps foretold their victims, "Tomorrow you'll be wiggling skyward as smoke from this chimney," bespeaks the indifference of each individual life that is the direction of history. Even in his formal freedom, the individual is as fungible and replaceable as he will be under the liquidators' boots.

But since, in a world whose law is universal individual profit, the individual has nothing but this self that has become indifferent, the performance of the old, familiar tendency is at the same time the most dreadful of things. There is no getting out of this, no more than out of the electrified barbed wire around the camps. Perennial suffering has as much right to expression as a tortured man has to scream; hence it may have been wrong to say that after Auschwitz you could no longer write poems. But it is not wrong to raise the less cultural question whether after Auschwitz you can go on living—especially whether one who escaped by accident, one who by rights should have been killed, may go on living. His mere survival calls for the coldness, the basic principle of bourgeois subjectivity, without which there could have been no Auschwitz; this is the drastic guilt of him who was spared. By way of atonement he will be plagued by dreams such as that he is no longer living at all, that he was sent to the ovens in 1944 and his whole existence since has been imaginary, an emanation of the insane wish of a man killed twenty years earlier.

Thinking men and artists have not infrequently described a sense of being not quite there, of not playing along, a feeling as if they were not themselves at all, but a kind of spectator. Others often find this repulsive; it was the basis of Kierkegaard's polemic against what he called the esthetic sphere. A critique of philosophical personalism indicates, however, that this attitude toward immediacy, this disavowal of every existential posture, has a moment of objective truth that goes beyond the appearance of the self-preserving motive. "What does it really matter?" is a line we like to associate with bourgeois callousness, but it is the line most likely to make the individual aware, without dread, of the insignificance of his existence. The inhuman part of it, the ability to keep one's distance as a spectator and to rise above things, is in the final analysis the human part, the very part resisted by its ideologists.

It is not altogether implausible that the immortal part is the one that acts in this fashion. The scene of Shaw on his way to the theater, showing a beggar his identification with the hurried remark, "Press," hides a sense of that beneath the cynicism. It would help to explain the fact that startled Schopenhauer: that affections in the face of death, not only other people's but our own, are frequently so feeble. People, of course, are spellbound without exception, and none of them are capable of love, which is why everyone feels loved too little. But the spectator's posture simultaneously expresses doubt that this could be all—when the individual, so relevant to himself in his delusion, still has nothing but that poor and emotionally animal-like ephemerality.

Spellbound, the living have a choice between involuntary ataraxy —an esthetic life due to weakness—and the bestiality of the involved. Both are wrong ways of living. But some of both would be required for the right *désinvolture* and sympathy. Once overcome, the culpable self-preservation urge has been confirmed, confirmed precisely, perhaps, by the threat that has come to be ceaselessly present. The only trouble with self-preservation is that we cannot help suspecting the life to which it attaches us of turning into something that makes us shudder: into a specter, a piece of the world of ghosts, which our waking consciousness perceives to be nonexistent. The guilt of a life which purely as a fact will strangle other life, according to statistics that eke out an overwhelming number of killed with a minimal number of rescued, as if this were provided in the theory of probabilities—this guilt is irreconcilable with living. And the guilt does not cease to reproduce itself, because not for an instant can it be made fully, presently conscious.

This, nothing else, is what compels us to philosophize. And in philosophy we experience a shock: the deeper, the more vigorous its penetration, the greater our suspicion that philosophy removes us from things as they are—that an unveiling of the essence might enable the most superficial and trivial views to prevail over the views that aim at the essence. This throws a glaring light on truth itself. In speculation we feel a certain duty to grant the position of a corrective to common sense, the opponent of speculation. Life feeds the horror of a premonition: what must come to be known may resemble the down-to-earth more than it resembles the sublime; it might be that this premonition will be confirmed even beyond the pedestrian realm, although the happiness of thought, the promise of its truth, lies in sublimity alone.

If the pedestrian had the last word, if it were the truth, truth would be degraded. The trivial consciousness, as it is theoretically expressed in positivism and unreflected nominalism, may be closer than the sublime consciousness to an *adaequatio rei atque cogitationis*; its sneering mockery of truth may be truer than a superior consciousness, unless the formation of a truth concept other than that of *adaequatio* should succeed. The innervation that metaphysics might win only by discarding itself applies to such other truth, and it is not the last among the motivations for the passage to materialism. We can trace the leaning to it from the Hegelian Marx to Benjamin's rescue of induction; Kafka's work may be the apotheosis of the trend. If negative dialectics calls for the self-reflection of thinking, the tangible implication is that if thinking is to be true—if if it is to be true today, in any case—it must also be a thinking against itself. If thought is not measured by the extremity that eludes the concept, it is from the outset in the nature of the musical accompaniment with which the SS liked to drown out the screams of its victims.

2. Metaphysics and Culture

A new categorical imperative has been imposed by Hitler upon unfree mankind: to arrange their thoughts and actions so that Auschwitz will not repeat itself, so that nothing similar will happen. When we want to find reasons for it, this imperative is as refractory as the given one of Kant was once upon a time. Dealing discursively with it would be an outrage, for the new imperative gives us a bodily sensation of the moral addendum—bodily, because it is now the practical abhorrence of the unbearable physical agony to which individuals are exposed even with individuality about to vanish as a form of mental reflection. It is in the unvarnished materialistic motive only that morality survives.

The course of history forces materialism upon metaphysics, traditionally the direct antithesis of materialism. What the mind once boasted of defining or construing as its like moves in the direction of what is unlike the mind, in the direction of that which eludes the rule of the mind and yet manifests that rule as absolute evil. The somatic, unmeaningful stratum of life is the stage of suffering, of the suffering which in the camps, without any consolation, burned every soothing feature out of the mind, and out of culture, the mind's objectification. The point of no return has been reached in the process which irresistibly forced metaphysics to join what it was once conceived against. Not since the youthful Hegel has philosophy—unless selling out for authorized cerebration—been able to repress how very much it slipped into material questions of existence.

Children sense some of this in the fascination that issues from the flayer's zone, from carcasses, from the repulsively sweet odor of putrefaction, and from the opprobrious terms used for that zone. The unconscious power of that realm may be as great as that of infantile sexuality; the two intermingle in the anal fixation, but they are scarcely the same. An unconscious knowledge whispers to the child what is repressed by civilized education; this is what matters, says the whispering voice. And the wretched physical existence strikes a spark in the supreme interest that is scarcely less repressed; it kindles a "What is that?" and "Where is it going?" The man who managed to recall what used to strike him in the words "dung hill" and "pig sty" might be closer to absolute knowledge than Hegel's chapter in which readers are promised such knowledge only to have it withheld with a superior mien. The integration of physical death into culture should be rescinded in theory—not, however, for the sake of an ontologically pure being named Death, but for the sake of that which the stench of cadavers expresses and we are fooled about by their transfiguration into "remains."

A child, fond of an innkeeper named Adam, watched him club the rats pouring out of holes in the courtyard; it was in his image that the child made its own image of the first man. That this has been forgotten, that we no longer know what we used to feel before the dogcatcher's van, is both the triumph of culture and its failure. Culture, which keeps emulating the old Adam, cannot bear to be reminded of that zone, and precisely this is not to be reconciled with the conception that culture has of itself. It abhors stench because it stinks—because, as Brecht put it in a magnificent line, its mansion is built of dogshit. Years after that line was written, Auschwitz demonstrated irrefutably that culture has failed.

That this could happen in the midst of the traditions of philosophy, of art, and of the enlightening sciences says more than that these traditions and their spirit lacked the power to take hold of men and work a change in them. There is untruth in those fields themselves, in the autarky that is emphatically claimed for them. All post-Auschwitz culture, including its urgent critique, is garbage. In restoring itself after the things that happened without resistance in its own countryside, culture has turned entirely into the ideology it had been potentially—had been ever since it presumed, in opposition to material existence, to inspire that existence with the light denied it by the separation of the mind from manual labor. Whoever pleads for the maintenance of this radically culpable and shabby culture becomes its accomplice, while the man who says no to culture is directly furthering the barbarism which our culture showed itself to be.

Not even silence gets us out of the circle. In silence we simply use the state of objective truth to rationalize our subjective incapacity, once more degrading truth into a lie. When countries of the East, for all their drivel to the contrary, abolished culture or transformed it into rubbish as a mere means of control, the culture that moans about it is getting what it deserves, and what on its part, in the name of people's democratic right to their own likeness, it is zealously heading for. The only difference is that when the apparatchiks over there acclaim their administrative barbarism as culture and guard its mischief as an inalienable heritage, they convict its reality, the infrastructure, of being as barbarian as the superstructure they are dismantling by taking it under their management. In the West, at least, one is allowed to say so.

The theology of the crisis registered the fact it was abstractly and therefore idly rebelling against: that metaphysics has merged with culture. The aureole of culture, the principle that the mind is absolute, was the same which tirelessly violated what it was pretending to express. After Auschwitz there is no word tinged from on high, not even a theological one, that has any right unless it underwent a transformation. The judgment passed on the ideas long before, by Nietzsche, was carried out on the victims, reiterating the challenge of the traditional words and the test whether God would permit this without intervening in his wrath.

A man whose admirable strength enabled him to survive Auschwitz and other camps said in an outburst against Beckett that if Beckett had been in Auschwitz he would be writing differently, more positively, with the front-line creed of the escapee. The escapee is right in a fashion other than he thinks. Beckett, and whoever else remained in control of himself, would have been broken in Auschwitz and probably forced to confess that frontline creed which the escapee clothed in the words "Trying to give men courage"—as if this were up to any structure of the mind; as if the intent to address men, to adjust to them, did not rob them of what is their due even if they believe the contrary. That is what we have come to in metaphysics.

3. Dying Today

And this lends suggestive force to the wish for a fresh start in metaphysics or, as they call it, for radical questioning—the wish to scrape off the delusions which a culture that had failed was papering over its guilt and over truth. But yielding to the urge for an unspoiled basic stratum will make that supposed demolition even more of a conspiracy with the culture one boasts of razing. While the fascists raged against destructive cultural bolshevism, Heidegger was making destruction respectable as a means to penetrate Being. The practical test followed promptly. Metaphysical reflections that seek to get rid of their cultural, indirect elements deny the relation of their allegedly pure categories to their social substance. They disregard society, but encourage its continuation in existing forms, in the forms which in turn block both the cognition of truth and its realization. The idol of pure original experience is no less of a hoax than that which has been culturally processed, the obsolete categorial stock of what is θέσει [Thesis]. The only possible escape route would be to define both by their indirectness: culture as the lid on the trash; and nature, even where it takes itself for the bedrock of Being, as the projection of the wretched cultural wish that in all change things must stay the same. Not even the experience of death suffices as the ultimate and undoubted, as a metaphysics like the one Descartes deduced once from the nugatory *ego cogitans.*

The deterioration of the death metaphysics, whether into advertisements for heroic dying or to the triviality of purely restating the unmistakable fact that men must die—all this ideological mischief probably rests on the fact that human consciousness to this day is too weak to sustain the experience of death, perhaps even too weak for its conscious acceptance. No man who deals candidly and freely with the objects has a life sufficient to accomplish what every man's life potentially contains; life and death cleave asunder. The reflections that give death a meaning are as helpless as the tautological ones. The more our consciousness is extricated from animality and comes to strike us as solid and lasting in its forms, the more stubbornly will it resist anything that would cause it to doubt its own eternity.

Coupled with the subject's historic enthronement as a mind was the delusion of its inalienability. Early forms of property coincided with magical practices designed to banish death, and as all human relations come to be more completely determined by property, the *ratio* exorcises death as obstinately as rites ever did. At a final stage, in despair, death itself becomes property. Its metaphysical uplifting relieves us of the its experience. Our current death metaphysics is nothing but society's impotent solace for the fact that social change has robbed men of what was once said to make death bearable for them, of the feeling of its epic unity with a full life.

In that feeling, too, the dominion of death may have been only transfigured by the weariness of the aged, of those who are tired of life and imagine it is right for them to die because the laborious life they had before was not living either, because it left them not even strong enough to resist death. In the socialized society, however, in the inescapably dense web of immanence, death is felt exclusively as external and strange. Men have lost the illusion that it is commensurable with their lives. They cannot absorb the fact that they must die. Attached to this is a perverse, dislocated bit of hope: that death does not constitute the entirety of existence—as it does to Heidegger—is the very reason why a man who is not yet debilitated will experience death and its envoys, the ailments, as heterogeneous and alien to the ego.

The reason, one may say nimbly, is that the ego is nothing but the self-preserving principle opposed to death, and that death therefore defies absorption in consciousness, which is the ego. But our experience of consciousness scarcely supports this view: in the face of death, consciousness does not necessarily take the form of defiance, as one would expect. Hardly any subject bears out Hegel's doctrine that whatever is will perish of itself. Even to the aging who perceive the signs of their debility, the fact that they must die seems rather like an accident caused by their own physis, with traits of the same contingency as that of the external accidents typical nowadays.

This strengthens a speculation in counterpoint to the insight of the object's supremacy: whether the mind has not an element of independence, an unmixed element, liberated at the very times when the mind is not devouring everything and by itself reproducing the doom of death. Despite the deceptive concern with self-preservation, it would hardly be possible without that mental element to explain the resistant strength of the idea of immortality, as Kant still harbored it. Of course, those powers of resistance seem to wane in the history of the species as they do in decrepit individuals. After the decline—long ratified in secret—of the objective religions that had pledged to rid it of its sting, death is now rendered completely and utterly alien by the socially determined decline of continuous experience as such.

As the subjects live less, death grows more precipitous, more terrifying. The fact that it literally turns them into things makes them aware of reification, their permanent death and the form of their relations that is partly their fault. The integration of death in civilization, a process without power over death and a ridiculous cosmetic procedure in the face of death, is the shaping of a reaction to this social phenomenon, a clumsy attempt of the barter society to stop up the last holes left open by the world of merchandise.

Death and history, particularly the collective history of the individual category, form a constellation. Once upon a time the individual, Hamlet, inferred his absolute essentiality from the dawning awareness of the irrevocability of death; now the downfall of the individual brings the entire construction of bourgeois existence down with it. What is destroyed is a nonentity, in itself and perhaps even for itself. Hence the constant panic in view of death, a panic not to be quelled any more except by repressing the thought of death. Death as such, or as a primal biological phenomenon, is not to be extracted from the convolutions of history; for that, the individual as the carrier of the experience of death is far too much of a historical category. The statement that death is always the same is as abstract as it is untrue. The manner of people's coming to terms with death varies all the way into their physical side, along with the concrete conditions of their dying.

In the camps death has a novel horror; since Auschwitz, fearing death means fearing worse than death. What death does to the socially condemned can be anticipated biologically on old people we love; not only their bodies but their egos, all the things that justified their definition as human, crumble without illness, without violence from outside. The remnant of confidence in their transcendent duration vanishes during their life on earth, so to speak: what should be the part of them that is not dying? The comfort of faith—that even in such disintegration, or in madness, the core of men continuous to exist—sounds foolish and cynical in its indifference to such experiences. It extends, into infinity, a pearl of pompous philistine wisdom: "One always remains what he is."

The man who turns his back on the negation of a possible fulfillment of his metaphysical need is sneering at that need.

Even so, it is impossible to think of death as the last thing pure and simple. Attempts to express death in language are futile, all the way into logic, for who should be the subject of which we predicate that it is dead, here and now? Lust—which wants eternity, according to a luminous word of Nietzsche's—is not the only one to balk at passing. If death were that absolute which philosophy tried in vain to conjure positively, everything is nothing; all that we think, too, is thought into the void; none of it is truly thinkable. For it is a feature of truth that it will last, along with its temporal core. Without any duration at all there would be no truth, and the last trace of it would be engulfed in death, the absolute.

The idea of absolute death is hardly less unthinkable than that of immortality. But for all its being unthinkable, the thought of death is not proof against the unreliability of any kind of metaphysical experience. The web of semblance in which men are caught extends to their imagined ways of tearing the veil. Kant's epistemological question, "How is metaphysics possible?" yields to a question from the philosophy of history: "Is it still possible to have a metaphysical experience?" That experience was never located so far beyond the temporal as the academic use of the word metaphysics suggests. It has been observed that mysticism—whose very name expresses the hope that institutionalization may save the immediacy of metaphysical experience from being lost altogether—establishes social traditions and comes from tradition, across the lines of demarcation drawn by religions that regard each other as heretical. Cabbala, the name of the body of Jewish mysticism, means tradition. In its farthest ventures, metaphysical immediacy did not deny how much of it is not immediate.

If it cites tradition, however, it must also admit its dependence upon the historic state of mind. Kant's metaphysical ideas were removed from the existential judgments of an experience that required material for its fulfillment, yet the place he assigned to them, despite the antinomies, was in consistence with pure reason. Today, those ideas would be as absurd as the ideas expressing their absence are said to be, in a deliberately defensive classification. But if I will not deny that the philosophy of history has overthrown the metaphysical ideas, and yet I cannot bear that overthrow unless I am to deny my own consciousness as well—then a confusion that goes beyond mere semantics tends straightway to promote the fate of metaphysical ideas to a metaphysical rank of its own. The secret paralogism is that despair of the world, a despair that is true, based on facts, and neither esthetic *weltschmerz* nor a wrong, reprehensible consciousness, guarantees to us that the hopelessly missed things exist, though existence at large has become a universal guilt context.

Of all the disgrace deservedly reaped by theology, the worst is the positive religions' howl of rejoicing at the unbelievers' despair. They have gradually come to intone their *Te Deum* wherever God is denied, because at least his name is mentioned. As the means usurp the end in the ideology swallowed by all populations on earth, so, in the metaphysics that has risen nowadays, does the need usurp that which is lacking. The truth content of the deficiency becomes a matter of indifference; people assert it as being good for people. The advocates of metaphysics argue in unison with the pragmatism they hold in contempt, with the pragmatism that dissolves metaphysics *a priori*. Likewise, despair is the final ideology, historically and socially as conditioned as the course of cognition that has been gnawing at the metaphysical ideas and cannot be stopped by a *cui bono*.

4. Happiness and Idle Waiting

What is a metaphysical experience? If we disdain projecting it upon allegedly primal religious experiences, we are most likely to visualize it as Proust did, in the happiness, for instance, that is promised by village names like Applebachsville, Wind Gap, or Lords Valley. One thinks that going there would bring the fulfillment, as if there were such a thing. Being really there makes the promise recede like a rainbow. And yet one is not disappointed; the feeling now is one of being too close, rather, and not seeing it for that reason. And the difference between the landscapes and regions that determine the imagery of a childhood is presumably not great at all; what Proust saw in Illiers must have happened elsewhere to many children of the same social stratum. But what it takes to form this universal, this authentic part of Proust's presentation is to be entranced in one place without squinting at the universal.

To the child it is self-evident that what delights him in his favorite village is found only there, there alone and nowhere else. He is mistaken; but his mistake creates the model of experience, of a concept that will end up as the concept of the thing itself, not as a poor projection from things. The wedding where Proust's narrator as a child gets his first look at the Duchess de Guermantes may have occurred just that way, with the same power over his later life, at a different place and time. Only in the face of absolute, indissoluble individuation can we hope that this, exactly this has existed and is going to exist; fulfilling this hope alone would fulfill the concept of the concept. But the concept clings to the promised happiness, while the world that denies us our happiness is the world of the reigning universal, the world stubbornly opposed by Proust's reconstruction of experience.

Happiness, the only part of metaphysical experience that is more than impotent longing, gives us the inside of objects as something removed from the objects. Yet the man who enjoys this kind of experience naïvely, as though putting his hands on what the experience suggests, is acceding to the terms of the empirical world—terms he wants to transcend, though they alone give him the chance of transcending. The concept of metaphysical experience is antinomical, not only as taught by Kantian transcendental dialectics, but in other ways. A metaphysics proclaimed without recourse to subjective experience, without the immediate presence of the subject, is helpless before the autonomous subject's refusal to have imposed upon it what it cannot understand. And yet, whatever is directly evident to the subject suffers of fallibility and relativity.

The category of reification, which was inspired by the wishful image of unbroken subjective immediacy, no longer merits the key position accorded to it, overzealously, by an apologetic thinking happy to absorb materialist thinking. This acts back upon whatever goes under the concept of metaphysical experience. From the young Hegel on, philosophers have been attacking objective theological categories as reifications, and those categories are by no means mere residues which dialectics eliminate. They are complementary to the weakness of idealistic dialectics, of an identitarian thought that lays claim to what lies outside thought—although there is no possible definition of something contrasted with thought as its mere otherness. Deposited in the objectivity of the metaphysical categories was not congealed society alone, as the Existentialists would have it; that objectivity was also a deposit of the object's supremacy as a moment of dialectics. The total liquefaction of everything thinglike regressed to the subjectivism of the pure act. It hypostatized the indirect as direct. Pure immediacy and fetishism are equally untrue. In our insistence on immediacy against reification we are (as perceived in Hegel's institutionalism) relinquishing the element of otherness in dialectics—as arbitrary a procedure as the later Hegel's unfeasible practice to arrest dialectics in something solid beyond it. Yet the surplus over the subject, which a subjective metaphysical experience will not be talked out of, and the element of truth in reity—these two extremes touch in the idea of truth. For there could no more be truth without a subject freeing itself from delusions than there could be truth without that which is not the subject, that in which truth has its archetype.

Pure metaphysical experience grows unmistakably paler and more desultory in the course of the secularization process, and that softens the substantiality of the older type. Negatively, that type holds out in the demand "Can this be all?"—a demand most likely to be actualized as waiting in vain. Artists have registered it; in *Wozzek*, Alban Berg gave the highest rank to bars that express idle waiting as music alone can express it, and he cited the harmony of those bars in the crucial caesuras and at the close of *Lulu*. Yet no such innervation, none of what Bloch called "symbolic intentionality," is proof against adulteration by mere life. Idle waiting does not guarantee what we expect; it reflects the condition measured by its denial. The less of life remains, the greater the temptation for our consciousness to take the sparse and abrupt living remnants for the phenomenal absolute.

Even so, nothing could be experienced as truly alive if something that transcends life were not promised also; no straining of the concept leads beyond that. The transcendent is, and it is not. We despair of what is, and our despair spreads to the transcendental ideas that used to call a halt to despair. That the finite world of infinite agony might be encompassed by a divine cosmic plan must impress anyone not engaged in the world's business as the kind of madness that goes so well with positive normalcy. The theological conception of the paradox, that last, starved-out bastion, is past rescuing—a fact ratified by the course of the world in which the *skandalon* that caught Kierkegaard's eye is translated into outright blasphemy.

5. "Nihilism"

The metaphysical categories live on, secularized, in what the vulgar drive to higher things calls the question of the meaning of life. The word has a ring of *weltanschauung* which condemns the question. All but inevitably, it will fetch the answer that life makes whatever sense the questioner gives it. Not even a Marxism debased to an official creed will say much else, as witness the late Lukács. But the answer is false. The concept of sense involves an objectivity beyond all "making": a sense that is "made" is already fictitious. It duplicates the subject, however collective, and defrauds it of what it seemingly granted. Metaphysics deals with an objectivity without being free to dispense with subjective reflection. The subjects are embedded in themselves, in their "constitution": what metaphysics has to ponder is the extent to which they are nonetheless able to see beyond themselves.

Philosophems that relieve themselves of this task are disqualified as counsel. The activity of someone linked with that sphere was characterized decades ago: "He travels around giving lectures on meaning to employees." People who sigh with relief when life shows some similarity to life, for once—when it is not, as Karl Kraus put it, kept going only for production's and consumption's sake—will eagerly and directly take this for a sign of a transcendent presence. The depravation of speculative idealism into the question of meaning retroactively condemns that idealism which even at its peak proclaimed such a meaning, though in somewhat different words—which proclaimed the mind as the absolute that cannot get rid of its origin in the inadequate subject, and that satisfies its need in its own image.

This is a primal phenomenon of ideology. The very totality of the question exerts a spell that comes to naught before real adversity, all affirmative poses notwithstanding. When a desperate man who wants to kill himself asks one who tries to talk him out of it about the point of living, the helpless helper will be at a loss to name one. His every attempt can be refuted as the echo of a general consensus, the core of which appeared in the old adage that the Emperor needs soldiers. A life that had any point would not need to inquire about it; the question puts the point to flight. But the opposite, abstract nihilism, would be silenced by the counter-question: "And what are you living for?" To go after the whole, to calculate the net profit of life—this is death, which the so-called question of meaning seeks to evade even if the lack of another way out makes it enthuse about the meaning of death.

What might not have to be ashamed of the name of meaning lies in candor, not in self-seclusion. As a positive statement, the thesis that life is senseless would be as foolish as it is false to avow the contrary; the thesis is true only as a blow at the high-flown avowal. Nor is Schopenhauer's inclination to identify the essence of the world, the blind will, as absolutely negative from a humane viewpoint any longer fitting. The claim of total subsumption is far too analogous to the positive claim of Schopenhauer's despised contemporaries, the idealists. What flickers up here again is the nature religion, the fear of demons, which the enlightenment of Epicurus once opposed by depicting the wretched idea of disinterested divine spectators as something better. Compared with Schopenhauer's irrationalism, the monotheism he attacked in a spirit of enlightenment has some truth to it also.

Schopenhauer's metaphysics regresses to a phase before the awakening of genius amidst the mute world. He denies the motive of freedom, the motive men remember for the time being and even, perhaps, in the phase of total unfreedom. Schopenhauer gets to the bottom of the delusiveness of individuation, but his recipe for freedom in Book Four, to deny the will to live, is no less delusive—as if the ephemerally individualized could have the slightest power over its negative absolute, the will as a thing in itself; as if it could escape from the spell of that will without either deceiving itself or allowing the whole metaphysics of the will to get away through the gap. Total determinism is no less mythical than are the totalities of Hegel's logic.

Schopenhauer was an idealist *malgré lui-même*, a spokesman of the spell. The *totum* is the totem. Grayness could not fill us with despair if our minds did not harbor the concept of different colors, scattered traces of which are not absent from the negative whole. The traces always come from the past, and our hopes come from their counterpart, from that which was or is doomed; such an interpretation may very well fit the last line of Benjamin's text on *Elective Affinities*: "For the sake of the hopeless only are we given hope." And yet it is tempting to look for sense, not in life at large, but in the fulfilled moments—in the moments of present existence that make up for its refusal to tolerate anything outside it.

Incomparable power flows from Proust the metaphysician because he surrendered to this temptation with the unbridled urge to happiness of no other man, with no wish to hold back his ego. Yet in the course of his novel the incorruptible Proust confirmed that even this fullness, the instant saved by remembrance, is not it. For all his proximity to the realm of experience of Bergson, who built a theory on the conception of life as meaningful in its concretion, Proust was an heir to the French novel of disillusionment and as such a critic of

Bergsonianism. The talk of the fullness of life—a *lucus a non lucendo* even where it radiates—is rendered idle by its immeasurable discrepancy with death. Since death is irrevocable, it is ideological to assert that a meaning might rise in the light of fragmentary, albeit genuine, experience. This is why one of the central points of his work, the death of Bergotte, finds Proust helping, gropingly, to express hope for a resurrection—against all the philosophy of life, yet without seeking cover from the positive religions.

The idea of a fullness of life, including the one held out to mankind by the socialist conceptions, is therefore not the utopianism one mistakes it for. It is not, because that fullness is inseparable from the craving, from what the *fin de siècle* called "living life to the full," from a desire in which violence and subjugation are inherent. If there is no hope without quenching the desire, the desire in turn is harnessed to the infamous context of like for like—and that precisely is hopeless. There is no fullness without biceps-flexing. Negatively, due to the sense of nonentity, theology turns out to be right against the believers in this life on earth. That much of the Jeremiads about the emptiness of life is true. But that emptiness would not be curable from within, by men having a change of heart; it could only be cured by abolishing the principle of denial. With that, the cycle of fulfillment and appropriation would also vanish in the end—so very much intertwined are metaphysics and the arrangement of life.

Associated with the slogans of "emptiness" and "senselessness" is that of "nihilism." Jacobi first put the term to philosophical use, and Nietzsche adopted it, presumably from newspaper accounts of terrorist acts in Russia. With an irony to which our ears have been dulled in the meantime, he used the word to denounce the opposite of what it meant in the practice of political conspirators: to denounce Christianity as the institutionalized negation of the will to live.

Philosophers would not give up the word any more. In a direction contrary to Nietzsche's, they re-functioned it conformistically into the epitome of a condition that was accused, or was accusing itself, of being null and void. For thinking habits that consider nihilism bad in any case, this condition is waiting to be injected with meaning, no matter whether the critique of the meaning, the critique attributed to nihilism, is well-founded or unfounded. Though noncommittal, such talk of nihilism lends itself to demagoguery; but it knocks down a straw man it put up itself. "Everything is nothing" is a statement as empty as the word "being" with which Hegel's motion of the concept identified it—not to hold on to the identity of the two, but to replace it, advancing and then recurring again behind abstract nihility, with something definite which by its mere definition would be more than nothing.

That men might want nothingness, as Nietzsche suggests on occasion, would be ridiculous hubris for each definite individual will. It would be that even if organized society managed to make the earth uninhabitable or to blow it up. By "believing in nothingness" we can mean scarcely more than by nothingness itself; by virtue of its own meaning, the "something" which, legitimately or not, we mean by the word "believing" is not nothing. Faith in nothingness would be as insipid as would faith in Being. It would be the palliative of a mind proudly content to see through the whole swindle. The indignation at nihilism that has today been turned on again is hardly aimed at mysticism, which finds the negated something even in nothingness, in the *nihil privativum*, and which enters into the dialectics unleashed by the word nothingness itself. The more likely point, therefore, is simply moral defamation—by mobilizing a word generally loathed and incompatible with universal good cheer—of the man who refuses to accept the Western legacy of positivity and to subscribe to any meaning of things as they exist.

When some prate of "value nihilism," on the other hand, of there being nothing to hold on to, this cries for the "overcoming" that is at home in the same subaltern language sphere. What they caulk up there is the perspective whether a condition with nothing left to hold on to would not be the only condition worthy of men, the condition that would at last allow human thought to behave as autonomously as philosophy had always merely asked it to, only to prevent it in the same breath from so behaving. Acts of overcoming—even of nihilism, along with the Nietzschean type that was meant differently and yet supplied fascism with slogans—are always worse than what they overcome. The medieval *nihil privativum* in which the concept of nothingness was recognized as the negation of something rather than as autosemantical, is as superior to the diligent "overcomings" as the image of Nirvana, of nothingness as something.

People to whom despair is not a technical term may ask whether it would be better for nothing at all to be than something. Not even to this is there a general answer. For a man in a concentration camp it would be better not to have been born—if one who escaped in time is permitted to venture any judgment about this. And yet the lighting up of an eye, indeed the feeble tail-wagging of a dog one gave a tidbit it promptly forgets, would make the ideal of nothingness evaporate. A thinking man's true answer to the question whether he is a nihilist would probably be "Not enough"—out of callousness, perhaps, because of insufficient sympathy with anything that suffers. Nothingness is the acme of abstraction, and the abstract is the abominable.

Beckett has given us the only fitting reaction to the situation of the concentration camps—a situation he never calls by name, as if it were subject to an image ban. What is, he says, is like a concentration camp. At one time he speaks of a lifelong death penalty. The only dawning hope is that there will be nothing any more. This, too, he rejects. From the fissure of inconsistency that comes about in this fashion, the image world of nothingness as something emerges to stabilize his poetry. The legacy of action in it is a carrying-on which seems stoical but is full of inaudible cries that things should be different. Such nihilism implies the contrary of identification with nothingness. To Beckett, as to the Gnostics, the created world is radically evil, and its negation is the chance of another world that is not yet. As long as the world is as it is, all pictures of reconciliation, peace, and quiet resemble the picture of death. The slightest difference between nothingness and coming to rest would be the haven of hope, the no man's land between the border posts of being and nothingness. Rather than overcome that zone, consciousness would have to extricate from it what is not in the power of the alternative. The true nihilists are the ones who oppose nihilism with their more and more faded positivities, the ones who are thus conspiring with all extant malice, and eventually with the destructive principle itself. Thought honors itself by defending what is damned as nihilism

6. Kant's Resignation

The antinomical structure of the Kantian system expressed more than contradictions in which speculation on metaphysical objects necessarily entangles itself. It expressed something from the philosophy of history. The powerful effect which *Critique of Pure Reason* exerted far beyond its epistemological substance must be laid to the faithfulness with which it registered the state of the experience of consciousness. Historiographers of philosophy see the achievement of the work primarily in the succinct separation of valid cognition and metaphysics. In fact, it first appears as a theory of scientific judgments, nothing more. Epistemology and logic in the broader sense of the word are concerned with exploring the empirical world under laws. Kant, however, does intend more. Through the medium of epistemological reflection he answers the so-called metaphysical questions in a far from metaphysically neutral way: they really must not be asked, he tells us. In that sense, *Critique of Pure Reason* anticipates both the Hegelian doctrine that logic and metaphysics are the same and the positivistic doctrine in which the questions everything depends upon are dodged by abolishing them and decided by indirect negation.

German idealism extrapolated its metaphysics from epistemology's fundamental claim to be the carrier of the whole. If we think it through to the end, it is precisely by its denial of objectively valid cognition of the absolute that the critique of reason makes an absolute judgment. This is what idealism stressed. Still, its consistency bends the motif into its opposite and into untruth. The thesis imputed to Kant's objectively far more modest doctrines on the theory of science is a thesis he had reason to protest against, despite its inescapability. By means of conclusions stringently drawn from him, Kant was—against himself—expanded beyond the theory of science. By its consistency, idealism violated Kant's metaphysical reservation. A thought that is purely consistent will irresistibly turn into an absolute for itself.

Kant's confession that reason cannot but entangle itself in those antinomies which he proceeds to resolve by means of reason was antipositivistic;[1] and yet he did not spurn the positivistic comfort that a man might make himself at home in the narrow domain left to reason by the critique of the faculty of reason, that he might be content to have solid ground under his feet. Kant chimes in with the eminently bourgeois affirmation of one's own confinement. According to Hegel's critique of Kant, letting reason judge whether it had passed the bounds of possible experience, and whether it was free to do so, presupposes already that there is a position beyond the realms separated on the Kantian map, that there is a court of last resort, so to speak.[2] As a possibility of decision, and without accounting for it, the intellectual realm was confronted by Kant's topological zeal with the very transcendence on which he banned positive judgments.

German idealism came to vest this authority in the absolute subject "Mind," which was said to be producing the subject-object dichotomy and thus the limit of finite cognition. Once this metaphysical view of the mind has lost its potency, however, the delimiting intention ceases to restrict anything but the cognitive subject. The critical subject turns into a resigned one. No longer trusting the infinity of its animating essence, it goes against that essence to reinforce its own finiteness, to affix itself to the finite. That subject wants to be undisturbed all the way into metaphysical sublimation; the absolute becomes for it an idle concern. This is the repressive side of Criticism. Its idealist successors were as far ahead of their class as they were in rebellion against it.

Originally lurking in what Nietzsche still extolled as intellectual honesty is the self-hatred of the mind, the internalized Protestant rage at the harlot Reason. A rationality that eliminates imagination—still ranking high for the Enlightenment and for Saint-Simon, and drying up, complementarily, on its own— such a rationality is tainted with irrationalism. A change also occurs in the function of critique: it repeats the transformation of the bourgeoisie from a revolutionary class into a conservative one. An echo of this condition is the now world-wide and pervasive malice of a common sense proud of its own obtuseness. This malice argues, *e contrario*, for disregarding the boundary upon the cult of which all are by now agreed. It is a "positive" malice, marked by the same arbitrariness of subjective arrangement which the common sense incarnated in Babbitt attributes to speculative thought.

Kant's metaphor for the land of truth, the island in the ocean, objectively characterizes the Robinson Crusoe style of the ivory tower, just as the dynamics of productive forces was quick enough to destroy the idyll in which the petty bourgeoisie, rightly suspicious of dynamics, would have liked to linger. The homeliness of Kant's doctrine is in crass conflict with his pathos of the infinite. If practical reason has primacy over the theoretical one, the latter, itself a mode

192 · The Frankfurt School on Religion

of conduct, would have to approach the alleged capacity of its superior if the caesura between intellect and reason is not to void reason's very concept. Yet this is precisely the direction in which Kant is pushed by his idea of scientificality. He must not say so, and yet he cannot help saying so; the discrepancy, which in intellectual history is so easily put down as a relic of the older metaphysics, lies in the matter itself. Kant boasts of having surveyed the Isle of Cognition, but its own narrow self righteousness moves that isle into the area of untruth, which he projects on the cognition of the infinite. It is impossible to endow the cognition of finite things with a truth derived, in its turn, from the absolute—in Kantian terms, from reason—which cognition cannot reach. At every moment, the ocean of Kant's metaphor threatens to engulf the island.

7. Rescuing Urge and Block

That metaphysical philosophy, which historically coincides in essence with the great systems, has more glamour to it than the empiricist and positivist systems is not just a matter of esthetics, as the inane word "conceptual poetry" would have us believe. Nor is it psychological wish fulfillment. If the immanent quality of a type of thinking, the strength manifested in it, the resistance, the imagination, the unity of critique with its opposite—if all this is not an *index veri*, it is at least an indication. Even if it were a fact, it could not be the truth that Carnap and Mieses are truer than Kant and Hegel. The Kant of *Critique of Pure Reason* said in the doctrine of ideas that theory without metaphysics is not possible. The fact that it *is* possible implies that metaphysics has its justification, the justification advanced by the same Kant whose work effectively crushed metaphysics.

Kant's rescue of the intelligible sphere is not merely the Protestant apologetics known to all; it is also an attempted intervention in the dialectics of enlightenment, at the point where this dialectics terminates in the abolition of reason. That the ground of the Kantian rescuing urge lies far deeper than just in the pious wish to have, amidst nominalism and against it, some of the traditional ideas in hand—this is attested by the construction of immortality as a postulate of practical reason. The postulate condemns the intolerability of extant things and confirms the spirit of its recognition. That no reforms within the world sufficed to do justice to the dead, that none of them touched upon the wrong of death—this is what moves Kantian reason to hope against reason. The secret of his philosophy is the unthinkability of despair.

Constrained by the convergence of all thoughts in something absolute, he did not leave it at the absolute line between absoluteness and existence; but he was no less constrained to draw that line. He held on to the metaphysical ideas, and yet he forbade jumping from thoughts of the absolute which might one day be realized, like eternal peace, to the conclusion that therefore the absolute exists. His philosophy—as probably every other, by the way—circles about the ontological argument for God's existence; but his own position remained open, in a grandiose ambiguity. There is the motif of "*Muss ein ewiger Vater wohnen*— must live an eternal Father," which Beethoven's composition of Schiller's Kantian Hymn to Joy accentuated in true Kantian spirit, on the word "must." And there are the passages in which Kant—as close to Schopenhauer here as Schopenhauer later claimed—spurned the metaphysical ideas, particularly that of immortality, as imprisoned in our views of space and time and thus restricted on their part. He disdained the passage to affirmation.

Even according to Hegel's critique, the so-called "Kantian block," the theory of the bounds of possible positive cognition, derives from the form-content dualism. Human consciousness, says the anthropological argument, is condemned, as it were, to eternal detention in the forms it happens once to have been given. What affects those forms is said to lack all definition, to need the forms of consciousness to acquire definition. But the forms are not that ultimate which Kant described. By virtue of the reciprocity between them and their existing content, they too go through an evolution. Yet this cannot be reconciled with the conception of the indestructible block. Once the forms are elements of a dynamics—as would be truly in keeping with the view of the subject as original apperception—their positive appearance can no more be stipulated for all future cognition than any one of the contents without which they do not exist, and with which they change. The dichotomy of form and content would have to be absolute to allow Kant to say that it forbids any content to be derived only from the forms, not form the matter. If the material element lies in the forms themselves, the block is shown to have been made by the very subject it inhibits. The subject is both exalted and debased if the line is drawn inside it, in its transcendental logical organization. The naïve consciousness, to which Goethe too probably tended—that we do not know yet, but that some day, perhaps, the mystery will be solved after all—comes closer to metaphysical truth than does Kant's *ignoramus*. His anti-idealist doctrine of the absolute barrier and the idealist doctrine of absolute knowledge are far less inimical to one another than the adherents of both thought they were; the idealist doctrine, according to the train of thought of Hegel's *Phenomenology*, comes also to the net result that absolute knowledge is nothing but the train of thought of *Phenomenology* itself, and thus in no way a transcending.

Kant, who forbids straying into the intelligible world, equates the subjective side of Newtonian science with cognition, and its objective side with truth. The question how metaphysics is possible as a science must be taken precisely: whether metaphysics satisfies the criteria of a cognition that takes its bearings from the ideal of mathematics and so-called classical physics. Mindful of his assumption that metaphysics is a natural disposition, Kant poses the problem with reference to the "how" of generally valid and necessarily supposed cognition; but what he means is the "what" of that cognition, its possibility itself. He denies the possibility, measured by that scientific ideal.

Yet science, whose imposing results make him relieve it of further misgivings, is a product of bourgeois society. The rigidly dualistic basic structure of Kant's model for criticizing reason duplicates the structure of a production process where the merchandise drops out of the machines as his phenomena drop out of the cognitive mechanism, and where the material and its own definition are matters of indifference vis-à-vis the profit, much as appearance is a matter of indifference to Kant, who had it stenciled. The final product with its exchange value is like the Kantian objects, which are made subjectively and are accepted as objectivities. The permanent *reductio ad hominem* of all appearance prepares cognition for purposes of internal and external dominance. Its supreme expression is the principle of unity, a principle borrowed from production, which has been split into partial acts.

The moment of dominance in Kant's theory of reason is that it really concerns itself only with the domain in which scientific theses hold sway. Kant's confinement of his questioning to empirically organized natural science, his orientation of it by validity, and his subjectivist critique of knowledge are so entwined that none could be without the others. As long as the subjective inquiry is to be a testing of validities, cognitions which have no scientific sanction—in other words, which are not necessary and not universal—are second-rate; this is why all efforts to emancipate Kantian epistemology from the realm of natural science had to fail. We cannot supplement and make up within the identifying rudiment what that rudiment eliminates by nature; the most we can do is change the rudiment because we recognize its insufficiency. The fact, however, that the rudiment does so little justice to the living experience which cognition is—this fact indicates that the rudiment is false, that it is incapable of doing what it sets out to do, namely, to provide a basis for experience. For such a rigid and invariant basis contradicts that which experience tells us about itself, about the change that occurs constantly in the forms of experience, the more open it is, and the more it is actualized. To be incapable of this change is to be incapable of experience.

To Kant we can add no theorems of knowledge that were not developed by him, because their exclusion is central to his epistemology; the systematic claim of the doctrine of pure reason makes this exclusion unmistakable enough. The Kantian system is a system of stop signals. The subjectively directed constitutional analysis does not alter the world as it is given to a naïve bourgeois consciousness; rather, it takes pride in its "empirical realism." But it sees the height of the validity it claims as one with the level of abstraction. Obsessed with the apriority of its synthetic judgments, it tends to expurgate any part of cognition that does not bow to their rules. The social division of labor is respected without reflection, along with the flaw that has become strikingly clear in the two hundred years since: that the sciences organized by a division of labor have usurped an illegitimate monopoly on truth. Put in bourgeois and very Kantian terms, the paralogisms of Kant's epistemology are the bad checks that went to protest with the unfoldment of science into a mechanical activity. The authority of the Kantian concept of truth turned terroristic with the ban on thinking the absolute. Irresistibly, it drifts toward a ban on all thinking. What the Kantian block projects on truth is the self-maiming of reason, the mutilation reason inflicted upon itself as a rite of initiation into its own scientific character. Hence the scantiness of what happens in Kant as cognition, compared with the experience of the living, by which the idealistic systems wished to do right, even though in the wrong fashion.

Kant would hardly have denied that the idea of truth mocks the scientivistic ideal. But the discrepancy is by no means revealed only in view of the *mundus intelligibilis;* it shows in every cognition that is accomplished by a consciousness free of leading strings. In that sense the Kantian block is a phenomenon blaspheming against the spirit in which Hölderlin's late hymns philosophically outstripped philosophy. The idealists were well aware of this, but what was manifest to them came under the same spell which forced Kant to contaminate experience and science. Though many an idealistic stirring aimed at openness, the idealists would pursue it by extending the Kantian principle, and the contents grew even more unfree to them than to Kant. And this in turn invests the Kantian block with its moment of truth: it forestalled a mythology of the concept.

Socially there is good reason to suspect that block, the bar erected against the absolute, of being one with the necessity to labor, which in reality keeps mankind under the same spell that Kant transfigured into a philosophy. The imprisonment in immanence to which he honestly and brutally condemns the mind is the imprisonment in self-preservation, as it is imposed on men by a society that conserves nothing but the denials that would not be necessary any more. Once the natural-historic cares we share with beetles were broken through, a change would occur in the attitude which human consciousness takes toward truth. Its present attitude is dictated by the objectivity that keeps men in the state they are in. Even if Kant's doctrine of the block was part of a social delusion, it is still based as solidly as the factual rule of the delusion. The separation of the sensual and intellectual realms, the nerve of the argument in favor of the block, is a social product; by the *chorismos,* sensuality is designated as a victim of the intellect because, all arrangements to the contrary notwithstanding, the state of the world fails to content sensuality.

The social qualification of the sensual realm might well permit the split to disappear one day—whereas the idealists are ideologues, either glorifying the reconciliation of the unreconciled as accomplished or attributing it to the unreconciled totality. The idealistic efforts to explicate the mind as its own union with that which is not identical with it were as consistent as they were futile. Such self-reflection happens even to the thesis of the primacy of practical reason, a thesis which from Kant, via the idealists, leads straight to Marx. Moreover, the dialectics of practice called for the abolition of practice, of production for production's sake, of the universal cover for the wrong practice. This is the materialistic ground of the traits which in negative dialectics rebel against the official doctrinal concept of materialism. The elements of independence and irreducibility in the mind may well accord with the supremacy of the object. As soon as the mind calls its chains by name, the chains it gets into by chaining others, it grows independent here and now. It begins to anticipate, and what it anticipates is freedom, not entangled practice. The idealists made a heaven of the mind, but woe betide the man who had a mind.

8. Mundus Intelligibilis

Kant confronts the construction of his block with the positive construction of metaphysics in *Critique of Practical Reason*. He did not pass in silence over its moment of despair: "Even if a transcendental faculty of freedom may serve as a supplement, perhaps, to initiate changes in the world, this faculty would have to be solely outside the world, at least (although it always remains an audacious presumption to assume, outside the totality of all possible views, an object that cannot be given to any possible perception)."

The parenthesis about the "audacious presumption" shows how skeptical Kant is of his own *mundus intelligibilis*. This formulation from the footnote to the Antithesis of the Third Antinomy comes close to atheism. What is so zealously postulated later is here called theoretically presumptuous; Kant's desperate reluctance to imagine the postulate as an existential judgment is strenuously evaded. According to the passage, it would have to be possible to conceive as an object of possible visuality, at least, what must at the same time be conceived as removed from all visuality. Reason would have to capitulate to the contradiction, unless the *hubris* of prescribing its own bounds had first irrationalistically narrowed reason's domain without tying it to those bounds objectively, as reason. But if—as by the idealists and also by the Neo-Kantians—visuality too were included in infinite reason, transcendence would be virtually cashiered by the immanence of the mind.

What Kant alludes to with respect to freedom would apply to God and immortality as well, only more so. For these do not refer to any pure possibility of conduct; their own concepts make them postulates of things in being, no matter of what kind. These entities need a "matter," and in Kant's case they would depend entirely upon that visuality whose possibility he excludes from the transcendent ideas. The pathos of Kantian intelligibility complements the difficulty of ascertaining it in any way, and if it were only in the medium of the self-sufficient thought designated by the word "intelligible." The word must not refer to anything real.

But the motion of *Critique of Practical Reason* proceeds to a positive *mundus intelligibilis* that could not be envisioned in Kant's intention. What ought to be—emphatically distinguished from what is—can no sooner be established as a realm of its own and equipped with absolute authority than the procedure will, albeit involuntarily, make it assume the character of a second existence. A thought in which we do not think something is not a thought. The ideas, the substance of metaphysics, are not visual, but neither could they be "airy nothings" of thought, lest they be stripped of all objectivity. The intelligible would be devoured by the very subject which the intelligible sphere was to transcend. A century after Kant, such flattening of the intelligible into the imaginary came to be the cardinal sin of the neo-romanticists of the fin de siècle, and of the phenomenological philosophy tailor-made to their measure.

The concept of the intelligible is not one of a reality, nor is it a concept of something imaginary. It is aporetical, rather. Nothing on earth and nothing in the empty heavens is to be saved by defending it. The "yes, but" answer to the critical argument, the refusal to have anything wrested away—these are already forms of obstinate insistence on existence, forms of a clutching that cannot be reconciled with the idea of rescue in which the spasm of such prolonged self-preservation would be eased. Nothing can be saved unchanged, nothing that has not passed through the portal of its death. If rescue is the inmost impulse of any man's spirit, there is no hope but unreserved surrender: of that which is to be rescued as well as of the hopeful spirit. The posture of hope is to hold lightly what the subject will hold on to, what the subject expects to endure. The intelligible, in the spirit of Kantian delimitation no less than in that of the Hegelian method, would be to transcend the limits drawn by both of these, to think in negations alone. Paradoxically, the intelligible sphere which Kant envisioned would once again be "appearance": it would be what that which is hidden from the finite mind shows to that mind, what the mind is forced to think and, due to its own finiteness, to disfigure. The concept of the intelligible is the self-negation of the finite mind.

In the mind, mere entity becomes aware of its deficiency; the departure from an existence obdurate in itself is the source of what separates the mind from its nature-controlling principle. The point of this turn is that the mind should not become existent in its own eyes either, to avoid an endless repetition of the eversame. The side of the mind that is hostile to life would be sheer depravity if it did not climax in its self-reflection. The asceticism which the mind demands of others is wrong, but its own asceticism is good; in its self-negation, the mind transcends itself—a step not so alien to Kant's subsequent *Metaphysics of Morals* as might be expected. To be a mind at all, it must know that what it touches upon does not exhaust it, that the finiteness that is its like does not exhaust it. The mind thinks what would be beyond it.

Such metaphysical experience is the inspiration of Kantian philosophy, once that philosophy is drawn out of the armor of its method. The question whether metaphysics is still possible at all must reflect the negation of the finite which finiteness requires. Its enigma animates the word "intelligible." The conception of that word is not wholly unmotivated, thanks to that independent moment which the mind lost by being absolutized, and which—as not identical with entity—it obtains as soon as we insist upon nonidentity, as soon as all there is does not evaporate in things of the mind. The mind, for all its indirectness, shares in existence, the substitute for its alleged transcendental purity. Although its moment of transcendent objectivity cannot be split off and ontologized, that moment is the unobtrusive site of metaphysical possibility.

The concept of the intelligible realm would be the concept of something which is not, and yet it is not a pure nonbeing. Under the rules of the sphere whose negation is the intelligible sphere, the intelligible one would have to be rejected without resistance, as imaginary. Nowhere else is truth so fragile. It may deteriorate into the hypostasis of something thought up for no reason, something in which thought means to possess what it has lost; and then again the effort to comprehend it is easy to confuse with things that are. If in our thinking we mistake thoughts for realities—in the paralogism of the ontological argument for the existence of God, which Kant demolished—our thinking is void. But the fallacy is the direct elevation of negativity, the critique of what merely is, into positivity as if the insufficiency of what is might guarantee that what is will be rid of that insufficiency. Even *in extremis* a negated negative is not a positive.

Kant called transcendental dialectics a logic of semblance: the doctrine of the contradictions in which any treatment of transcendent things as positively knowable is bound to become entangled. His verdict is not made obsolete by Hegel's effort to vindicate the logic of semblance as a logic of truth. But reflection is not cut short by the verdict on semblance. Once made conscious, the semblance is no longer the same. What finite beings say about transcendence is the semblance of transcendence; but as Kant well knew, it is a necessary semblance. Hence the incomparable metaphysical relevance of the rescue of semblance, the object of esthetics.

9. Neutralization

In Anglo-Saxon countries Kant is often euphemistically called an agnostic. However little this leaves of the wealth of his philosophy, the awful oversimplification is not barefaced nonsense. The antinomical structure of the Kantian doctrine survives the resolution of the antinomies, and it can be crudely translated into a directive to thought: to refrain from idle questions. It is above the vulgar form of bourgeois skepticism, whose solidity is serious only about what one has safely in hand—though Kant was not utterly free of such states of mind either. His authority in Germany was surely strengthened far beyond the effect of his thoughts by the fact that in the Categorical Imperative, and indeed in the ideas of *Critique of Pure Reason*, that disdained sublimity was added with raised forefinger, as a bonus with which the bourgeoisie is as loath to dispense as with its Sunday, that parody of freedom from toil.

The element of noncommittal conciliatoriness in rigorism went rather well with the decorative tendency to neutralize all things of the mind. After the triumph of the revolution—or, where there was no revolution, after the imperceptible advance of general "bourgeoisation"—that tendency conquered the entire scenery of the mind, along with the theorems previously used as weapons of bourgeois emancipation. No longer needed for the interests of the victorious class, those theorems became uninteresting in a two-fold sense, as Spengler astutely noted in Rousseau's case. Society, for all its ideological praise of the spirit, subordinates the function of the spirit. The Kantian *non liquet* contributed to transforming the critique of feudalism's ally, religion, into that indifference which donned the mantle of humanity under the name of tolerance. The spirit, in the form of metaphysics no less than in the form of art, grows only more neutralized as the culture of which society prided itself loses its relation to any possible practice.

In Kant's metaphysical ideas that relation was still unmistakable. In those ideas bourgeois society sought to transcend its own limited principle, to void itself, as it were. Such a spirit becomes unacceptable, and culture turns into a compromise between its form of bourgeois utility and the side of it which in neo-German nomenclature is "undesirable" and projected into an unattainable distance. Material circumstances add their part. Capital, compelled to expand its investments, possesses itself of the spirit whose own inevitable objectifications spur it to transform them into property, into merchandise. Esthetics, by its disinterested approbation of the spirit, transfigures and debases it at the same time, satisfied to observe, to admire, and finally blindly and unrelatedly to revere all those things that were created and thought once upon a time, irrespective of their truth content. Objectively it is a mockery how the increasing merchandise character of culture estheticizes it for utility's sake. Philosophy becomes the manifestation of the spirit as a showpiece.

What Bernard Groethuysen traced back to the eighteenth and seventeenth centuries in religion—that the devil is no longer to be feared, and God, no longer to be hoped for—this expands beyond metaphysics, in which the memories of God and the devil live on even where it is a critical reflection on that fear and hope. What in a highly unideological sense ought to be the most urgent concern of men has vanished. Objectively it has become problematical; subjectively, the social network and the permanently overtaxing pressure to adjust leaves men neither the time nor the strength to think about it. The questions are not solved, and not even their insolubility is proven. They are forgotten, and any talk of them lulls them so much more deeply to their evil sleep. Goethe's fatal dictum that Eckermann need not read Kant because Kant's philosophy had done its job and entered into the universal consciousness—this line has triumphed in the socialization of metaphysical indifference.

The indifference of consciousness to metaphysical questions—questions that have by no means been laid to rest by satisfaction in this world—is hardly a matter of indifference to metaphysics itself, however. Hidden in it is a horror that would take men's breath away if they did not repress it. We might be tempted to speculate anthropologically whether the turn in evolutionary history that gave the human species its open consciousness and thus an awareness of death— whether this turn does not contradict a continuing animal constitution which prohibits men to bear that consciousness. The price to be paid for the possibility to go on living would be a restriction of consciousness, then, a means to shield it from what consciousness is, after all: the consciousness of death.

It is a hopeless perspective that biologically, so to speak, the obtuseness of all ideologues might be due to a necessity of self-preservation, and that the right arrangement of society would by no means have to make it disappear—although, of course, it is only in the right society that chances for the right life will arise. The present society still tells us lies about death not having to be feared, and it sabotages any reflection upon it. Schopenhauer, the pessimist, was struck by the fact how little men *in media vita* are apt to bother with death.[3] Like Heidegger a hundred years later, Schopenhauer read this indifference in human nature rather than in men as products of history. Both of them came to regard the lack of metaphysical sense as a metaphysical phenomenon. In any case, it is a measure of the depth reached by neutralization, an existential of the bourgeois consciousness.

This depth makes us doubt whether—as has been drilled into the mind by a romantic tradition that survived all romanticism—things were so very different in times allegedly steeped in metaphysics, in the times which the young Lukács called "replete with meaning." The tradition carries a paralogism with it. The truth of metaphysical views is not assured by their collective obligatoriness, by the power they exert over life in closed cultures. Rather, the possibility of metaphysical experience is akin to the possibility of freedom, and it takes an unfolded subject, one that has torn the bonds advertised as salutary, to be capable of freedom. The dull captive of socially authorized views on allegedly blessed times, on the other hand, is related to the positivistic believer in facts. The ego must have been historically strengthened if, beyond the immediacy of the reality principle, it is to conceive the idea of what is more than entity. An order that shuts itself up in its own meaning will shut itself away from the possibility above order.

Vis-à-vis theology, metaphysics is not just a historically later stage, as it is according to positivistic doctrine. It is not only theology secularized into a concept. It preserves theology in its critique, by uncovering the possibility of what theology may force upon men and thus desecrate. The cosmos of the spirit was exploded by the forces it had bound; it received its just deserts. The autonomous Beethoven is more metaphysical, and therefore more true, than Bach's *ordo*. Subjectively liberated experience and metaphysical experience converge in humanity. Even in an age when they fall silent, great works of art express hope more powerfully than the traditional theological texts, and any such expression is configurative with that of the human side—nowhere as unequivocally as in moments of Beethoven. Signs that not everything is futile come from sympathy with the human, from the self-reflection of the subjects' natural side; it is only in experiencing its own naturalness that genius soars above nature.

What remains venerable about Kant is that in his theory of the intelligible he registered the constellation of the human and the transcendent as no philosopher beside him. Before humanity opened its eyes, the objective pressure of the miseries of life made men exhaust themselves in their neighbor's shame, and the immanence of meaning in life is the cover of their imprisonment. Ever since there appeared something like organized society, a solidly built autarkic context, the urge to leave it has been weak. A child who has not been prepared already could not help noticing in his Protestant hymn book how poor and tenuous the part entitled "The Last Things" is in comparison with all the training exercises for what the faithful should believe and how they ought to behave. That magic and superstition might continue to flourish in religions has long been suspected, and the reverse of that suspicion is that the core, the hope for a Beyond, was hardly ever so important to the positive religions as their concept required. Metaphysical speculation unites with speculation in the philosophy of history; for the chance of the right consciousness even of those last things it will trust nothing but a future without life's miseries.

The curse of these miseries is that instead of spurring us beyond mere existence, they disguise existence and confirm it as a metaphysical authority. "All is vanity," the word with which immanence has been endowed by great theologians ever since Solomon, is too abstract to guide us beyond immanence. Where men are assured that their existence is a matter of indifference, they are not going to lodge any protest; as long as their attitude toward existence remains unchanged, the rest seems vain to them also. If one accuses entity of nonentity without differentiation, and without a perspective of possibility, he aids and abets the dull bustle. The bestiality which such total practice amounts to is worse than the original bestiality: it comes to be a principle unto itself. The Capuchin sermon of the vanity of immanence secretly liquidates transcendence as well, for transcendence feeds on nothing but the experiences we have in immanence. But neutralization, profoundly sworn to that immanence, has survived even the catastrophes which according to the clarion calls of the apologists were to have thrown men back upon their radical concerns.

For there has been no change in society's basic condition. The theology and metaphysics which necessity resurrected are condemned, despite some valiant Protestant resistance, to serve as ideological passports for conformism. No rebellion of mere consciousness will lead beyond that. In the minds of the subjects, too, a bourgeois society will choose total destruction, its objective potential, rather than rise to reflections that would threaten its basic stratum. The metaphysical interests of men would require that their material ones be fully looked after. While their material interests are shrouded from them, they live under Maya's veil. What is must be changeable if it is not to be all.

10. "Only a Parable"

Decades after Arnold Schönberg set Stefan George's "Rapture" to music, he wrote a commentary praising the poem as a prophetic anticipation of the feelings of astronauts. In this naïve reduction of one of his most important works to the level of science fiction he was involuntarily acting out the metaphysical need. The subject matter of that neo-romanticist poem, the face of a man setting foot on another planet, is beyond doubt a parable for something internal, for an ecstasy and exaltation recalling Maximinus. The ecstasy is not one in space, not even in the space of cosmic experience, although it must take its images from that experience. But precisely this shows the objective ground of the excessively earthly interpretation.

Taking literally what theology promises would be as barbarian as that interpretation. Historically accumulated respect alone prevents our consciousness from doing so, and like the symbolic language of that entire cycle, poetic exaltation has been pilfered from the theological realm. Religion à la lettre would be like science fiction; space travel would take us to the really promised heaven. Theologians have been unable to refrain from childishly pondering the consequences of rocket trips for their Christology, and the other way round, the infantile interest in space travel brings to light the infantilism that is latent in messages of salvation. Yet if these messages were cleansed of all subject matter, if their sublimation were complete, their disseminators would be acutely embarrassed if asked to say what the messages stand for. If every symbol symbolizes nothing but another symbol, another conceptuality, their core remains empty—and so does religion.

This is the antinomy of theological consciousness today. Getting along with it would be easiest for the anachronistic primitive Christianity of Tolstoy, a *successio Christi* here and now, with closed eyes and without reflection. Goethe's construction of Faust already has a touch of the antinomy. When Faust says *"Die Botschaft hör ich wohl, allein mir fehlt der Glaube*—I hear the message, yet I lack the faith," the depth of the emotions that hold him back from suicide is interpreted by him as a return of deceptively consoling childhood traditions. And yet he is saved into the Marian heaven. The dramatic poem leaves unsettled whether its gradual progress refutes the skepticism of the thinking adult, or whether its last word is another symbol (*"nur ein Gleichnis*—only a parable") and transcendence is secularized, in more or less Hegelian fashion, into a picture of the whole of fulfilled immanence.

Any man who would nail down transcendence can rightly be charged—as by Karl Kraus, for instance—with lack of imagination, anti-intellectualism, and thus a betrayal of transcendence. On the other hand, if the possibility, however feeble and distant, of redemption in existence is cut off altogether, the human spirit would become an illusion, and the finite, conditioned, merely existing subject would eventually be deified as carrier of the spirit. An answer to this paradox of the transcendent was Rimbaud's vision of a mankind freed from oppression as being the true deity. At a later date, the Old-Kantian Mynona undisguisedly mythologized the subject and made idealism manifest as *hubris.* With speculative consequences of this sort, science fiction and rocketry found it easy to come to an understanding. If indeed the earth alone among all heavenly bodies were inhabited by rational beings, the idiocy of such a metaphysical phenomenon would amount to a denunciation of metaphysics; in the end, men would really be gods—and what gods!—only under a spell that prevents them from knowing it, and without dominion over the cosmos. Luckily, the latter fact made such speculations null and void again.

All metaphysical speculations are fatally thrust into the apocryphal, however. The ideological untruth in the conception of transcendence is the separation of body and soul, a reflex of the division of labor. It leads to idolization of the *res cogitans* as the nature-controlling principle, and to the material denials that would founder on the concept of a transcendence beyond the context of guilt. But what hope clings to, as in Mignon's song, is the transfigured body.

Metaphysics will not hear of that. It will not demean itself to material things, and this is why it passes the line to an inferior faith in spirits. Between the hypostasis of a noncorporeal and yet individuated spirit—and what would theology have in hand without this?—and spiritualism, the mendacious assertion that purely spiritual beings exist, the only difference is the historical dignity clothing the concept of "spirit." The effect of this dignity is that power, social success, comes to be the criterion of metaphysical truth. The English language drops the German distinction between *Spiritismus*, the German word for spiritualism, and *Spiritualismus*—in German the doctrine of the spirit as the individual-substantial principle. The equivocation comes from the epistemological need which once upon a time moved the idealists to go beyond the analysis of individual consciousness and to construe a transcendental or absolute one. Individual consciousness is a piece of the spatial-temporal world, a piece without any prerogatives over that world and not conceivable by human faculties as detached from the corporeal world. Yet the idealistic construction, which proposes to eliminate the earthly remains, becomes void as soon as it wholly expunges that egoity which served as the model for the concept of "spirit." Hence the assumption of a nonsensory egoity—which as existence, contrary to its own definition, is nonetheless to manifest itself in space and time.

According to the present state of cosmology, heaven and hell as entities in space are simple archaicisms. This would relegate immortality to one of spirits, lending it a spectral and unreal character that mocks its own concept. Christian dogmatics, in which the souls were conceived as awakening simultaneously with the resurrection of the flesh, was metaphysically more consistent—more enlightened, if you will—than speculative metaphysics, just as hope means a physical resurrection and feels defrauded of the best part by its spiritualization. With that, however, the impositions of metaphysical speculation wax intolerably. Cognition weighs heavily in the scale of absolute mortality—something speculation cannot bear, something that makes it a matter of absolute indifference to itself. The idea of truth is supreme among the metaphysical ideas, and this is where it takes us. It is why one who believes in God cannot believe in God, why the possibility represented by the divine name is maintained, rather, by him who does not believe. Once upon a time the image ban extended to pronouncing the name; now the ban itself has in that form come to evoke suspicions of superstition. The ban has been exacerbated: the mere thought of hope is a transgression against it, an act of working against it.

Thus deeply embedded is the history of metaphysical truth—of the truth that vainly denies history, which is progressive demythologization. Yet demythologization devours itself, as the mythical gods liked to devour their children. Leaving behind nothing but what merely is, demythologization recoils into the mythus; for the mythus is nothing else than the closed system of immanence, of that which is. This contradiction is what metaphysics has now coalesced into. To a thinking that tries to remove the contradiction, untruth threatens here and there.

11. The Semblance of Otherness

In spite of and, so to speak, absorbing the Kantian critique, the ontological argument for the existence of God was resurrected in Hegelian dialectics. In vain, however. In Hegel's consistent resolution of nonidentity into pure identity, the concept comes to be the guarantor of the nonconceptual. Transcendence, captured by the immanence of the human spirit, is at the same time turned into the totality of the spirit and abolished altogether. Thereafter, the more transcendence crumbles under enlightenment, both in the world and in the human mind, the more arcane will it be, as though concentrating in an outermost point above all mediations. In this sense, the anti-historical theology of downright otherness has its historical index. The question of metaphysics is sharpened into the question whether this utter tenuousness, abstractness, indefiniteness is the last, already lost defensive position of metaphysics—or whether metaphysics survives only in the meanest and shabbiest, whether a state of consummate insignificance will let it restore reason to the autocratic reason that performs its office without resistance or reflection.

The thesis of positivism is that even a metaphysics that has escaped to profanity is void. Even the idea of truth, on whose account positivism was initiated, is sacrificed. Credit is due to Wittgenstein for having pointed this out, however well his commandment of silence may otherwise go with a dogmatic, falsely resurrected metaphysics that can no longer be distinguished from the wordless rapture of believers in Being. What demythologization would not affect without making it apologetically available is not an argument—the sphere of arguments is antinomical pure and simple—but the experience that if thought is not decapitated it will flow into transcendence, down to the idea of a world that would not only abolish extant suffering but revoke the suffering that is irrevocably past.

To have all thoughts converge upon the concept of something that would differ from the unspeakable world that is—this is not the same as the infinitesimal principle whereby Leibniz and Kant meant to make the idea of transcendence commensurable with a science whose fallibility, the confusion of control of nature with being-in-itself, is needed to motivate the correcting experience of convergence. The world is worse than hell, and it is better. It is worse, because even nihility could not be that absolute as which it finally appears conciliatory in Schopenhauer's Nirvana. There is no way out of the closed context of immanence; it denies the world even the measure of sense accorded to it by the Hindu philosophem that views it as the dream of an evil demon. The mistake in Schopenhauer's thinking is that the law which keeps immanence under its own spell is directly said to be that essence which immanence blocks, the essence that would not be conceivable as other than transcendent. But the world is better than hell because the absolute conclusiveness which Schopenhauer attributes to the world's course is borrowed in turn from the idealistic system. It is a pure identity principle, and as deceptive as any identity principle.

As in Kafka's writings, the disturbed and damaged course of the world is incommensurable also with the sense of its sheer senselessness and blindness; we cannot stringently construe it according to their principle. It resists all attempts of a desperate consciousness to posit despair as an absolute. The world's course is not absolutely conclusive, nor is absolute despair; rather, despair is its conclusiveness. However void every trace of otherness in it, however much all happiness is marred by revocability: in the breaks that belie identity, entity is still pervaded by the ever-broken pledges of that otherness. All happiness is but a fragment of the entire happiness men are denied, and are denied by themselves.

Convergence, the humanly promised otherness of history, points unswervingly to what ontology illegitimately locates before history, or exempts from history. The concept is not real, as the ontological argument would have it, but there would be no conceiving it if we were not urged to conceive it by something in the matter. Karl Kraus, armored against every tangible, imaginatively unimaginative assertion of transcendence, preferred to read transcendence longingly rather than to strike it out; and he was not a romantically liberal metaphoricist. Metaphysics cannot rise again—the concept of resurrection belongs to creatures, not to something created, and in structures of the mind it is an indication of untruth—but it may originate only with the realization of what has been thought in its sign.

Art anticipates some of this. Nietzsche's work is brimful of anti-metaphysical invective, but no formula describes metaphysics as faithfully as Zarathustra's "Pure fool, pure poet." The thinking artist understood the unthought art. A thought that does not capitulate to the wretchedly ontical will founder upon its criteria; truth will turn into untruth, philosophy into folly. And yet philosophy cannot abdicate if stupidity is not to triumph in realized unreason. *Aux sots je préfère les fous.* Folly is truth in the form which men are struck with as amid untruth they will not let truth go. Art is semblance even at its highest peaks; but its semblance, the irresistible part of it, is given to it by what is not semblance. What art, notably the art decried as nihilistic, says in refraining from judgments is that everything is not just nothing. If it were, whatever is would be pale, colorless, indifferent. No light falls on men and things without reflecting transcendence. Indelible from the resistance to the fungible world of barter is the resistance of the eye that does not want the colors of the world to fade. Semblance is a promise of nonsemblance.

12. Self-Reflection of Dialectics

The question is whether metaphysics as a knowledge of the absolute is at all possible without the construction of an absolute knowledge—without that idealism which supplied the title for the last chapter of Hegel's *Phenomenology.* Is a man who deals with the absolute not necessarily claiming to be the thinking organ with the capacity to do so, and thus the absolute himself? And on the other hand, if dialectics turned into a metaphysics that is not simply like dialectics, would it not violate its own strict concept of negativity?

Dialectics, the epitome of negative knowledge, will have nothing beside it; even a negative dialectics drags along the commandment of exclusiveness from the positive one, from the system. Such reasoning would require a nondialectical consciousness to be negated as finite and fallible. In all its historical forms, dialectics prohibited stepping out of it. Willy-nilly, it played the part of a conceptual mediator between the unconditional spirit and the finite one; this is what intermittently kept making theology its enemy. Although dialectics allows us to think the absolute, the absolute as transmitted by dialectics remains in bondage to conditioned thinking. If Hegel's absolute was a secularization of the deity, it was still the deity's secularization; even as the totality of mind and spirit, that absolute remained chained to its finite human model.

But if our thought, fully aware of what it is doing, gropes beyond itself—if in otherness it recognizes something which is downright incommensurable with it, but which it thinks anyway—then the only shelter it will find lies in the dogmatic tradition. In such thoughts our thinking is estranged from its content, unreconciled, and newly condemned to two kinds of truth, and that in turn would be incompatible with the idea of truth. Metaphysics depends upon whether we can get out of this aporia otherwise than by stealth. To this end, dialectics is obliged to make a final move: being at once the impression and the critique of the universal delusive context, it must now turn even against itself. The critique of every self-absolutizing particular is a critique of the shadow which absoluteness casts upon the critique; it is a critique of the fact that critique itself, contrary to its own tendency, must remain within the medium of the concept. It destroys the claim of identity by testing and honoring it; therefore, it can reach no farther than that claim. The claim is a magic circle that stamps critique with the appearance of absolute knowledge. It is up to the self-reflection of critique to extinguish that claim, to extinguish it in the very negation of negation that will not become a positing.

Dialectics is the self-consciousness of the objective context of delusion; it does not mean to have escaped from that context. Its objective goal is to break out of the context from within. The strength required from the break grows in dialectics from the context of immanence; what would apply to it once more is Hegel's dictum that in dialectics an opponent's strength is absorbed and turned against him, not just in the dialectical particular, but eventually in the whole. By means of logic, dialectics grasps the coercive character of logic, hoping that it may yield—for that coercion itself is the mythical delusion, the compulsory identity. But the absolute, as it hovers before metaphysics, would be the nonidentical that refuses to emerge until the compulsion of identity has dissolved. Without a thesis of identity, dialectics is not the whole; but neither will it be a cardinal sin to depart from it in a dialectical step.

It lies in the definition of negative dialectics that it will not come to rest in itself, as if it were total. This is its form of hope. Kant registered some of this in his doctrine of the transcendent thing-in-itself, beyond the mechanisms of identification. His successors, however stringently they criticized the doctrine, were reinforcing the spell, regressing like the post-revolutionary bourgeoisie as a whole: they hypostatized coercion itself as the absolute. Kant on his part, in defining the thing-in-itself as the intelligible being, had indeed conceived transcendence as nonidentical, but in equating it with the absolute subject he had bowed to the identity principle after all. The cognitive process that is supposed to bring us asymptotically close to the transcendent thing is pushing that thing ahead of it, so to speak, and removing it from our consciousness.

The identifications of the absolute transpose it upon man, the source of the identity principle. As they will admit now and then, and as enlightenment can strikingly point out to them every time, they are anthropomorphisms. This is why, at the approach of the mind, the absolute flees from the mind: its approach is a mirage. Probably, however, the successful elimination of any anthropomorphism, the elimination with which the delusive content seems removed, coincides in the end with that context, with absolute identity. Denying the mystery by identification, by ripping more and more scraps out of it, does not resolve it. Rather, as though in play, the mystery belies our control of nature by reminding us of the impotence of our power.

Enlightenment leaves practically nothing of the metaphysical content of truth—*presque rien*, to use a modern musical term. That which recedes keeps getting smaller and smaller, as Goethe describes it in the parable of New Melusine's box, designating an extremity. It grows more and more insignificant; this is why, in the critique of cognition as well as in the philosophy of history, metaphysics immigrates into micrology. Micrology is the place where metaphysics finds a haven from totality. No absolute can be expressed otherwise than in topics and categories of immanence, although neither in its conditionality nor as its totality is immanence to be deified.

According to its own concept, metaphysics cannot be a deductive context of judgments about things in being, and neither can it be conceived after the model of an absolute otherness terribly defying thought. It would be possible only as a legible constellation of things in being. From those it would get the material without which it would not be; it would not transfigure the existence of its elements, however, but would bring them into a configuration in which the elements unite to form a script. To that end, metaphysics must know how to wish. That the wish is a poor father to the thought has been one of the general theses of European enlightenment ever since Xenophanes, and the thesis applies undiminished to the attempts to restore ontology. But thinking, itself a mode of conduct, contains the need—the vital need, at the outset—in itself. The need is what we think from, even where we disdain wishful thinking. The motor of the need is the effort that involves thought as action. The object of critique is not the need in thinking, but the relationship between the two.

Yet the need in thinking is what makes us think. It asks to be negated by thinking; it must disappear in thought if it is to be really satisfied; and in this negation it survives. Represented in the inmost cell of thought is that which is unlike thought. The smallest intramundane traits would be of relevance to the absolute, for the micrological view cracks the shells of what, measured by the subsuming cover concept, is helplessly isolated and explodes its identity, the delusion that it is but a specimen. There is solidarity between such thinking and metaphysics at the time of its fall.

Notes

1. "A dialectical thesis of pure reason must therefore have this element to distinguish it from all sophistical tenets: that it does not concern an arbitrary question posed to a certain random purpose only, but a question that must necessarily be encountered in the course of each human reason; and secondly, that in its antithesis it does not bear with it a mere artificial delusion which, once perceived, will fade at once, but a natural and inevitable delusion—one that even when it has ceased to deceive us is still delusive, although not deceptive, and can thus be rendered harmless but never expunged." (Kant, *Kritik der reinen Vernunft*, Works III, p. 290f.)

2. "Usually . . . great store is set by the barriers to thought, to reason, and so forth, and those barriers are said to be impassable. Behind this contention lies unawareness that by its very definition as a barrier a thing is already passed. For a definite thing, a limit, is defined as a barrier—opposed to its otherness at large—only against that which it does not bar; the otherness of a barrier is its transcending." (Hegel, *Works* 4, p. 153.)

3. "Man alone bears the certainty of his death with him in abstract concepts; and yet—a fact that is very strange—this certainty can frighten him only at specific moments, when an occasion recalls it to his imagination. Reflection can do little against nature's powerful voice. The permanent condition holding sway in man, as in the unthinking animal, is an assurance sprung from the innermost feeling that he is nature, the world itself; due to this assurance, no man is notably troubled by the thought of certain and never distant death, but each one lives as if he had to live forever. Which goes so far that we might say: No one really has a living conviction of the certainty of his death, else no man's mood could differ so greatly from a condemned criminal's. We might say, rather, that everyone admits that certainty in abstracto and theoretically, but puts it aside like other theoretical truths that do not apply in practice, without the slightest acceptance of it into his living consciousness." (Schopenhauer, *Die Welt als Wille und Vorstellung I*, Works, ed. Frauenstädt, II, Leipzig 1888, p. 332 — *The World as Will and Idea*, trans. R. B. Haldane and J. Kemp, Humanities Press, New York 1964.)

VI
Max Horkheimer

11
Theism and Atheism

Max Horkheimer

Crimes committed in the name of God are a recurrent theme in the history of Christian Europe. The ancients practiced torture and murder in war, on slaves (who were supplied by the wars) and as a form of entertainment: the *circenses*. But in spiritual matters the emperors were relatively tolerant. If the Christians were singled out as scapegoats, it was because they did not yet at that time place the state above all else and still recognized something higher than the empire. But since Constantine in his unscrupulous way singled out Christianity from among the existing religions to fill in the cracks in his crumbling empire and elevated it to the state religion, Europe has stood under the sign of that doctrine and betrayed it again and again. If the words of the founder, his recorded will, his precepts had been put in practice instead of being interpreted by the scholars, neither the unified Christians of the middle ages nor the disunited Christians of the modern period would have had their splendid careers. Whatever teachings could have been taken over from the Old Testament, glory in battle was no part of it. Under the heathen emperors, the commandment to render unto Caesar what was Caesar's could bring Christians into conflict with the state and, when they rightly refused to observe it, to the cross. But the Christian emperors would have undertaken no wars of conquest, they would have named no tribunals to punish those who had offended against them. The victorious course of Christianity since Nicaea and especially since Augustine, which was not unlike the expansion of Buddhism since the reign of Asoka, sealed its pact with that worldly wisdom which it had originally professed to renounce. Its readiness for fanaticism, without which its ascendancy would have been unthinkable, testified to a

213

secret and indomitable hatred for that attitude of mind for which its founder had earlier been put to death.

Initially, when the Christians themselves were the persecuted, the divinity appeared to them as a guarantor of justice. There was to be no more suppression in the world beyond, and the last would be the first; it was for the sake of heaven and not because of hell, out of hope and not for fear that the martyrs and their disciples professed their faith. Suppression, even death under torture, was but a transition into eternal blessedness; apparently inescapable conditions were but a moment of false defeats or triumph. All were the likeness of the divinity, even the lowest, and especially the lowest. The man at the stake, on the gallows, on the cross was the symbol of Christianity. It was not the ruling order of the time which determined who were to be the first; the prison and the gas chamber were at least no further from the followers of the divine delinquent than headquarters. If the barbarian masters, the men of quick decision, the generals and their confidants were included in the divine love, it was because of their poor souls. The pact concerned first of all those who were poor in spirit, those whose lives were not primarily oriented toward riches, power, affairs of state, or even towards prestige. In the first centuries of the Christian era, when the self-confidence of the senate and the people was shaken by the aspirations of the tribes outside and the resulting growth of barbarism inside, the gospel of a goal beyond this world gave a new meaning to the lives of the masses, enslaved and unruly under their masters. If it was possible for the primitive Christians to follow the gospel without unconscious resistance, it was because they knew nothing except that heaven was open to them. But the closer their doctrine came to gaining absolute power, the more it had to conform to the requirements of self-preservation under existing conditions, to come to terms with the law of this world—though its main idea had been the relativity of this law—and to conclude the pact it has kept ever since. Darkness gained in importance. As evil became increasingly necessary for it to carry out its plans for this world, hell became increasingly important to it in its thinking of the world beyond.

Theology has always tried to reconcile the demands of the Gospels and of power. In view of the clear utterances of the founder, enormous ingenuity was required. Theology drew its strength from the fact that whatever is to be permanent on earth must conform to the laws of nature: the right of the stronger. Its indispensable task was to reconcile Christianity and power, to give a satisfactory self-awareness to both high and low with which they could do their work in a corrupt world. Like the founder, who paid the price for refusing to show any concern for his own life and was murdered for it, and like all who really followed him and shared his fate or at least were left to perish helplessly, his later followers would have perished like fools if they had not concluded a pact or at least found a *modus vivendi* with the blood-thirsty Merovingians and Carolingians, with the demagogues of the crusades and with the holy inquisition.

Civilization with its tall cathedrals, the madonnas of Raphael and even the poetry of Baudelaire owes its existence to the terror once perpetrated by such tyrants and their accomplices. There is blood sticking to all good things, as Nietzsche remarked whose sensitivity was unsurpassed even by a saint. If the great had taken the conflict of Christianity and Christendom as seriously as Kierkegaard did in the end, there would exist no monument of Christian culture. Without the artful patchwork of scholastic theology, neither the works of pro-Christian nor of anti-Christian philosophy would have come into being, nor the struggle for human rights, which found in John XXIII a late high-minded spokesman, nor the remote village with its old church, which was at first allowed to remain intact by the traffic, the sign of a more advanced civilization, in its barbaric and at the same time benevolent manner. Building on the foundation of enlightenment and renewal which had been laid by church fathers, Pelagians, and gnostics against the superstitions of a decaying antiquity, the Scholastics developed the view of the world on which the freemen of the middle ages organized their government and established their cities. The combination of acuteness and precision, knowledge and imagination to be found in the Summas rivals the interpretations of the Torah which have been admired and disparaged as products of the Talmudic spirit. Scholasticism signifies the great age of theology. But while its comprehensive system lent ideological support to a relatively static society, it could not in the end prevent the dissolution of Christian unity.

Scholasticism lived on its inheritance from classical philosophy. Eternal ideals, which are supposed to reveal themselves to the mind like numbers, formed according to it the intellectual structure of reality. Scholastic wisdom was accepted by all believers as an interpretation of revelation, as knowledge of the world, of the temporal and eternal, of past and future. The lord and the saints were enthroned on the highest plane. Above the earth dwelt the angels and the blessed. Then came spiritual and secular dignitaries, lords, freemen and serfs. The ladder of nature stretched into the darkness of non-living things, and at the bottom was the place of the damned. Men had a picture of the universe in which divine and natural knowledge, divine and natural laws were one. In spite of predestination and grace, a man's future in other regions was largely determined by his conduct on earth which had implications beyond the moment. Each man's life had a meaning, not just the lives of the prominent. The political divisions led to the disappearance of the belief in eternal concepts, in the harmony of natural and supernatural knowledge, and in the unity of theory and practice which the Scholastics had in common with the Marxists, though the former glorified the continuation of existing conditions and the latter their transformation. In the end the medieval order was set in motion not only by wars, but as a result of the widening of the world, through economic activity, the misery of the masses, inflation, the beginnings of modern science and the backwardness of the religious professions. The educated reacted with scepticism and humanism, and the threatened powers with a religious renewal. The reformers, who had been preceded by the nominalists, the followers of Cusa and by others, renounced the system as a way of rationalizing the union of Christianity and worldliness. The opposition was all too apparent. They acknowledged it and made it the central part of their teaching. The Protestant way of reconciling the commandments of Christ with those human activities that appealed to them was to declare any reconciliation to be impossible. Nothing could be said, either about the will of God or about the right order of things, which would set up a general connection between the two. Knowledge and science were concerned with transitory things in a transitory world. Luther hated Scholasticism, theories of eternal relations, systematic philosophy, "the whore Reason." The view that men could justify their private or collective lives in theological terms and determine whether they were in harmony with the divine seemed to him sheer pride and superstition. Even though he judged Christians to be high above other men, especially Jews and Turks, his final judgment about right action remained suspended. In the end nobody knew what good works were—the church as little as a secular board of censors. Luther's verdict against theological speculation, which anticipated Kant's limitation of metaphysical speculation, left reason free to roam this vale of tears—in empirical research, in commerce, and especially in secular government. The interest of the individual and the state became the criterion of action in this world. Whether the troops waded in the blood of peasants who had risen from hunger, or whether a man sacrificed himself out of political blindness to share his last bread with them, one action was as "Christian" as the other, provided each agent sincerely believed that he was following the Word. The Reformation introduced the era of civil liberty. Hate and treachery, the "scab of time," had its origin in the inscrutable counsels of God, and would remain till the end of pre-history, till "all enemies of the Word have become like dung in the street." The idealist philosophers in Germany, who outdid the classics of liberalism in England in their glorification of progress, came to regard the ruthless competition between individuals and nations as the unfolding of the absolute spirit. God's ways are peculiar. His Word stands: We must love our enemies. But whether this means burning the heretic and the witch, sending children to work before they can read, making bombs and blessing them, or whether it means the opposite, each believer has to decide for himself without even suspecting what the true will of God might be. A guiding light, though a deceptive one, is provided by the interest of the fatherland, of which there is little mention in the Gospels. In the last few centuries, an incomparably greater number of believers have staked their lives for their country than for the forbidden love of its enemies. The idealists from Fichte to Hegel have also taken an active part in this development. In Europe, faith in God has now become faith in one's own people. The motto, "Right or wrong, my country," together with the tolerance of other religions with similar views, takes us back into that ancient world from which the primitive Christians had turned away. Specific faith in God is growing dim.

Theology was able to adapt itself to the triumphs of the new science and technology in the last few centuries. In those European countries which had resisted the Reformation, especially in France and Italy, the intellectual and political struggles produced a form of life in which the consciousness of civil liberty was allowed to flourish while Christianity in its traditional form was able to retain a place in connection with it. There the social forces which had found expression in the Enlightenment were able to assert themselves in political reality, whereas in the German states they were confined to the subjective realm, to the benefit of romantic poetry, great music and idealist philosophy. Here the way to bliss led again through faith, through the idea. Similarly religion, whether Catholic or Protestant, survived the nineteenth century as an element of bourgeois life, even though it changed its role. Much of the credit for its survival belonged to the militant atheists. Even when the great atheists did not themselves suffer martyrdom for their beliefs like Bruno and Vanini, it was so obvious that the antithesis—their radical or not so radical departure—was inspired by the thesis—the spirit of the Gospels—that they were far more capable of deepening the interest in religion than of extinguishing it. Voltaire, the foremost among them, was still so generous as to let theism pass, and his work remained as foreign to the general consciousness as Goethe's, which resembled his. The popular figure of atheism, metaphysical materialism, was too barren to become a serious threat to Christianity as long as it lacked a dialectical and idealistic— or in reality, a utopian and messianic—theory of history. As long as government was not yet in control of everything, from the co-operation of political and economic forces in commerce and industry to the conduct of one's private life—the struggle with solitude which is called "spare time"—preaching the love of God and trust in His guidance continued to be the better way. The Absolute of the theologians was incomparably more effective in providing consolation, incentive and admonition than any concept which the philosophical materialists had to offer. True, their critique of theism sounded plausible enough. "It has always been in the womb of ignorance, fear and misery that men have formed their first conceptions of the divinity," writes Holbach in his *System of Nature*, the bible of eighteenth-century materialism. This shows that those teachings "were either doubtful or false and in any case deplorable. In fact, whatever part of the globe we look at, whether the icy regions of the North, the torrid ones of the South, or the most moderate zones, we find that people everywhere have trembled and, as a result of their fears and their misery, either created their own national gods or adored those brought to them from elsewhere. It is ignorance and fear which have created the gods; conceit, passion and deceit which have adorned and disfigured them; it is weakness which adores them, credulity which nourishes them, and tyranny which supports them in order to

218 • The Frankfurt School on Religion

profit from the delusions of men." So much for the materialist's account of the origin of religion. In place of the rejected divinity they offer Nature. "Nature," continues Holbach at a later place, "tells the pervert to blush at his vices, at his shameful inclinations, his misdeeds; she shows him that his most secret disorders will necessarily affect his happiness. . . . Nature tells the civilized man to love the country in which he was born, to serve it faithfully, to enter with it into a community of interests against all those who might try to harm it." In the name of Nature the enlightened Holbach calls for the defense of one's country not only against external enemies but against internal tyrants. But what does he mean by "Nature?" There is nothing outside her; she is one and all at once. Man shall discover her laws, admire her inexhaustible energy, use his discoveries for his own happiness, and resign himself to his ignorance of her last, her ultimate causes which are impenetrable. With his whole being man belongs to her. The abstract entity which, according to such materialists, forms the basis of right conduct is as indeterminate as the *Deus absconditus* of the Protestants, and the promise of happiness in this world is as problematical as bliss in the next, which is extremely uncertain. The naturalistic doctrine agrees with the theological doctrine it opposes in identifying what is most permanent and powerful with what is most exalted and worthy of love—as if this were a matter of course. In their fear of death men turn to the One, eternal and immortal—which is their own wishful thinking hypostatized—as if in obedience to a superior power. The ancient materialists were still inclined to stop with a plurality of atoms; the worshippers of Nature, like the pantheists, ontologists and theologians, will hear of nothing less than the One. But Nature does not say anything, as little as Being, which has been tried recently and which is supposed to deliver its oracles through the mouths of professors. The place of God is taken in each case by an impersonal concept. The Scholastics had already depersonalized the humanity and individuality of the murdered Jesus by multiplying them as it were into the Oneness of God. The *ipsum esse*, the true identity of the divinity, his humanity could hardly be distinguished any longer from the radiant Being of the neo-Platonists, because of the ceaseless interpretation of being and being-in-the-world—the unity of essence and existence—in which all differences disappeared. When they build a system, theists and atheists alike posit an entity at the top. The dogma of a Nature which can speak and command—or at least serve as a principle for deducing moral truths—was an inadequate attempt to go along with science without giving up the age-old longing for an eternal guideline. But nature could only teach self-preservation and the right of the stronger, not for example liberty and justice. The liberal bourgeois order was always forced to pursue non-rational interests. Traditional institutionalized religion was still in a far better position to arouse these interests than atheism of whatever kind. The French materialists of the eighteenth century and especially the socalled "free-thinkers" and the pale monists of the nineteenth century were only a passing threat to Christianity.

The upheavals which began with the present century—the era of world wars, of nations awakening all over the globe, of stupendous population growth—can only be compared with the decline of antiquity or the middle ages. Christianity and theism in general are far more seriously called in question than in the *Siècle des Lumières.* In the nineteenth century, individual advancement depended in relatively wide areas on general education, initiative, responsibility and foresight. In a changing economy, the decisive qualities are now versatility, ability to react precisely to stimuli, specialized skill, reliability. We are witnessing a rapid decline in the importance of highly differentiated and independently acquired attitudes, along with a decline in the role of those qualities and of the family which produced them. But qualities which lose their social utility become obstacles, the marks of the provincial, of backwardness. These changes in the psychological structure are part of a comprehensive process in which political and religious institutions are also involved. Democracy is being undermined, at least as Locke and Rousseau conceived it and as it was still functioning under the French Third Republic and even in imperial Germany: as a conflict between the different commercial, industrial and agrarian interests of independent groups. (The relationship between workers and employers formed as it were a surd which could not be expressed in parliament.) There has been a radical change in the character of the deputies, in their relationship to their party, in their ability to form their own independent judgments on the questions under debate. When faced with important matters of state, especially in foreign policy and even more so in case of conflict, the clumsy democratic apparatus calls for its own transformation into a fast and efficient instrument operated by strong men. Theology had to adapt not only to structural changes in the social mechanism and to the related transformation of the family and the individual; a powerful enemy, called "communism" by friend and foe alike, sprang up at the same time. This threat, which concerns not only religion but civilization as such, comes not so much from the theory of Marx and Engels which is itself among the greatest achievements of civilization. Dialectical materialism was, moreover, quickly transformed into a mere ideology, like the bourgeois Enlightenment after its victory in the French Revolution and like theistic religions wherever they come to power. Much more important is a social mechanism which is also operative in other countries where it is about to integrate religion completely with the state, and which ensures that the only serious interest transcending the horizon of individual self-preservation is collective power, the rule of one's own nation or supra-national block. National socialism was a case in point. It had no longer any need of Christianity and felt it as a threat in spite of mutual concessions. Anybody, whether theist or atheist, who did not belong without

reservations was an enemy of the national atheism. Even today the Third Reich—
the savage collective will to power—tends everywhere to suppress the thought
of another Reich and to achieve thereby what the *civitas terrena*—in spite of
the gruesome deeds it committed in the name of the *civitas Dei* throughout
history—was unable to accomplish earlier because of its backward technology:
a world without shelter.

The changes with which Catholics and Protestants alike are trying to meet
the threat in the developed countries are no less far-reaching than the most
fundamental changes in the history of theology. Rome these days (May 1963)
is both progressive and conservative. The new spirit seeks to improve the lot of
the workers, to give them a share of the wealth in free countries and to liberate
them from brutal suppression under backward dictatorships. Social movements
are judged without hatred even when they derive from an anti-religious doctrine.
Who could deny, we are asked in *Pacem in terris*, the papal encyclical, "that
something good and worthy of recognition is to be found in such movements,
as long as they conform to the law and order of reason and take into account
the just demands of the human person?" The inevitability of social change is
being acknowledged and affirmed. But tolerance of social progress is combined,
by internal necessity, with the endeavor to salvage as many middle-class virtues
as possible and to build them into the new order even at the risk of making
quick adaptation to existing conditions impossible. It is by remaining within
the tradition while giving it a new sense that the Church is trying to take an
active part in shaping society. Its efforts to keep up with the times appear modest
when compared with the conclusions that Protestant theologians have already
drawn. The latter have eliminated the possibility of any conflict not only with
science—which science in its positivistic form has been avoiding in any case—
but even with all moral principles, no matter what their content may be. Further,
the assertion that God really exists as a person or even as a trinity—not to
mention the other world—is true only in a mythical sense. According to a popular work, *Honest to God*, by John Robinson, an Anglican bishop, which is now
being debated in several countries, the whole conception of a God who "visited"
the earth in the person of His Son is as mythical as the prince in the fairy tale.
The "supernatural scheme" which includes for example the Christmas story
and corresponding legends can, we are told, survive and take its place as a myth
"quite legitimately." The only reason why it ought to survive is that it points to
the spiritual meaning of our lives. Robinson is only putting into simpler words
the thoughts of Paul Tillich and other philosophical theologians: The stories of
the Bible are symbolic. When the New Testament tells us that God was in Christ
and that the Word was God, this only means according to Robinson that God is
the ultimate "depth" of our being, the unconditioned within the conditioned.
The so-called "transcendent"—God, love, or whatever name we might give it—
is not "outside" but is to be found in, with and below the Thou of all finite

relationships as their ultimate depth, their ground, their meaning. But if we must talk of ultimate, then Schopenhauer was closer to the truth when he denounced it in each creature as the instinct for self-preservation, the will to be and to be well. However well-intentioned, the bishop's words turn out to be mere verbiage, unctuous words which to German ears are nothing but well-worn clichés. And even though theism is to be sacrificed for an anti-dogmatic attitude, the rejected view is being presupposed in a perfectly naive way. Truth—eternal truth outlasting human error—cannot as such be separated from theism. The only alternative is positivism, with which the latest theology is in accord irrespective of contradictions. On the positivist view, truth consists in calculations that work, thoughts are instruments, and consciousness becomes superfluous to the extent that purposive behavior, which was mediated by it, merges into the collective whole. Without God one will try in vain to preserve absolute meaning. No matter how independent a given form of expression may be within its own sphere as in art or religion, and no matter how distinct and how necessary in itself, with the belief in God it will have to surrender all claim to being objectively something higher than a practical convenience. Without reference to something divine, a good deed like the rescue of a man who is being persecuted unjustly loses all its glory, unless it happens to be in the interest of some collective whole inside the national boundaries or beyond them. While the latest Protestant theologians still permit the desperate to call themselves Christians, they subvert the dogma whose truth alone would give their words a meaning. The death of God is also the death of eternal truth.

Having retreated to their last position, Protestant theologians, unconscious of this philosophical dilemma, try to rescue the idea that the life of each individual has its own meaning. It is essential for life in this world to mean something more than this world. What more? Their answer is: Love. The reason why love remains to determine what cannot be determined is obviously the memory of the Christian heritage. But love as an abstraction—as it appears in recent writings—remains as obscure as the hidden God whom it is supposed to replace. If its consequences for thought and action are not to be left entirely to chance, it is essential that the various implications contained in this principle be made explicit. The meaning of the concept would become apparent if it were explicated in the form of a theory of reality—of those real situations in which it should be tested. One would then deduce from the concept of Christian love how the world appeared today within its horizons, in which direction it could work within society, and especially, to what extent it would have to be negated to be able to express itself—not to speak of finding the strength to assert itself. As the theory was being developed, it would in turn affect the principle behind it by defining it more fully and by modifying it. Even the will to eradicate all hunger and injustice is still an abstraction, though it is already more concrete than empty talk about values, eternal meaning and genuine being. The idea of a better world has not only been given shape in theological treatises, but often just as well in the so-called "nihilistic" works—the critique of political economy, the theory of Marx and Engels, psychoanalysis—works which have been black-listed, whether in the East or in the West, and provoked the wrath of the mighty as the inflammatory speeches of Christ did among his contemporaries. The opposition between theism and atheism has ceased to be actual. Atheism was once a sign of inner independence and incredible courage, and it continues to be one in authoritarian or semi-authoritarian countries where it is regarded as a symptom of the hated liberal spirit. But under totalitarian rule of whatever denomination, which is nowadays the universal threat, its place tends to be taken by honest theism. Atheism includes infinitely many different things. The term "theism" on the other hand is definite enough to allow one to brand as a hypocrite whoever hates in its name. When theism adopts eternal justice as a pre-text for temporal injustice, it is as bad as atheism insofar as it leaves no room for thoughts of anything else. Both of them have been responsible for good and evil throughout the history of Europe, and both of them have had their tyrants and their martyrs. There remains the hope that, in the period of world history which is now beginning, the period of docile masses governed by clocks, some men can still be found to offer resistance, like the victims of the past and, among them, the founder of Christianity.

Even though Catholics and Protestants are nowadays both on the defensive, theism is again becoming an actual force in the period of its decline. This follows from the very meaning of "atheism." Only those who used "atheism" as a term of abuse meant by it the exact opposite of religion. Those who professed them-selves to be atheists at a time when religion was still in power tended to identify themselves more deeply with the theistic commandment to love one's neighbor and indeed all created things than most adherents and fellow-travelers of the various denominations. Such selflessness, such a sublimation of self-love into love of others had its origin in Europe in the Judaeo-Christian idea that truth, love and justice were one, an idea which found expression in the teachings of the Messiah. The necessary connection between the theistic tradition and the overcoming of self-seeking becomes very much clearer to a reflective thinker of our time than it was to the critics of religion in by-gone days. Besides, what is called "theism" here has very little in common with the philosophical movement of the seventeenth and eighteenth centuries which went by that name. That movement was mostly an attempt to reconcile the concept of God with the new science of nature in a plausible manner. The longing for something other than this world, the standing-apart from existing conditions played only a sub-ordinate part in it and mostly no part at all. The meanings of the two concepts do not remain unaffected by history, and their changes are infinitely varied. At a time when both the national socialists and the nationalistic communists de-spised the Christian faith, a man like Robespierre, the disciple of Rousseau, but not a man like Voltaire, would also have become an atheist and declared nationalism as a religion. Nowadays atheism is in fact the attitude of those who follow whatever power happens to be dominant, no matter whether they pay lip-service to a religion or whether they can afford to disavow it openly. On the other hand, those who resist the prevailing wind are trying to hold on to what was once the spiritual basis of the civilization to which they still belong. This is hardly what the philosophical "theists" had in mind: the conception of a divine guarantor of the laws of nature. It is on the contrary the thought of something other than the world, something over which the fixed rules of nature, the perennial source of doom, have no dominion.

12

The Jews and Europe

Max Horkheimer
Translated by Mark Ritter

Whoever wants to explain anti-Semitism must speak of National Socialism. Without a conception of what has happened in Germany, speaking about anti-Semitism in Siam or Africa remains senseless. The new anti-Semitism is the emissary of the totalitarian order, which has developed from the liberal one. One must thus go back to consider the tendencies within capitalism. But it is as if the refugee intellectuals have been robbed not only of their citizenship, but also of their minds. Thinking, the only mode of behavior that would be appropriate for them, has fallen into discredit. The "Jewish-Hegelian jargon," which once carried all the way from London to the German Left and even then had to be translated into the ringing tones of the union functionaries, now seems completely eccentric. With a sigh of relief they throw away the troublesome weapon and turn to neohumanism, to Goethe's personality, to the true Germany and other cultural assets. International solidarity is said to have failed. Because the worldwide revolution did not come to pass, the theoretical conceptions in which it appeared as the salvation from barbarism are now considered worthless. At present, we have really reached the point where the harmony of capitalist society along with the opportunities to reform it have been exposed as the very illusions always denounced by the critique of the free market economy; now, as predicted, the contradictions of technical progress have created a permanent economic crisis, and the descendants of the free entrepreneurs can maintain their positions only by the abolition of bourgeois freedoms; now the literary opponents of totalitarian society praise the very conditions to which they owe their present

225

existence, and deny the theory which, when there was still time, revealed its secrets.

No one can demand that, in the very countries that have granted them asylum, the emigres put a mirror to the world that has created fascism. But whoever is not willing to talk about capitalism should also keep quiet about fascism. The English hosts today fare better than Frederick the Great did with the acid-tongued Voltaire. No matter if the hymn the intellectuals intone to liberalism often comes too late, because the countries turn totalitarian faster than the books can find publishers; the intellectuals have not abandoned hope that somewhere the reformation of Western capitalism will proceed more mildly than in Germany and that well-recommended foreigners will have a future after all. But the totalitarian order differs from its bourgeois predecessor only in that it has lost its inhibitions. Just as old people sometimes become as evil as they basically always were, at the end of the epoch class rule has taken the form of the "folk community" [*Volksgemeinschaft*]. The theory has destroyed the myth of the harmony of interests [between capital and labor]; it has presented the liberal economic process as the reproduction of power relations by means of free contracts, which are compelled by the inequality of the property. Mediation has now been abolished. Fascism is that truth of modern society which has been realized by the theory from the beginning. Fascism solidifies the extreme class differences which the law of surplus value ultimately produced.

No revision of economic theory is required to understand fascism. Equal and just exchange has driven itself to the point of absurdity, and the totalitarian order is this absurdity. The transition from liberalism has occurred logically enough, and less brutally than from the mercantile system into that of the nineteenth century. The same economic tendencies that create an ever higher productivity of labor through the mechanism of competition have suddenly turned into forces of social disorganization. The pride of liberalism, industry developed technically to the utmost, ruins its own principle because great parts of the population can no longer sell their labor. The reproduction of what exists by the labor market becomes inefficient. Previously the bourgeoisie was decentralized, a many-headed ruler; the expansion of the plant was the condition for every entrepreneur to increase his portion of the social surplus. He needed workers in order to prevail in the competition of the market. In the age of monopolies, the investment of more and more new capital no longer promises any great increase in profits. The mass of workers, from whom surplus value flows, diminishes in comparison to the apparatus which it serves. In recent times, industrial production has existed only as a condition for profit, for the expansion of the power of groups and individuals over human labor. Hunger itself provides no reason for the production of consumer goods. To produce for the insolvent demand, for the unemployed masses, would run counter to the laws of economy and religion that hold the order together; no bread without work.

Even the facade betrays the obsolescence of the market economy. The advertising signs in all countries are its monuments. Their expression is ridiculous. They speak to the passers-by as shallow adults do to children or animals, in a falsely familiar slang. The masses, like children, are deluded: they believe that as independent subjects they have the freedom to choose the goods for themselves. But the choice has already largely been dictated. For decades there have been entire spheres of consumption in which only the labels change. The panoply of different qualities in which consumers revel exists only on paper. If advertising was always characteristic of the *faux frais* of the bourgeois commodity economy, still, it formerly performed a positive function as a means of increasing demand. Today the buyer is still paid an ideological reverence which he is not even supposed to believe entirely. He already knows enough to interpret the advertising for the great brand-name products as national slogans that one is not allowed to contradict. The discipline to which advertising appeals comes into its own in the fascist countries. In the posters the people find out what they really are: soldiers. Advertising becomes correct. The strict governmental command which threatens from every wall during totalitarian elections corresponds more exactly to the modern organization of the economy than the monotonously colorful lighting effects in the shopping centers and amusement quarters of the world.

The economic programs of the good European statesmen are illusory. In the final phase of liberalism they want to compensate with government orders for the disintegrating market economy's inability to support the populace. Along with the economically powerful they seek to stimulate the economy so that it will provide everyone with a living, but they forget that the aversion to new investments is no whim. The industrialists have no desire to get their factories going via the indirect means of taxes they must pay to an all-too-impartial government simply to help the bankrupt farmers and other draft animals out of a jam. For their class such a procedure does not pay. No matter how much progovernmental economists may lecture the entrepreneurs that it is for their own benefit, the powerful have a better sense of their interests and have greater goals than a makeshift boomlet with strikes and whatever else belongs to the proletarian class struggle. The statesmen who, after all this, still wish to run liberalism humanely, misunderstand its character. They may represent education and be surrounded by experts, but their efforts are nonetheless absurd: they wish to subordinate to the general populace that class whose particular interests by nature run contrary to the general ones. A government that would make the objects of welfare into subjects of free contracts by garnering the taxes of employers, must fail in the end: otherwise it would involuntarily degenerate from the proxy of the employers into the executive agency of the unemployed, indeed, of the dependent classes in general. Nearly confiscatory taxes, such as the inheritance tax, which are forced not only by the layoffs in industry, but also by the insoluble agriculture crisis, already threaten to make the weak into the "exploiters" of the capitalists. Such a reversal of circumstances will not be permitted in the long run by the employers in any empire. In the parliaments and all of public life, the employers sabotage neoliberal welfare policies. Even if these would help the economy, the employers would remain unreconciled: economic cycles are no longer enough for them. The relations of production prevail against the humanitarian governments. The pioneers from the employers' associations create a new apparatus and their advocates take the social order into their hands; in place of fragmented command over particular factories, there arises the totalitarian rule of particular interests over the entire people. Individuals are subjected to a new discipline which threatens the foundations of the social order. The transformation of the downtrodden jobseeker from the nineteenth century into the solicitous member of a fascist organization recalls in its historical significance the transformation of the medieval master craftsman into the protestant burgher of the Reformation, or of the English village pauper into the modern industrial worker. Considering the fundamental nature of this change, the statesmen pursuing moderate progress appear reactionary.

The labor market is replaced by coerced labor. If over the past decades people went from exchange partners to beggars, objects of welfare, now they become direct objects of domination. In the prefascist stage the unemployed threatened the order. The transition to an economy which would unite the separated elements, which would give the people ownership of the idle machines and the useless grain, seemed unavoidable in Germany, and the world-wide danger of socialism seemed serious. With socialism's enemies stood everyone who had anything to say in the Republic. Governing was carried out by welfare payments, by former imperial civil servants, and by reactionary officers. The trade unions wished to transform themselves from organs of class struggle into state institutions which distribute governmental largesse, inculcate a loyal attitude in the recipients, and participate in social control. Such help, however, was suspect to the powerful. Once German capital had resumed imperialist policies, it dropped the labor bureaucrats, political and trade unions, who had helped it into power. Despite their most honest intentions, the bureaucrats could not measure up to the new conditions. The masses were not activated for the improvement of their own lives, not to eat, but to obey—such is the task of the fascist apparatus. Governing has acquired a new meaning there. Instead of practiced functionaries, imaginative organizers and overseers are needed; they must be well removed from the influence of ideologies of freedom and human dignity. In late capitalism, peoples metamorphose first into welfare recipients and then into followers [*Gefolgschaften*].

Long before the fascist revolution, the unemployed constituted an irresistible temptation for industrialists and agrarians, who wished to organize them for their purposes. As at the beginning of the epoch, uprooted masses are again available, but one cannot force them into manufacturing as one did then; the time of private enterprise is past. The fascist agitator unites his people for the battle against democratic governments. If during the transformation it becomes less and less attractive to invest capital in useful production, then the money is put into the organization of the masses one wishes to wrest away from the prefascist governments. Once that has been accomplished at home, then it is tried internationally. Even in foreign countries the fascist states appear as organizers of power against obstinate governments. Their emissaries prepare the ground for fascist conquests; they are the descendants of the Christian missionaries who preceded the merchants. Today it is not English but German imperialism which strives for expansion.

If fascism in fact follows from the capitalist principle, it is not adapted only to the poor, the "have-not" countries, in contrast to the rich ones. The fact that fascism was initially supported by bankrupt industries concerns its specific development, not its suitability as a universal principle. Already during the time of greatest profitability, heavy industry extorted its share of the class profit by means of its position of economic power. The average profit rate, which applied to it as well, always exceeded the surplus value produced in its own area. Krupp and Thyssen obeyed the principle of competition less than others. Thus, the bankruptcy that the balance eventually revealed showed nothing of the harmony between heavy industry and the needs of the status quo. The fact that the chemical industry was superior in the market to heavy industry in terms of profitability was not socially decisive. In late capitalism the task assigned is to remodel the populace into a combat-ready collective for civil and military purposes, so that it will function in the hands of the newly formed ruling class. Poor profitability thus merely stimulated certain parts of German industry before others to force the development.

The ruling class has changed. Its members are not identical with the owners of capitalist property. The fragmented majority of the shareholders have long since fallen under the leadership of the directors. With the progression of the enterprise from one among many competing economic units to the impregnable position of social power of the modern conglomerate, management gained absolute power. The scope and differentiation of the factories has created a bureaucracy, whose apex pursues its own goals with the capital of the shareholders and, if need be, against them. The same degree of organic conglomeration of capital that limits the economic incentive for further investment allows the directors to put the brakes on production in the course of political machinations, and even to halt it, without being affected much themselves. Directors' salaries at times free themselves from the balance sheets. The high industrial bureaucracy takes the place of the legal owners. It turns out that actual disposition, physical possession, and not nominal ownership are socially decisive.

Juridical form, which actually determined the happiness of individuals, has always been considered a product of ideology. The dispossessed groups in the bourgeoisie cling now to the hypostatized form of private property and denounce fascism as a new Bolshevism, while the latter theoretically hypostatizes a given form of socializing property and in practice cannot stop the monopolization of the production apparatus. It ultimately matters little whether the state takes care of its own by regulating private profits or the salaries of civil servants. The fascist ideology conceals the same relationship as the old harmonizing ideology: domination by a minority on the basis of actual possession of the tools of production. The aspiration for profit today ends in what it always was: striving for social power. The true self of the juridical owner of the means of production confronts him as the fascist commander of battalions of workers. Social dominance, which could not be maintained by economic means, because private property has outlived itself, is continued by directly political means. In the face of this situation, liberalism, even in its decadent form, represents the greatest good for the greatest number, since the amount of misfortune suffered by the majority in the capitalist mother countries is less than that concentrated today upon the persecuted minorities [in totalitarian countries].

Liberalism cannot be re-established. It leaves behind a demoralized proletariat betrayed by its leaders, in which the unemployed form a sort of amorphous class that fairly screams for organization from above, along with farmers, whose methods of production and forms of consciousness have lagged far behind technological development, and finally the generals of industry, the army, and the administration, who agree with each other and embrace the new order.

After the century-long interlude of liberalism, the upper class in the fascist countries has returned to its basic insights. In the twentieth century, the existence of individuals is once again being controlled in all its details. Whether totalitarian repression can persist after the unleashing of productive forces within industrial society cannot be deduced. The economic collapse was predictable, not the revolution. Theory and practice are not directly identical. After the war the question was posed in practical terms. The German workers possessed the qualifications to rearrange the world. They were defeated. How far fascism reaches its goal will depend on the struggles of the present epoch. The adaptation of individuals to fascism, however, also expresses a certain rationality. After their betrayal by their own bureaucracy since 1914, after the development of the parties into world-spanning machineries for the destruction of spontaneity, after the murder of revolutionaries, the neutrality of workers with respect to the totalitarian order is no sign of idiocy. Remembering the fourteen years [of the Weimar Republic] has more attraction for the intellectuals than for the proletariat. Fascism may have no less to offer them than the Weimar Republic, which brought up fascism.

Totalitarian society may survive economically in the long run. Collapses are not a short-term prospect. Crises were rational signs, the alienated critiques of the market economy, which, though blind, was oriented to needs. In the totalitarian economy, hunger in war and peacetime appears less as a disruption than as a patriotic duty. For fascism as a world system, no economic end is visible. Exploitation no longer reproduces itself aimlessly via the market, but rather in the conscious exercise of power. The categories of political economy—exchange of equivalents, concentration, centralization, falling rate of profit, and so on— still have a tangible validity, except that their consequence, the end of political economy, has been attained. In the fascist countries, economic concentration proceeds rapidly. It has entered, however, into the practice of methodical violence, which seeks to master social antagonisms directly. The economy no longer has any independent dynamism. It loses its power to the economically powerful. The failure of the free market reveals the inability of further progress in the forms of antagonistic society of any kind. Despite the war, fascism can survive, unless the peoples of the world understand that the knowledge and machines they possess must serve their own happiness, rather than the perpetuation of power and injustice. Fascism is retrograde not in comparison to the bankrupt principle of laissez-faire, but in terms of what could be attained.

Even if it had been possible to limit armaments and divide the world, by following the example of the conglomerates (one should recall the efforts at a British-German, and beyond that, a European coal cartel),[1] even then fascism would not have needed to fear for its survival. There are innumerable tasks to be done which would provide food and work and yet not allow individuals to become arrogant. Mandeville, who knew what was needed, already designated the distant goal of fascism at the beginning of capitalism: "We have work for a hundred thousand more paupers than we actually have, work for three or four hundred years to come. In order to make our land useful and well populated everywhere, many rivers would need to be made navigable and many canals built. Many regions would need to be drained and protected for the future against floods. Large expanses of dry soil would have to be made fertile, many square miles of land more accessible and thus more profitable. *Dei laboribus omni vendunt.* There are no difficulties in this area that work and perseverance cannot overcome. The highest mountains can be toppled into the valleys that stand ready to receive them, and bridges can be built in places where we would not dare think of it. . . . It is the state's business to correct social ills, and take on those things first which are most neglected by private persons. Antagonisms are best cured by antagonisms; and since in the case of national failure an example accomplishes more than an order, the government should decide on some great undertaking that would require an immense amount of work for a long period, and thus convince the world that it does nothing without anxious concern for the most distant posterity. This will have a solidifying effect on the wavering spirit and the flighty mind of the people; it will remind us we do not live only for ourselves and will ultimately make people less distrustful, and thus will instill in them greater patriotism and loyal affection for their home soil, which, more than anything else, is necessary for the higher development of a nation.[2]

The terror in which the ruling class now takes refuge has been recommended by authorities ever since Machiavelli. "The wild animal called the people necessarily requires iron leadership: you will be lost immediately if you allow it to become aware of its strength. . . . The ruled individual needs no other virtue than patience and subordination; mind, talents, sciences belong on the side of the government. The greatest misfortune results from the overthrow of these principles. The real authority of the government will cease to exist, if everyone feels called to share in it; the horror of anarchy comes from such extravagance. The only means to avoid these dangers is to tighten the chain as much as possible, to pass the strictest laws, to avoid the enlightenment of the people, above all to resist the fatal freedom of the press, which is the source of all the knowledge that emancipates the people, and finally to terrify them by means of severe and frequent punishments. . . . Do not delude yourself that I understand by 'people' the class one designates as the third estate; certainly not. I call 'people' the venal and corrupt class that, thrown upon our earth like the scum of Nature, is only able to exist in the sweat of its brow."[3] What the National Socialists know was already known a hundred years ago. "One should only assemble people in church or in arms; then they don't think, they only listen and obey."[4] The place of St. Peter's is taken by the Berlin Sport Palace [where Nazi rallies were staged].

Not merely the dark, pessimistic [*dunklen*] philosophers, who are considered inhumane by their ideological descendants, have declared the subordination of the people the precondition for stable conditions; they have only designated the circumstances more clearly than the idealists. The later Kant is not much more convinced of the lower classes' right to freedom than Sade and de Bonald. According to practical reason, the people must obey as if in prison, only with the difference that it also should have its own conscience as warden and overseer, alongside the agents of the regime in power. "The origin of the highest power is for practical purposes inscrutable for the people which is subject to it, i.e., the subject should not practically reason . . . about its origin; for if the subject who had pondered out the ultimate origin were to resist that now prevailing authority, then by the laws of the latter, i.e., with complete justification, he would be punished, destroyed, or (outlawed, *exlex*) expelled."[5] Kant embraces the theory "that whoever is in possession of the supreme ruling and legislating power over a people, must be obeyed, and so juridically-absolutely, that even to research the title to this acquisition in public, that is, to doubt it, in order to resist it in case of some failing, is itself punishable; that it is a categorical imperative: Obey authority that has power over you (in everything which does not contradict the inwardly moral)."[6] But the scholar of Kant knows: the inwardly moral can never protest against an onerous task ordered by the respective authority.

Fascist nationalization, the installation of a terroristic party apparatus alongside the administration, is the opposite of socialization. As usual, the whole functions in the interests of a set group. The command of outside labor by the bureaucracy is now formally the last resort; the command of competing firms is delegated, but the contrasts blur: the owners become bureaucrats and the bureaucrats owners. The concept of the state completely loses its contradiction to the concept of a dominant particularity, it is the apparatus of the ruling clique, a tool of private power, and this is more true the more it is idolized. In Italy as well as in Germany, large public enterprises are being reprivatized. In Italy, electric factories, the monopolies on telephones and life insurance, and other governmental and municipal operations, and in Germany the banks above all, have gone into private hands.[7] Of course, only the powerful profit from that. In the long run, the protection of the small businessman proves to be a pure propaganda hoax. The number of corporations which dominate the entire industry grows steadily smaller. Under the surface of the Führer-state a furious battle takes place among interested parties for the spoils. The German and other elites in Europe, which share the intention of keeping the populace in check, would long ago have started an internal and external war without this binding tie. Inside the totalitarian states, this tension is so great that Germany could dissolve overnight into a chaos of gangster battles. From the beginning, the tragic gestures as well as the incessant assurances of a multi-millennial permanence in National Socialist propaganda reflect the intimation of such a frailty. Only because the justified fear of the masses constantly brings them together do the subordinate leaders allow themselves to be integrated and if necessary massacred by the mightiest one. More than was ever the case under capitalism, anarchy is hidden behind the unity and harmony, atomistic private interest behind the planned economy. An equalization occurs which is no less coincidental to human needs than the previous price range of free markets. Despite all the directives, the forces which bring about the distribution of social energies to the various branches of production are as irrational as the mechanisms of the profit economy, which were formerly removed from human power. Freedom is no less a delusion for the leaders than for the businessman; as he depends on the market, they now depend on blind constellations of power. Arms build-ups are dictated to them by the interplay among the groups, by fear of one's own and foreign peoples, by dependence on certain parts of the world of business, just as the expansion of factories is dictated to entrepreneurs in industrial society by social antagonisms, not by the contest of people against nature, which is the only criterion for determining a rational society. The stability of fascism rests on an alliance against the revolution and on the elimination of the economic remedy. The atomistic principle, according to which the success of one person is tied to the misery of the other, has even been intensified today. In the fascist organizations, equality and brotherliness prevail only on the surface. The struggle to rise in the barbarian hierarchy makes one's comrades presumptive opponents. The fact that in a war economy more jobs are available than workers does not abolish the struggle of all against all. Wage differentials in the individual factories, for men and women, for blue-collar and white-collar workers, for various categories of proletarians are crasser than ever. With the abolition of unemployment the isolation of human beings has not been broken. Fear of unemployment is supplanted by fear of the state. Fear atomizes.

The common interest of the exploited is harder than ever to recognize today, when it is stronger than ever. Despite all the crises, at the height of liberalism, the proletariat remained tied to the process of commodity production, the unemployment of the individual passed. The proletarians' labor in industry formed the basis of solidarity, as it was still understood by social democracy. In the time immediately preceding fascism, a great part of the population became permanently unemployed and lost its backbone. The goons from the Technicians' Emergency League [*Technische Nothilfe*, an organization devoted to strike-breaking in the interest of "national security"] showed even the employed German workers their own weakness. In addition, the further the destruction of all spontaneity, conditioned by economic impotence, was driven by the old mass parties, the easier it was for the victims to be captured by the new one. In the new party, as in the old one, collectivism is the ideology of the atomized mass, which is completely the object of dominance. Like work under the dictates of the state, the belief in Führer and community propagated by the state appears to be an escape from a bleak existence. Everyone knows what he has to do and more or less what tomorrow will be like. One is no longer a beggar, and if there is war, one won't die alone. The "folk community" continues the ideology of 1914. National outbursts are the approved substitute for the revolution. Unconsciously, the workers realize the horror of their existence, which they are nevertheless unable to change. Salvation must come from above. Insincere as may be the belief in the insignificance of the individual, the survival of the "folk," or the leaders as personalities, it at least expresses an experience, in contrast to apathetic Christianity. The society is abandoned by the idolized leaders, but not quite as abandoned as it always was by the True God.

Fascism surpasses the conditions before its advent not just negatively, but positively as well. If the life forms of liberal capitalism had an inhibiting function, if idealistic culture had already become a laughing-stock, then their demolition by fascism must also set forces free. The individual is robbed of false securities; the fascist rescue of property, family, and religion scarcely leaves them intact. The masses become powerful instruments and the power of the totalitarian organization, suffused by another's will, is superior to the sluggishness of the Reichstag, which was led by the will of the people. The centralization of administration carried out by National Socialism in Germany meets an old bourgeois demand, which was fulfilled elsewhere in the seventeenth century. The democratic trait of the new Germany, the formal abolition of the classes, is rational for the bourgeois. Of course, Richelieu dealt with the feudal lords more energetically than Hitler with the so-called reactionaries. Large landholders still enjoy the well-camouflaged protection of the so-called settlement policy. The successes of fascist foreign policy correspond to its domestic striking power. They authenticate the promises of the regime. The most important reason for the indolence with which fascism is tolerated by the masses is the sober expectation that it might bully something out of the fragile states all around, something that would benefit even the little man. After the phase of conquests, which to be sure has only begun, National Socialism hopes to give as much as possible to the masses as long as there is no subversion of discipline or the will to sacrifice. In fascism, the number of accidents in factories rises at the same time as the turnover of champagne factories increases, but the certainty that there will continue to be jobs ultimately seems better than democracy. The people are not respected any less under Hitler than under Wilhelm. They will hardly permit a long war.

True, the productive forces are more strongly repressed in fascism than ever before. The invention of artificial materials offers no excuse for the mutilation of human talents, which leads to the annihilation of the humane. But this only continues a process that had already assumed a catastrophic dimension. In the latest phase, the fascist one, the countertendencies also grow stronger. The ideas of nationalism and race are overturned. At bottom, the Germans no longer believe in them. The conflict between liberalism and the totalitarian state no longer runs along national boundaries. Fascism conquers from abroad and from within at the same time. For the first time, the whole world has been pulled into the same political development. India and China are no longer mere peripheral areas, historical entities of a secondary order; now they manifest the same tensions as the advanced capitalist countries.

The lie of justice within modern society, the lie of the reward for achievement, the lie of success as a divine judgment, all the cultural lies that poisoned life, have either become transparent or been abolished. Bureaucracy decides on life and death. It does not shift the responsibility for the failure of individuals to God, as did the old capitalists, but rather to the necessity of the state. The inhuman people who now dispose over lives probably are no more unjust than the market, which was moved only by the will to profit, in selecting who will live and who will die. Fascism has rescued disposition over the means of production for that minority which emerged from the competition as the most determined. It is the up-to-date form. Even where fascism is not in power in Europe, strong social tendencies are at work, which wish to prepare the administrative, legal, and political apparatus for authoritarianism. For reasons of competition alone, the real liberal motive, the capitalists and their supporters are driven to that view. "If the British Government," the Whaley-Eaton Service writes, "is forced to choose between active inflation and totalitarian control of finance and industry, it will take the latter course."[8] Whether people will be content to stay with half-measures and compromises is still undecided.

That is how it is with the Jews. They shed many a tear for the past. That they fared better under liberalism does not guarantee the justice of the latter. Even the French Revolution, which helped the bourgeois economy to victory and gave the Jews equality, was more ambivalent than they dare imagine today. Not ideas but utility are decisive for the bourgeoisie: "It was only decided to bring about the revolutionary changes because people had thought it over. Such thinking was not the province of a few advanced minds; it was a very numerous elite, throughout France, which discussed the causes of the evils and the nature of the remedy."[9] Here, thinking over means calculating. So far as the Revolution overshot the economically desirable goals, things were set right later. People were less concerned with philosophy than with the administration's sluggishness, with provincial and governmental reforms. The bourgeois were always pragmatists; they always kept an eye on their property. For its sake the privileges fell. Even the more radical development, interrupted by the fall of the terrorists, did not point only in the direction of greater freedom. Even then, people were faced with choosing between various forms of dictatorship. Robespierre's and Saint Just's plans envisioned statist elements, a strengthening of the bureaucratic apparatus, similar to the authoritarian systems of the present. The order which set out as the progressive one in 1789 carried the germs of National Socialism from the beginning.

Despite all the fundamental differences between the Committee of Public Safety and the leaders of the Third Reich, which can be confronted with surprising parallels, the practice of both springs from the same political necessity: to preserve control of the means of production for those groups which already own them, so that the others are subject to their direction at work. Political freedom for everyone, equality for the Jews, and all the humane institutions were accepted as means to utilize wealth productively. The democratic institutions fostered the supply of cheap labor, the possibility of planning with assurance, and the spread of free trade. With the changing of circumstances the institutions lost the utilitarian character to which they owed their existence. Rationality which ran counter to the specific commercial conditions at any given stage was also considered eccentric or subversive by the Jewish entrepreneur. This kind of rationality now turns against him. A national morality was immanent to the reality in which the Jews lived their lives, according to which they are now found wanting, the morality of economic power. The same rationality of economic expediency, according to which the defeated competitors have always sunk into the proletariat and been cheated of their lives, has now pronounced judgment on the Jews. Once again a large elite, this time not only throughout France, is discussing "the cause of the evils and the nature of their remedy." The result is bad for the Jews. They are being run over. Others are the most capable today: the leaders of the new order in the economy and the state. The same economic necessity that irrationally created the army of the unemployed has now turned, in the form of carefully considered regulations, against entire minority groups.

The sphere of circulation, which was decisive for the fate of the Jews in a dual fashion, as the site of their livelihood and the foundation of bourgeois democracy, is losing its economic importance. The famous power of money is on the wane today. In liberalism it connected the power of capital to the fulfillment of useful functions. From the growth or loss of finance capital, which accrued to the entrepreneur as the result of every venture, he could see whether and to what extent that venture was useful to the existing society. The judgment of the market on the salability of goods attested to their effect on the progress of general economic life. With the increasing elimination of the market, the importance of money, as the material in which such evidence was given, also diminishes. Needs are not satisfied any more appropriately or justly than they were by the mechanical balancing of variously equipped capital interests. Only now, the verdict of the market on how everyone may live, the verdict over prosperity and misery, hunger and power, is made directly by the ruling economic groups themselves. The anonymity of the market has turned into planning, but instead of the free planning of united humanity, it is the crafty planning of the archenemies of humanity. Previously, the economic fate was not only anonymous, it also took aim at the sinners and the elect without regard to their human particularities; it did people the honor of ignoring them. To that extent it was humane in its inhumanity. In the Führer-state, those who are to live and those who are to die are deliberately designated. The Jews are stripped of power as agents of circulation, because the modern structure of the economy largely puts that whole sphere out of action. They are the first victims of the ruling group that has taken over the canceled function. The governmental manipulation of money, which already has robbery as its necessary function, turns into the brutal manipulation of money's representatives.

The Jews become aware of their despair, at least those who have been victimized. Whoever in England or France is still permitted to curse taxes with the Aryans does not like to see his coreligionists coming across the border; the fascists reckon in advance with that type of embarrassment. The newcomers often have a bad accent or uncouth manners in their new country. This is tolerated in the prominent persons. The others are like Eastern Jews or worse yet—political undesirables. They compromise the established Jews, who feel at home there and in turn get on the nerves of the resident Christians. As if the very concept "at home" in a horrible reality were not a sign of lies and scorn for every single member of Jewry, which has experienced it for millennia; as if the Jews who fancy themselves established anywhere did not know inwardly that the tidy housekeeping from which they now profit could turn against them tomorrow. The newcomers are discomforting in any case. The ideological practice in which people tend to demean the objects of social injustice all over again in their own minds, so as to give the injustice a veneer of rationality—this practice of the ruling classes that has been classical ever since Aristotle, and from which anti-Semitism also lives, is neither Jewish nor gentile; it belongs to every antagonistic society. Whoever fails in this economy may as a rule expect nothing more from those who worship it than the recognition of the economic verdict which has ruined him, anonymously or by name. Probably those affected are not so innocent after all. How should nouveau riche Jews and Aryans abroad, who have always acquiesced in the impoverishment of other social and national groups, in mass poverty in mother countries and colonies, and in the conditions in prisons and insane asylums, how should they come to their senses in the presence of German Jews?

The National Socialist plan to force what remains of the Jews down into the Lumpenproletariat testifies once again how well its authors know the environment. Once the Jews have become shabby, they will no longer even benefit from the fleeting sentiment of bourgeois class solidarity: the outrage that even rich people are no longer safe. Poor Jews are less pitiable. There have to be poor people; they can't change the world. Between the unfulfilled needs of the powerless and the unfulfillable needs of the powerful there exists a preordained harmony. The lower classes must not become too happy, or else they cease to be objects. The rage produced by misery, however, the deep, fervent, secret rage of those dependent in body and soul, becomes active where opportunity presents itself, that is, against the weak and dependent itself. The workers in Germany, schooled in revolutionary teachings, watched the pogroms with disgust; how the populace of other countries would behave is not precisely known. Wherever the emigrating Jews end up, the novelty soon subsides and daily routine takes over. Then the emigres find, despite all the well-wishes of enlightened souls, the callousness of competition and the vague, aimless hate of the crowd, nourished by the sight of them, for more than one reason.

To appeal today to the liberal mentality of the nineteenth century against fascism means appealing to what brought fascism to power. The phrase "make way for the achiever" can be claimed by the victor. He has withstood the national economic competition so well that he can abolish it. Laissez-faire, laissez-aller, he can ask, why shouldn't I do what I want? I am the employer and source of sustenance for no fewer people than any economic champion of the free market countries. I am also ahead in the chemical industry. Proletarians, colonial peoples, and malcontents complain. My God, haven't they always done that?

The hope of the Jews, which attaches itself to the Second World War, is miserable. However it comes out, a seamless militarization will lead the world further into authoritarian-collectivistic ways of life. The German war economy in the First World War was a precursor of modern multiyear plans; the compulsory conscription employed during that war is now a main part of the totalitarian technique. Mobilization brings little that is new, except perhaps the mass grave, to the work battalions assigned to the arms industry, to the construction of more and more new motor highways, subways, and community buildings. The incessant excavation of the earth in peacetime was already a type of trench war. Whether there is a war on remains unclear today, even to the combatants themselves. The concepts are no longer clearly distinguishable as in the nineteenth century. The resettlement of whole peoples into the bomb shelter is Hitler's triumph, even if he is defeated. Perhaps in the initial fright the Jews will not be noticed, but in the long run they must tremble, along with everyone else, at what is now coming over the Earth.

A large portion of the masses being led against the totalitarian order does not, at bottom, fear fascism. Preserving the status quo is no more sensible a goal for war than for peace. Perhaps after a long war the old economic conditions will be re-established in individual territories for a short time. Then the economic development will repeat itself—fascism did not arise by chance. Since the failure of the market economy, people have faced, once and for all, the choice between freedom and fascist dictatorship. As agents of circulation, the Jews have no future. They will not be able to live as human beings until human beings finally put an end to prehistory.

Anti-Semitism will come to a natural end in the totalitarian order when nothing humane remains, although a few Jews might. The hatred of Jews belongs to the ascendant phase of fascism. At most, anti-Semitism in Germany is a safety valve for the younger members of the SA. It serves to intimidate the populace by showing that the system will stop at nothing. The pogroms are aimed politically more at the spectators than the Jews. Will anyone react? There is nothing more to be gained. The great anti-Semitic propaganda is addressed to foreign countries. Prominent Aryans in business and other areas may express all the outrage they wish, especially if their countries are far from the action; their prospectively fascist masses do not take it very seriously. People can secretly appreciate the cruelty by which they are so outraged. In continents from whose produce all of humanity could live, every beggar fears that the Jewish emigre might deprive him of his living. Reserve armies of the unemployed and the petty bourgeoisie love Hitler all over the world for his anti-Semitism, and the core of the ruling class agrees with that love. By increasing cruelty to the level of absurdity, its horror is mollified. That the offended divine power leaves the evildoers unpunished proves once again that it does not exist at all. In the reproduction of inhumanity, people confirm to themselves that the old humanity and religion along with the entire liberal ideology no longer have any value. Pity is really the last sin.

Even an unnatural end is foreseeable: the leap into freedom. Liberalism contained the elements of a better society. The law still possessed a generality that also applied to the rulers. The state was not directly their instrument. Someone who spoke up independently has not necessarily lost. Of course, such protection existed only in a small part of the world, in those countries to which the others were handed over. Even this fragile justice was limited to a few geographical areas. Anyone who participates in a limited human order must not be surprised if he occasionally falls victim to the limitations himself. One of the greatest bourgeois philosophers stated approvingly: "That some evil or other be done to an innocent man who is not a subject, if it occurs for the common good and without violating any previous agreements, is no violation of the natural law. For all people who are not subjects are either enemies or have ceased through prior agreements to be such. Against enemies, however, who in the view of the state are dangerous to it, one may wage war according to the original natural law; in this case the sword reaches no judgment, nor does the victor distinguish between innocent and guilty with respect to the past, nor does he give any particular consideration to mercy, unless that happens in the interest of his people."[10] Someone who does not belong, who is not protected by treaties, who is not backed up by any power, a stranger, a mere human being, is completely abandoned.

Even in the upright language of the classical economist, the limitation of the bourgeois concept of the human being constantly shows through. "Our goodwill has no limits, it can embrace the endless universe. The administration of the universe, however, the care for the general happiness of all reasonable and intelligent beings, concerns God and not man. . . . The part allotted to man is smaller . . . the care for his own well-being, the happiness of his family, his friends and his country; having the higher in mind never excuses his neglecting his more modest part."[11] The concern for family, country, and nation was a reality in bourgeois society—regard for humanity an ideology. As long as a person is miserable by virtue of the mere organization of this society, however, the identification with it in the name of humanity contains an absurdity. Practical adaptation may be necessary for the individual, but the concealment of the antagonism between the concept of the human being and the capitalist reality deprives thinking of any truth. If the Jews, in an understandable homesickness, glorify the prehistory of the totalitarian state, monopoly capitalism and the Weimar Republic, then the fascists, who always had an open eye for the decrepitude of those conditions, will be vindicated. Even before 1933, today's refugees could be reproached for gentleness with respect to the flaws of bourgeois democracy, flirtation with the forces of reaction, so long as they were not too openly anti-Semitic, arranging themselves in the status quo. The German people, which spasmodically displays its faith in the Führer, has already seen through him better than those who call Hitler a madman and Bismarck a genius.

Nothing can be hoped for from the alliance between the great powers. There can be no relying on the collapse of the totalitarian economy. Fascism sets in place the results of the collapse of capitalism. It is utterly naive to encourage the German workers from abroad to revolution. Someone who can only play at politics should keep away from it. The confusion has become so general that the truth receives more practical dignity the less it eyes self-styled praxis. Theoretical insight is needed and its transmission to those who eventually will lead the way. The optimism of the political appeal arises today from dejection. The fact that the progressive forces have been defeated and fascism can last indefinitely takes away the intellectuals' ability to think. They believe everything that works must also be good, and thus they prove that fascism cannot function. But there are periods in which the status quo in its strength and competence has become evil. The Jews were once proud of abstract monotheism, their rejection of idolatry, their refusal to make something finite an absolute. Their distress today points them back. Disrespect for anything mortal that puffs itself up as a god is the religion of those who cannot resist devoting their life to the preparation of something better, even in the Europe of the Iron Heel.

Notes

1. *Frankfurter Zeitung*, February 2 and March 9, 1939.
2. "Eine Abhandlung über Barmherzigkeit, Armenpflege und Armenschule," in Otto Bobertag and Georg Müller, ed., *Mandevilles Bienenfabel* (Munich, 1914), pp. 283f. and 286f.
3. De Sade, *Histoire de Justine* (Holland, 1797), vol. IV, pp. 275–278.
4. De Bonald, "Pensées sur divers subjets et discours politiques," *Oeuvres* (Paris, 1817), p. 147.
5. Kant, *Die Metaphysik der Sitten*, part I; *Metaphysische Anfangsgründe der Rechttslehre*, part II, section 1 (Akademieausgabe), vol. VI, pp. 318f.
6. Kant, op. cit., p. 371.
7. For Italy, see Perroux, "Economic corporative et système capitaliste," *Revue d'économic politique*, Sept.—Oct. 1933; for Germany, *Frankfurter Zeitung*, July 21, 1936 and Feb. 26, 1937.
8. *Whaley-Eaton Foreign Service*, Letter 1046, May 2, 1939.
9. D. Mornet, *Les origines intellectuelles de la Révolution Française* (Paris, 1933), p. 3.
10. "The Second Part of Commonwealth," *The English Works of Thomas Hobbes* (John Bohn: London, 1839), vol. III, p. 305. See also *The Latin Works of Thomas Hobbes*, p. 228.
11. Adam Smith, *The Theory of Moral Sentiments* (Basel, 1793), pp. 79, 83.

13
Religion and Philosophy

Max Horkheimer
Translated by Eduardo Mendieta

To speak today of the relation between philosophy and religion without thinking of Paul Tillich is not possible. Like no one else, he has united both of them in his thought, and his death has left a deep void in intellectual life. When in 1929 he accepted the invitation to a chair of philosophy at the University of Frankfurt, he remained a Protestant theologian, and above all a Christian. In contrast to many of his faith, academic and lay, he took the commandment to love one's neighbor at every moment absolutely seriously. If he had not left Germany immediately after the beginning of the radical anti-Christianity movement, he would have been exterminated fairly soon. He had seen the ascendancy of Nazism, and he had opposed to it the ideal of a just society. He adhered to religious socialism. In the idea of the just society is superseded love for one's neighbor, the respect for the rights of each. A politics that, even if it were highly unreflexive, were it not to preserve in itself theology, would remain, no matter how adroit it would like to be, mere business. Tillich also had the presentiment that in Marx's work, in an unconscious way but logically inseparable from its content, theological postulates are decisive. In the contemporary period these are rapidly disempowered, not only in politics and science, in which already for a long time they serve as phrases, but also in those spheres, such as advanced art, in which they find expression today, although if only as openly negated. Instead of adapting, whether as ontology or positivism, to specialization, philosophy ought, against conformism, to give expression to the destruction of religion as well as to the consequences for Western civilization, as inevitable as this might be.

European thinking, its decisive concepts, is closely bound up with theology. As much as progressive theologians, with Tillich united in this with Judaism, would like to define the essence of the Highest, even if only to name it in a proper manner, the Highest and the One have a linguistic priority that loses its sense with religion. Why should God be one and not many, high and not deep, above and not under? Is singularity more important that plurality? How should we consider life in the world that is thoroughly dominated by science, the universe conceived as the creation of the Highest, the One, when above all, the nature of the Highest harkens back to the most primitive, from which it stems, if not as an inversion? Linguistically, the good remains associated with that which is above and is the first, and this corresponds with the prince that at that time, although he was the founder of Christian thinking, was highly nonconformist, and always sought the good for the lowest and last. Already in the Renaissance, with the beginning of the new science, the representation of heaven above loses its sense.

Like the concepts of creation, of above and below, the one and the many, the concepts of finitude and infinity, body and spirit are also immersed in crisis. It is certain that after death the body returns to the earth, from which in the last instance it comes. The emergence of the spirit, the soul, their eternity, appear however as antithesis to its fragility and subtlety. Small physical affections can transform it. The I cannot even resist wine or drugs. It lets itself be sundered and overwhelmed, losing itself. To think that after the collapse of the nervous system, the spiritual, constantly threatened in life, should remain in its individuality, when individuality, singular properly of the individual, always carried the trace of the ephemeral, makes mockery of all experience. Theology has given preference, as the best, to the infinite over the finite, eternal duration over what is transitory; the soul over the flesh, and such a hierarchy is not to be dissolved from language.

The progress of science, content-wise as well as formally, condemns thought to function, to instrument. The word is a sign for a fact, itself a fact in the infinity of facts, in which as much the sun, the moon and the Earth as the Milky Way, to which they belong, the one and everything, disappear never to be seen again. What transcends facts in the sense of an eternal sense becomes an unsustainable illusion, into a field of free speculation, an interpretation of the world proper to earlier stages of human development that have been superseded. The foul peace between science and faith understood as different disciplines, one oriented to the progress of life, economy, politics, and the defense of the nation, in one word, reality, and the other oriented to the soul, means the resignation of theology. The victor is generous. Our concepts, concedes the scientist, are methodologically speaking fruitful fictions, mechanisms for organization, signs for the predicting with exactitude events at the right moment and place. Science is a means for the domination of nature, for construction of automata and rockets, for the rationalization of society; absolute truth, whatever that may mean, is with pleasure abandoned for the exact investigation of priests and artists of whatever allegiance. To the extent that philosophy makes do with secondary logical labors, with the abstract history of philosophers and philosophemes, or busies itself with words such as being and entity, essence or presence, or with eternal values, the more it is reserved to an academic discipline.

Religion also succumbs to the division of labor. Its place as a not evidently necessary discipline in the actual functioning of contemporary knowledge, such as it is performed in the schools and universities, means a regress, as with the civilization for which religion was once significant for its conception of the world and life. To the extent that since the Renaissance, emergent science, the expansion of its mode of thinking entered increasingly into contradiction with theology, so much more that philosophy took over the task of supporting the Christian teaching, at least its postulates, through rational methods used by science. The concept of God as the creator, lawgiver and judge, and above all the most important maxims for the functioning of society, should be as rational truths brought into harmony with science. Independently from the dangerous idea of revelation, its postulates were considered through thinking's reflection on itself as eternal maxims. On this conviction converged philosophical systems of different orientation. The tendency to save European culture in the face of the growing knowledge of the world, led to the origin of humanism as well as to the emergence of modern philosophy. This was linked more closely than the other to the conviction that without God morality, the immortality of the soul, and society's life must decline. Although Descartes, Leibniz, and Kant, are indebted to rigorous science, their legitimation of supreme religious principles through the mediation of their identification with the concept of reason constitute a decisive moment in their thinking. Against them, David Hume, among the greatest of that period of the English bourgeoisie, remitted morality to rationally neutral human love, and reduce religion to a mere convention.

Luther had already anticipated the futility of the rationalist attempts. For this reason, he came to hate Erasmus and philosophy as such. "Reason, you are a prostitute, I will not follow you."[1] Since he had abandoned to the irrational principle with all its consequences, to grace, and deprecated to deduce concrete behavior from reason, he had no other social alternative but to deify the state and administration, the established authority. His teaching represented an attempt to save religion. Beyond science there is nothing, there is only error and superstition. Among the representations that cannot be grounded through experience and reason, Christian ones ought to be considered valid inasmuch as they are beliefs. Beyond what is right and false there is a third, God's word. Had High Scholastic thought not acknowledged any contradiction between theological and secular knowledge, and sought only to describe the highest truths of Christianity through supernatural light, few of these truths would remain.

This is the case after Luther's perspective, who with the Bible's own world perspective challenged the new scientific outlook, unmediated by philosophy. There is a relation among earth, heaven, hell, humans, soul, and God that the developing knowledge is not close; it is the realm of the Greek Gods or astrology and magic and nonetheless must be valid as holy text. This sums up news, theses and commandments, which are sanctioned through the tradition and institutions, which are separated from experience and evidence by a deepening abyss; for "religion will be repressed by the developing education of the understanding."[2] The part of the youth, which due to the transformed family life does not preserve religion as a moment of its own substance, but rather acknowledges a bifurcated tradition, remains fundamentally helpless.

The last great philosophical attempt to salvage the core of Christianity was Schopenhauer's work. He agreed with Tillich in some important thoughts. "If you take Christian dogma *sensu propio*, then Voltaire is right. Taken allegorically, on the other hand, it is a sacred myth, a vehicle for bringing to the people truths which would otherwise be altogether inaccessible to them."[3] He anticipated the symbolism that Tillich would develop in a differentiated way. Christianity is "thoroughly symbolic in nature."[4] What Schopenhauer calls the "weakest point for all religions," Tillich wanted to supersede, namely "the they cannot be openly but only surreptitiously allegorical."[5] Man, according to Tillich, receives revelation according to his own finite, delimited situation, "under the conditions of man's estranged character."[6] The parables are to be understood symbolically, taken literally they would be superstition, at least in the contemporary epoch. Schopenhauer's metaphysics, distantly separated from Tillich's unwavering confidence, offers an explicitly formulated theory of the relation between the beyond and the worldly, transience and eternity, the conditioned and the unconditional. In a determined way, no longer distanced from science, it gives expression to what Tillich, and before him, Kant, held for unsayable.

That the world, how humans know it, the products of their intellect apparatus, which is capable of perception and understanding, is a phenomenon that is mediated by transitory functions, Kant had already made clear. Technical results that would like to preserve in many other constellations the control of the nature of the earth leave undisturbed the relation of the finite to the absolute truth. Conceptual digressions into reality independent from the subject, as it is in itself, speculation about appearances not constituted through a human-mental realm of forms of experience, are a fraud. Human consciousness remains enclosed within the gestalt of the universe that is dependent on him, no matter how much he would like to reach the truth despite the fact this project is infinite. The world in itself, the other of the subjectively conditioned, is related to thought, knowledge corresponds only to relatives. Kant's disciple Schopenhauer dissociated himself from such agnosticism. While in Tillich, the unknown Other, "God above God," meant to approximate the Higher and

Highest, and is at the same time an opposition to horrible reality, becomes in Schopenhauer the absolute that denounces the eternally blind, insatiable will, which serves and belongs to the last end, what is manifest in the world. To him what can lead to the only substance does not mean in the same sense objectification as knowledge from appearances or speculation about another world. What deeply moves me is neither the realm of the perceptive nor the conceivable, the sagaciously disclosed or constructed; rather everyone can feel this inner movement in their conviction that their thoughts, plans, actions, their picture and conception of the world, which they may owe to their own meditation or however they may have been acquired, have risen from strivings of the will, which all expression of life thoroughly dominates as the identical. The individual, insofar as he reflects upon himself, experiences this, the psychic power, not unlike the libido in Freud's sense, as what belongs to him, a durable impulse, as one of its many inner essences. In truth, he is in different points, blindness and non-infirmities still the same: plurality is appearance, the affirmation of one man over another is foolishness. The "in itself" is One, struggle, oppression, domination, bloody world history is in an emphatic sense meaningless. The Kantian commandment, which wonders out of the world, will disclose the realization that unity is not reconstituted as truer than multiplicity, as is usual for theology, but instead that both are categorical instruments of understanding that make possible for the new interpretation of the world as a whole.

This summary recollection of Schopenhauer's ideas should clarify the indication that his philosophical salvation of the Christian faith is accomplished through these theorems, which are contrary to faith itself. This is disconcerting to the believers who worship the creator of the world, even a good one, even when the destiny of everything that is living, including humanity, contradicts openly this dogma, and only with an escape like that offered by the doctrine of an inscrutable divine design can it go against the absurd. It would be more rational, as is the case in Buddhism and Hinduism, to worship a "world overcomer and in a sense world destroyer," and preferable to place Christianity among these Asiatic religions.[7] Nothing would be better than what is. The justification of Christian morality is derived from this negation. If the realm of phenomena, reality that can be experienced, is not work of a positive power, expression of being in itself good and eternal, but instead of the will that affirms itself in everything that is finite, that is reflected, disfigures, and in multiplicity and is, with everything, profoundly identical, then every entity has reason to feel like any other entity, not with its specific motives, but with its very condition of being trapped in the illusion, responsible and moved by the same passion, in enjoyment and decline. The life and destiny of the founder of Christianity becomes thus an exemplar, no longer by reason of a commandment, but from the knowledge of the intimate essence of the world. With respect to itself, his founding of morality, the thesis of the "despicable character" of the world, as Schopenhauer says, his teaching could be considered "the genuine Christian philosophy."[8] Who acknowledges his work as truth does not affirm in any way the dogmas, but instead the spirit of the gospels.

The arguments of pessimist philosophy that point to Christianity, even if today they can only be taken on with extreme caution, are in any case more plausible than those of the rationalists, even including those of criticism that in their practical part are extremely close to them. The conviction that moral prescriptions form a part of reason is superseded. The doctrine according to which the categorical imperative is found in every being that thinks is an absolutization of the product of the tradition. Kant attempted to secure philosophically the dream of the great enlightenment. Voltaire's conviction that "dans le coeur Dieu se grave lui-méme"[9] has a long prehistory and reaches to the most significant literature of our times. The beautiful proclamation of morality as the will written in the heart by God—espoused by Tolstoy in his work *Resurrection*—that Kant, more scientifically, named practical reason, rests however on a precipitated induction. Even when in all acts the thinking being is completely confident that in their place each would act as him, reason acts neutrally towards the categorical imperative. Next to moral acts, reason also justifies actions whose maxim can hardly be universalized. The categorical imperative characterizes the civilized mentality, but not reason as such. It is no more evident that morality is to be derived from it than are divine precepts. Jealousy and ambition are as far and close to reason as are love and abnegation, and they are absolutely no less productive. Notwithstanding its geniality and veracity, the way out proposed by Kant is no more viable than is the theological. The grounding of love for our neighbor, departing from the idea that everything that exists is in the last instance one, contains more critical consciousness than recourse to the supreme essence. Schopenhauer's unconventional solution also easily includes fatalism and means in a certain sense resignation. No less than the Kantian and Voltairian thought, his thinking on the Reformation, so presented, shows how he virtually negates the free will, and with it responsibility, without laying specific values with reference to the freedom of action: "Je pense que vous croyez à la destinée; pour moi c'est mon dogme favori. Toutes les affaires de ce monde me paraissent des boules poussées les unes par les autres."[10]

The Christian civilization is, as has been said, inseparable from the Christian-Theological picture of the world, even when this was opposed at every moment. When moral impulses have been transmitted to the youth, even when these, free from confessional commitments, go together with conscious atheism, they become, as soon as reference to a transcendent is eliminated, a matter of taste and mood, the same as its opposite. Moral engagement, no less than erotic engagement, appears today as something left behind. For this reason, philosophical help appears more necessary than ever, as it becomes simultaneously more superfluous, since morality loses all social significance. The more regulated are the details of individual life by administration, and one's personal decision becomes reduced to the precise reaction to determined signs, the more personal work is rigidly dictated according to tasks and goals, not only by the overarching apparatus and by specialization that that same apparatus conditions, but also by the gigantic social and political constellations, the narrower the game field for the development of the individual becomes. Relations with others, already predetermined in the sense of utility by the gigantic apparatus, stays marginalized to the field of the useful, just like every other non-required activity, and thus remains relegated to the so called free time. Work and interest, once closely united in the bourgeoisie, have become separate parts. Religion appears today with a right to existence, for it keeps humans united through the church and the community, keeping them partially busy during the free time, thus working against solitude. To believe in its doctrines, even today, confers to many a comforting support without too great a risk. Not few of the services that the religious and their organizations offer society could be turned over to secular institutions, and the functions that still perform the strictly theological passes over frequently to a secondary plane. The fading of thinking on an Other that is distinct from empirical reality affects language itself. For science as well as with administration, more precise forms of communication are appropriate. Without nationalisms, the transition to more functional systems already appeared a long time ago as a fortunate transformation, and the more so inasmuch that the different situations of the individual, to which belong fully the thin walls of homes and the instruments of listening, is not in any way whatsoever appropriate for differentiated expression.

The historical process, which includes the demise of cultural spheres, does not dissolve domination. The feudal, absolutistic, bourgeois forms of society, in which many could still make use of religion, and which in the face of a gross injustice points to a threatening and promising beyond, translate however into structures that are no longer a system of two classes, and that cannot be thought rightly anymore as a transition to a realm of freedom. If the diagnosis by the founder of historical materialism, that the crisis would exacerbate itself, as it has proven itself so far, this theory in its totality is outstripped by reality. In the Eastern countries, Marxism functions under rejection of its theological as well as idealist elements as the seeming actual religion. This serves as an instrument of inward, as well as outward, manipulation. In contrast, for the workers in the Western countries, the residues of *The Communist Manifesto*, and the critique of political economy are no more than fading traditions, analogous to the fate of the confessions under bourgeois society. The relativization of what is extant, whether it is as the finite, as in Christianity, or as prehistory, as in Marxism, appears in the administered world as a romantic symptom. It would seem assured that, aside from that which has not befallen catastrophe, a transition in highly industrialized societies to a totally organized and automated society is being realized, in opposition to messianic time and its secularized form, the Marxist utopia. A system of reactions, proper to the state of technique, will become part of human nature. If the individual does not function with security, if he is not normal, but is no longer immoral; he needs medical treatment: a repair. Perfect socialization is mediated through total administration, and if it is necessary through a dictatorship, for a long time already appropriate. The inexhaustible yearning, the lack of an internal support, which is concomitant with the need for community, momentarily offers a chance for a demagogue to alter history. An unconditional end is no longer such, and real aims, that once accomplished immediately become means, are, despite so much rationality, in themselves so empty that a good part of the youth protests against every glorification of the quotidian through their identification with the Beatles, provocateurs and *happenings*. The service that philosophy may still offer to what is disappearing resides in expressing this loss and its consequences. The effort is a paradox since the traditional form of the pronouncement and the words themselves presuppose precisely that sense whose loss they themselves try to give expression to.

Notes

1. Citation in Hartman Grisar, *Luther*, III (Freiburg im Breisgau: Herder, 1911), 836.
2. Arthur Schopenhauer, *Aus Arthur Schopenhauers Handschriftlicher Nachlaß: Abhandlungen, Anmerkungen, Aphorismen und Fragmente*, edited by Julius von Frauenstädt (Leipzing: F. A. Brockhaus, 1864), 429.
3. Arthur Schopenhauer, *Parerga und Paraliponema: Kleine philosophische Schriften* vol. 2 (Zürich: Diogenes Verlag, 1977), ¶ 177, p. 401. [English translation, Arthur Schopenhauer, *Essays and Aphorisms*, trans. R. J. Hollingdale (New York: Penguin Books, 1970), p. 182.]
4. Ibid.
5. Ibid.
6. Paul Tillich, *The Future of Religions* (New York: Harper & Row, 1966), 81.
7. A. Schopenhauer, *Aus Arthur Schopenhauers Handschriftlicher*, 430.
8. Schopenhauer, *Parerga und Paraliponema*, ¶ 163.
9. See Voltaire, *Oeuvres complètes* X, (Paris: Garnier Frères, 1877-82), 130, and many other places.
10. Voltaire, *Oevres Complètes*, Vol. 45, 98.

14
Observations on the Liberalization of Religion

Max Horkheimer
Translated by Eduardo Mendieta

I would like to undertake the attempt to confront my idea of religion, which originated in a determined cultural and theoretical context, with the situation in which we all find ourselves today, but which is seldom comprehended in its full reach.[1]

If one had affirmed a hundred, or even fifty, years ago that the dominant religions in Europe could continue to exist without having to contain explicitly within themselves faith in God, this would have only evoked laughter or a head-shake. We have come so far today that occasionally even bishops put in question the traditional faith in an almighty God, and they nonetheless continue to be representatives of the official Church and to identify themselves as Christians. In view of these facts, the question is raised about the permanent substance of religion. According to an expansive modern conception, the divine expresses itself only in the community of humans, in their encounter and relations. The supposition of a God that exists independently of this human figure, who surpasses and grounds it, becomes problematic. Such a God no longer forms part, so it seems, of what we call religion.

Religion in a genuine sense, in the sense that has now become problematic within the community of believers, exists, as I see it, only at first, since the medieval scholastic that made religion into its vital realm and gave it an intellectual foundation, in such a way that the non-believers were considered not only sinners, but also fools, whose reason did not work in an orderly manner. In this conception, that remained in effect until the nineteenth century and remains so in some places, the idea of a world that is not grounded in an almighty creator to which existence is owed has no place. An almighty being and, notwithstanding all the suffering of the world, at the same time infinitely good, ought to be, according to this conception, the origin and end of the cosmos.

Religion, however, has not been able to translate its conviction of the existence of an infinitely good God into the praxis of history marked and dominated by it. Its representatives have not made credible the acceptance of an infinitely good God, and they have not acted in accordance with idea of divine creator and legislator, but instead have committed numerous atrocities and infamies that have put religion at the service of the worst human inclinations. The crusades and the witch burnings are only two sad examples of this. The indignation of the masses forced to live in inhuman conditions was redirected, precisely with the help of established religion, towards innocent victims and objects of aggression. From this praxis arose serious dangers for religion. Communism has also experimented with a similar fate. Communism, which rose up with the idea of bringing about the peaceful unification of all nations, and in the first place, of all the men within a nation, and of eliminating class society, established in the dominated nations, by the domination of classes that supersedes in rigor, that of the non-communist world. The aggression of oppressed men here is also turned towards threats and external enemies, to the nations where no similar domination of classes exist.

Religion, to return to our topic, suffered then, due to the praxis of its representatives and believers, a serious threat, to which was added in the modern period the spiritual threat raised by science. It was from this threat, that was felt with greater strength since the Renaissance, due to the discoveries by Galileo, Copernicus, Newton and Kepler that transformed the earth from the center of the cosmos into a small sphere in the midst of a universe of galaxies, that religion attempted to escape by delinking itself from the sphere of knowledge, which since the Scholastic period was linked to religion, thus becoming a third independent magnitude next to the secure results of science and the hypotheses still awaiting scientific confirmation. Especially Luther and the reformers emphasized strongly, for this reason, the autonomy of faith over against all forms of knowledge.

But this solution, also with which a danger was evaded, made another one appear on the scene. To the theoretical separation between world and faith there followed a separation between quotidian life and religious forms of life; thus emerging a rupture between the morality of this life and the business and relation among men with what is beyond. Man as a unity broke up into fragments and was at the mercy of different disciplines. This tendency to the fragmentation of human reality is carried over in modern reality into two spheres: for example, the different disciplines of medicine no longer project a global gaze over the totality of human existence. This specialization forms part of the decline of culture.

Another attempt to overcome the chasm between God and world was undertaken by pantheism, which identified God with the world, and which had in Giordano Bruno one of its most important representatives at the beginning of the modern period. This pantheism was a complete challenge to religions and human thinking, and continues to be so until today. For this raises the question of why the assumption of *one* God is logically superior to the existence of *many* gods. In order to explain the fact that for a given culture (for example, in the Greek) there is polytheism, and in another a basically monotheistic attitude, calls for sociology, which, as a branch of modern science, has the specific task of deducing the contents of representations of individuals and groups in a given social context from the conditions of life of those individuals and groups. Metaphysical and theological representations also reflect the conditions of existence of a society. In the sociomorphic picture of the world, man contemplates the higher world according to the standard of his relations to the world. To a society with a plurality of lords and slaves corresponds a polytheistic cosmovision, while to a society with a strong concentration and centralization of coercive command corresponds a monotheistic vision of the world. That unity will be preferred to multiplicity has realistic but no theoretical reasons.

Modern philosophy also wanted to bring about a reconciliation between science and faith inasmuch as many of its representatives attempted to satisfy the need felt by men of wanting to harmonize both spheres. The great thinkers of modernity tried to provide rational arguments for the foundation of faith. Indeed, when involved in this endeavor they frequently lapsed behind their normal critical level. Thus, Descartes, who stands at the beginning of modern philosophy, and who is truly one of the great ones in the history of human thinking, wanted to deduce the existence of God, against his own convictions that only the facts of experience can offer a secure knowledge, from the idea of a singular essence and to ground it with the reasoning that the singular effect can never be stronger than the cause. From this follows that God himself must be the originating cause of our idea of the supreme plenitude, of the essence of God. These arguments are not very persuasive; nor are other subsequent attempts that follow the same path. This judgment applies as well to Leibniz, with his optimistic view of the world and the future; as for Kant, who developed next to the great insight that all we recognize and know is only a manifestation, phenomena, also developed the naïve doctrine, not very different from the Cartesian one, of the categorical imperative. The categorical imperative has two versions. In its simple form it commands that humans should not be treated as mere means, but always as ends. In its second version it says that we ought to act in such a way that the maxim of our action can at every instant become a principle of universal legislation. The supposition of this categorical imperative

254 • The Frankfurt School on Religion

that is inherent to every human has not been precisely confirmed by the history of human behavior and, nonetheless, it led Kant to the postulates of freedom and the existence of God as a guarantee of this freedom. No matter how questionable these postulates and their foundations may be, one thing is certain: they respond to the social need, in that historical moment, of a scientific grounding of morality and religion.

Other thinkers gave, in their inclination to science, one more step and made matter absolute. This philosophical materialism has also been superseded today. Humans trust, openly or covertly, only science and dispense with a philosophical elevation or integration of its results. Religion has become a problem. Instead of the attempts to reconcile faith and knowledge through science, now what we call the "liberation" of religion has been imposed. Theology itself attempts to accommodate itself to the social needs and the conceptions of the time in order not to have to ask men to believe in things that today can only appear as comic and extraordinary. For this reason, the Jewish youth finds it unbearable to have to wear temple locks and caftan. Where these customs still exist they are practically symbolic for the antiquatedness of religion.

If, in view of these events, we dare to take a look at the future of religion, we are forced, following the immanent logic of history, to take note of the regression of the meaning of the individual as the main tendency. While religion attributes to the individual an immortal soul, social, and above all economic, development increasingly marches over the individual. The emphasis on the singularity of each individual turns into mere memory. And with the socially conditioned marginalization of the individual comes in hand that of religion and philosophy in higher education and universities. Philosophy does not cease to be an object of teaching and attention; in a world oriented to the immediate and the practical, philosophy will be valued only because of its utility and, consequently, devalued.

To illustrate this, I will recall an episode that I experienced in the United States a few years ago. I was speaking with the manager of a hotel in Nevada about my project of establishing a museum of all the games since the beginning of history. The man seemed at the beginning in favor of my project and wanted to carry it out immediately. During the length of the conversation, he asked me, however, about my profession. I responded: professor. That shocked him to speechlessness; for until that moment he had held me as an intelligent man. Then he asked me, as is almost always the case in the United States, "Professor of what?" and I answered: "Philosophy." Then everything was finished.

To conclude, I would like to say something about my own idea of "liberalization," we could also say here of the preservation of religion. The already mentioned Immanuel Kant has made us aware, beyond every doubt, that what we call reality, world, that which can be investigated by science, is a product of subjective and intellectual factors. The work of our brain, as Schopenhauer held expanding on the Kantian teaching, consists, from the beginning, in ordering the facts of consciousness, as Descartes would say, in such a way that they fit appropriately with our form of life. Our subjective organization is responsible that the world appears before us as an objective reality; the world is not a simple "in itself," but a function. But if this is the case, then knowledge of the relations between the appearances, the phenomena of this world, are not the last word about reality; it is not an absolute. The ultimate truth cannot be translated into human language because all of our concepts proceed from a subjective organization. But, given the ultimate truth, which has to find expression in religion, cannot be translated into language and to the human conceptual world, we can only speak of religion acknowledging that the reality known by us is not the ultimate reality. We are not capable of saying what is the absolute and where this stands. Dogmatic atheists also infringe upon this conviction when, as with Schopenhauer, they make nothing the ultimate reality that liberates humans from the suffering on this world. This metaphysics is as little sustainable as any other, for the concept of "nothing" is no less subjective than the concepts of "God" or "ethics." All our concepts are subjective. Nevertheless, or rather because of it, we can say that the surrounding world is not the ultimate reality. An authentic liberalization of religion ought to concentrate on this insight. Over against it, the questions about the change in beliefs and customs are much less important. What is essential is, as I see it, the new human conception of God. God as positive dogma acts as a disaggregating moment. Against it, the yearning that the reality of the world, with all of its horror, not be the ultimate unites and relates all humans that cannot or do not want to resign themselves to the injustices of this world. God thus becomes an object of yearning and veneration of humans and ceases to be object of knowledge and possession.

A faith so understood belongs necessarily to what we call human culture. We must strive to unite all humans that do not want to consider as definitive the horrors of the past; who find themselves in the same, conscious yearning that there exists an absolute that is opposed to the world that is mere appearance. Religious customs can continue to manifest, since it is comprehensible that the humans who share the same yearning, the same deep conviction that something is wrong with that exists, and this conviction is shared by religion with Marx, also have common customs to preserve alive this yearning. Such is, I think, the task of those who want to preserve what is good of the past inasmuch as it is possible. They are not opposed, in an abstract, general, way, to progress, but they defend themselves against the negation of the individual in a world perfectly administered. My modest contribution to the development of the liberalization of religion consists, essentially, in making reference to this yearning.

Note

1. This is the text of a lecture given on September 25th, 1970 in Salzburg in the conversations about humanism and "the future of religion" and was published in O. Schatz, ed., *Hat die Religion Zukunft?* (Graz-Wien-Köln, 1971), 113–19. The manuscript of this lecture was worked over by Norbert Leser and Alfred Schmidt without the cooperation of the author.

VII
Walter Benjamin

15
Capitalism as Religion

Walter Benjamin
Translated by Chad Kautzer

[Fragment 74][1]

One can behold in capitalism a religion, that is to say, capitalism essentially serves to satisfy the same worries, anguish, and disquiet formerly answered by so-called religion. The proof of capitalism's religious structure—as not only a religiously conditioned construction, as Weber thought, but as an essentially religious phenomenon—still today misleads one to a boundless, universal polemic. We cannot draw close the net in which we stand. A commanding view will, however, later become possible.

Three characteristics of the religious structure of capitalism are, however, recognizable at present. First, capitalism is a pure religious cult, perhaps the most extreme there ever was. Within it everything only has meaning in direct relation to the cult: it knows no special dogma, no theology. From this standpoint, utilitarianism gains its religious coloring. This concretization of the cult connects with a second characteristic of capitalism: the permanent duration of the cult. Capitalism is the celebration of the cult *sans rêve et sans merci*.[2] Here there is no "weekday," no day that would not be a holiday in the awful sense of exhibiting all sacred pomp—the extreme exertion of worship. Third, this is a cult that engenders blame. Capitalism is presumably the first case of a blaming, rather than a repenting cult. Herein stands this religious system in the fall of a tremendous movement. An enormous feeling of guilt not itself knowing how to repent, grasps at the cult, not in order to repent for this guilt, but to make it universal, to hammer it into consciousness and finally and above all to include God himself in this guilt, in order to finally interest him in repentance. This

259

[repentance] is thus not to be expected in the cult itself, nor in the reformation of this religion—which must hold on to something certain within it—nor yet in the denial of it. In the essence of this religious movement that is capitalism lies—bearing until the end, until the finally complete infusion of blame into God—the attainment of a world of despair still only hoped for. Therein lies the historical enormity of capitalism: religion is no longer the reform of being, but rather its obliteration. From this expansion of despair in the religious state of the world, healing is expected. God's transcendence has fallen, but he is not dead. He is drawn into the fate of man. This passage of "planetary man" [*Planeten Mensch*] through the house of despair is, in the absolute loneliness of his path, the ethos Nietzsche describes. This man is the *Übermensch*, the first who knowingly begins to realize the capitalist religion. The fourth characteristic [of the religious structure of capitalism] is that its God must become concealed and may only be spoken of in the zenith of his culpability. The cult becomes celebrated before an immature deity, [while] every image, every idea of it injures the secret of its maturity.

Freudean theory also belongs to the priestly rule of this cult. It is thoroughly capitalistic in thought. The repressed, the sinful imagination, is, at bottom, still an illuminating analogy to capital—to which the hell of the unconscious pays interest.

This type of capitalist, religious thinking magnificently reconciles itself in Nietzsche's philosophy. The thought of the *Übermensch* loses the apocalyptic "leap" not by changing its ways, atonement, purification, [or] penitence, but in the apparently continuous, but in the end, rupturing, discontinuous intensification. That is why intensification and evolution are incompatible in the sense of "non facit saltum."[3] The *Übermensch* is the one who without changing, arrived, who streaked through the heavens—historical man.

Nietzsche prejudged [preached] that [in] this breaking open of the heavens through increased humanization [Menschhaftigkeit], the religious (also for Nietzsche) blame is and remains. And similarly [with] Marx: the non-inverting [*nicht umkehrende*] capitalism becomes socialism with interest and compound interest, which [are the] functions of blame (note the demonic ambiguity of this concept).[4]

Capitalism is a purely cultic religion, without dogma. Capitalism itself developed parasitically on Christianity in the West–not in Calvinism alone, but also, as must be shown, in the remaining orthodox Christian movements—in such a way that, in the end, its history is essentially the history of its parasites, of capitalism. Compare the holy iconography [*Heiligenbildern*] of various religions on the one hand with the banknotes of various countries on the other: The spirit that speaks from the ornamentation of banknotes.

Capitalism and law [*Recht*]. Pagan character of law. Sorel *Réflexions sur la violence* p. 262.[5]

Overcoming of capitalism through journeying [Wanderung]. Unger *Politik und Metaphysic* S44[6]

Fuchs: *Struktur der kapitalistischen Gesellschaft* o.ä. [?][7]

Max Weber: *Ges. Aufsätze zur Religionssoziologie* 2 Bd 1919/20[8]

Ernst Troeltsch: *Die Soziallehren der chr. Kirchen und Gruppen* (*Ges. W.* I. 1912)[9]

See above all the Schönbergean bibliography under II.

Landauer: *Aufuf zum Sozialismus* p.144[10]

The worries: a mental illness, which suits the capitalist epoch. Spiritual (not material) hopelessness in poverty, vagabondism-begging-monasticism. A condition that is so hopeless it is culpable [*verschuldend*]. The "worries" are the index of this guilty conscience of hopelessness: "Worries" originating in the fear of hopelessness that is community-based, not individual-material.

Christianity in the time of the Reformation did not encourage the emergence of capitalism, but rather changed itself into capitalism.

Methodologically [it] would be [productive] to first examine what associations money has adopted with myth in the course of history—until it could draw from Christianity enough mythical elements in order to constitute its own myth.

Wergild[11]/Thesaurus of good works/The salary that is owed to the priest. Pluto as God of the rich.

Adam Müller: *Reden übr die Beredsamkeit*[12] 1816 S56ff.

Connection of the dogma of the nature of knowledge—which, in its quality of resolving [*auflösenden*], is, to us, at the same time a liberating and killing—with capitalism. The end result is a liberating and ruining [*erledigende*] knowledge.

It contributes to the knowledge of capitalism as a religion to imagine that the original paganism certainly and most proximately grasped religion not as a "higher" "moral" interest, but as the most immediately practical—that it had with other words been aware of its "ideal" or "transcendent" nature, just as today's capitalism is, but saw in the irreligious or individual of different faith an infallible member of its community, in precisely the same sense the modern bourgeoisie [sees] its non-earning members [*nicht erwerbenden Angehörigen*].

Notes

1. "Capitalism as Religion" is a translation of Fragment 74, entitled "Kapitalismus als Religion," from Volume VI of Benjamin's *Gesammelte Schriften*, edited by Rolf Tiedemann and Hermann Schweppenhäuser (Suhrkamp), 100–03. In the notes of that volume (pp. 690–91), the editors have cited the texts Benjamin references in his manuscript in the editions that he would have read at the time. These are provided with slight emendations in the following footnotes, along with corresponding available English translations. Bracketed English words in the text are added merely to assist the reader in completing fragmentary sentences. All footnotes are those of the translator.

2. The literal translation of "sans rêve et sans merci" is "without dream and without mercy," but this is most likely the result of a typo or error in the transcription of Benjamin's manuscript. The phrase should probably read "sans trêve et sans merci," which is found in the sixth principle of the Medieval decalogue of chivalry, as catalogued by the influential 19th century French literary historian Leon Gautier. The sixth principle refers to the medieval knight's method of fighting the infidels, and is in concert with Benjamin's description of capitalism's development and Georges Sorel's treatment of Christianity and capitalism in his *Réflexions sur la violence*, which Benjamin later cites in this manuscript. See Leon Gautier, *Chivalry, The Everyday Life of the Medieval Knight* (New York: Crown Publishers 1989). I would like to thank Devah Pager and Paul Humphrey for their assistance in tracing this connection.

3. Benjamin's use of "non facit saltum" is a truncated version of the evolutionary adage, *Natura non facit saltum* or "Nature makes no leaps," which figured prominently in Leibniz's *Nouveaux essais sur l'entendement humain* of 1704 (translated as *New Essays on Human Understanding* (Cambridge: Cambridge University Press 1996)), Charles Darwin's *On the Origin of Species* (London: John Murray 1859), and Alfred Marshall's *Principles of Economics* (London: Macmillan 1920).

4. Benjamin is noting the ambiguity of the German word *Schuld*, which can mean either blame, guilt, or debt.

5. Georges Sorel, *Réflexions sur la violence*, 5th edition (Paris: *Marcel Rivière et Cie* 1919). Translated as *Reflections on Violence* (New York: Peter Smith 1941).

6. Erich Unger, *Politik und Metaphysic. Die Theorie. Versuche zu philosophischer Politik*, I. (Berlin: Verlag David 1921).

7. Bruno Archibald Fuchs, *Der Geist der bürgerlich-kapitalischen Gesellschaft. Eine Untersuchung über seine Grundlage und Voraussetzungen* (Berlin, München 1914).

8. Max Weber, *Gesammlte Aufsätze zur Religionssoziologie* 2 Bd. (Tübingen: Mohr 1920).

9. Ernst Troeltsch, *Die Soziallehren der christlichen Kirchen und Gruppen. Gesammlte Schriften*, Bd. I. (Tübingen: Scientia Aalen 1912). Translated as *The Social Teaching of the Christian Churches* (New York: The Macmillan Company 1931).

10. Gustav Landauer, *Aufruf zum Sozialismus* (Berlin: Verlegt bei Paul Cassirer 1920).

11. In Teutonic and Old English law, *wergild* (or *Wergeld*) is the value set for a human life and is paid to the family or lord of the dead.

12. Adam Müller, *Zwölf Reden uber die Beredsamkeit und deren Verfall in Deutschland* (München: Drei Masken Verlag 1816).

16

Theologico-Political Fragment

Walter Benjamin
Translated by Edmund Jephcott

Only the Messiah himself consummates all history, in the sense that he alone redeems, completes, creates its relation to the Messianic. For this reason nothing historical can relate itself on its own account to anything Messianic. Therefore the Kingdom of God is not the *telos* of the historical dynamic; it cannot be set as a goal. From the standpoint of history it is not the goal, but the end. Therefore the order of the profane cannot be built up on the idea of the Divine Kingdom, and therefore theocracy has no political, but only a religious meaning. To have repudiated with utmost vehemence the political significance of theocracy is the cardinal merit of Bloch's *Spirit of Utopia*.

The order of the profane should be erected on the idea of happiness. The relation of this order to the Messianic is one of the essential teachings of the philosophy of history. It is the precondition of a mystical conception of history, containing a problem that can be represented figuratively. If one arrow points to the goal toward which the profane dynamic acts, and another marks the direction of Messianic intensity, then certainly the quest of free humanity for happiness runs counter to the Messianic direction; but just as a force can, through acting, increase another that is acting in the opposite direction, so the order of the profane assists, through being profane, the coming of the Messianic Kingdom. The profane, therefore, although not itself a category of this Kingdom, is a decisive category of its quietest approach. For in happiness all that is earthly seeks its downfall, and only in good fortune is its downfall destined to find it. Whereas, admittedly, the immediate Messianic intensity of the heart, of the inner man in isolation, passes through misfortune, as suffering. To the spiritual *restitutio in integrum*, which introduces immortality, corresponds a worldly restitution that leads to the eternity of downfall, and the rhythm of this eternally transient worldly existence, transient in its totality, in its spatial but also in its temporal totality, the rhythm of Messianic nature, is happiness. For nature is Messianic by reason of its eternal and total passing away.

To strive after such passing, even for those stages of man that are nature, is the task of world politics, whose method must be called nihilism.

17
Theses on the Philosophy of History

Walter Benjamin
Translated by Harry Zohn

I

The story is told of an automaton constructed in such a way that it could play a winning game of chess, answering each move of an opponent with a counter-move. A puppet in Turkish attire and with a hookah in its mouth sat before a chessboard placed on a large table. A system of mirrors created the illusion that this table was transparent from all sides. Actually, a little hunchback who was an expert chess player sat inside and guided the puppet's hand by means of strings. One can imagine a philosophical counterpart to this device. The puppet called "historical materialism" is to win all the time. It can easily be a match for anyone if it enlists the services of theology, which today, as we know, is wizened and has to keep out of sight.

II

"One of the most remarkable characteristics of human nature," writes Lotze, "is, alongside so much selfishness in specific instances, the freedom from envy which the present displays toward the future." Reflection shows us that our image of happiness is thoroughly colored by the time to which the course of our own existence has assigned us. The kind of happiness that could arouse envy in us exists only in the air we have breathed, among people we could have talked to, women who could have given themselves to us. In other words, our image of happiness is indissolubly bound up with the image of redemption. The same applies to our view of the past, which is the concern of history. The past carries with it a temporal index by which it is referred to redemption. There is a secret agreement between past generations and the present one. Our coming was expected on earth. Like every generation that preceded us, we have been endowed with a *weak* Messianic power, a power to which the past has a claim. That claim cannot be settled cheaply. Historical materialists are aware of that.

III

A chronicler who recites events without distinguishing between major and minor ones acts in accordance with the following truth: nothing that has ever happened should be regarded as lost for history. To be sure, only a redeemed mankind receives the fullness of its past—which is to say, only for a redeemed mankind has its past become citable in all its moments. Each moment it has lived becomes a *citation à l'ordre du jour*—and that day is Judgment Day.

IV

> *Seek for food and clothing first, then the Kingdom of God*
> *shall be added unto you.*
> —Hegel, 1807

The class struggle, which is always present to a historian influenced by Marx, is a fight for the crude and material things without which no refined and spiritual things could exist. Nevertheless, it is not in the form of the spoils which fall to the victor that the latter make their presence felt in the class struggle. They manifest themselves in this struggle as courage, humor, cunning, and fortitude. They have retroactive force and will constantly call in question every victory, past and present, of the rulers. As flowers turn toward the sun, by dint of a secret heliotropism the past strives to turn toward that sun which is rising in the sky of history. A historical materialist must be aware of this most inconspicuous of all transformations.

V

The true picture of the past flits by. The past can be seized only as an image which flashes up at the instant when it can be recognized and is never seen again. "The truth will not run away from us": in the historical outlook of historicism these words of Gottfried Keller mark the exact point where historical materialism cuts through historicism. For every image of the past that is not recognized by the present as one of its own concerns threatens to disappear irretrievably. (The good tidings which the historian of the past brings with throbbing heart may be lost in a void the very moment he opens his mouth.)

VI

To articulate the past historically does not mean to recognize it "the way it really was" (Ranke). It means to seize hold of a memory as it flashes up at a moment of danger. Historical materialism wishes to retain that image of the past which unexpectedly appears to man singled out by history at a moment of danger. The danger affects both the content of the tradition and its receivers. The same threat hangs over both: that of becoming a tool of the ruling classes. In every era the attempt must be made anew to wrest tradition away from a conformism that is about to overpower it. The Messiah comes not only as the redeemer, he comes as the subduer of Antichrist. Only that historian will have the gift of fanning the spark of hope in the past who is firmly convinced that *even the dead* will not be safe from the enemy if he wins. And this enemy has not ceased to be victorious.

VII

> *Consider the darkness and the great cold*
> *In this vale which resounds with mysery.*
> —Brecht, "The Threepenny Opera"

To historians who wish to relive an era, Fustel de Coulanges recommends that they blot out everything they know about the later course of history. There is no better way of characterizing the method with which historical materialism has broken. It is a process of empathy whose origin is the indolence of the heart, *acedia*, which despairs of grasping and holding the genuine historical image as it flares up briefly. Among medieval theologians it was regarded as the root cause of sadness. Flaubert, who was familiar with it, wrote: "*Peu de gens devineront combien il a fallu être triste pour ressusciter Carthage.*"[1] The nature of this sadness stands out more clearly if one asks with whom the adherents of historicism actually empathize. The answer is inevitable: with the victor. And all rulers are the heirs of those who conquered before them. Hence, empathy with the victor invariably benefits the rulers. Historical materialists know what that means. Whoever has emerged victorious participates to this day in the triumphal procession in which the present rulers step over those who are lying prostrate. According to traditional practice, the spoils are carried along in the procession. They are called cultural treasures, and a historical materialist views them with cautious detachment. For without exception the cultural treasures he surveys have an origin which he cannot contemplate without horror. They owe their existence not only to the efforts of the great minds and talents who have created them, but also to the anonymous toil of their contemporaries. There is no document of civilization which is not at the same time a document of barbarism. And just as such a document is not free of barbarism, barbarism taints also the manner in which it was transmitted from one owner to another. A historical materialist therefore dissociates himself from it as far as possible. He regards it as his task to brush history against the grain.

VIII

The tradition of the oppressed teaches us that the "state of emergency" in which we live is not the exception but the rule. We must attain to a conception of history that is in keeping with this insight. Then we shall clearly realize that it is our task to bring about a real state of emergency, and this will improve our position in the struggle against Fascism. One reason why Fascism has a chance is that in the name of progress its opponents treat it as a historical norm. The current amazement that the things we are experiencing are "still" possible in the twentieth century is *not* philosophical. This amazement is not the beginning of knowledge—unless it is the knowledge that the view of history which gives rise to it is untenable.

IX

> *Mein Flügel ist zum Schwung bereit,*
> *ich kehrte gern zurück,*
> *denn blieb ich auch lebendige Zeit,*
> *ich hätte wenig Glück.*
> —Gerhard Scholem, "Gruss vom Angelus"[2]

A Klee painting named "Angelus Novus" shows an angel looking as though he is about to move away from something he is fixedly contemplating. His eyes are staring, his mouth is open, his wings are spread. This is how one pictures the angel of history. His face is turned toward the past. Where we perceive a chain of events, he sees one single catastrophe which keeps piling wreckage upon wreckage and hurls it in front of his feet. The angel would like to stay, awaken the dead, and make whole what has been smashed. But a storm is blowing from Paradise; it has got caught in his wings with such violence that the angel can no longer close them. This storm irresistibly propels him into the future to which his back is turned, while the pile of debris before him growrs skyward. This storm is what we call progress.

X

The themes which monastic discipline assigned to friars for meditation were designed to turn them away from the world and its affairs. The thoughts which we are developing here originate from similar considerations. At a moment when the politicians in whom the opponents of Fascism had placed their hopes are prostrate and confirm their defeat by betraying their own cause, these observations are intended to disentangle the political worldlings from the snares in which the traitors have entrapped them. Our consideration proceeds from the insight that the politicians' stubborn faith in progress, their confidence in their "mass basis," and, finally, their servile integration in an uncontrollable apparatus have been three aspects of the same thing. It seeks to convey an idea of the high price our accustomed thinking will have to pay for a conception of history that avoids any complicity with the thinking to which these politicians continue to adhere.

XI

The conformism which has been part and parcel of Social Democracy from the beginning attaches not only to its political tactics but to its economic views as well. It is one reason for its later breakdown. Nothing has corrupted the German working class so much as the notion that it was moving with the current. It regarded technological developments as the fall of the stream with which it thought it was moving. From there it was but a step to the illusion that the factory work which was supposed to tend toward technological progress constituted a political achievement. The old Protestant ethics of work was resurrected among German workers in secularized form. The Gotha Program[3] already bears traces of this confusion, defining labor as "the source of all wealth and all culture." Smelling a rat, Marx countered that ". . . the man who possesses no other property than his labor power" must of necessity become "the slave of other men who have made themselves the owners. . . ." However, the confusion spread, and soon thereafter Josef Dietzgen proclaimed: "The savior of modern times is called work. The . . . improvement . . . of labor constitutes the wealth which is now able to accomplish what no redeemer has ever been able to do." This vulgar-Marxist conception of the nature of labor bypasses the question of how its products might benefit the workers while still not being at their disposal. It recognizes only the progress in the mastery of nature, not the retrogression of society; it already displays the technocratic features later encountered in Fascism. Among these is a conception of nature which differs ominously from the one in the Socialist utopias before the 1848 revolution. The new conception of labor amounts to the exploitation of nature, which with naïve complacency is contrasted with the exploitation of the proletariat. Compared with this positivistic conception, Fourier's fantasies, which have so often been ridiculed, prove to be surprisingly sound. According to Fourier, as a result of efficient cooperative labor, four moons would illuminate the earthly night, the ice would recede from the poles, sea water would no longer taste salty, and beasts of prey would do man's bidding. All this illustrates a kind of labor which, far from exploiting nature, is capable of delivering her of the creations which lie dormant in her womb as potentials. Nature, which, as Dietzgen puts it, "exists gratis," is a complement to the corrupted conception of labor.

XII

We need history, but not the way a spoiled loafer in the garden
of knowledge needs it.
—Nietzsche, "Of the Use and Abuse of History"

Not man or men but the struggling, oppressed class itself is the depository of historical knowledge. In Marx it appears as the last enslaved class, as the avenger that completes the task of liberation in the name of generations of the downtrodden. This conviction, which had a brief resurgence in the Spartacist group,[4] has always been objectionable to Social Democrats. Within three decades they managed virtually to erase the name of Blanqui, though it had been the rallying sound that had reverberated through the preceding century. Social Democracy thought fit to assign to the working class the role of the redeemer of future generations, in this way cutting the sinews of its greatest strength. This training made the working class forget both its hatred and its spirit of sacrifice, for both are nourished by the image of enslaved ancestors rather than that of liberated grandchildren.

XIII

Every day our cause becomes clearer and people get smarter.
—Wilhelm Dietzgen, "Die Religion der Sozialdemokratie"

Social Democratic theory, and even more its practice, have been formed by a conception of progress which did not adhere to reality but made dogmatic claims. Progress as pictured in the minds of Social Democrats was, first of all, the progress of mankind itself (and not just advances in men's ability and knowledge). Second, it was something boundless, in keeping with the infinite perfectibility of mankind. Third, progress was regarded as irresistible, something that automatically pursued a straight or spiral course. Each of these predicates is controversial and open to criticism. However, when the chips are down, criticism must penetrate beyond these predicates and focus on something that they have in common. The concept of the historical progress of mankind cannot be sundered from the concept of its progression through a homogeneous, empty time. A critique of the concept of such a progression must be the basis of any criticism of the concept of progress itself.

XIV

Origin is the goal.
—Karl Kraus, "Worte in Versen, Vol. I"

History is the subject of a structure whose site is not homogeneous, empty time, but time filled by the presence of the now [*Jetztzeit*].[5] Thus, to Robespierre ancient Rome was a past charged with the time of the now which he blasted out of the continuum of history. The French Revolution viewed itself as Rome reincarnate. It evoked ancient Rome the way fashion evokes costumes of the past. Fashion has a flair for the topical, no matter where it stirs in the thickets of long ago; it is a tiger's leap into the past. This jump, however, takes place in an arena where the ruling class gives the commands. The same leap in the open air of history is the dialectical one, which is how Marx understood the revolution.

XV

The awareness that they are about to make the continuum of history explode is characteristic of the revolutionary classes at the moment of their action. The great revolution introduced a new calendar. The initial day of a calendar serves as a historical time-lapse camera. And, basically, it is the same day that keeps recurring in the guise of holidays, which are days of remembrance. Thus the calendars do not measure time as clocks do; they are monuments of a historical consciousness of which not the slightest trace has been apparent in Europe in the past hundred years. In the July revolution an incident occurred which showed this consciousness still alive. On the first evening of fighting it turned out that the clocks in the towers were being fired on simultaneously and independently from several places in Paris. An eye-witness, who may have owed his insight to the rhyme, wrote as follows:

> Qui le croiraít! on dit, qu'irrités contre l'heure
> De nouveaux Josués au pied de chaque tour,
> Tiraient sur les cadrans pour arrêter le jour.[6]

XVI

A historical materialist cannot do without the notion of a present which is not a transition, but in which time stands still and has come to a stop. For this notion defines the present in which he himself is writing history. Historicism gives the "eternal" image of the past; historical materialism supplies a unique experience with the past. The historical materialist leaves it to others to be drained by the whore called "Once upon a time" in historicism's bordello. He remains in control of his powers, man enough to blast open the continuum of history.

XVII

Historicism rightly culminates in universal history. Materialistic historiography differs from it as to method more clearly than from any other kind. Universal history has no theoretical armature. Its method is additive; it musters a mass of data to fill the homogeneous, empty time. Materialistic historiography, on the other hand, is based on a constructive principle. Thinking involves not only the flow of thoughts, but their arrest as well. Where thinking suddenly stops in a configuration pregnant with tensions, it gives that configuration a shock, by which it crystallizes into a monad. A historical materialist approaches a historical subject only where he encounters it as a monad. In this structure he recognizes the sign of a Messianic cessation of happening, or, put differently, a revolutionary chance in the fight for the oppressed past. He takes cognizance of it in order to blast a specific era out of the homogeneous course of history—blasting a specific life out of the era or a specific work out of the lifework. As a result of this method, the lifework is preserved in this work and at the same time canceled;[7] in the lifework, the era; and in the era, the entire course of history. The nourishing fruit of the historically understood contains time as a precious but tasteless seed.

XVIII

"In relation to the history of organic life on earth," writes a modern biologist, "the paltry fifty millennia of *homo sapiens* constitute something like two seconds at the close of a twenty-four-hour day. On this scale, the history of civilized mankind would fill one-fifth of the last second of the last hour." The present, which, as a model of Messianic time, comprises the entire history of mankind in an enormous abridgment, coincides exactly with the stature which the history of mankind has in the universe.

A

Historicism contents itself with establishing a causal connection between various moments in history. But no fact that is a cause is for that very reason historical. It became historical posthumously, as it were, through events that may be separated from it by thousands of years. A historian who takes this as his point of departure stops telling the sequence of events like the beads of a rosary. Instead, he grasps the constellation which his own era has formed with a definite earlier one. Thus he establishes a conception of the present as the "time of the now" which is shot through with chips of Messianic time.

B

The soothsayers who found out from time what it had in store certainly did not experience time as either homogeneous or empty. Anyone who keeps this in mind will perhaps get an idea of how past times were experienced in remembrance-namely, in just the same way. We know that the Jews were prohibited from investigating the future. The Torah and the prayers instruct them in remembrance, however. This stripped the future of its magic, to which all those succumb who turn to the soothsayers for enlightenment. This does not imply, however, that for the Jews the future turned into homogeneous, empty time. For every second of time was the strait gate through which the Messiah might enter.

Notes

1. "Few will be able to guess how sad one had to be in order to resuscitate Carthage."
2. *My wing is ready for flight,*
   I would like to turn back,
   If I stayed timeless time,
   I would have little luck.
3. The Gotha Congress of 1875 united the two German Socialist parties, one led by Ferdinand Lassalle, the other by Karl Marx and Wilhelm Liebknecht. The program, drafted by Liebknecht and Lassalle, was severely attacked by Marx in London. See his "Critique of the Gotha Program."
4. Leftist group, founded by Karl Liebknecht and Rosa Luxemburg at the beginning of World War I in opposition to the pro-war policies of the German Socialist party, later absorbed by the Communist party.
5. Benjamin says "*Jetztzeit*" and indicates by the quotation marks that he does not simply mean an equivalent to *Gegenwart*, that is, present. He clearly is thinking of the mystical *nunc stans*.
6. Who would have believed it! we are told that new Joshuas at the foot of every tower, as though irritated with time itself, fired at the dials in order to stop the day.
7. The Hegelian term *aufheben* in its threefold meaning: to preserve, to elevate, to cancel.

VIII

Johann Baptist Metz

18
Productive Noncontemporaneity

Johann Baptist Metz
Translated by Andrew Buchwalter

I

What can a contemporary so noncontemporaneous as a theologian, and a Catholic at that, have to say about the temper of the age? Perhaps this; it is high time to develop a better understanding of noncontemporaneity. Above all, it is high time that the leftist intellectuals of this country develop a better understanding of noncontemporaneity. In so doing they might establish closer ties with a still noncontemporaneous people and thus will not be left to lament impotently about, among other things, a revived populism. And they might also free themselves from their all too many subjectless theories and from an abstract rigor that is not made "radical" by the fact that they so gladly label it that way. Only if the left sheds the nervous anxiety it experiences in the face of noncontemporaneous phenomena can it successfully counter the reactionary flight into a wholly noncontemporaneous life, a flight that—considering the increasing social conflicts in our country as well as, say, the United States—is characteristic of the present mood and tendency.

II

A Christian religion worthy of the name, one that has not yet been secularized into a utopia (which, as everyone knows, is not the object of anyone's prayers), is in the highest degree and almost irritatingly noncontemporaneous. It is indeed informed of this by all parties. For the left, Christian religion serves as a special example of a noncontemporaneous residue left from the period preceding the

277

Enlightenment; it is perceived as professing a purely perfunctory interest in universal justice and liberation. As for the right and the center, the situation at first appears different. Indeed there is even talk of an ideological shift (*Tendenzwende*) in society toward religion; and religious terminology is once again appearing in political programs. Yet it must be asked whether what is at issue here is really a matter of religion. Is this shift a timely form of inspiration and irritation wrought by religious noncontemporaneity? Or is it instead an indication of society's interest in its own security, a type of protective ideology for affluent bourgeois societies that, confronted everywhere by increasingly insistent demands and challenges, refuse to alter their priorities and look to religion as a supposedly reliable and time-tested accomplice in their efforts to safeguard the status quo?

In any case there seems to be agreement on at least one point: religion is a phenomenon of noncontemporaneity, a patina phenomenon, of which today even many who view themselves as religious dare make only ceremonial and not serious or radical use. In fact a religion that has not been rendered superfluous through the abandonment of its aspirations is permeated with this atmosphere of noncontemporaneity, with this scent of the anachronistic. It comes from afar, from the depths of the history of humankind, which from a standpoint of dialectics or of a logic of evolution, is now held to be transparent or at least capable of being rendered transparent.

Of parallel significance is the way in which the major societal systems of our day react to religious noncontemporaneity. In the West, in bourgeois-liberal societies, this noncontemporaneity of religion is—somewhat grudgingly— privatized: "To each his own noncontemporaneity!" In Eastern countries, those bearing the imprint of Marxist socialism, that aspect of religion not regarded as bald alienation have long ago been incorporated into and stood on its feet by the dialectical process of a socialist history of liberation. Finally, we know from our recent past that fascism has its own way of dealing with a noncontemporaneous religion; time and again it has attempted to politicize and exploit in populist manner the cultural and political resentments often bottled up in a religion owing to its noncontemporaneity, such as a latent animosity toward enlightenment and democracy.

III

I would like to clarify the experience of religious noncontemporaneity first by way of a few autobiographical observations. Religious noncontemporaneity is not simply a position; it is a comprehensive way of life, a mode of presenting oneself, of learning and experiencing—a social-psychological life rhythm. I come from an arch-Catholic Bavarian village. One comes from far away when one comes from there. It is as if one were born not fifty years ago, but somewhere along the receding edges of the Middle Ages. I had to approach many things slowly at first, had to exert great effort to discover things that others and that society had long ago discovered and that had since become common practice, like democracy in daily political life, dealing with a diffuse public sphere, and rules of the game of conflict even in family life. Much appeared alien and in fact continued to be alienating. Only gradually did I adjust to urban life. (To this very day, it seems to me, Catholicism remains essentially a rural religion; I am referring to the Catholics who, in the diaspora of our fully secularized cities, are shaken almost to the core.) Later I was depressed by the cognitive isolation experienced by Catholic theology, especially within our universities. In general, I made an observation about the theoretical-theological domain similar to one I made about the domain of everyday religion: from a point quite removed, I had to work my way into the academic and social discussion fronts, had to learn to comprehend things that supposedly my theology and I had already discovered and comprehended long ago, had to gain access to phenomena that my contemporaries seemed to master through clichés: enlightenment, pluralism, emancipation, secularization, the critique of capitalism, and Marxism. And I had to learn how difficult and problematic it was to connect these parameters of contemporaneity, or however one wishes to designate the signals for the "height of the age," with that religion already so familiar to me before I had begun reflecting upon it.

IV

With reference to the situation in Catholic theology, I would like to distinguish three ways in which it deals with this experience of non-contemporaneity. I am making these distinctions with extreme caution and with the expressed recognition that they serve only as ideal types, for in reality we always confront only mixed forms. I am more interested in sketching out mentalities than positions.

First, there is theology as the systematic consolidation of noncontemporaneity. Here the tensive contradictions contained in the experience of religious noncontemporaneity are relaxed. The experience of noncontemporaneity is fashioned into an immediate expression of the intrinsic untimeliness and foreignness of religion and its message. This in fact involves a retreat to earlier theological and cultural-political positions. Without wishing to denigrate the merits of the so-called neo-Scholasticism of nineteenth- and twentieth-century Catholic theology, I must nonetheless characterize it as a prototype for the traditionalist approach to the experience of religious noncontemporaneity. It is sufficiently telling that this school's classic work during the last century was entitled *Theologie der Vorzeit* [Theology of the premodern period]. This fixation of theology on premodernity was accompanied by a process of spiritual and social isolation in which Catholics were consolidated into a firm and, not least of all, political *corpus catholicum,* a rather weak imitation of the great *corpus christianum* of the Middle Ages. *Kulturkämpfe* in the sociopolitical sphere and controversial theology in the confessional sphere testified to the strictly defensive character of the treatment of the experience of religious noncontemporaneity. Ecclesiastic religion, which adapted only with great difficulty to the conditions and requirements of the industrial revolution, appeared more rigorous than radical; dike-plugging strategies began to dominate the Church's pastoral practice. Ecclesiastic religion displayed features especially characteristic of a traditionalist welfare religion (*Betreuungsreligion*). Unfortunately this depiction of the historical situation is even today only too apt!

Second, there is the catch-up mentality in theology: the energetic attempt to shed noncontemporaneity and install theology "at the height of the age," with which it is not (or is no longer) identified. Here all forms of progress since the Reformation are painstakingly and meticulously incorporated into theology. The goal is a consciousness that is as contemporaneous as possible with bourgeois-liberal society and scientific-technological civilization. Thus even in Catholicism there has now emerged a type of bourgeois theology. In this country the model is not infrequently Protestant theology, which is always regarded as being more contemporaneous. Clearly this also has the consequence that this type of Catholic theology, while commonly viewed as particularly progressive or critical within Catholicism, has been accorded less attention by Protestant thinkers, who too often expect to find in it only a reproduction of the problems and questions with which they have already become familiar as a result of their own recent history. The churchly basis for this kind of theological treatment of a non-contemporaneous religion consists in the fact that in our society even Catholic Christianity is assuming more and more the character of a bourgeois religion, with a contemporaneity bonus similar to that long enjoyed by Protestantism.

Finally, there is the theological attempt to specify the creative character of religious noncontemporaneity. I would like to shed some light on the creative component in noncontemporaneity first by way of comparison. In a biography of Einstein I recently read that this great physicist was constantly asked how he had managed to arrive at his revolutionary insights. In reply he suggested that it might be connected with the fact that in school he had always learned more slowly and comprehended with greater difficulty than others; that even later he had experienced more difficulty with physics than some of his colleagues and that for this reason he had to devote himself to a problem for a longer time and with greater tenacity than did others, continuing to play, as it were, with the same ball long after others were already juggling new ones. The biographer noted that as a child Einstein had in fact so many learning difficulties that he could have been designated learning-disabled. People who are religiously devout, particularly Catholics, are like learning-disabled students in the school of progress! And indeed why not, if one bears in mind the "Einstein effect," thus viewing the noncontemporaneity of the devout not merely as a form of backwardness to be overcome as quickly as possible but as a trenchant and ultimately revolutionary way of relating to reality and its conditions, a form of timely inspiration and irritation through noncontemporaneous religion.

With reference to Catholicism, G. K. Chesterton once spoke of the "adventure of orthodoxy." I would like to refashion this phrase into the "adventure of religious noncontemporaneity." Certainly this adventure remains as removed from every progressive approach to religion as from every traditionalist one, the latter neither deriving strength from nor finding inspiration in the tension of noncontemporaneity. I see the impetus for a theological approach to religion, which attempts to make visible religion's creative noncontemporaneity for social life, in the theology of Karl Rahner, who as no one else has influenced the Catholic theology of our day. Rahner's thought is particularly apparent or at least invoked in the approach of the new political theologians and especially the liberation theologians, whose significance within Catholicism as a whole is far less marginal than the left's within West German society. For this theological left the Christian religion is primarily a messianic religion of emulation, certainly not in the elitist sense but in terms of impulses emanating from the social base. After many setbacks it has tenaciously taken root and asserted its presence within Church life as part of a process in which the entire ecumenical situation, with its tremendous tensions and challenges, has become an internal element in the individual situation of every Church. For instance, as a result of this process, the Church in this country, much more so than the society as a whole, has been forced to abandon a strictly European orientation and to view and judge itself through the eyes of the other—through the eyes of the victim, in this case through the eyes of members of the impoverished Churches of the Third World. So noncontemporaneous a notion as the community of believers, the Eucharistic fellowship of the devout, is ever more compelled to set free that kernel of radical praxis often concealed within the lawlike rigidity of Church life. Our Latin American brothers might also interpret for us the noncontemporaneous language of mortal sin in the sense of those sins through which quite literally we bring death to others as long as we fail to change ourselves radically.

V

And yet the question remains: Can talk of the creative noncontemporaneity of religion, of a religion that intervenes not just in our private life, be anything more than the creation of modern theology? Will it not founder on the reality of the church, on the practice, say, of "Catholicism" in this country? I am, of course, aware that there are sufficient grounds to pose these and related questions, and I myself have done so frequently and repeatedly to my Church. Of course, I understand what by now has become the near-constitutional distrust of those, particularly on the left, who no longer believe that ecclesiastic religion, with its notion of redemption, also pleads for the liberation of the oppressed; who no longer believe in its intention to combine prayer with struggle, love with a solidarity partial to the damaged life; and finally who no longer believe that its living faith can also give voice to a passionate opposition to that world of exploitation and consumerism that desecrates humanity's divine image. Not only must the Church be found wanting; there are also pitiful clichés about the Church that are sorely wanting. For instance, I regard as foolish and ignorant the view (held at times by Christians) in which the Church is seen only as a feudal relic that has since been refashioned into agent and advocate for the interests of monopoly capitalism.

But where is one to observe in the practice of ecclesiastic religion something of a connection between a noncontemporaneous religion and a form of political life that is creative and not oriented to backwardness and accommodation? Admittedly an answer to this question cannot go much beyond intimations and first approximations. In any case I would like to call attention to the Christian base communities (*Basisgemeinde*) that have sprung up primarily in the Churches of the Third World (although not only there); in the very terms used to define these communities one detects something of this connection. In them the noncontemporaneous social form of a cultic community has become societally differentiated, incorporating fundamental social conflicts and afflictions. In this way they reveal as a rule far greater orientational and integrational force than does a base oriented exclusively to strategies for socioeconomic transformation. To be sure, in this country these Christian base communities are not held in particularly high regard. Although their specific developmental validity for Third World Churches is affirmed in certain circumstances, this is done to stress their nontransferability and to reinforce the ideal of a "purely religious community" whose peace is only disturbed by the incorporation of conflicts emanating from the social base—as if love rendered social suffering and the suffering of the afflicted invisible, rather than making it all the more visible; as if in some meek way love were general and impartial! (Hate is selfish, individually as well as collectively, but love is partial.) The price our congregations pay for this type of social insouciance is high. It reveals only too clearly those features one would want to avoid in societal uniformization and in the political pseudoneutrality of religious communities, such as relationlessness, lack of warmth, alienation, and lack of compelling and identificational force (especially among the young).

But, most importantly, our congregations renounce in this way the possibility of becoming a productive model in our society for a new mediation of public and private affairs. If today politics and morality can, in a clearly diffuse and rather helpless albeit ineluctable fashion, establish contact with one another (one speaks of renunciation and asceticism, of changing life priorities or abandoning consumerism, of conversion as a maxim of political survival), then the classic bourgeois distinction between public and private once again becomes a topic of discussion. And indeed not simply to dismiss it, which would be possible only at the price of a denial of the individual and ultimately of barbarism, but in order to constitute it in new fashion. In the form of base communities religion could and would have to intervene in this process, which is accessible neither through sound political pragmatism nor through selfless moral rigor. These base communities could become exemplary social localities, where political life becomes personal through its moral claims and where personal life, through the radical way in which it can be affected, nears political life. Here it could be demonstrated that a greater political potency and capacity for resistance can be found in the noncontemporaneous elements of Christian religion than in their purely secular counterparts. For in terms of their origin such notions as sin, conversion, sacrifice, and grace all clearly stand opposed to any pure internalization and therefore make more radical claims on individuals.

VI

In this context I would like to add a few remarks about the relation of noncontemporaneous religion to a question for which the left has evinced a special sensitivity. This question concerns the possibility for a new culture of solidarity in political life, a new principle of political individuation that does not renounce the achievements of a bourgeois principle (such as the basic political rights of the individual, the right to dissent, the right to popular sovereignty) but rather extends and surpasses that principle. Whence comes the forces for a new, quasi-postbourgeois principle of individuation, no longer based on the repression of others? Whence comes the power to resist a solidarity systematically distorted by hate or depersonalization without simultaneously jettisoning the hope for a solidarity that unconditionally enjoins individuals to assert their identity not against but with the meek, the socially and economically disenfranchised, the dependent groups and classes?

Who wants to place trust in the pure reserves of contemporaneity, in the exclusively contemporaneous man, who is in any case so horrified by his own future that, unlike members of all preceding generations, he no longer envies his successors? Is not a contemporaneity in which all the wrinkles of a noncontemporaneous life have been ironed out too narrow, too fortuitous, and too devoid of fantasy to generate any vision of a new individual that differs from the tiny unit of labor power, from the cunningly adaptive animal, from the smoothly functioning machine, or from the individual as a potentially criminal clog in a totalitarian grip?

The future, especially that of a new life dedicated to solidarity, is not nourished merely on the stuff of contemporaneity or on a noncontemporaneity rendered contemporaneous. The future of the village is not simply the urban center; the future of the cathedral is not simply the bank or the politically cultified mausoleum (as architecture may wish to insinuate); the future of childhood dreams is not simply the adult world of reason; and the future of religion is not simply a pallid utopia. Precisely for the sake of a future life of solidarity, noncontemporaneity demands more respect—and not only from traditionalists and conservatives, who, after all, only confirm themselves in it and who derive from it no spark of promise.

Why is it that on the left only artists and writers find sustenance in the tough, resistant stuff of noncontemporaneous religion? Does the left indeed deal with noncontemporaneity only in aesthetic fashion? I believe it is high time to think about this.

19

Anamnestic Reason
A Theologian's Remarks on the Crisis in the Geisteswissenschaften

Johann Baptist Metz
Translated by Barbara Fultner

I

I believe there are parallels that can be drawn between two crises. The crisis in Christianity is a crisis of intact traditions—that is, traditions that are capable of truth and that determine one's life; the crisis in the *Geisteswissenschaften* or human sciences, as I see it, is a crisis of the anamnestic constitution of *Geist* or Spirit and thus rooted in the loss or—more hopefully—in the occlusion of this underlying anamnestic structure of Spirit. Could it be that the two crises share a common origin in what we call European intellectual history?

II

The particular weakness of Christianity in this critical situation lies in an early division of its spirit. I want to elucidate this "division of Christian Spirit" with reference to the debate about the so-called Hellenization of Christianity, a debate dating as far back as the Renaissance but of interest in the present context in its most recent incarnation.

The Hellenization of Christianity refers to the reception of late Greek, Hellenistic philosophy into Christianity. This contributed to the universalization of Christianity, on the one hand, and to the development of its dogmatic character, on the other. (Early Christian dogmatism, after all, arose primarily under the categorial influence of Middle Platonism and of the Neoplatonism coined by Plotinus.) Because of its dogmatizing effects, the liberal A. V. Harnack rejected

285

Hellenization as a process of Christianity's self-alienation. Other historians of Christian dogma and systematic philosophers of both denominations have objected and continue to object to him. They do so not just in the interest of defending Christian dogma but also—as, for example, J. Ratzinger and W. Pannenberg have done recently—in the interest of a Christianity that thinks and engages in argument in an effort to develop its universal claim beyond a positivistic faith and a sharp, zealotous rhetoric of faith: by this very reception of Greek Spirit. This, of course, then leads to definitions of Christianity such as Ratzinger's: "Christianity is the synthesis—mediated by Jesus Christ—of Hebrew faith and Greek intellect."[1]

Without underestimating, let alone denying, the significance of Greek thought for Christianity, the question, however, remains: Did Israel have nothing spiritual to offer to Christianity and to Europe? Is there a "logic," something to think about, to be found in the New Testament only where that New Testament is already, as, for example, in the scriptures of Paul and John, under the influence of late Greek thought? No; Israel, too, brings something new and original to Christianity, both spiritually and intellectually: meditative thought (*Angedenken*) *qua* historical mindfulness or remembrance (*Eingedenken*). This kind of thought has been persistently concealed in the very tradition of Christian theology itself and concerns the basic anamnestic constitution of Spirit that cannot be identified with Platonic anamnesia, which is exempt from time and history.[2] In this sense, Israel ought to be included not only in the religious history but also in the intellectual history of Christianity and, hence, in European intellectual history more generally.[3] And thought *qua* remembrance must be included in the history of reason.[4] I believe this to be relevant for the diagnosis and treatment of the spiritual crisis in the *Geisteswissenschaften* and the crisis of enlightenment.

III

In connection with the crisis in the *Geisteswissenschaften*, there is much talk at present of a crisis of reason and a crisis of enlightenment, if not of a crisis of modernity *tout court*. The advocates of reason and enlightenment in this context like to speak of a fateful domination of "divided" reason that has brought the age of reason and enlightenment into disrepute. But if that is so, what would nondivided reason be? Jürgen Habermas is known for discussing the basic communicative structure of reason. This determination of reason orients itself on a model of linguistification and of discourse and therefore imposes a privileging of contemporaneity on the readiness of reason to recognize the Other. Hence it absolutely must be related and connected to the anamnestic constitution of reason (no doubt also for the sake of a narrower determination of its bearers in the lifeworld). Only as anamnestically constituted does reason prevent abstract understanding from taking progressive lack of recollection, progressive amnesia, for actual progress. Only anamnestic reason enables enlightenment to enlighten itself again concerning the harm it has caused.[5]

The most recent so-called *Historikerstreit*, to which Habermas has contributed incisively and with great sensitivity, has again and again made me wonder whether our coming to terms with the catastrophe of Auschwitz is so uncertain and discordant because we lack the spirit that was to have been irrevocably extinguished in Auschwitz; because we lack the anamnestically constituted Spirit necessary to perceive adequately what happened to us in this catastrophe—and to what we call "Spirit" and "reason"; in a word: because we lack a culture of anamnestic Spirit. In place of remembrance, there is an evolutionarily colored history that presupposes that what is past is past and that no longer considers it a challenge to reason that every time a part of our past is successfully historicized, it is also forgotten in a sense. Memory, which keeps track of this forgetting, is split off from historical reason and reduced to a compensatory category removed from history and pregnant with myth; it becomes the museum piece of traditionalism and of counterenlightenment—or it drifts off into the postmodern fictionalization of history.

Anamnestically constituted reason opposes this. It does not by any means take its cue from counterenlightenment, for it discloses the traditions that gave rise to the interest in freedom—thus creating, the theologian adds, the recognition of the capacity for guilt as a dignity of freedom.[6] Anamnestic reason opposes the oblivion of past suffering. The authority of those who suffer denies its "receptive" character. It does not serve the leveling rationalization of discontinuities and historical ruptures in the interest of securing individual and collective identities of those alive today. Rather, it ensures that the public use of history remains unpopular. It is and continues to be "dangerous" in this sense, for it opposes the conception of our lifeworld as the "air-tight normality of what has come to be established" (as Habermas pointedly criticizes it).[7]

IV

I want to return to the crisis of the *Geisteswissenschaften* and conclude by listing three points concerning the implications of the notions of the anamnestic constitution of Spirit and of anamnestic reason, respectively, that I have defended.

1. The first point is fundamental (and in a particularly vulnerable way, speculative): I take memory *qua* remembrance not to be a compensatory but a constitutive category of the human mind or Spirit and of the way it perceives the world—and it is only in the light of this presupposition that the human sciences represent not a purely compensatory but a defining

and innovative knowledge in our perception of the world. A detailed argument for this constitutive significance of remembrance cannot avoid taking up once again the theme of the century "being and time," though not, as in Nietzsche and, somewhat differently, Heidegger, by reverting to Dionysian or Presocratic thought, but rather by keeping in mind biblical thought, which perceives the world from within the horizon of a fixed period of time. This perception does not by any means rule out science and technology, but it keeps them firmly tied to their instrumental character, thus giving rise to possibilities for limiting the modernizing processes that are increasingly self-propelled and subject-less. In addition, language, on this view, becomes ever more exclusively oriented toward information rather than communication; in the end, human beings are nothing but their own infinite experiment and no longer mindful of themselves.[8]

2. In my view, only the anamnestically constituted Spirit of the *Geisteswissenschaften* can successfully oppose the "death of man"—as we know him from history and as history has entrusted him to us—that scientific theory has already predicted and that culture and industry increasingly promote. After all, the scientific knowledge whose categories are dominant today is not interested in the subjective foundation of knowledge. It considers subject, freedom, the individual, and so forth to be anthropomorphisms, and the human being we know, his or her subjective identity, possibilities of communication, and sense of justice are becoming increasingly anachronistic. It is only by disclosing its basic anamnestic constitution that the Spirit of the *Geisteswissenschaften* will be able to withstand the anonymous pressure of this scientific knowledge and to maintain the distinction between communicative and instrumental reason.

3. The ethnic-cultural diversification of our world and its cultural polycentrism can be saved only in the face of a civilization of world unity without substance, if, in so-called intercultural exchange, the *Geisteswissenschaften* elaborate and hermeneutically secure the communicative superiority of the language of memory against the subject-less language or argumentation of Greek metaphysics and also of the predominant scientific language of Occidental rationality.

Notes

1. J. Ratzinger, in F. König and K. Rahner, eds., *Europa: Horizonte und Hoffnungen* (Graz/Wien/Köln, 1983), p. 68.
2. Johann Baptist Metz, "Erinnerung," in H. Krings, H. M. Baumgartner, and C. Wild, eds., *Handbuch philosophischer Grundbegriffe* (Munich, 1973), vol. 1.
3. Perhaps one may now, more than fifty years after the "Reichskristallnacht," put it as follows: Not until the Spirit of Israel has gained a right of settlement in European intellectual history will synagogues no longer be threatened—more, no longer be merely tolerated but recognized. Consider, for instance. Fichte's claim: "They [the Jews] must have human rights. . . . But

to grant them civil rights, to that end I see no other means than to cut off their heads one night and to replace them with ones that contain not a single Jewish idea."

4. It is again not by accident that in contemporary philosophy, Jewish voices are the ones to draw attention to this basic anamnestic constitution of reason: the old Frankfurt School (not just Walter Benjamin but also Theodor W. Adorno, who was still in a position to object to the Enlightenment's abstract idea of autonomy on the grounds that tradition or memory of any critical reason remains immanent as a mediating moment of its objects), F. Rosenzweig and E. Levinas, as well as H. Jonas and E. Bloch, who despite all their differences seem to agree that thinking is remembrance and that undivided reason has an anamnestic deep structure.

5. As long as European enlightenment has nothing further to say on the subject of Judaism except that the emancipation of the Jews is to be achieved by their emancipation from the Jewish Spirit of remembrance, it will not be able to extricate itself from the calamities in which Horkheimer and Adorno in the *Dialectic of Enlightenment* saw it to be ensnared.

6. See my "Erinnerung."

7. In *Eine Art Schadenabwicklung* (Frankfurt, 1987), p. 175. It seems to me to be typical and worth considering in this context that, in contrast to Alan Bloom's *The Closing of the American Mind* (New York, 1987), R. Bellah et al. in their most recent diagnosis of "Individualism and Commitment in American Life," in *Habits of the Heart* (Berkeley, 1985) refer to just such "Communities of Memory" as grass-roots loci of resistance to the decline of the possible orientations and the readiness to assume them in American life.

8. See the abridged prepublication of my paper at the Giessen Philosophy Conference (1987) entitled "Theologie gegen Mythologie: Kleine Apologie des biblischen Monotheismus" in *Herder Korrespondenz* (April 1988).

IX
Jürgen Habermas

20
Israel and Athens, or to Whom Does Anamnestic Reason Belong?

Jürgen Habermas
Translated by Eduardo Mendieta

On Unity in Multicultural Diversity

Johann Baptist Metz's way of thinking fascinates me because, overlooking certain distances, I recognize our common intentions. The fact that someone who, from a philosophical perspective adopts the position of methodical atheism, asks the same questions as the theologians is even less astonishing than the parallelism of the answers. In attempting to clarify these parallelisms, I would like to demonstrate my gratitude to the contemporary theologian.

Metz once illustrated with his own life history the factum of the contemporaneity of the non-contemporaneous [*Gleichzeitigkeit des Ungleichzeitigen*], which confronts us today in the multicultural kaleidoscope of a de-centered global society:

> I come from a small Bavarian city profoundly Catholic. Coming from there, one comes from very far. It is not as if one had been born fifty years ago (or sixty five), but in some point at the margins of the dawn of the middle ages. It took me a great effort to discover things that others, that "society," as it seems, had long ago already discovered [. . .]: democracy in everyday politics, for instance, the dealings with a diffused public sphere, rules of game of conflict even in the family life, etc. Much appeared strange and, in reality, it always continued being strange. (Metz 1980, 13)

Against the background of these experiences, Metz has opposed a defensive position of the pre-modern Catholic church and has advocated a productive participation in the processes of the bourgeois and post-bourgeois enlightenment. The biblical vision of salvation includes not only the redemption from individual guilt but the collective liberation from situations of misery and oppression as well (which, therefore, together with the mystical element, also contains a political element). The eschatological march towards salvation of those who suffer unjustly enters into contact with the impulses of the history of freedom in the European modernity.

In the same way, the consequences of the insensibility before the emancipatory potential of this history are as grave as the blindness before the dialectic of the Enlightenment. The barbaric reversal of its own mirror remained hidden for too long to the Enlightenment; under the light of its universalistic pretensions it deceived itself about the particularistic nucleus of its Western origins. This inveterate rationalism has become the silent violence of a capitalistic civilization of global reach that assimilates alien cultures, forgetting its own traditions. Christianity, which believed it could use this civilization as an "innocent catalyst for the universal propagation of its hope," and the church, which believed it could send its missionaries following the footsteps of the European colonizers, unwillingly participated in this dialectic of disenchantment and loss of memory. This explains the diagnosis that Metz presents of theology and the practical demand with which he confronts his church.

The diagnostic says: through the philosophical reason of Greek origin, a Hellenized Christianity has become so distanced from its own origin in the spirit of Israel that theology has become insensitive before the cry of suffering and before the demand for universal justice (Metz 1981; Kuschel 1990, 23 ff.). The demand is that: the eurocentric church that emerged from the soil of Hellenism must overcome its mono-cultural self-understanding and, taking into account its original Judaic context, develop itself into a culturally polycentric universal church (Metz 1981).

Israel vs. Athens

Metz does not tire of claiming for Christianity the inheritance of Israel. With the provocative formulation that "Jesus was not a Christian, but a Jew," Metz not only opposed Christian anti-semitism, but also called to account the *ecclesia triumphans* for its victorious, profoundly questionable, attitude before a shut down and humiliated synagogue. This formulation opposes above all the apathy of a theology that appears not to have been affected by Auschwitz (Kuschel 1990, 23 ff; Metz 1981). This critique obeys a practical-existential impulse. But it also means that a Hellenized Christianity, when rejecting its Judaic origin, has separated itself from the source of anamnestic reason and has become the expression of an erratic and idealistic reason, incapacitated for memory and historical remembrance. Understanding Christianity in an "Augustinian" fashion as a synthesis of reason and faith—reason deriving from Athens and faith from Israel—sunders in two the spirit of Christianity (Metz 1992, 189). Against the division of labor between philosophical reason and religious faith, Metz insists on the rational content of the tradition of Israel; he conceives of the force of historical remembrance as an element of reason: "This anamnestic reason resists forgetting, even the forgetting of the forgetting that nests in every simple historization of the past" (Metz 1992a, 24). From this point of view the philosophy with Greek roots appears as the administrator of Ratio, of the forces of understanding that is made to reason only through the linkage with the memory that remits us to Moses and his promise. In this sense, a theology that, departing from its Hellenistic alienation by returning to its own origins has, before philosophy, the last word: "[this theology] appeals to the indissoluble nexus between Ratio and Memoria (expressed in late modern terms: to the grounding of communicative reason in anamnestic reason)" (Metz 1992a, 24).

If we contemplate this pronouncement in a philosophical counter-light, it is more than the relation of grounding that suggests contradictions. The sketch of a philosophical tradition that is not exhausted in Platonism, but which in the course of history has appropriated the Judeo-Christian tradition and, through the inheritance of Israel, been shaken to the depths of its Greek roots, also appears too superficial. Philosophical idealism from Saint Augustine to Hegel, going through Saint Aquinas, has produced a synthesis in which the God who confronts Job has been transformed into the God of the philosophers. But the history of philosophy is not only the history of Platonism, but also of the protest against it. We can conceive of these protests, whether they appeared under the sign of nominalism or empiricism, of individualism or existentialism, of negativism or historical materialism, as attempts to rescue the semantic potential of the salvific thought in the universe of the grounding speech. With this potential, practical intuitions that in themselves are foreign to ontological thought and to the transformations undergone at the hands of the theory of knowledge and the philosophy of language have penetrated philosophy.

Metz gathers these non-Greek themes in the *one* focus of the act of remembrance (*Eingedenkens*). He understands the force of remembrance in Freud's sense, as the analytic force of the "making conscious," and in Benjamin's sense, as the mystical force of a retroactive reconciliation. Remembrance saves from ruin that which we do not want to lose and that, nevertheless, finds itself in the greatest of dangers. This religious concept of "salvation" undoubtedly exceeds the horizon of that which philosophy can make plausible under the conditions of post-metaphysical thinking. But departing from the concept of salvific remembrance, opens the field of experiences and religious motives that made themselves heard long before the doors of philosophical idealism opened, until they were finally taken seriously and, from within, planted uncertainty in a reason directed in principle only to the cosmos. But not everything remained in disquiet. In the course of an evolution that leads from the intellectual contemplation of the cosmos to a linguistically incarnated reason, passing through the self-reflexivity of a knowing subject, the Greek Logos has been transformed. Today, it no longer centers only on the cognitive relation with the world—on beings as beings, on the knowing of knowing, or on the meaning of sentences that can be true or false. What has also unfolded within philosophy, making possible that argumentative reason be receptive to the practical experiences of historically existing yet threatened identities of beings, is the idea of an alliance of the people of God and of a justice that is imposed on a history of suffering. It is the idea of an alliance that links freedom and solidarity in the horizon of an undamaged intersubjectivity.

Without this filtering of genuinely Jewish and Christian ideas into Greek metaphysics, we could not have constituted the modern network of concepts that converge in a concept of reason that is simultaneously communicative and historically situated. I mean the concept of subjective freedom and the demand for equal respect for all, including and precisely for the foreign in its particularity and difference. I mean the concept of autonomy, of a self-constraint of the will by virtue of a moral reasoning that is contingent on relations of reciprocal acknowledgement. I mean the concept of a socialized subject that is individualized in the course of its life and that as an unsubstitutable individual is at the same time member of a community, who can only carry out an authentic life in solidarity with others. I mean the concept of liberation, as much in the sense of emancipation from denigrating conditions as in the sense of an utopian project of a fulfilling life-form. The irruption of historical thinking into philosophy has finally encouraged the understanding of the "deferred" character of vital time; it has made us aware of the narrative structure of the history in which we find ourselves involved and of the contingent character of all that happens to us. To that also belongs the awareness of the fallibility of the human mind and the contingency of the condition under which it continues to still maintain unconditional claims.

The tension between the spirit of Athens and the inheritance of Israel has had profound consequence in philosophy as well as in theology. But if philosophical thinking is not resolved simply in the synthetic labour of the idealism that led to the paleo-Christianity of the West—conceived ecclesiastically—to be thought in theological terms, then the critique of Hellenized Christianity can not direct itself against argumentative reason "per se," nor against the impersonal reason of the philosophers as such. Anamnesis and narrative can also offer reasons and insofar give impulse to the philosophical discourse, although they do not decide its march. Although profane reason remains skeptical before the mystical causality of an act of remembrance inspired in salvific terms and does not offer any credence to the mere promise of restitution, it is not necessary that philosophers leave only to the hands of theologians that which

Metz calls "anamnestic reason." I would like to clarify this by referring to two questions that for Metz are of special interest in theological terms or for ecclesiastical politics.

The Problem of Theodicy

The question of the salvation of those who suffer unjustly is perhaps the most important in maintaining the discourse about God. Metz rebels decidedly against a Platonizing weakening of this question which, after Auschwitz, formulates itself to Christians with greater radicalness than ever (Metz 1984, 382–389). It was once again the means of reflection of the Greek tradition that distinguished between a redemptive God and a creator God of the Old Testament, who was thus exonerated from the responsibility for the barbarities of a sinful humanity. God himself could not be implicated in his creation "stricken with suffering." Against this idealistic mitigation of suffering, Metz evokes a "culture of regret [Kultur des Vermissens]," a culture of remembrance that keeps alive, without a false need of consolation, the existential restlessness proper to the vehement interpellation to God, stimulating with that an eschatologically fueled hope in a future that, although in stasis, almost reaches reality (Metz 1992a, 15–34). According to the Nietzchean doctrine of the eternal return, the biblical hope in the future cannot founder in the element of an eternity understood in Greek terms (Theunissen 1991, 368).

Even for this protest, which reaches to the farthest depths of religious experience, there is a parallelism in that subterranean current of the philosophical thinking that, before the Neoplatonic attempt to establish a gradation between the good and the true, insists on the positivity and in the unique sense of the negative. Just as it occurs with theology, which leads to its extreme ends in eschatology, the philosophical tradition—from Jakob Böhme through Baader, Schelling, and Hegel to Bloch and Adorno—hopes to transform the experience of negativity of the existing into the propelling dialectical force of a reflection that must break with the dominion of the past over the future. Since philosophy does not depart from the premise of a God that is omnipotent and just, it becomes clear that it cannot redeem a "culture of regret"—or a sense for all that has been pillaged or has been the object of dispossession—basing itself in the question of theodicy. In any event, today philosophy has less to do with the idealist glorification of a reality in need of redemption than with the indifference before a world reduced empiristically to a figure without contours and totally deaf to the normative.

The fronts have inverted. Today's historicism is an empiricism of a second level that denies seriousness to the validity claim of universalist character that stands behind every affirmation and negation of the subject who takes a position, a validity claim that although is always held "here and now," in a local context, overflows all merely provincial criteria. If a paradigm or a world view has the same value as the next, if different discourses codify in their own way everything that can be true or false, good or bad, then the normative dimension that allows us to identify the characteristics of a human life damaged, adulterated, and without dignity, and thus to experience it as a privation, is liquidated. For this reason, before the historicist forgetfulness of forgetfulness itself, philosophy also takes recourse to the force of anamnesis. But not its argumentative reason itself, which, in the deepest layers of its pragmatic presuppositions, discloses the conditions for the appellation of an unconditional sense and, with that, maintains open the dimension of the validity claims that transcend the social spaces and historical time. In this fashion, it opens a rift in the normality of a inner worldly happening that lacks all promissory characteristics—a normativity that in another way would remain sealed shut before any experience of *absence* of solidarity and justice. Evidently, this philosophy, which incorporates the idea of the alliance in the concept of a communicative reason historically situated, cannot offer any firm hope; it finds itself under the sign of a transcendence from within and must content itself with the grounded exhortation to a skeptical resistance, not defeatist, but rather, "against the idols and demons of a world that scorns the human being."

That the relationship between philosophy and theology once again varies in terms of an ecclesiastical politics and history concerns Metz the most. Here philosophy not only tries, as in the question of theodicy, to appropriate the semantic potentials that have been preserved in the religious tradition, but can aid a theology that must clarify the self-understanding of Christianity and the church with respect to the pluralism of cultures and world views (Metz 1984a, 14 ff.).

The Universal Polycentric Church

Since Vatican II, the Church finds itself faced with the double task of: internally, opening itself to the multiplicity of cultures in which Christian Catholism has taken root; and, externally, searching for a dialogue with the religions of non-Christian origins that does not evade the confrontation or persist with a defensive apologetic. The same problem is formulated in both directions: how to maintain the identity of the Christian church in the cultural multiplicity of its voices? And, how can the Christian doctrine maintain the authenticity of its quest for truth in the discursive dispute with competing world views? Metz offers suggestive answers. The Church, which reflects on the limits of its Eurocentric history in order to harmonize the Christian doctrine with the original hermeneutical situation of non-Western cultures, cannot depart from the "idea of an ahistorical Christianity, situated above cultures and ethnically innocent," instead it ought to have in mind as much the history of its theological origins as its institutional complicity with the history of European colonialism. A Christianity which in a dialogue with other religions, adopts a reflexive position with respect to its own truth claim cannot be satisfied with a "pluralism without mutual relationships or merely condescending"; rather it must abide firmly, without monopolizing and renouncing every means of power, by the universal validity of its offer of salvation (Metz 1987, 93–115).

With that the polycentric church appears to adopt almost an exemplary function for the political coming to terms with multiculturalism. In its internal relations it appears a commendable model for a democratic state of law that wishes to do justice to the different forms of life of a multicultural society; and in its external relationships a church of this type could be taken as a model for a community of peoples that regulate its international relations on the basis of reciprocal acknowledgement. However, looked at closely, matters work in reverse. It is the idea of the polycentric church that, in turn, feeds on the convictions of an European enlightenment and its political philosophy.

Metz himself refers affirmatively to the bequest of a rational, enlightened, natural law illustrated in hermeneutical terms beyond its eurocentric limits. Europe is the:

> political and cultural home of a universalism which in essence is strictly anti-eurocentric. . . . Certainly, the universalism of the Enlightenment, with its quest after freedom and justice, was only universal in the semantic sense at the beginning and, its concrete process of execution, has remained particularist even to this day. However, it established a new political and hermeneutical culture that aims at the acknowledgement of the inherent freedom of the subject and the dignity of all human beings. This universalism of human rights, developed in the European traditions, cannot renounce to cultural alterity. Through it is assured that cultural pluralism does not simply disintegrate into vague relativism and that the postulated culture of sensibility maintains its capacity to be true. (Metz 1992b)

Christianity cannot expect for its conceptions of the history of salvation and of the order of creation—impregnated with ethical contents—an universal acknowledgement *in the same sense* that a procedural theory of law and morality does with respect to human rights and the principles of the state of the rule of law that it purports to ground, basing itself on the concept of procedural justice (Rawls 1971; Habermas 1992). For this reason, Metz himself understands the universality of the offer of salvation as an "invitation" directed to everyone and not as that universal claim of rational acceptability with which, for instance, rational natural law is presented. Even the polycentric universal church remains, in modern societies, *one* community of interpretation among many, where each one articulates its own conception of salvation, and its own idea of an accomplished life, and that debate among themselves on the interpretation of justice, solidarity, and liberation from misery and humiliation. The Church must internalize this external point of view and appropriate it as a view directed at itself. To this end, it makes use of the ideas developed in the European Enlightenment, precisely those ideas that must prevail as much in democratic multicultural societies as in the relations of acknowledgment—structured in terms of human rights—between the peoples and cultures of this world.

The fundamental rights and principles of the state of the rule of law constitute, in multicultural societies, the points of crystallization for a political culture that includes all citizens, this political culture is, in turn, the foundation for an egalitarian co-existence of different groups and sub-cultures, each possessing their own origin and identity. The *uncoupling between these two levels of integration* is the presupposition that the majority culture no longer exercises the power to define the common political culture, but rather it submits and opens itself to an exchange, free of coercion, with the minority cultures. A comparable situation is that which exists inside the universal polycentric church: in it a common Christian self-understanding must form that stops coinciding with the historically determined Western traditions that represent merely the background against which such traditions take note of their limitations and eurocentric specificity.

But, with respect to its relation with other religions, from Catholic Christianity another type of hermeneutical self-reflection is demanded. Here analogy with a Western world bent on maintaining a de-centered and open attitude towards learning with non-Western cultures breaks down. For that, we presuppose as a common basis certain human rights that presumably enjoy a general and rationally motivated acknowledgment. However, in the dialogic debate between religious and metaphysical views of the world a common conception is lacking of the good that would serve as equivalent to that common legal-moral basis. This dispute must be resolved with full reflexive consciousness that all involved parties move in the same universe of discourse and respect one another as cooperative participants in the search for the ethical-existential truth. For that, a culture of acknowledgment is required whose first principles are derived from the secularized world of the universalism of morality as rational natural law. Thus, in this question, it is the philosophical spirit of the political illustration that offers to theology concepts that allow it to explain the sense of a march towards a polycentric church. I do not say this for the simple haste of wanting to have the reason, but because such political philosophy is marked by the idea of the alliance at least as deeply as it is by the idea of the polis. For this reason I also invoke a biblical inheritance, to which Metz appeals when he reminds the contemporary church that "in the name of its mission" it "search for freedom and justice for all" and that it be guided by "a culture of acknowledgment of others in their different ways of being" (Metz 1987, 118).

Works Cited

Habermas, Jürgen. 1992. *Faktizit und Geltung.* Frankfurt: Suhrkamp Verlan.

―――. 1992a. "Kommunikativen Freiheit und negative Theologie," in E. Angehrn, et al. eds., *Dialektischer Negativismus.* Frankfurt: Suhrkamp Verlag.

Kuschel, K. J., ed. 1990. *Dorothee Sölle und Johann Baptist Metz im Gespräch.* Stuttgarkreuzt.

Metz, Johann Baptist 1992. "Anamnestic Reason: A Theologian's Remarks on the Crisis in the *Geistewissenschafter"* in Axel Honneth, Thomas McCarthy, Claus Ofe, and Albrecht Wellmer, eds. *Cultural-Political Interventions in the Unfinished Project of Enlightenment,* trans. Barbara Fultner. Cambridge: The MIT Press.

―――. 1992a. "Die Rede von Gott angesichts der Leidensgeschichte der Welt," *Stimmen der Zeit,* 5, 247.

―――. 1992b. *Perspetkiven eines multikulturellen Christentum.* Manuscript.

―――. 1986. "Im Aufbruch zu einer kulturell polyzentrischen Welkirche," in *Zeitschrift für Missionwissenschaft un Religionwissenschaft* vol 70, No. 2–3 (1986).

―――. 1984. "Im Angesicht der Juden. christiliche Theologie nach Auschwitz," in *Concilium,* 20, 382–9.

―――. 1984. "Theologie im Angesicht und vor dem Ende der Moderne," in *Concilium,* 20, 14–18.

―――. 1981. *The Emergent Church: The Future of Christianity in a Postbourgeoise World* trans. Peter Mann. New York: Crossroad.

―――. 1980. *Unterbrechungen.* Güterlosher Verlaghaus Mohr.

Rawls, John. 1971. *A Theory of Justice.* Cambridge: Harvard University Press.

Theunissen, M. 1991. *Negative Theologie der Zeit.* Frankfurt: Suhrkamp Verlag.

21

Transcendence from Within, Transcendence in this World

Jürgen Habermas
Translated by Eric Crump and Peter P. Kenny

Allow me to make a personal remark to facilitate the start of a difficult discussion. I have continually responded to objections from my colleagues in philosophy and sociology.[1] Here, I again gladly respond to the criticism of Fred Dallmayr and Robert Wuthnow. Up until now, I have held back from a discussion with theologians; I would also prefer to continue to remain silent. A silence on the grounds of embarrassment would also be justified, for I am not really familiar with the theological discussion, and only reluctantly move about in an insufficiently reconnoitered terrain. On the other hand, for decades theologians both in Germany and in the United States have included me in their discussions. They have referred in general to the tradition of critical theory,[2] and have reacted to my writings.[3] In this situation, silence would be a false response: the person who is addressed and remains silent, clothes himself or herself in an aura of indeterminate significance and imposes silence. For this, Heidegger is one example among many. Because of this authoritarian character, Sartre has rightly called silence "reactionary."

I will start by first ascertaining a few premises under which theologians and philosophers today speak to one another, insofar as they share a self-critical assessment of modernity. Then, I will make an attempt to understand the status and truth claim of theological discourse. Following this, I will take up the most important objections from the theological side and, at the end, take a position on the criticism of the nontheologians in this volume.

Common Premises

From a distance, it is easier to speak about one another than with one another. For sociologists, it is easier to explain religious traditions and their roles from the perspective of an observer than to approach them in a performative stance. For sociologists, as long as they do not step out of their professional role, the change to the stance of an actual participant in religious discourse can only have the methodological sense of a hermeneutical intermediary step. A slightly different situation results for philosophers, at least for one who has grown up at German universities with Fichte, Schelling, and Hegel, including the latter's Marxist legacy. For, from this perspective, there is excluded from the start an approach that would merely objectify Jewish and Christian traditions, especially the speculatively fruitful Jewish and Protestant mysticism of the early modern period as mediated through the Swabian pietism of Bengel and Oetinger. Just as German Idealism with the concept of the Absolute appropriated theoretically the God of creation and of gracious love, it also with a logical reconstruction of the process of the world as a whole appropriated theoretically the traces of salvation history. Also, Kant cannot be understood without recognizing the motive of conceiving the essentially practical contents of the Christian tradition in such a way that these could perdure before the forum of reason. But contemporaries were fully aware of the ambiguity of these attempts at transformation. With the concept of "sublation" [Aufhebung] Hegel included this ambiguity in the dialectical method itself. The sublation of the world of religious representation in the philosophical concept enabled the saving of its essential contents only by casting off the substance of its piety. Certainly, the atheistic core, enveloped in esoteric insight, was reserved for the philosophers. Thus the later Hegel trusted philosophical reason only with the power of *partial* reconciliation. He had given up his hope in the concrete universality of that public religion which—according to the "Oldest System Program"—was to make the people rational and the philosophers sensible. The people are abandoned by their priests, now become philosophers.[4]

The *methodical* atheism of Hegelian philosophy and of all philosophical appropriation of essentially religious contents (which does not assert anything about the personal self-understanding of the philosophical author) became an open scandal only after Hegel's death as the "process of decay of the absolute spirit" (Marx) set in. The right-Hegelians, who to this day have reacted only defensively to this scandal, have yet to furnish a convincing response. For under the conditions of postmetaphysical thinking, it is not enough to take shelter behind a concept of the Absolute which can neither be freed from the concepts of the Hegelian "logic," nor be defended without a reconstruction of Hegelian dialectic that would be insightful *today* and would be joined to our philosophical discourse.[5] Clearly, the Young Hegelians did not recognize with equal acuity that along with fundamental metaphysical concepts, a metaphysically affirmed atheism is also no longer tenable. In whatever form materialism may appear, within the horizon of a scientific, fallibilistic mode of thinking it is a hypothesis which at best can claim plausibility for the present moment.

In our parts of the world, the grounds for a politically motivated atheism or, better, for a militant *laicism* have also, by and large, fallen away. During my time as a student, it was, above all, theologians such as Gollwitzer and Iwand who had given morally responsible answers to the political questions that challenged us after the war. It was the Confessing Church which at that time with its acknowledgment of guilt at least attempted a new beginning. In both confessions, leftist associations were formed, by lay people as well as theologians, who sought to free the church from its comfortable alliances with the power of the state and the existing social conditions. They sought renewal instead of restoration and to establish universal standards of judgment in the public political realm. With this exemplary witness and widely effective change of mentality there arose the model of a religious engagement which broke away from the conventionality and interiority of a merely private confession. With an undogmatic understanding of transcendence and faith, this engagement took seriously this-worldly goals of human dignity and social emancipation. It joined in a multivoiced arena with other forces pressing for radical democratization.

Against the background of a praxis which all would respect, we encounter a critical theology that interprets the self-understanding of this praxis in such a way that it helps express our best moral intuitions without tearing down the bridges to secular languages and cultures. Schüssler Fiorenza's fundamental theology offers a good example of a political theology that is in touch with contemporary investigations in morality and in social theory.[6] He first characterizes in a threefold manner the transformations that both religion and theology undergo under the conditions of postmetaphysical thinking, conditions that have become inescapable in modernity.[7] He emphasizes the uncoupling of a religion which is both interiorized and at the same time open to the secularized world from the explanatory claims of cosmological world views. The *Glaubenslehre* [*The Christian Faith*] in Schleiermacher's sense casts off the character of a cosmological world view. As a consequence of the recognition of the pluralism of religious forces, there ensues a reflective relationship to the particularity of one's own faith within the horizon of the universality of the religious as such. Joined with this is the insight that the ethical approaches which have emerged from the contexts of various world religions agree in the basic principles of a universalist morality. In a further step, Schüssler Fiorenza expounds the limits of a philosophical theory of morality which confines itself to the explanation and the grounding of the moral standpoint. He also discusses subsequent problems which arise from the abstractions of such an ethics of justice.

Since a philosophy which has become self-critical does not trust itself any longer to offer universal assertions about the concrete whole of exemplary forms of life, it must refer those affected to discourses in which they answer their substantial questions themselves. The parties should examine in moral argumentation what is equally good for all. But first they must become clear about what the good is for themselves in their respective contexts. These ethical questions in a stricter sense, concerning a life that is worthwhile [*nichtverfehlten*] or is preferable, can find an answer only in context-dependent discourses of self-understanding. These answers will be more differentiated and more appropriate depending upon how rich the identity-building traditions are that support self-reassurance [*Selbstvergewisserung*]. As Schüssler Fiorenza states using the words of Rawls, the question about one's own identity—who we are and desire to be—requires a "thick concept of the good." Thus each party must bring into the discussion his or her conceptions of the good and preferable life in order to find out with other parties what they all might desire. He suggests a "dialectic between universalizable principles of justice and the reconstructive hermeneutic of normative tradition" and attributes to the churches in modern society the role of being "communities of interpretation in which issues of justice and conceptions of goodness are publicly discussed" (86). Today the ecclesial communities are in competition with other communities of interpretation that are rooted in secular traditions. Even viewed from outside, it could turn out that monotheistic traditions have at their disposal a language whose semantic potential is not yet exhausted [*unabgegoltenen*], that shows itself to be superior in its power to disclose the world and to form identity, in its capability for renewal, its differentiation, and its range.

What I find interesting to observe in this example is that where theological argumentation is pushed so far into the neighborhood of other discourses, the perspectives from within and without meet without restraint. In this sense, I also understand those "correlational methods," which David Tracy employs for the "public theologies" widespread in the United States. These methods have the goal of placing in a relation of mutual critique interpretations of modernity proceeding from philosophical and social-theoretical approaches with theological interpretations of the Christian tradition. Thus, their goal is to bring these interpretations into a relation where arguments are used. This intention is facilitated when the projects of Enlightenment and of theology that Helmut Peukert discusses are described in similar ways from both sides: "The thesis seems plausible to me that the unsolved problem of advanced civilizations is that of mastering the tendency toward power accumulation."[8] Matthew Lamb observes how this tendency becomes critical in modernity and brings forth two false reactions, a romantic one and a historicist one. He pleads for a self-reassurance of modernity which breaks out of the cycle of a pernicious back and forth between nihilistic condemnation and dogmatic self-assertion: "Modern dogmatic self-assertion is profoundly nihilistic, just as modern nihilism is irresponsibly dogmatic."[9] Tracy specifies the concept of reason which guides a diagnosis of this kind. The dual failure of positivism and of the philosophy of consciousness confirms the pragmatic turn that took place from Peirce through Dewey toward a non-fundamentalist concept of communicative reason. At the same time, this concept opposes the conclusions that Rorty and Derrida draw from this failure, whether in the form of a radical contextualism or by way of an aesthetization of theory. Just as strongly, Tracy objects to selective modes of reading that leave out the ambivalent sense of modernization and perceive it merely as the history of the decay of a subject-centered reason that progresses forward in a linear manner and inflates itself up to be the totality. Even in modernity, reason has not withered into instrumental reason: "If understanding is dialogical, it is also . . . both historical and contextual. But . . . [a]ny act of understanding implicitly puts forward a claim to more than subjective understanding. Any act of understanding addresses all others with a claim to its validity—a validity that, in principle, the inquirer is obliged to redeem if challenged."[10]

Tracy draws from this pragmatic insight consequences also for the activity of theology itself which would be disciplined [*wissenschaftliche*] work and in no way simply a gift of faith. Peukert understands the work of theology as a methodically controlled form of religion. Gary Simpson compares the lifeworld, which reproduces itself through communicative action and validity claims that are open to critique, with a "forensically fraught world" and suggests that on the cross even God submits to this forum. Hence, none of the lifeworld's segments can immunize themselves against the demands for an argumentative justification, not even—as I understand the sentence—theology.[11] If this, however, is the *common ground* of theology, science, and philosophy, what then still constitutes the distinctiveness of theological discourse? What separates the internal perspective of theology from the external perspective of those who enter into a dialogue with theology? It cannot be the relation to religious discourses in general, but only the nature of the reference to the discourse conducted within each particular religious community.

The Truth Claim of Theological Discourse

Schüssler Fiorenza appeals to the line of tradition from Schleiermacher down to Bultmann and Niebuhr when he distinguishes a critical theology from neo-Aristotelian and neo-Thomist theologies. The great example of Karl Barth demonstrates, indeed, that the consistent unburdening of theology from metaphysical-cosmological explanatory claims does not mean *eo ipso* the willingness to assert that theological arguments have the power to convince in the debate with scientific discourses. From the Barthian viewpoint, the biblically witnessed event of revelation in its historical facticity rejects a mode of argumentation based on reason alone.[12] In the Protestant-shaped milieu of German universities, theological faculties have always enjoyed a special status. The young history of the University of Frankfurt dramatically shows this tension. When in the 1920s theological lectureships were to be introduced there, controversies broke out which could then only be settled by refusing to recognize the Catholic, Protestant, and Jewish subjects of study as specifically *theological* teaching. At this university, which grew out of a business college, it is interesting that in its social science atmosphere personalities such as Steinbüchel, Buber, and Tillich were able to establish themselves. It was thus political theologians in the broadest sense who could move about with ease in the discourses of the humanities and the social sciences.[13] In the Federal Republic of Germany, if I am right, it was primarily a group of Catholic theologians who, having always maintained a less troubled relation to the *lumen naturale*, were able to draw upon this tradition. Yet, the more that theology opens itself in general to the discourses of the human sciences, the greater is the danger that its own status will be lost in the network of alternating takeover attempts.

The *religious* discourse conducted within the communities of the faithful takes place in the context of a specific tradition with substantive norms and an elaborated dogmatics. It refers to a common ritual praxis and bases itself on the specifically religious experiences of the individual. It is, however, more than the non-objectifying, hermeneutically understanding reference to religious discourse and to the experiences underlying this discourse that characterizes theology. For the same would hold for a philosophy which understands itself as the critical appropriation and transformation, as the retrieval, of essential religious contents in the universe of argumentative discourse. This Hegelian self-understanding of philosophy has also not been abandoned by the materialistic students of Hegel. It lives on especially in Bloch, Benjamin, and in critical theory. True, Hegel was the last in an idealistic tradition that upheld the claim of metaphysics in a transformed shape, and completed the philosophical appropriation of the Judeo-Christian tradition as much as was possible under the conditions of metaphysical thinking. Hegel's philosophy is the result of that great experiment, crucially defining European intellectual history, which sought to produce a synthesis between the faith of Israel and the Greek spirit—a synthesis that, on the one side, led to the Hellenization of Christianity and, on the other, to the ambiguous Christianization of Greek metaphysics. The dialectical God of the philosophers allows the alter ego of prayer to fade away into anonymous thoughts of the Absolute. At least since Kierkegaard, this synthesis has become fragile, because it has been put into question from *both* sides.

In the same way as Adorno's philosophical critique, the theological protest of Johann Baptist Metz is directed against the fundamental concepts of a metaphysics which, even when they have been dialectically set in motion, remain too rigid to be able to retrieve rationally those experiences of redemption, universal alliance, and irreplaceable individuality which have been articulated in the language of the Judeo-Christian history of salvation without truncating them and reducing the fullness of their specific meanings. Metz insists with Benjamin upon the anamnestic constitution of reason and wants to understand the faith of Israel also from its own historical spirit.[14] Adorno circumscribes the non-identical and seeks to think with the aid of concepts beyond all objectifying concepts, because he follows the same impulse: to save intuitions that have not been exhausted in philosophy. Here it is the experience of an equality that does not level out difference and of a togetherness that individualizes. It is the experience of a closeness across distance to an other acknowledged in his or her difference. It is the experience of a combination of autonomy and self-surrender, a reconciliation which does not extinguish the differences, a future-oriented justice that is in solidarity with the unreconciled suffering of past generations. It is the experience of the reciprocity of freely granted acknowledgment, of a relationship in which a subject is associated to another without being submitted to the degrading violence of exchange—a derisive violence that allows for the happiness and power of the one only at the price of the unhappiness and powerlessness of the other.

If, however, this *anti-Platonic turn* takes place on both sides, then it cannot be the postmetaphysical kind of reference to religious discourse that today separates philosophy from a theology open to conversation. Rather, under the conditions of postmetaphysical thought another difference, which was surrounded by ambiguities up until Hegel, clearly emerges: methodical atheism in the manner of the philosophical reference to the contents of religious experience. Philosophy cannot appropriate what is talked about in religious discourse *as* religious experiences. These experiences could only be added to the fund of philosophy's resources, recognized as philosophy's own basis of experience, if philosophy identifies these experiences using a description that is no longer borrowed from the language of a specific religious tradition, but from the universe of argumentative discourse that is uncoupled from the event of revelation. At those fracture points where a neutralizing translation of this type can no longer succeed, philosophical discourse must confess its failure. The metaphorical use of words such as "redemption," "messianic light," "restoration of nature," etc., makes religious experience a mere citation. In these moments of its powerlessness, argumentative speech passes over beyond religion and science into literature, into a mode of presentation that is no longer directly measured by truth claims. In an analogical way, theology also loses its identity if it only cites religious experiences, and under the descriptions of religious discourse no longer acknowledges them as its own basis. Therefore, I hold that a conversation cannot succeed between a theology and a philosophy which use the language of religious authorship and which meet on the bridge of religious experiences that have become literary expressions.

Admittedly, theology which wants to subject itself without reservation to scientific argumentation, as Tracy and Peukert emphasize, will not be satisfied with the limiting criterion that I have proposed. What does "methodical atheism" really mean? To answer this question, I would like to digress a moment.

Religious discourse is closely joined to a ritual praxis that, in comparison with profane everyday praxis, is limited in the degree of its freedom of communication in a specific way. If a functionalist description is permitted, then it could be said that faith is protected against a radical problematization by its being rooted in cult. This problematization unavoidably occurs when the ontic, normative, and expressive aspects of validity, which must remain fused together in the conception of the creator and redeemer God, of theodicy, and of the event of salvation, are separated analytically from one another.[15] Theological discourse, however, distinguishes itself from religious by separating itself from ritual praxis in the act of explaining it, for example that it *interprets* sacraments such as baptism or the eucharist. Theology for its assertions also aspires to a truth claim that is differentiated from the spectrum of the other validity claims. Yet, beyond the measure of uncertainty that all reflection brings as it intrudes upon practical knowledge, theology did not present a danger to the faith of the community as long as it used the basic concepts of metaphysics. Indeed, these metaphysical concepts were immune to a differentiation of the aspects of validity in a fashion similar to the basic religious concepts. This situation only changed with the collapse of metaphysics. Under the conditions of postmetaphysical thinking, whoever puts forth a truth claim today must, nevertheless, translate experiences that have their home in religious discourse into the language of a scientific expert culture—and from this language retranslate them back into praxis.

This task of translation demanded by critical theology can be formally compared with that which modern philosophy also has to undertake. For philosophy stands in a similarly intimate relationship to common sense which it reconstructs and at the same time undermines. In the opposite direction, philosophy functions in the role of an interpreter that should carry essential contents of the expert culture back into everyday praxis. This task of mediation is not free of a certain paradox, because in the expert cultures knowledge is treated under respectively separate aspects of validity, whereas in everyday praxis *all* linguistic functions and aspects of validity are interwoven and form a syndrome.[16] Nevertheless, philosophy, in a way, has an easier task dealing with common sense, from which it lives and which it at the same time reforms, than does theology with the religious discourses given to it. Today, between these discourses and profane everyday praxis, there is certainly no longer the same distance that once existed between the sacred and the profane spheres of life—and this distance even continues to decrease as the ideas of a "public theology" gain acceptance. But against the reform to which common sense is subject in modern societies, whether with the assistance of philosophers or not, that syndrome of revelation faith, held together in ritualized praxis, still forms a specific barrier. For religious discourses would lose their identity if they were to open themselves up to a type of interpretation which no longer allows the religious experiences to be valid *as* religious.

One must expect, after all, such a far-reaching problematization if theological discourse no longer chooses either of the two premises that are characteristic of modern theology. After Kierkegaard, theology has either taken the "Protestant path" and appealed to the kerygma and faith as a source of religious insight absolutely independent of reason, or has chosen the path of "enlightened Catholicism" in the sense that it relinquishes the status of a special discourse and exposes its assertions to the whole range of scientific discussion. Admittedly, it does this without renouncing the acknowledgment of the experiences articulated in the language of the Judeo-Christian tradition as its *own* base of experience. It is this reservation alone which permits a distanciation from the language game of religious discourses without invalidating it. It leaves the religious language game intact. The third way, however, is characterized by what I have called "methodical atheism." It is this way that leads to a program of demythologization that is tantamount to an experiment. Without reservation it is left to the realization of this program to see whether the theological (not just a history of religions) interpretation of the religious discourses by virtue of its argumentation alone permits a joining to the scientific discussion in such a manner that the religious language game remains intact, or collapses. I see the "political dogmatics" of the Copenhagen theologian Jens Glebe-Möller as an example of such an experiment.

Building upon the theoretical approaches of Apel, Döbert, and myself and supported by a discourse ethics, Glebe-Möller subjects the Christian dogmas to a demythologizing interpretation, which recalls for me a saying of Hugo Ball: God is the freedom of the lowliest in the spiritual communication of all. Glebe-Möller interprets baptism, the eucharist, the imitation of Christ, the role of the church, and eschatology in the sense of a theology of liberation based on a theory of communication, which opens up the Bible in a fascinating (for me, also convincing) way, even in those passages that have become foreign to modern ears. But I ask myself *who* recognizes himself or herself in this interpretation.

Does the Christian language game remain intact if one understands the idea of God in the way that Glebe-Möller proposes it? "The thought of a personified divine power necessarily involves heteronomy, and this is an idea that goes directly against the modern concept of human autonomy. A political dogmatic in the modern context must therefore be atheistic. But this does not mean that there is no thinking about God or that the thought of God is emptied of all content."[17] Taking up a reflection of Peukert's, he explains this as follows:

If we desire to hold on to solidarity with everyone else in the communicative fellowship, even the dead . . . then we must claim a reality that can reach beyond the here and how, or that can connect our selves beyond our own death with those who went innocently to their destruction before us. And it is this reality that the Christian tradition calls God. (110)

But in contrast to Peukert, Glebe-Möller insists on an *atheistic version* of this idea in that he poses the question:

But are we not then back at the point where only faith in a divine deliverance can rescue us—where, with Peukert, we have to reintroduce the thought of God? I continue to be convinced that we are today unable to think that thought. This means that the guilt remains in effect. Instead of resigning ourselves to it, however, we must make the consciousness of guilt into something positive, something that spurs us to fight against the conditions that have produced the guilt. That can happen when we hold fast to our solidarity with all who have suffered and died, now and before. This solidarity or fellowship contains within itself a "messianic" power that transforms any passive consciousness of guilt into an active struggle against the conditions for guilt—just as it was when Jesus, who, two thousand years ago, forgave sinners and set people free to continue that struggle.

But *can* we be in solidarity? In the last analysis, we can be nothing else, for solidarity—the ideal communicative fellowship—is presupposed in everything we say and do! (112)

Theological Objections

The theologians who in this volume have entered into a dialogue with me would hardly want to be bound to one of the three alternatives that I have named. They want to follow the path of radical demythologizations as little as they want to follow the classical Protestant path which in our century led to Karl Barth. Yet these same theologians may not consider valid for themselves the reservation that I associated with the characterization and the name of "enlightened Catholicism." For settling on a basis of experience which remains bound *a priori* to the language of a specific tradition signifies a particularistic limitation of the truth claims of theology. Yet, as truth claims they extend beyond all merely local contexts—and for David Tracy this is not open to negotiation. Consistent with this, my theological dialogue partners therefore choose the indirect procedure of apologetic argumentation and attempt to force the secular opponent into a corner by way of an immanent critique such that the opponent can find a way out of the aporias demonstrated only by conceding the theologically defended affirmations.

Helmut Peukert masterfully employs this technique in his major investigation, *Science, Action, and Fundamental Theology*.[18] He first of all criticizes, as does David Tracy, the one-sided, functionalist description that I gave of religion in *The Theory of Communicative Action*. Even in traditional societies, the world religions do *not* function *exclusively* as a legitimation of governmental authority: "in their origin and in their core, they are often protest movements against the basic trend of a society's development and attempt to ground other ways for human beings to relate to one another and to reality as a whole."[19] I will not dispute this. I would also admit that I subsumed rather too hastily the development of religion in modernity with Max Weber under the "privatization of the powers of faith" and suggested too quickly an affirmative answer to the question as to "whether then from religious truths, after the religious world views have collapsed, nothing more and nothing other than the secular principles of a universalist ethics of responsibility can be salvaged, and this means: can be accepted for good reasons, on the basis of insight."[20] This question has to *remain open* from the view of the social scientist who proceeds reconstructively and who is careful not simply to project developing trends forward in a straight line. It must also remain open from the viewpoint of the philosopher who appropriates tradition and who in a performative stance has the experience that intuitions which had long been articulated in religious language can neither be rejected nor simply retrieved rationally—as I have shown with the example of the concept of individuality.[21] The process of a critical appropriation of the essential contents of religious tradition is still underway and the outcome is difficult to predict. I willingly repeat my position: "As long as religious language bears with itself inspiring, indeed, unrelinquishable semantic contents which elude (for the moment?) the expressive power of a philosophical language and still await translation into a discourse that gives reasons for its positions, philosophy, even in its postmetaphysical form, will neither be able to replace nor to repress religion."[22]

This still does not imply any agreement with Peukert's thesis that the discourse theory of morality and ethics gets so entangled in limit questions that it finds itself in need of a theological foundation. Of course, effective socializing or pedagogical praxis, which under the aegis of an anticipated autonomy [*Mündigkeit*] seeks to provoke freedom in the other, must take into account the appearance of circumstances and spontaneous forces that it cannot at the same time control. And, with an orientation toward unconditional moral expectations, the subject increases the degree of his or her vulnerability. This then makes the subject especially dependent upon a considerate moral treatment from other persons. Yet, the risk of failure, indeed, of the annihilation of freedom precisely in the processes that should promote and realize freedom, only attests to the constitution of our finite existence. I refer to the necessity, which Peirce emphasized again and again, of a self-relinquishing, transcending anticipation of an unlimited community of communication. This anticipation is simultaneously conceded to us and demanded of us. In communicative action, we orient ourselves toward validity claims that, practically, we can raise only in the context of *our* languages and of our forms of life, even if the convertibility

[*Einlösbarkeit*] that we implicitly co-posit *points beyond* the provinciality of our respective historical standpoints. We are exposed to the movement of a transcendence from within, which is just as little at our disposal as the actuality of the spoken word turns us into masters of the structure of language (or of the Logos). The anamnestically constituted reason, which Metz and Peukert, rightly, continually advocate in opposition to a Platonically reduced communicative reason that is insensitive to the temporal dimension, confronts us with the conscientious question about deliverance for the annihilated victims. In this way we become aware of the limits of that transcendence from within which is directed to this world. But this does not enable us to ascertain the *counter-movement* of a compensating transcendence from beyond.

That the universal covenant of fellowship would be able to be effective retro-actively, toward the past, only in the weak medium of our memory, of the remembrance of the living generations, and of the anamnestic witnesses handed down falls short of our moral need. But the painful experience of a deficit is still not a sufficient argument for the assumption of an "absolute freedom which saves in death."[23] The postulate of a God "which is outlined in temporal, finite, self-transcending intersubjective action in the form of a hopeful expectation [*Erwartung*]"[24] relies upon an experience that is either recognized as such in the language of religious discourse—or loses its evidence. Peukert himself resorts to an experience *accessible only in the language of the Christian tradition*, inter-woven inseparably with religious discourse: that with the death on the cross, the disastrous web of evil has been broken. Without this "anticipatory" [*zuvorkommende*] goodness of God, a solidarity among human beings who acknowledge one another unconditionally remains without the guarantee of an outcome that extends beyond the individual act and the moment of illumination this ignites in the eye of the other. It is, indeed, true that whatever human beings succeed in doing they owe to those rare constellations in which their own powers are able to be joined with the favorableness of the historical moment. But the experience that we are dependent upon this favorableness is still no license for the assumption of a divine promise of salvation.

Charles Davis takes up the same apologetic figure of thought when he wants to show that the moral viewpoint implied in the structure of a praxis directed toward reaching agreement, as well as the perspective of living together in solidarity and justice, remain ungrounded without a foundation in Christian hope: "A secular hope without religion cannot affirm with certainty . . . a future fulfillment."[25] Once again I do not see why a *superadditum* is indispensable in order that we would endeavor to act according to moral commands and ethical insights as long as these require something that is objectively possible. It is true that a philosophy that thinks postmetaphysically cannot answer the question that Tracy also calls attention to: why be moral at all? At the same time, however, this philosophy can show why this question does not arise meaningfully for communicatively socialized individuals. We acquire our moral intuitions in our parents' home, not in school. And moral insights tell us that we do not have any good reasons for behaving otherwise: for this, no self-surpassing of morality is necessary. It is true that we often behave otherwise, but we do so with a bad conscience. The first half of the sentence attests to the weakness of the motivational power of good reasons; the second half attests that rational motivation by reasons is more than nothing [*auch nicht nichts ist*]—moral convictions do not allow themselves to be overridden without resistance.

All of this does not yet treat that struggle against the conditions that have caused us to fail again and again. Glebe-Möller, Davis, Peukert, and others have in view not only the observance of concrete obligations. They also seek a far-reaching engagement for the abolition of unjust conditions and the promotion of forms of life that would not only make solidary action more likely but first make it possible for this action to be reasonably expected. Who or what gives us the courage for such a total engagement that in situations of deprivation and degradation is already being expressed when the destitute and deprived summon the energy each morning to carry on anew? The question about the meaning of life is not meaningless. Nevertheless, the circumstance that penultimate arguments inspire no great confidence is not enough for the grounding of a hope that can be kept alive only in a religious language. The thoughts and expectations directed toward the common good have, after metaphysics has collapsed, only an unstable status. In the place of an Aristotelian politics and a Hegelian philosophy of history, a post-Marxist social theory that has become more humble has appeared. This social theory attempts to exhaust the potential for argumentation in the human sciences in order to contribute to assertions about the genesis, constitution, and ambivalent development of modernity. These diagnoses, even if they are somewhat reliably grounded, remain controversial. Above all they perform a critical service. They can take apart the mutual prejudices of affirmative theories of progress and of negativist theories of decline, of patchwork ideologies and premature totalizations. But, in the passage through the discursive universes of science and philosophy, not even the Peircean hope in a fallible theory of the development of being as a whole, including that of the *summum bonum*, will be able to be realized. Kant had already answered the question "What may be hoped for?" with a *postulate* of practical reason, not with a premodern certainty that could inspire us with *confidence*.

I believe to have shown that in communicative action we have no choice but to presuppose the idea of an undistorted intersubjectivity. This, again, can be understood as the formal characterization of the necessary conditions for the forms, not able to be anticipated, of a worthwhile life. There is no theory for these totalities themselves. Certainly, praxis requires encouragement; it is inspired by intuitive anticipations of the whole. There is an intuition that impresses me deeply which I have occasionally formulated: If historical progress consists in lessening, abolishing, or preventing the suffering of vulnerable creatures, and if historical experience teaches that on the heels of advances finally achieved, consuming disaster closely follows, then there are grounds for supposing that the balance of what can be endured remains intact only if we give our utmost for the sake of the possible advances.[26] Perhaps it is such assumptions which, indeed, can give no confidence for a praxis whose certainties have been taken away, yet can still leave it some hope.

To reject apologetic figures of thought is one thing; it is another thing to learn from the worthy objections of my theological colleagues. I leave aside here the reservations that David Tracy brings forth against approaches based on an evolutionary theory and shall concentrate on his thesis that dialogue, and not argumentation, offers the more encompassing approach for the investigation of communicative action.

Argumentative discourse is certainly the more specialized form of communication. In it, validity claims, which previously remained implicit because they arose performatively, are expressly thematized. Therefore, they have a reflexive character that requires the more exacting presuppositions of communication. The presuppositions of action oriented toward reaching understanding are more easily accessible in argumentation. This preference as part of a research strategy does not imply an ontological distinction, as if argumentation would be more important or even more fundamental than conversation or the communicative everyday praxis constituted in the lifeworld. This everyday praxis forms the most encompassing horizon. In this sense, even the analysis of speech acts enjoys only a heuristic preference. This analysis of speech acts forms the key for a pragmatic analysis which, as Tracy rightly insists, must comprise the entire spectrum of the world of symbolic forms: symbols and images, indicators and expressive gestures, as well as relations of similarity. Thus, it must extend to all signs that lie beneath the level of propositionally differentiated speech, signs that can represent semantic contents even if they have no author who bestows meaning upon them. The semiotics of Charles S. Peirce has made accessible this archaeology of signs. The richness of this theory is far from being exhausted; this is also true for an aesthetics that points out the world-disclosing function of works of art in their speechless materiality.

Tracy repeats the criticism concerning the reductions of an expressivistic aesthetics which *The Theory of Communicative Action* at least suggested. In the meantime, in response to the works of Albrecht Wellmer and Martin Seel,[27] I have corrected this.[28] Although an innovative world-disclosing power belongs to both prophetic speech as well as to art that has become autonomous, I would hesitate to name religious and aesthetic symbols in the same breath. I am certain that David Tracy in no way wants to suggest an aesthetic understanding of the religious. Aesthetic experience has become an integral component of the modern world in that it has become independent as a cultural sphere of value. Religion would be stabilized by a similar differentiation into a social subsystem specialized, as Niklas Luhmann holds, in coping with contingency, but only at the price of the complete neutralization of its experiential content. In opposition to this, political theology also fights for a public role for religion and precisely in modern societies. Yet then religious symbolism should not conform to the aesthetic, that is, to the forms of expression of an expert culture, but must maintain its *holistic* position in the lifeworld.

Furthermore, I take very seriously Peukert's warning to take into account the temporal dimensions of action that is oriented toward reaching understanding. Nevertheless, phenomenological analyses in the style of *Being and Time* cannot simply be transplanted into a theory of communication. Possibly, Peirce's semiotics offers a better and, until now, unused entry point. Karl-Otto Apel and I have, up to now, appropriated only the fundamental insight of his theory of truth, that a transcending power dwells within validity claims which assures a relation to the future for every speech act: "Thus thought is rational only so far as it recommends itself to a possible future thought. Or in other words the rationality of thought lies in its reference to a possible future."[29] But the young Peirce had already given an interesting reference to the ability of the sign process to establish continuity. In epistemological contexts, he ascribes to the individual symbol the power to produce that continuity in the flow of our experiences that Kant wanted to ascertain through the accompanying "I-think" of transcendental apperception. Because the individual experience itself assumes the threefold structure of a sign that refers simultaneously to a past object and to a future interpretant, this experience can come into a semantic relation to other experiences across temporal distances and thus establish a temporal connection upon a diversity which otherwise, as in a kaleidoscope, would fall apart.[30] In this way, Peirce explains temporal relations that are only first produced through the structure of signs. The medium of language could borrow from this semiotic structure its dynamic of temporalization that is unfolded in the continuities of tradition.

Finally, I respond to the objections that are not motivated by specifically theological considerations.

Response to the Nontheologians

1. Sheila Briggs makes distinctions within the paradigm of praxis philosophy that I find plausible. However, I still do not quite see how under her premises one can reach the type of dialogical ethics that will ground the universal accountability and the integrity of the particular identity of each person without claiming the universalist viewpoints of equality and justice. Seyla Benhabib, on whose works Briggs supports her feminist critique, also remains faithful to the

universalist intentions of Kant and Hegel. Benhabib develops her conception thoroughly in agreement with me:

> While agreeing that normative disputes can be rationally settled, and that fairness, reciprocity, and some procedure of universalizability are constituents, that is necessary conditions of the moral standpoint, interactive universalism regard difference as a starting point for reflection and action. In this sense "universality" is a regulative ideal that does not deny our embodied and embedded identity, but aims at developing moral attitudes and encouraging political transformations that can yield a view acceptable to all. Universality is not the ideal consensus of fictitiously defined selves, but the concrete process in politics and morals of the struggle of concrete, embodied selves, striving for autonomy.[31]

Nevertheless, Benhabib questions the limitation of moral argumentation to problems of justice, because she believes that the logical distinction between questions of justice and questions about the good life is based on or, at least, corresponds to the sociological distinction between the public and private spheres. A morality curtailed legalistically, so she thinks, would have to restrict itself to questions of political justice. All private relations and personal spheres of life, which a patriarchal society leaves principally to women, are then excluded *per definitionem* from the sphere of responsibility of morality. This assumption, however, is not correct. For the logical distinction between problems of justice and of the good life is independent from the sociological distinction between spheres of life. We make a *moral* use of practical reason when we ask what is equally good for everyone; we make an *ethical* use when we ask what is respectively good for me or for us. Questions of justice permit under the moral viewpoint what all could will: answers that in principle are universally valid. Ethical questions, on the other hand, can be rationally clarified only in the context of a specific life-history or a particular form of life. For these questions are perspectively focused on the individual or on a specific collective who want to know who they are and, at the same time, who they want to be. Such processes of self-understanding distinguish themselves from moral argumentation in the way they pose the question, not however, in the gender-specific location of their themes.

That certainly does not mean that in moral questions we have to abstract from the concrete other. Briggs and Benhabib distinguish between two perspectives according to whether we respectively consider all those concerned in their entirety, or the particular individual in his or her situation. In moral argumentation, both perspectives must come into play. But they have to be intertwined. In *justification discourses* [*Begründungsdiskursen*], practical reason becomes effective through a principle of universalization, while individual cases are considered only as illustrative examples. Justified norms, admittedly, can claim only *prima facie* validity. Which norm in the individual case is held to be the most appropriate and, to that extent, has precedence over other, likewise *prima facie* valid norms cannot be decided in the same way. This application of norms requires instead a discourse of another type. Such *application discourses* [*Anwendungsdiskurse*] follow a logic different than that for justification discourses. Here, in fact, it is a question of the concrete other in the context of the respective given circumstances, the particular social relationships, the unique identity and life-history. Which norm is respectively the *appropriate* one can only be judged in the light of a description of all the relevant features that is as complete as possible.[32] If there is anything to hold against Lawrence Kohlberg, against whom Benhabib advances considerations from Carol Gilligan, then it is not his explanation of the moral principle on the basis of the process of the ideal role-taking, an explanation based upon George Herbert Mead, but his neglect of the problem of application.

2. At this point, I can react only with a few remarks to the very thoughtful, but rather allusively presented criticism of Robert Wuthnow. A great deal of hermeneutical preparatory work would probably be necessary on both sides. Wuthnow is uneasy about the whole undertaking of a critical theory of society that reflexively retrieves, in a way, its context of origin, and which relies upon a rational potential found in the linguistic medium of socialization itself.[33] He does not keep separate the different analytical levels and does not bear in mind the methodical difference between a formal-pragmatically performed theory of language, of argumentation, and of action, on the one hand, and a sociological theory of action and of systems, on the other hand. He does not distinguish between the concept of the lifeworld employed formal-pragmatically or sociologically. He also does not distinguish between a discourse theory of truth, of morality, and of justice which proceeds normatively, on the one hand, empirically substantive attempts at reconstruction that have a descriptive claim, on the other hand. This theoretical framework is certainly not unproblematic. But I don't see how his *ad hoc* objections can be properly discussed if there is not a closer understanding of the architectural plan.

For example, it is not the case that I oppose a radiant future to a devalued past. The proceduralist concept of rationality that I propose cannot sustain utopian projects for concrete forms of life as a whole. The theory of society within which my analyses take place can at best lead to diagnostic descriptions which allow the ambivalence of contrary tendencies of development to emerge more clearly. It is not a case of idealizing the future; if anything, in *The Structural Transformation of the Public Sphere*, there was on my part an idealization of the past.

It is correct that I advocate a pragmatic theory of meaning according to which a hearer understands an expression when he or she knows the conditions under which it can be accepted as valid. The basic idea is simple: one understands an expression only if one knows how one could utilize it in order to come to an understanding with anyone about something in the world. This internal relation between the process of reaching agreement and rationality is inferred from the methodically assumed attitude of a virtual participant. But from here there is no direct path that leads to a social-scientific rationalism which remains deaf to "personal freedom, willful violations of established norms, pluralism, and nonreductive modes of expressivity."[34] Wuthnow can recognize in communicative rationality, which is inherent in the medium of language, only an extension of instrumental rationality. In doing this, he is relying upon the analyses that were put forth at the beginning of the first volume of *The Theory of Communicative Action*, namely, that of the use of propositional knowledge in affirmations, on the one hand, and purposive-rational actions, on the other hand. He does not take into consideration that these two model cases form merely the starting point for a progressively expanded analysis. By the way, I consider information [*Mitteilung*] and norm-regulated action (as also expressive self-presentation) only as limit cases of communicative action. The contrast between an innovative and idiosyncratic use of language serves only the explanation of the use of evaluative expressions.

All these things must first be set right before Wuthnow's interesting remark concerning a resacralization of the lifeworld could be discussed. That is probably the real point of dispute: whether the liberation of everyday praxis from alienation and colonialization is to be described more in the sense that I hold, as a rationalization of the lifeworld, or in the sense of Odo Marquard as a "reenchantment."[35]

3. Fred Dallmayr's paper on "Critical Theory and Reconciliation" presents me with some difficulties. With great understanding Dallmayr traces important religious background motifs in Horkheimer and Adorno's *Dialectic of Enlightenment* as well as in Adorno's later philosophy. He analyses in a manner similar to my own the aporias in which critical theory gets entangled. Against this background, he then subjects *The Theory of Communicative Action* to an astonishingly prejudiced critique. It is astonishing for the reason that Dallmayr is thoroughly acquainted with my writings. For decades, he has commented upon my publications not uncritically, but rather with great sensitivity and a comprehensive knowledge of the German discussion and its context.[36]

Dallmayr has set the course for the present dispute in an interesting essay on the question: "Is Critical Theory a Humanism?" In it the expression "humanism" is used pejoratively as with Heidegger and means as much as anthropocentrism. Dallmayr thinks that I merely exchange the transcendental subject for a quasi-transcendental intersubjectivity. To him, the linguistic turn of critical theory only veils the fact that beyond language subjectivity is reinstated in its Cartesian rights:

Habermas's outlook . . . can with some legitimacy be described as a "human-ism"—where this term stands for a more or less man- or subject-focused orientation. The distinctions between empiricism and hermeneutics, system and lifeworld and propositional and reflexive speech can, without undue violence, be reconciled with the Cartesian and Kantian subject-object bifurcation [and thus with the basic framework of metaphysics).[37]

This focus, naturally, must surprise an author who, in his own understanding, has pursued the pragmatic-linguistic turn as the critique of any form of a philosophy of the subject—certainly with enough caution as not to fall from the frying pan of subject-centered reason into the fire of a history of Being circumscribed by a negative metaphysics. Precisely this anti-Heideggerian accent to the paradigm shift might provoke Dallmayr into disavowing the paradigm shift itself.

This is especially difficult for me to understand in view of a book like *The Philosophical Discourse of Modernity*, in which I develop the new paradigm of the process of understanding from its context in the history of philosophy. My intention is to show how one can avoid the traps of the philosophy of the subject without entangling oneself at the same time in the aporias of a self-referential and totalizing critique of reason—neither in the deconstructionist version of the late Heideggerians nor in the contextualistic version of the late Wittgensteinians.[38] Since the argumentative substance of the third, critical part of Dallmayr's contribution is not sufficient for an extensive debate, I limit myself to a few cursory remarks.

A. Dallmayr supports his assertion of a "continuity" between the paradigm of the process of understanding and that of the subject-object relation with the point that speech acts demonstrate the same teleological structure as do purposive activities.[39] Yet, as I have argued elsewhere, the teleological language game has a different meaning in the theory of language than in the theory of action.[40] The same fundamental concepts are respectively interpreted in each case in a different sense—and, indeed, interpreted differently in a sense that is relevant for our question. In contrast to teleological actions, speech acts are directed toward illocutionary goals, which do not have the status of a purpose that is to be realized *innerworldly*. These goals also cannot be realized without the *uncoerced* cooperation and agreement of the one addressed and, finally, can be explained only through recourse to the concept of reaching agreement that is *inherent* in the medium of language itself. As opposed to teleological actions, speech acts in addition interpret themselves on the basis of their twofold illocutionary-propositional structure itself: by performing speech acts, one states at the same time what one does.

B. Dallmayr believes further that the theory of speech acts privileges the role of the speaker and does not take into account the accomplishments of the hearer (143). The opposite is the case for an analysis which insists (against Searle) that every action of speech remains incomplete without the "Yes" or "No" response of a potential hearer. The hearer must take the position of a second person, give up the perspective of an observer in favor of that of a participant, and enter into a lifeworld that is intersubjectively shared by a linguistic community if he or she wants to take advantage of the characteristic reflexivity of natural language. This thoroughly hermeneutical conception of language is directed against the theoreticism of the causalistic model of linguistic understanding shared by Quine, Davidson, and others.

C. Dallmayr then emphasizes the complementarity of speaking and silence: "language . . . reverberates with its own silence" (143). This reference to the ontological "unfathomability" of language clearly remains in needs of further elaboration beyond the mystical language allusions of the later Heidegger. If Dallmayr does not want to withdraw from the start the phenomenon of silence from an analysis of language, he can make use of my theory of communication: nonauratic silence draws from the specific context a more or less unmistakable meaning. Moreover, every speech act is, of course, situated, and every speech situation is embedded in an intersubjectively shared lifeworld context, which silently wreathes what is spoken in a mute presence.[41]

D. Furthermore, Dallmayr accuses me of having an instrumentalist conception of language (142ff.). This linguistic empiricism has already been overcome by Hamann and Humboldt. I, too, do not develop my theory of communication from Locke, but from hermeneutics and from American pragmatism. Clearly, the act of naming, which from the Romantic philosophy of language up to Benjamin has played a paradigmatic role (a role rich in associations with respect to Christian speculations about the Logos), has proved to be a rather one-sided model for the explanation of linguistically creative powers. In a strict interpretation, it leads to a conception of language based upon a semantics of reference. According to it, expressions should represent states of affairs in the same way that a name stands for an object—which is false. Just as incorrect is the speculative interpretation of the model of naming, which hypostatizes the constitutive, i.e., world-disclosing power of language and thereby neglects the relevance of the validity of language-enabled practices in the world (the confrontation with whatever is encountered in the world).

E. Finally, Dallmayr blames me for the restoration of a "shallow" (as it was called in Germany until 1945) Enlightenment Rationalism (132ff.). The shallow and the profound have their own pitfalls. I have always attempted to steer between the Scylla of a leveling, transcendence-less empiricism and the Charybdis of a high-flying idealism that glorifies transcendence. I hope to have learned much from Kant, and still I have not become a Dallmayrian Kantian because the theory of communicative action *integrates* the transcendental tension between the intelligible and the world of appearances in communicative everyday praxis, yet does not thereby *level* it out. The Logos of language founds the intersubjectivity of the lifeworld, in which we find ourselves already preunderstood, in order that we can encounter one another face to face as subjects. Indeed, we meet as subjects who impute to each other accountability, that is, the capability to guide our actions according to transcending validity claims. At the same time, the lifeworld reproduces itself through the medium of our communicative action which are to be accounted for by us. Yet, this does not mean that the lifeworld would be at our disposal. As agents of communicative action, we are exposed to a transcendence that is integrated in the linguistic conditions of reproduction without being *delivered up* to it. This conception can hardly be identified with the productivist illusion of a species that generates itself and which puts itself in the place of a disavowed Absolute. Linguistic intersubjectivity goes beyond the subjects without putting them in *bondage* [*hörig*]. It is not a higher-level subjectivity and therefore, without sacrificing a transcendence from within, it can do without the concept of an Absolute. We can dispense with this legacy of Hellenized Christianity as well as with any subsequent right-Hegelian constructions, upon which Dallmayr still seems to rely.

Notes

1. See my "A Postscript to *Knowledge and Human Interests,*" in *Philosophy of the Social Sciences* 3 (1975): 157–89, as well as my replies in John B. Thompson and David Held, eds., *Habermas: Critical Debates* (Cambridge, Mass.: MIT Press, 1982); Richard J. Bernstein, ed., *Habermas and Modernity* (Cambridge, Mass.: MIT Press, 1985); and Axel Honneth and Hans Joas, eds., *Kommunikatives Handeln* (Frankfurt am Main: Suhrkamp, 1986) [Axel Honneth and Hans Joas, eds., *Communicative Action* (Cambridge, Mass.: MIT Press, 1990)].
2. Hans-Georg Geyer, Hans-Norbert Janowski, and Alfred Schmidt, *Theologie und Soziologie* (Stuttgart: Kohlhammer, 1970); Rodolf J. Siebert, *The Critical Theory of Religion: The Frankfurt School* (Berlin/New York/Amsterdam: Mouton, 1985).
3. See the impressive bibliography compiled by Edmund Arens in *Habermas und die Theologie. Beiträge zur theologischen Rezeption, Diskussion und Kritik der Theorie kommunikativen Handelns*, ed. Edmund Arens (Düsseldorf: Patmos, 1989), 9–38.
4. Jürgen Habermas, *The Philosophical Discourse of Modernity*, trans. Frederick Lawrence (Cambridge, Mass.: MIT Press, 1987), 35–41; see also Karl Löwith, "Hegels Aufhebung der christlichen Religion," in Karl Löwith, *Vorträge und Abhandlungen. Zur Kritik der christlichen Überlieferung* (Stuttgart: Kohlhammer, 1966), 54–96.
5. This appears to me to be the awkward situation in which Fred Dallmayr finds himself.
6. Francis Schüssler Fiorenza, *Foundational Theology: Jesus and the Church* (New York: Crossroad, 1984).
7. Francis Schüssler Fiorenza, "The Church as a Community of Interpretation: Political Theology between Discourse Ethics and Hermeneutical Reconstruction," in Don S. Browning and Francis Schüssler Fiorenza, eds., *Habermas, Modernity, and Public Theology* (New York, Crossroads, 1992). The page numbers in the text refer to this essay.
8. Helmut Peukert, "Enlightenment and Theology as Unfinished Projects," in Browning and Schüssler Fiorenza, eds., *Habermas, Modernity, and Public Theology*, 44.
9. Matthew Lamb, "Communicative Praxis and Theology: Beyond Modern Nihilism and Dogmatism," in Browning and Schüssler Fiorenza, eds., *Habermas, Modernity, and Public Theology*, 95.
10. David Tracy, "Theology, Critical Social Theory, and the Public Realm," in Browning and Schüssler Fiorenza, eds., *Habermas, Modernity, and Public Theology*, 23–24.

324 • The Frankfurt School on Religion

11. Gary M. Simpson, "Die Versprachlichung (und Verflüssigung?) des Sakralen," in *Habermas und die Theologie*, 158f.; also as "The Linguistification (and Liquefaction?) of the Sacred: A Theological Consideration of Jürgen Habermas's Theory of Religion," *Exploration* 7 (1989): 21–35.
12. See Peter Eicher, "Die Botschaft von der Versöhnung und die Theorie des kommunikativen Handelns," in *Habermas und die Theologie*, 199f.
13. Paul Kluke, *Die Stiftunguniversität Frankfurt am Main 1914–1932* (Frankfurt am Main, 1972); Notker Hammerstein, *Die Johann-Wolfgang-Goethe-Universität*, vol. 1 (Frankfurt am Main: Luchterhand, 1989).
14. Johann Baptist Metz, "Erinnerung," in Hermann Krings et al. eds., *Handbuch philosophischer Grundbegriffe* (München: Kösel, 1973) 2: 386–96; Metz, "Anamnetische Vernunft," in Axel Honneth, Thomas McCarthy, Claus Offe, and Albrecht Wellmer, eds., *Zwischenbetrachtungen* (Frankfurt am Main: Suhrkamp 1989), 733f.
15. Jürgen Habermas, *The Theory of Communicative Action* (Boston: Beacon Press, 1984, 1987), 2: 281ff.
16. Habermas, *The Philosophical Discourse of Modernity*, 245f.; see also my article "Die Philosophie als Platzhalter und Interpret," in Habermas, *Moralbewubtsein und kommunikatives Handeln* (Frankfurt am Main: Suhrkamp, 1983), 9–28 [*Moral Consciousness and Communicative Action* (Cambridge, Mass.: MIT Press, 1990)].
17. Jens Glebe-Möller, *A Political Dogmatic* (Philadelphia: Fortress, 1987), 102. The page numbers in the text refer to this book.
18. Trans. James Bohman (Cambridge, Mass: MIT Press, 1986) [ET of *Wissenschaftstheorie – Handlungstheorie – Fundamentale Theologie* (Düsseldorf: Patmos, 1976; Frankfurt am Main: Suhrkamp, 1978)].
19. Peukert, "Enlightenment and Theology," in Browning and Schüssler Fiorenza, eds., *Habermas, Modernity, and Public Theology*, 56.
20. Jürgen Habermas, *Die neue Unübersichtlichkeit* (Frankfurt am Main: Suhrkamp, 1985), 52.
21. Jürgen Habermas, "Individuierung durch Vergesellschaftung," in *Nachmetaphysisches Denken* (Frankfurt am Main: Suhrkamp, 1988), 187–241, esp. 192ff.
22. Habermas, *Nachmetaphysisches Denken*, 60.
23. For a more extensive treatment of this argument, see Thomas McCarthy, "Philosophical Foundations of Political Theology: Kant, Peukert and the Frankfurt School," in Leroy S. Rouner, ed., *Civil Religion and Political Theology* (Notre Dame, Ind.: University of Notre Dame Press, 1986), 23–40.
24. Peukert, "Enlightenment and Theology," 60.
25. Charles Davis, "Kommunikative Rationalität und die Grundlegung christlicher Hoffnung," in *Habermas und die Theologie*, 111.
26. Jürgen Habermas, *Eine Art Schadensabwicklung* (Frankfurt am Main: Suhrkamp, 1987), 146.
27. Albrecht Wellmer, "Wahrheit, Schein, Versöhnung. Adornos ästhetische Rettung der Modernität," in Albrecht Wellmer, *Zur Dialektik von Moderne und Postmoderne* (Frankfurt am Main: Suhrkamp, 1985), 9–47; Martin Seel, *Die Kunst der Entzweiung* (Frankfurt am Main: Suhrkamp, 1986).
28. J. Habermas, "Questions and Counterquestions," in Bernstein, ed., *Habermas and Modernity*, 192ff., here 202f.; further, Habermas, *The Philosophical Discourse of Modernity*, 204ff.
29. Charles S. Peirce, *Writings of Charles S. Peirce: A Chronological Edition, Vol. 3: 1872–1878*, ed. Max H. Fisch et al. (Bloomington, Ind.: University of Indiana Press, 1986), 3: 108.
30. Ibid., 3: 68–71.
31. Seyla Benhabib, "The Generalized and the Concrete Other," *Praxis International* 5 (1986), 406.
32. Klaus Günther, *Der Sinn für Angemessenheit. Anwendungsdiskurse in Moral und Recht* (Frankfurt am Main: Suhrkamp, 1988).
33. See the Introduction to my *Theory and Practice*, trans. John Viertel (Boston: Beacon Press, 1973), 1–40.
34. Robert Wuthnow, "Rationality and the Limits of Rational Theory," in Browning and Schüssler Fiorenza, eds., *Habermas, Modernity, and Public Theology*, 216.
35. Odo Marquard, *Abschied vom Prinzipiellen: Philosophische Studien* (Stuttgart: Reclam, 1981).

36. Fred Dallmayr, *Beyond Dogma and Despair* (Notre Dame, Ind.: University of Notre Dame Press, 1981), 220ff. and 246ff.; Dallmayr, *Twilight of Subjectivity* (Amherst: University of Massachusetts Press, 1981), 179ff. and 279ff.
37. Fred Dallmayr, *Polis and Praxis* (Cambridge, Mass.: MIT Press, 1984), 158.
38. See Fred Dallmayr, "The Discourse of Modernity: Hegel, Nietzsche, Heidegger (and Habermas)," *Praxis International* 8 (1989): 377–406; see also the discussion about *Theorie des kommunikativen Handelns* in Fred Dallmayr, *Polis and Praxis*, 224–53. Dallmayr is similarly prejudicial in "Habermas and Rationality," *Political Theory* 16 (1988): 553–79. In his response, Richard J. Bernstein remarks about Dallmayr: "Considering his hermeneutical sensitivity, his most recent discussion of Habermas comes a bit as a shock. For although he makes use of extensive citations to create the impression that the 'author' is speaking for himself, the result is a distortion of Habermas' views" (ibid., 580).
39. See Browning and Schüssler Fiorenza, eds., *Habermas, Modernity, and Public Theology*, 141. The page numbers in the text refer to this essay.
40. Habermas, *Nachmetaphysisches Denken*, 64ff.
41. See my analysis of the lifeworld in ibid., 82–104.

22
Faith and Knowledge

Jürgen Habermas
Translated by Hella Beister and William Rehy

When restricted in one's choice of a subject by the depressing current events, one is severely tempted to compete with the John Waynes among us intellectuals to see who is the fastest shot. Only the other day, opinions differed about another issue—the question of whether, and how, we should, via genetic engineering, submit to self-instrumentalization or even pursue the goal of self-optimization. The first steps on this path led to a clash between the spokespersons of institutionalized science and those of the churches. One side feared obscurantism and the consolidation, based on skepticism toward science, of remnants of archaic emotions; the other side objected to the crude naturalism of a scientistic belief in progress supposedly undermining morality. But on September 11, 2001, the tension between secular society and religion exploded in an entirely different way.

As we now know from Atta's testament and from Bin Laden himself, the suicidal murderers who made living bombs of civil aircraft, directing them against the capitalist citadels of Western civilization, were motivated by religious beliefs. For them, the symbols of globalized modernity are an embodiment of the Great Satan. And we, too, the universal eyewitnesses of the "apocalyptic" events, were assailed by biblical images as we watched television repeat again and again, in a kind of masochistic attitude, the images of the crumbling Manhattan Twin Towers. And the language of retaliation—which the President of the United States was not the only one to resort to in response to the unbelievable—had an Old Testament ring to it. As if the blind fundamentalist attack had struck a religious chord in the very heart of secular society, synagogues, churches, and mosques everywhere began to fill. The hidden correspondence, however, failed to induce the civil-religious mourning congregation, gathering in the New York Stadium a week later, to assume a symmetrical attitude of hatred. For all its patriotism, not a single voice was heard calling for a warlike extension of national criminal law.[1]

In spite of its religious language, fundamentalism is an exclusively modern phenomenon and, therefore, not only a problem of others. What was immediately striking about the Islamic assailants was the perceptible time-lag between their motives and their means. This mirrors the time-lag between culture and society, which in their home countries has only come to exist as the result of an accelerated and radically uprooting modernization. What in our countries, under more propitious conditions, could after all be experienced as a process of *creative* destruction was, there, not bound up with the promise of compensation for the pain suffered through the disintegration of traditional forms of life. The prospect of seeing one's material conditions of life improved is but one thing. What is crucial is the shift in mentality, perhaps blocked so far by feelings of humiliation, which in the political realm comes to be expressed in the separation of church and state. Even in Europe, where under similar circumstances history allowed for much more time to be taken in developing a sensitive attitude toward Janus-faced modernity, feelings toward "secularization" are still highly ambivalent, as shown by the dispute over genetic engineering.

Orthodoxies exist in the Western world as well as in the Middle or Far East, among Christians and Jews as well as among Muslims. If we want to avoid a clash of civilizations, we must keep in mind that the dialectic of our own occidental process of secularization has as yet not come to a close. The "war against terrorism" is no war, and what comes to be expressed in terrorism is also the fatally speechless clash of worlds, which have to work out a common language beyond the mute violence of terrorists or missiles. Faced with a globalization imposing itself via deregulated markets, many of us hoped for a return of the political in a different form—not in the original Hobbesian form of the globalized security state, that is, in its dimensions of police activity, secret service, and the military, but as a worldwide civilizing force. What we are left with, for the moment, is little more than the bleak hope for a cunning of reason—and for some self-reflection. The rift of speechlessness strikes home, too. Only if we realize what secularization means in our own postsecular societies can we be far-sighted in our response to the risks involved in a secularization miscarrying in other parts of the world. Such is the intention which guides my taking up, once more, the topic of "Faith and Knowledge." I will speak neither on bioethics nor on a new kind of terrorism but on secularization in our postsecular societies. This self-reflection is one among several steps necessary if we want to present a different image of the West to other cultures. We do not want to be perceived as crusaders of a competing religion or as salespeople of instrumental reason and destructive secularization.

Secularization in Postsecular Society

In Europe, the term "secularization" first had the juridical meaning of a forced conveyance of church property to the secular state. This meaning was then extended to cover the rise and development of cultural and social modernity as a whole. Ever since, "secularization" has been subject to contrasting evaluations, depending on whether its main feature is seen as the successful *taming* of clerical authority, or as the act of unlawful *appropriation*. According to the first reading—"taming"—religious ways of thinking and forms of life are *replaced* by rational, in any case superior, equivalents; whereas in the second reading—"stealing"—these modern ways of thinking and forms of life are *discredited* as illegitimately appropriated goods. The replacement model suggests a progressivist interpretation in terms of disenchanted modernity, while the expropriation model leads to an interpretation in terms of a theory of decline, that is, unsheltered modernity. Both readings make the same mistake. They construe secularization as a kind of zero-sum game between the capitalistically unbridled productivity of science and technology on the one hand, and the conservative forces of religion and the church on the other hand. Gains on one side can only be achieved at the expense of the other side, and by liberal rules which act in favor of the driving forces of modernity.

This image is inconsistent with a postsecular society which adapts to the fact that religious communities continue to exist in a context of ongoing secularization. It obscures the civilizing role of a democratically shaped and enlightened common sense that makes its way as a third party, so to speak, amid the *Kulturkampf* confusion of competing voices. To be sure, from the perspective of the liberal state, only those religious communities which abstain, by their own lights, from violence in spreading their beliefs and imposing them on their own members, let alone manipulation inducing suicide attacks, deserve the predicate of "reasonable."[2] This restraint results from a triple reflection of the believers on their position in a pluralist society. Religious consciousness must, first, come to terms with the cognitive dissonance of encountering other denominations and religions. It must, second, adapt to the authority of the sciences which hold the societal monopoly of secular knowledge. It must, last, agree to the premises of a constitutional state grounded in a profane morality. Without this thrust of reflection, monotheisms in relentlessly modernized societies unleash a destructive potential. The term "thrust of reflection" [*Reflexionsschub*] suggests, however, the misleading image of a process carried out by one side only, and of one that has already come to a close. Actually, this reflection sets in again and again, and continues with each conflict of existential weight.

As soon as an issue of existential relevance makes it to the political agenda, citizens, whether believers or unbelievers, clash over beliefs impregnated by different worldviews; grappling with the strident dissonances of public dispute, they experience the offensive fact of an antagonistic coexistence of competing worldviews. If, aware of their own fallibility, they learn to deal with this fact of pluralism in a nonviolent way, that is, without disrupting the social cohesion of a political community, they realize what the secular grounds for the separation of religion from politics in a postsecular society actually mean. The neutral state, confronted with competing claims of knowledge and faith, abstains from prejudging political decisions in favor of one side or the other. The pluralized reason of the public of citizens follows a dynamic of secularization only insofar as the latter urges equal distance to be kept, *in the outcome*, from any strong traditions and comprehensive worldviews. In its willingness to learn, however, democratic common sense remains osmotically open to *both* sides, science and religion, without relinquishing its independence.

Science as an Agent of Informed Common Sense

Of course, common sense, being full of illusions about the world, needs to be informed, without any reservation, by the sciences. The scientific theories which intrude upon the lifeworld, however, do not essentially touch on the *framework* of our everyday knowledge, which is linked to the self-understanding of speakers and actors. Learning something new about the world, and about ourselves as beings in the world, changes the *content* of our self-understanding. Copernicus and Darwin revolutionized the geocentric and the anthropocentric worldview. As it is, the traces left by the destruction of the astronomical illusion about the orbits of the stars are less profound than those of the biological disillusionment about the position of man in natural history. The closer scientific findings approach our bodily existence, the more disconcerting they seem for our self-understanding. Brain research instructs us on the physiology of consciousness. But does it also change the intuitive awareness of authorship and responsibility which accompanies all our actions?

We realize what is at stake if, with Max Weber, we look at the beginnings of the "disenchantment of the world." To the extent that nature is made accessible to objectivating observation and causal explanation, it is depersonalized. Nature as an object of science is no longer part of the social frame of reference of persons who communicate and interact with one another and mutually ascribe intentions and motives. What, then, will become of these persons if they progressively subsume *themselves* under scientific descriptions? Will common sense, in the end, consent to being not only instructed, but completely absorbed by counterintuitive scientific knowledge? The philosopher Wilfrid Sellars addressed this question in 1960 (in a famous essay on "Philosophy and the Scientific Image of Man"), responding to it by the scenario of a society where the old-fashioned language games of our everyday life are invalidated in favor of the objectivating description of mental processes.

The vanishing point of this naturalization of the mind is a scientific image of man drawn up in the extensional concepts of physics, neurophysiology, or evolutionary theory, and resulting in a complete desocialization of our self-understanding as well. This naturalization of the mind can only be achieved, however, if the intentionality of human consciousness and the normativity of our actions are completely accounted for by such an objectivating self-description. The theories required would have to explain, for instance, how actors may follow, or break, rules, be they grammatical, conceptual, or moral.[3] Sellars's followers misconstrued the aporetic thought experiment of their teacher as a research program.[4] The project of a scientific "modernization" of our everyday psychology[5] led to attempts at a semantics—teleosemantics—explaining the contents of thought in terms of biology.[6] But even these most advanced efforts fail, it seems, because the concept of purposefulness with which we invest the Darwinian language game of mutation and adaptation, selection and survival is too poor to be adequate to the difference of "is" and "ought" which is implied if we violate rules—misapplying a predicate or violating a moral rule.[7]

In describing how a person did something she did not want to do, nor should have done, we *describe* her—but not in the same way as we describe a scientific object. The description of persons tacitly includes elements of the prescientific self-understanding of speakers and actors. If we describe an event as being a person's action, we know for instance that we describe something which can be not only *explained* like a natural process, but also, if need be, justified. In the background, there is the image of persons who may call upon one another to account for themselves, who are naturally involved in normatively regulated interactions and encounter one another in a universe of public reasons.

This perspective, going along with everyday life, explains the difference between the language games of justification and *mere* description. Even nonreductionist strategies of explanation end up against this dualism.[8] They too, after all, provide descriptions from the observer's perspective. But the participant's perspective of our everyday consciousness—in which the justificatory practices of research are grounded—can neither be easily integrated nor simply subordinated to the perspective of the observer. In our everyday dealings, we focus on others whom we address as a second person. Understanding the yes or no of the other, the contestable statements we owe and expect from one another, is bound up with this attitude toward second persons. The awareness of authorship implying accountability is the core of our self-understanding, disclosed only to the perspective of a participant, but eluding revisionary scientific description. The scientistic belief in a science which will one day not only supplement, but *replace* the self-understanding of actors as persons by an objectivating self-description is not science, but bad philosophy. No science will relieve common sense, even if scientifically informed, of the task of forming a judgment, for instance, on how we should deal with prepersonal human life under descriptions of molecular biology that make genetic interventions possible.

Democratic Common Sense and Religion

Thus, common sense is linked to the awareness of actors who can take initiatives, and make and correct mistakes. Against the sciences, it holds its own by persisting in its perspective. The same awareness of being autonomous which eludes naturalistic reduction is also the reason for keeping a distance, on the other hand, from a religious tradition whose normative substance we nevertheless feed on. By its insistence on rational justification, science seems in the end to succeed in getting on its side an informed common sense which has found its place in the edifice of the constitutional state. Of course, the contractualist tradition, too, has religious roots—roots in the very revolution of the ways of thinking that were brought about by the ascent of the great world religions. But this legitimation of law and politics in terms of modern natural law feeds on religious sources that have long since become secularized. Against religion, the democratic common sense insists on reasons which are acceptable not just for the members of *one* religious community. Therefore, the liberal state makes believers suspect that occidental secularization might be a one-way street bypassing religion as marginal.

The other side of religious freedom is in fact a pacification of the pluralism of worldviews that distribute burdens unequally. To date, only citizens committed to religious beliefs are required to split up their identities, as it were, into their public and private elements. They are the ones who have to translate their religious beliefs into a secular language before their arguments have any chance of gaining majority support. In Germany, just to give an example, Catholics and Protestants claim the status of a subject of human rights for the gamete fertilized ex utero; this is how they engage in an attempt (an unfortunate one, I think) to translate man's likeness to God into the secular language of the constitution. But only if the secular side, too, remains sensitive to the force of articulation inherent in religious languages will the search for reasons that aim at universal acceptability not lead to an unfair exclusion of religions from the public sphere, nor sever secular society from important resources of meaning. In any event, the boundaries between secular and religious reasons are fluid. Determining these disputed boundaries should therefore be seen as a cooperative task which requires *both* sides to take on the perspective of the other one.

Liberal politics must abstain from externalizing the perpetual dispute over the secular self-awareness of society, that is, from relegating it only to the religious segment of the population. Democratic common sense is not singular; it describes the mental state of a *many-voiced* public. Secular majorities must not reach decisions on such questions before the objections of opponents who feel that these decisions violate their beliefs have been heard; they have to consider these objections as a kind of dilatory plea in order to examine what may be learned from them. Considering the religious origins of its moral foundation, the liberal state should be aware of the possibility that Hegel's "culture of common sense" ["Kultur des gemeinen Menschenverstands"] may, in view of entirely novel challenges, fail to be up to the level of articulation which characterized its own origins. Today, the all-pervasive language of the market puts all interpersonal relations under the constraint of an egocentric orientation toward one's own preferences. The social bond, however, being made up of mutual recognition, cannot be spelled out in the concepts of contract, rational choice, and maximal benefit alone.[9]

Therefore, Kant refused to let the categorical "ought" be absorbed by the whirlpool of enlightened self-interest. He enlarged subjective freedom [*Willkür*] to autonomy (or free will), thus giving the first great example—after metaphysics—of a secularizing, but at the same time salvaging, deconstruction of religious truths. With Kant, the authority of divine commands is unmistakably echoed in the unconditional validity of moral duties. With his concept of autonomy, to be sure, he destroys the traditional image of men as children of God.[10] But he preempts the trivial consequences of such a deflation by a critical *assimilation* of religious contents. His further attempt to translate the notion of "radical evil" from biblical language into the language of rational religion may seem less convincing. The unrestrained way in which this biblical heritage is once more dealt with today shows that we still lack an adequate concept for the semantic difference between what is morally wrong and what is profoundly evil. There is no devil, but the fallen archangel still wreaks havoc—in the perverted good of the monstrous deed, but also in the unrestrained urge for retaliation that promptly follows.

Secular languages which only eliminate the substance once intended leave irritations. When sin was converted to culpability, and the breaking of divine commands to an offense against human laws, something was lost. The wish for forgiveness is still bound up with the unsentimental wish to undo the harm inflicted on others. What is even more disconcerting is the irreversibility of *past* sufferings—the injustice inflicted on innocent people who were abused, debased, and murdered, reaching far beyond any extent of reparation within human power. The lost hope for resurrection is keenly felt as a void. Horkheimer's justified skepticism—"The slaughtered are really slaughtered"—with which he countered Benjamin's emphatic, or rather excessive, hope for the anamnestic power of reparation inherent in human remembrance, is far from denying the helpless impulse to change what cannot be changed any more. The exchange of letters between Benjamin and Horkheimer dates from spring 1937. Both, the

334 • The Frankfurt School on Religion

true impulse and its impotence, were prolonged after the holocaust by the practice, as necessary as it was hopeless, of "coming to terms with the past" ["Aufarbeitung der Vergangenheit"] (Adorno). They are manifest as well in the rising lament over the inappropriateness of this practice. In moments like these, the unbelieving sons and daughters of modernity seem to believe that they owe more to one another, and need more for themselves, than what is accessible to them, in translation, of religious tradition—as if the semantic potential of the latter was still not exhausted.

Dispute Over a Heritage: Philosophy versus Religion

The history of German philosophy since Kant can be perceived in terms of a trial on this disputed heritage. By the end of the Middle Ages, the Hellenization of Christianity had resulted in a symbiosis of religion and metaphysics. This symbiosis was broken up again by Kant. He draws a sharp line between the moral belief of rational religion and the positive belief in revealed truths. From this perspective faith had certainly contributed to the "bettering of the soul" [*Seelenbesserung*], but "with its appendages of statutes and observances . . . bit by bit . . . became a fetter."[11] To Hegel, this is pure "dogmatism of enlightenment" ["Dogmatismus der Aufklärung"]. He derides the Pyrrhic victory of a reason which resembles those barbarians who are victorious, but succumb to the spirit of the conquered nation, in that it holds "the upper hand outwardly" only ["der äuberen Herrschaft nach die Oberhand behält"].[12] So, with Hegel, *delimiting* reason is replaced by a reason which *embraces*. Hegel makes death by crucifixion as suffered by the Son of God the center of a way of thinking that seeks to incorporate the positive form of Christianity. God's incarnation symbolizes the life of the philosophical spirit. Even the absolute must realize itself in its other because it will experience itself as absolute power only if it passes through the agonizing negativity of self-limitation. Thus, religious contents are saved in terms of philosophical concepts. But Hegel sacrifices together with sacred history [*Heilsgeschichte*] the promise of a salvaging future in exchange for a world process revolving *in itself*. Teleology is finally bent back into a circle.

Hegel's students and followers break with the fatalism of this dreary prospect of an eternal recurrence of the same. Rather than save religion in thought, they want to realize its profanized contents in a political effort of solidary praxis. This pathos of a desublimated earthly realization of the Kingdom of God is the driving force behind the critique of religion from Feuerbach and Marx to Bloch, Benjamin, and Adorno: "Nothing of theological content will persist without being transformed; every content will have to put itself to the test of migrating into the realm of the secular, the profane" ["Nichts an theologischem Gehalt wird unverwandelt fortbestehen; ein jeglicher wird der Probe sich stellen müssen, ins Säkulare, Profane einzuwandern"].[13] Meanwhile, it is true, it had become evident from the course of history that such a project was asking too much of reason. As reason was despairing of itself under these excessive demands, Adorno secured, albeit with a purely methodological intention, the help of the Messianic perspective: "Knowledge has no light but that shed on the world by redemption" ["Erkenntnis hat kein Licht als das von der Erlösung her auf die Welt scheint"].[14] What applies to Adorno here is a proposition by Horkheimer aiming at Critical Theory as a whole: "Knowing there is no God, it nevertheless believes in him" ["Sie weib, dass es keinen Gott gibt, und doch glaubt sie an ihn"].[15] Today, Jacques Derrida, from different premises, comes to a similar position—a worthy winner of the Adorno Prize also in this respect. All he wants to retain of Messianism is "messianicity, stripped of everything."[16]

The borders of philosophy and religion, however, are mined grounds. *Reason which disclaims itself* is easily tempted to merely borrow the authority, and the air, of a sacred that has been deprived of its core and become anonymous. With Heidegger, devotion [*Andacht*] mutates to become remembrance [*Andenken*]. But there is no new insight to be gained by having the day of the Last Judgement evaporate to an undetermined event in the history of being. If posthumanism is to be fulfilled in the return to the archaic beginnings *before* Christ and *before* Socrates, the hour of religious kitsch has come. Then the department stores of art open their doors to altars from all over the world, with priests and shamans flown in from all four points of the compass for exclusive exhibitions. *Profane*, but *nondefeatist* reason, by contrast, has too much respect for the glowing embers, rekindled time and again by the issue of theodicy, to offend religion. It knows that the profanation of the sacred begins with those world religions which disenchanted magic, overcame myth, sublimated sacrifice, and disclosed the secret. Thus, it can keep its distances from religion without ignoring its perspective.

The Example of Genetic Engineering

This ambivalence may also lead to the reasonable attitude of keeping one's distance from religion without closing one's mind to the perspective it offers. This attitude may help set the right course for the self-enlightenment of a civil society torn by *Kulturkampf*. Postsecular society continues the work, for religion itself, that religion did for myth. Not in the hybrid intention of a hostile takeover, to be sure, but out of a concern to counteract the insidious entropy of the scarce resource of meaning in its own realm. Democratic common sense must fear the media-induced indifference and the mindless conversational trivialization of all differences that make a difference. Those moral feelings which only religious language has as yet been able to give a sufficiently differentiated expression may find universal resonance once a salvaging formulation turns up for something almost forgotten, but implicitly missed. The mode for nondestructive secularization is translation. This is what the Western world, as the worldwide secularizing force, may learn from its own history. If it presents this complex image of itself to other cultures in a credible way, intercultural relations may find a language other than that of the military and the market alone.

In the controversy, for instance, about the way to deal with human embryos, many voices still evoke the first book of Moses, Genesis 1: 27: "So God created man in his own image, in the image of God created he him." In order to understand what *Gottesebenbildlichkeit*—"in the likeness of God"—means, one need not believe that the God who is love creates, with Adam and Eve, free creatures who are like him. One knows that there can be no love without recognition of the self in the other, nor freedom without mutual recognition. So, the other who has human form must himself be free in order to be able to return God's affection. In spite of his likeness to God, however, this other is also imagined as being God's creature. Regarding his origin, he cannot be of equal birth with God. This *creatural nature* of the image expresses an intuition which in the present context may even speak to those who are tonedeaf to religious connotations. Hegel had a feeling for this difference between divine "creation" and mere "coming from" God. God remains a "God of free men" only as long as we do not level out the absolute difference that exists between the creator and the creature. Only then, the fact that God gives form to human life does not imply a determination interfering with man's self-determination.

Because he is both in one, God the Creator and God the Redeemer, this creator does not need, in his actions, to abide by the laws of nature like a technician, or by the rules of a code like a biologist or computer scientist. From the very beginning, the voice of God calling into life communicates within a morally sensitive universe. Therefore God may "determine" man in the sense of enabling and, at the same time, obliging him to be free. Now, one need not believe in theological premises in order to understand what follows from this, namely, that an entirely different kind of dependence, perceived as a causal one, becomes involved if the difference assumed as inherent in the concept of creation were to disappear, and the place of God be taken by a peer—if, that is, a human being would intervene, according to his own preferences and without being justified in assuming, at least counterfactually, a consent of the concerned other, in the random combination of the parents' sets of chromosomes. This reading leads to the question I have dealt with elsewhere: Would not the first human being to determine, *at his own discretion*, the natural essence of another human being at the same time destroy the equal freedoms that exist among persons of equal birth in order to ensure their difference?

Notes

1. H. Prantl, "Das Weltgericht," *Süddeutsche Zeitung*, Sept. 18, 2001.
2. J. Rawls, *Politischer Liberalismus* (Frankfurt am Main, 1998), pp. 132–41, English edition *Political Liberalism* (New York: Columbia University Press, 1993); R. Forst, "Toleranz, Gerechtigkeit, Vernunft," in Forst (ed.), *Toleranz* (Frankfurt am Main: Campus, 2000), 144–61.
3. W. Sellars, *Science, Perception and Reality* (1963; Altascadero, Calif.: Ridgeview, 1991), 38.
4. P. M. Churchland, *Scientific Realism and the Plasticity of Mind* (Cambridge: Cambridge University Press, 1979).
5. J. D. Greenwood (ed.), *The Future of Folk Psychology: Intentionality and Cognitive Science* (Cambridge: Cambridge University Press, 1991), Introduction, 1–21.
6. W. Detel, "Teleosemantik. Ein neuer Blick auf den Geist?" *Deutsche Zeitschrift für Philosophie*, 49, no. 3 (2001), 465–91. Teleosemantics, based on neo-Darwinian assumptions and conceptual analyses, aims to show how the normative consciousness of living beings who use symbols and represent facts might have developed. According to this approach, the intentional frame of the human mind originates from the selective advantage of certain behaviors (e.g., the bees' dance) which are interpreted as representations by those belonging to the same species. Against the background of normalized copies of this kind, divergent behaviors are, then, supposed to be interpretable as misrepresentations – which provides a natural explanation for the origins of normativity.
7. W. Detel, "Haben Frösche und Sumpfmenschen Gedanken? Einige Probleme der Teleosemantik," *Deutsche Zeitschrift für Philosophie*, 49, no. 4 (2001), 601–26.
8. These research strategies account for the complexity of new properties (of organic life or of man) emerging on higher evolutionary stages by abstaining from describing processes of the higher evolutionary stage in concepts which apply to processes of a lower evolutionary stage.
9. A. Honneth, *The Struggle for Recognition*, trans. J. Anderson (Cambridge: Polity, 1995).
10. The Preface to the first edition of *Religion within the Limits of Reason Alone* (1793) begins with the sentence: "So far as morality is based upon the conception of man as a free agent who, just because he is free, binds himself through his reason to unconditioned laws, it stands in need neither of the idea of another Being over him, for him to apprehend his duty, nor of an incentive other than the law itself, for him to do his duty" (I. Kant, *Religion within the Limits of Reason Alone*, trans. and introd. T. M. Greene and H. H. Hudson (La Salle, Ill.: Open Court, 1934), 3).
11. Kant, *Religion within the Limits of Reason Alone*.
12. G. W. F. Hegel, *Faith and Knowledge*, trans. W. Cerf and H. S. Harris (Albany: State University of New York Press, 1977).
13. T.W. Adorno, *Critical Models: Interventions and Catchwords*, trans. H. W. Pickford (New York: Columbia University Press, 1998), 136.
14. T. W. Adorno, *Minima Moralia: Reflections from Damaged Life*, trans. E. F. N. Jephcott (London: New Left Books, 1974), 247.
15. M. Horkheimer, "Kritische Theorie und Theologie" (Dec. 1968), 507–9 of *Gesammelte Schriften*, vol. 14, at 508.
16. J. Derrida, "Faith and Knowledge: The Two Sources of 'Religion' at the Limits of Reason Alone," in J. Derrida and G. Vattimo (eds), *Religion* (Cambridge: Polity; Stanford: Stanford University Press, 1998), 18; cf. also J. Derrida, "Den Tod geben," in A. Haverkamp (ed.), *Gewalt und Gerechtigkeit* (Frankfurt am Main: Suhrkamp, 1994), 331–445.

23
On the Relation between
the Secular Liberal State
and Religion

Jürgen Habermas
Translated by Matthias Fritsch

The topic proposed for our discussion recalls a question that Ernst Wolfgang Böckenförde, in the mid-1960s, formulated quite precisely in the following manner: whether the liberal, secularized state is nourished by normative presuppositions which it itself cannot guarantee.[1] This question expresses doubt about whether the democratic constitutional state can renew the normative presuppositions of its own existence from out of its own resources. It also expresses the presumption that this state is dependent upon autochthonous world views or religious traditions—in any case, collectively binding ethical traditions. While, in the face of the "fact of pluralism" (Rawls), this would indeed bring a state obligated to world-view neutrality into trouble, this conclusion does not yet speak against the presumption itself.

I would first like to render the problem more specific in two respects. (1) In the cognitive respect, the doubt refers to the question whether political rule is, in view of the complete positivization of law, at all open to a secular, that is, non-religious or postmetaphysical, justification. (2) Even if such a legitimation is granted, doubts remain with respect to motivation about the issue of whether a society with pluralist worldviews may be stabilized normatively, that is, beyond a mere *modus vivendi*, by way of the supposition of an, at best, formal background consensus that is limited to procedures and principles. (3) Even if this doubt can be removed, a liberal state remains dependent upon the solidarity of its citizens. The sources of this solidarity, however, can peter out as a result of a "derailed" secularization of society as a whole. This diagnosis cannot be dismissed, but it must not be understood in such a way that the educated among the defenders of religion can, so to speak, "capitalize" on it. (4) Instead, I will propose to understand cultural and societal secularization as a double learning process which forces the Enlightenment traditions as well as religious doctrines to become reflexive about their respective limits. (5) With regard to postsecular societies, we finally come to the question as to which cognitive attitudes and normative expectations the liberal state must demand [*zumuten*] of citizens with and without faith in their interaction with one another.

1

Political liberalism—which I defend in the special version of a Kantian republicanism[2]—understands itself as a non-religious and postmetaphysical justification of the normative foundations of a democratic constitutional state. This theory belongs to a tradition of the law of reason [*Vernunftrecht*] which dispenses with the strong cosmological or soteriological assumptions of classical and religious doctrines of natural law. Of course, the history of Christian theology in the Middle Ages, in particular late Spanish Scholasticism, belongs to the genealogy of human rights. But in the end, the legitimating foundation of a state power that is neutral between world views derive from the profane sources of 17th and 18th century philosophy. Theology and church come to terms with the intellectual [*geistige*] challenges of the revolutionary constitutional state only much later. However, if my understanding is correct, Catholicism, which maintains a relaxed attitude toward the *lumen naturale*, is not fundamentally opposed to an autonomous justification of morality and law, a justification independent of the truths of revelation.

In the 20th century, a post-Kantian justification of liberal constitutional principles did not have to confront the after-effects of objective natural law (as in a material value ethics) so much as the historicist and empiricist forms of critique. In my view, weak assumptions regarding the normative content of the communicative condition of socio-cultural forms of life suffice to defend a non-defeatist concept of reason against contextualism and a non-decisionist concept of the validity of law against legal positivism. The central task is to explain:

- Why the democratic process is considered [*gilt*] a procedure of legitimate law-making: in so far as it meets the conditions of an inclusive and discursive opinion- and will-formation, the democratic process justifies the presumption of the rational acceptability of the results; and

• Why democracy and human rights are equiprimordially conjoined in the process of constitution-making: the legal institutionalization of the procedure of democratic law-making requires the simultaneous guarantee of political *as well as liberal* basic rights.[3]

The reference point of this strategy of justification is the constitution which the associated citizens grant themselves, and not the domestication of an existing state power, for the latter is first of all to be generated by way of democratic constitution-making. A "constituted" (and not only constitutionally tamed) state power is legalized down to its innermost core, so that law penetrates political power without remainder. Whereas the positivism of the will of the state, rooted in Imperial Germany [*Kaiserreich*] and advanced by the German school of state law (from Paul Laband and Georg Jellinek to Carl Schmitt), left a loophole for the non-legal ethical [*rechtsfreie sittliche*] substance "of the state" or "of the political," there is no ruling subject, nourished by a prelegal substance, in the constitutional state.[4] Of the preconstitutional sovereignty of the prince, no vacant site [*Leerstelle*] remains which would now have to be filled out—in the form of an ethos of a more or less homogenous people—by an equally substantial popular sovereignty.

In light of this problematic heritage, Böckenförde's question has been understood as implying that a fully positivized constitutional order necessitates religion or some other "sustaining power" for the cognitive assurance of its foundations of validity. According to this reading, the validity claim of positive law is dependent upon a foundation in the prepolitical ethical convictions of religious or national communities because such a legal order cannot be legitimized self-referentially on the basis of democratically generated legal procedures alone. By contrast, if one conceptualizes the democratic procedure not positivistically, as Hans Kelsen and Niklas Luhmann do, and instead as a method for the generation of legitimacy from legality, no validity deficit to be filled out by "ethicality" [*Sittlichkeit*] arises. As opposed to the understanding of the constitutional state advanced by right-wing Hegelians [*rechtshegelianisches Verständnis*], the proceduralist conception inspired by Kant insists upon an autonomous justification of basic constitutional principles, a justification that claims to be rationally acceptable to all citizens.

2

In what follows, I will assume that the constitution of a liberal state can provide for its legitimation needs self-sufficiently, that is, from the cognitive stock of argumentation that is independent of religious and metaphysical traditions. Even with this premise, however, a doubt regarding motivation remains. For the normative, existential presuppositions of the democratic constitutional state

are more demanding with respect to the role of citizens who understand themselves as authors of the law, than with respect to the role of societal citizens
who are the addressees of the law. Of the latter, it is merely expected that they
not transgress legal limits in the pursuit of their subjective freedoms (and
claims). As opposed to obedience to coercive laws of freedom, the situation is
different with regard to the motivations and attitudes expected of citizens in
the role of democratic co-legislators.

They should pursue their rights of communication and participation actively,
and indeed not only in their correctly understood personal interest, but in orientation to the common good. This demands a more costly motivational effort
that cannot be legally enforced. A *duty* of electoral participation would be as
alien to the democratic state of law as *prescribed* solidarity. The willingness, in
case of need, to stand in for alien co-citizens who remain anonymous, and to
accept sacrifices in favour of general interests can only be *suggested* to citizens
of a liberal society. That is why political virtues are essential for the existence of
a democracy, even if they are "charged" in small change only. They are a matter
of socialization and habituation to the practices and mentalities of a liberal
political culture. The status of a citizen is, so to speak, embedded in a civil
society which lives on spontaneous, if you will, "pre-political" sources.

It does not yet follow from this that the liberal state is unable to reproduce
its motivational presuppositions on the basis of its own, secular inventory. Certainly, the motives for citizens' participation in political opinion- and will-
formation are nourished by ethical [*ethischen*] life projects and cultural forms
of life. But democratic practices unfold their own political dynamic. Only a
state with the rule of law [*Rechtsstaat*] but without democracy, to which we
were used in Germany long enough, would suggest a negative response to
Böckenförde's question: "To what extent can a people united by a state live
merely on the basis of guaranteeing the freedom of the individual, without a
unifying tie that is prior to this freedom?"[5] For the democratically constituted
state of the rule of law does not only guarantee the negative liberties of societal
citizens concerned about their own well-being. By means of the release of communicative freedoms, it also *mobilizes* the participation of citizens in the public
debate about topics that concern all equally. The "unifying tie" whose absence
is regretted is a democratic process, in which ultimately the right understanding
of the constitution is open to discussion.

For instance, in the current debates about reforming the welfare state, im-
migration politics, the war in Iraq, and the abolition of coercive conscription,
what is at issue are not just individual policies, but also the controversial interpretation of constitutional principles—and implicitly, what is at issue is the question
as to how we want to understand ourselves as citizens of the Federal Republic
as well as Europeans in light of the diversity of our cultural ways of life, the

pluralism of world views and religious convictions. Certainly, in historical retrospect, a common religious background, a common language, and, above all, a newly awakened national consciousness were helpful for the emergence of a highly abstract civic solidarity. But in the meantime, republican convictions have largely freed themselves from these pre-political anchorings—that we are not prepared to die "for Nice" is precisely no longer an objection to a European constitution. Recall the politico-ethical discourses about the Holocaust and mass criminality: for the citizens of the Federal Republic, they brought to awareness the constitution as an achievement. The example of a self-critical "politics of memory"—which is no longer exceptional, but rather widespread in other countries, too—illustrates how constitutional-patriotic ties form and renew themselves in the medium of politics *itself*.

Contrary to a wide-spread misunderstanding, "constitutional patriotism" means that citizens appropriate the principles of a constitution not solely in their abstract content, but rather from within the historical context of their own national history in its concrete meaning. If the moral contents of basic rights are supposed to gain a foothold in convictions, cognitive primacy does not suffice. Only for the integration of a constitutional society of world citizens [*einer verfassten Weltbürgergesellschaft*]—if it is to come about one day—would moral insight and the global agreement on moral indignation about massive violations of human rights suffice. Among members of a political community, solidarity—however abstract and legally mediated it may be—emerges only when principles of justice enter into the thicker web of cultural value orientations.

3

According to the foregoing considerations, the secular nature of the democratic constitutional state does not expose a weakness internal to the political system as such, which would jeopardize its self-stabilization in cognitive or motivational respects. This does not exclude external reasons. A derailing modernization of society as a whole could very well wear down the democratic tie and deplete the kind of solidarity on which the democratic state remains dependent without being able to legally enforce it. In such a case, precisely the constellation Böckenförde had in mind would obtain: the transformation of the citizens of affluent and peaceful liberal societies into solitary, self-interestedly acting monads who merely turn their subjective rights like weapons against one another. Evidence for such a crumbling of civic solidarity shows itself in the larger context of a politically uncontrolled global economy and global society.

Markets—which, as is well-known, cannot be democratized as state administrations can—increasingly assume steering functions in domains of life that had previously been held together normatively, that is, either politically or by way of prepolitical forms of communication. Thereby, not only private spheres are increasingly switched over to mechanisms of success-oriented action that are oriented toward individual preferences: the area subject to the needs of public legitimation also shrinks. Civic privatism is reinforced by the discouraging loss of the function of a democratic opinion- and will-formation, which, until now, functions half-way only in national arenas, and hence, does not extend to the decision-making processes that have been displaced onto the supranational level. The dwindling hope for the political and formative power of the international community promotes the tendency to the depoliticization of citizens. In the face of conflicts and the crying social injustices of a highly fragmented global society, disappointment grows with every further failure on the path toward the constitutionalization of international law [*Völkerrechts*], a path that had initially been pursued after 1945.

Postmodern theories conceptualize the crises through a critique of reason, as the logical result of the program of a self-destructive intellectual [*geistige*] and societal rationalization, and not as a result of the selective utilization of the rational potential which is at least latent [*angelegt*] in Western modernity. To be sure, radical skepticism with regard to reason is foreign to the Catholic tradition from the beginning. But until the 1960s, Catholicism had a hard time with the secular thought of humanism, Enlightenment, and political liberalism. Thus, the theorem that a contrite modernity can only be helped out of its cul-de-sac through the religious orientation to a transcendent reference point, resonates well today again. In Teheran, a colleague asked me whether, from the viewpoint of a comparison of cultures and a sociology of religion, European secularization was the real *Sonderweg* in need of correction. The question recalls the mood of the Weimar Republic; it recalls Carl Schmitt, Heidegger, or Leo Strauss.

I think it is better not to dramatically heighten, in the manner of a critique of reason, the question as to whether an ambivalent modernity will stabilize itself from out of the secular powers of a communicative reason. Instead, the question should be treated undramatically as an open empirical question. I do not wish here to bring into play the phenomenon of the continued existence of religion in an environment of continuing secularization as a mere social fact. Philosophy has to take this phenomenon seriously, from the inside, as it were, as a *cognitive challenge*. Before I follow this path of the discussion, however, I want to mention a path of the dialogue that also suggests itself, but that takes us in a different direction. By way of the pull toward the radicalization of the critique of reason, philosophy has allowed itself to be moved to a self-reflection upon its own religious-metaphysical origins, and to get involved in conversations with a theology that itself looked for a connection with philosophical attempts at the post-Hegelian self-reflection of reason.[6]

Excursus

The point of contact for the philosophical discourse about reason and revelation is a perpetually recurring figure of thought: the reason that reflects upon its deepest ground discovers its origin in an alterity, whose fate-like power it has to recognize if it is not to lose its rational orientation in the cul-de-sac of hybrid self-possession. The exercise of a conversion of reason through reason, a turning-around accomplished, or at least initiated, through its own power, serves as the model here—no matter whether reflection, as in Schleiermacher, starts with the knowing and acting subject, or, as in Kierkegaard, with the historicity of an always individual existential self-assurance, or, as in Hegel, Feuerbach, and Marx, with the provocative fragmentation of ethical relations. Without an initially theological goal, a reason that becomes aware of its limits transcends itself toward some alterity: be it toward the mystical fusion with a cosmically comprehensive consciousness, the despairing hope for the historical event of the redeeming message, or in the form of progressive solidarity with the downtrodden and offended, a solidarity that wishes to accelerate messianic salvation. These anonymous gods of post-Hegelian metaphysics—a comprehensive consciousness, an event that could not be anticipated [*das unvordenkliche Ereignis*], a non-alienated society—are easy prey for theology. They offer themselves to be deciphered as pseudonyms for the trinity of a personal God imparting himself.

These attempts at a renewal of philosophical theology after Hegel are still more attractive than the Nietzscheanism which merely borrows the Christian connotations of hearing and listening, devotion and the expectation of grace, arrival and event in order to recall a propositionally denucleated [*entkerntes*] thinking back beyond Christ and Socrates into the indeterminately archaic. By contrast, a philosophy conscious of its fallibility and its fragile position in the differentiated framework of modern society insists upon the generic but not pejoratively intended distinction between secular speech, which claims to be publicly accessible, and religious speech, which is dependent upon the truths of revelation. As opposed to Kant and Hegel, this drawing of a grammatical limit is not connected with the philosophical claim to determine by itself which contents of religious traditions—beyond the societally institutionalized mundane knowledge [*Weltwissen*]—are true or false. The respect that goes along with this restraint in cognitive judgment is based upon the respect for persons and ways of life which openly draw their integrity and authenticity from religious convictions. But respect is not all: philosophy has reason to display a *willingness to learn* from religious traditions.

4

In contrast to the ethical abstinence of postmetaphysical thinking, which cannot be committed to any generally obligatory concept of the good and exemplary

life, holy scriptures and religious traditions articulate—as well as spelling out
in subtle ways and hermeneutically keeping awake over thousand of years—
intuitions about misconduct or failure [*Verfehlung*] and redemption, about
the saving exit from a life experienced as being without salvation [*heillos*]. That
is why, in the life of a religious congregation or community—as long as it avoids
dogmatism and an enforced conscience—something may stay alive which has
been lost elsewhere, and which cannot be reconstituted through the professional
knowledge of experts alone: what I mean are sufficiently differentiated powers
of expression and sensibilities for a failed life [*verfehltes Leben*], for societal
pathologies, for the failure of individual projects of life and the deformation of
disfigured life contexts. Philosophy's willingness to learn from religion may be
justified on the basis of the asymmetry of epistemic claims; to be sure, not for
functional reasons, but—reminiscent of successful "Hegelian" learning processes—for reasons of content.

The reciprocal interpenetration of Christianity and Greek metaphysics not
only generated the intellectual form [*geistige Gestalt*] of theological dogmatism and a Hellenization of Christianity, which is not beneficial in every respect.
It also promoted philosophy's appropriation of genuinely Christian content.
This work of appropriation crystallized in strongly charged, normative conceptual networks, such as responsibility, autonomy and justification, history
and memory, beginning anew, innovation and return, emancipation and fulfillment, externalization, internalization and incorporation, individuality and community. This work indeed transformed the originally religious meaning, but it
did not deflate and expend in such a way as to empty it out. The translation of
the human likeness to God [*Gottesebenbildlichkeit*] into the equal dignity of
all humans, a dignity to be respected unconditionally, is such a saving translation.
It captures the content of biblical concepts for the general public of non-believers
and people of a different faith, beyond the boundaries of a religious community.
Benjamin was one of those who at times succeeded in such translations.

On the basis of this experience of the secularizing releasement of religiously
encapsulated meaning potentials, we can give Böckenförde's theorem an in-
nocuous meaning. I mentioned the diagnosis according to which modernity's
balance between the three big media of societal integration becomes endan-
gered, because markets and administrative power drive out societal solidarity—
that is, action coordination by way of values, norms, and the use of language
oriented toward understanding—from more and more areas of life. Thus, it is
also in the ownmost interest of the constitutional state to treat sparingly all
those sources from which the normative consciousness and the solidarity of
citizens springs. This consciousness which has become conservative is reflected
in talk of a "postsecular society."[7]

The phrase does not only refer to the fact that religion maintains itself in an
increasingly secular environment, and that society for now expects the

continuing survival of religious communities. The expression "postsecular" also does not only express to religious communities public recognition for the functional contribution they accomplish for the reproduction of desired motives and attitudes. Rather, the public consciousness of a postsecular society reflects a normative insight which has consequences for the political relation between believing and non-believing citizens. In postsecular societies, the insight prevails that the "modernization of public consciousness" captures religious and secular [weltliche] mentalities in different phases and reflexively alters them. If they conceive of the secularization of society in common as a complementary learning process, both sides can then reciprocally take seriously, for cognitive reasons, their contributions to controversial topics in the public sphere.

5

On the one hand, religious consciousness was forced to adapt itself. Every religion is originally a "world view" or a "comprehensive doctrine," in the sense that it claims authority to structure a form of life as a whole. Religion had to surrender this claim on the monopoly of interpretation and comprehensive formation of life under conditions of the secularization of knowledge, the neutralization of state power, and the generalized freedom of religion. Along with the functional differentiation of societal subsystems, the life of a religious community also separates itself from its social environment. The role of the member of a congregation differentiates itself from the role of a societal citizen. And since the liberal state depends on a political integration of citizens that goes beyond a mere modus vivendi, this differentiation of memberships may not be exhausted by a cognitively unsophisticated adaptation of the religious ethos to imposed laws of secular society. Rather, the universalist order of law and the egalitarian morality of society must connect from within with the congregational ethos in such a way that one emerges consistently from the other. For this "embedding," John Rawls chose the image of a module: this module of secular justice is supposed to fit into the different orthodox contexts of justification, despite the fact that the former is constructed on the basis of reasons neutral between world views.[8]

This normative expectation with which the liberal state confronts religious congregations meets with their own interest in so far as, for them, the possibility opens up in this way to exert their own influence via the political public sphere on society as a whole. To be sure, the resulting costs of tolerance, as the more or less liberal regulation of abortion shows, are not divided symmetrically among believers and non-believers; but secular consciousness as well does not enjoy without cost the negative freedom of religion. It is expected to practice self-reflexive interaction with the limits of the Enlightenment. The understanding of tolerance in pluralistic societies with liberal constitutions does not only demand of believers, in their interaction with non-believers and those who hold a different faith, the insight that they have to *reasonably* count with the continuing existence of dissension. On the other side, the same insight is demanded of non-believers in interaction with believers within the context of a liberal political culture.

For religiously uninspired citizens, this implies the task, by no means trivial, to define the relationship between knowledge and belief from the perspective of mundane knowledge *in a self-critical way*. For the expectation of a continuing non-agreement of belief and knowledge in fact only earns the predicate "rational" when religious convictions are granted, even from the perspective of secular knowledge, an epistemic status that is not irrational as such. In the political public sphere, naturalistic world views, which owe themselves to a speculative processing of scientific information and are relevant to the ethical self-understanding of citizens,[9] thus in no way enjoy a *prima facie* priority over competing world-view or religious conceptions.

The world-view neutrality of state power, which guarantees equal ethical liberties for every citizen, is incompatible with the political generalization of a secularist world view. Secularized citizens, insofar as they are acting in their role as citizens of a state, should neither deny a truth potential to religious world views as a matter of principle, nor dispute the right of believing fellow citizens to make contributions to public discussions in religious language. A liberal political culture can even expect of its secularized citizens that they participate in efforts to translate contributions from the religious language into the publicly accessible one.[10]

Notes

1. E. W. Böckenförde, "Die Entstehung des Staates als Vorgang der Säkularisation" (1967), in: *Recht, Staat, Freiheit*. Frankfurt, 1991, 92 ff.; here, 112.
2. J. Habermas, *The Inclusion of the Other*, ed. C. Cronin, P. de Greiff, Cambridge: MIT Press, 1998.
3. J. Habermas, *Between Facts and Norms*, tr. W. Rehg, Cambridge: MIT Press, 1996, chapter III.
4. H. Brunkhorst, "Der lange Schatten des Staatswillenspositivismus" *Leviathan* 31, 2003, 362–81.
5. Böckenförde 1991, p. 111.
6. P. Neuner, G. Wenz (ed.), *Theologen des 20. Jahrhunderts*. Darmstadt, 2002.
7. K. Eder, "Europäische Säkularisierung—ein Sonderweg in die postsäkulare Gesellschaft?" *Berliner Journal für Soziologie*, vol. 3 (2002), 331–43.
8. J. Rawls, *Political Liberalism*, New York: Columbia University Press, 1996, 12 ff.
9. For an example, see W. Singer, "Keiner kann anders sein, als er ist. Verschaltungen legen uns fest: Wir sollten aufhören, von Freiheit zu reden" *Frankfurter Allgemeine Zeitung*, January 8, 2004, p. 33.
10. J. Habermas, *Glauben und Wissen*, Frankfurt: Suhrkamp Verlag, 2001.

X
Helmut Peukert

24

Enlightenment and Theology as Unfinished Projects

Helmut Peukert
Translated by Peter P. Kenny

The relationship between critical theory and theology can be correctly determined only when we take into account the challenge that confronts both of them in our historical situation. It is a situation in which it has become more and more apparent that certain trends within our social-cultural formation threaten us. It is a situation in which—to put it a bit dramatically—humanity as a whole has become the *object* of our political decisions and of our economic activity, yet in which it is not yet the *subject* of its activity: that we would have available regular forms of public decision making or even have the necessary insights at our disposal that would be adequate to the size of the problems. This may meanwhile appear as something banal. But it is still our situation, and nothing is more resistant to analysis than a banality or something that has been declared a banality.

Granted this situation, what is the significance of projects like that of critical theory or of theology? And what relationship do they have to each other?

Ever since its beginnings, the critical theory of the Frankfurt School has considered itself as standing in the tradition of the Enlightenment. Indeed, the authors of the *Dialectic of Enlightenment* specifically understand Enlightenment as the project of human culture in general. This project is founded on the ability of human persons to step out of their blind, prereflective bond with nature and to become more and more aware of the conditions of their own existence, and with the help of their distancing-reflective reason, to lead a life in which they themselves give it its direction on the basis of mutually shared, free insight.

Some might hesitate to also call theology a "project." It is true that at the core of religion there is something at stake that is simply not in our power, that therefore cannot simply be the result of our efforts. But Kierkegaard, who knew this quite well, did not hesitate to speak of the project of thinking that is assigned to us with the exacting demands of becoming a Christian.[1] The dimensions of this project are first clear when one admits that since the rise of the great world religions, theology, as a methodically controlled reflective form of religion, has been concerned with the basic problems of advanced civilizations that developed simultaneously with it. The thesis seems plausible to me that the unsolved fundamental problem of advanced civilizations is that of mastering the tendency toward power accumulation.[2]

The concept of power is multi-layered. Power denotes first of all the ability through an action to bring about certain effects. Power increases through the expansion of possibilities of action within the framework of the general cultural development. But its character is first revealed, according to Max Weber, when power appears as the ability in situations of social conflict to push through a will even against resistance, when along with this, the expanded possibilities of action are systemically organized, and when such systems of power engage in competition with one another and place themselves under the pressure through this competition to surpass each other by increasing their own power. The structure of power then manifests itself in the self-driven competition of systems accumulating power in the political-military, in the economic, and in the—media-determined—cultural realms. The fundamental problem of our historical situation then appears to be that these mechanisms of accumulation are barely controllable and threaten to lead toward self-destruction. In my opinion, religion, and in its reflected form, theology, at least since the beginning of the world religions, cannot be understood simply as the attempt to endorse these mechanisms. Rather, religion must be understood as the attempt to put them into question and to develop *alternative* ways of dealing with reality from a grounding in another kind of experience.

Both projects, that of the Enlightenment and that of theology, remain unfulfilled. This is true not only because both share in the fallibility of human knowledge, and therefore as projects are limitless and unfinishable. It is true also in a more radical sense: in an increasingly precarious social-cultural situation both theology and the Enlightenment find themselves placed under the suspicion of having contributed to the rise of this situation in their previous expressions and activity. If they are to be continued, it can only be after they undergo fundamental corrections.

This has been true of theology for a long time. Ever since modernity's critique of religion, theology is suspected of having covered up and also legitimizing the mechanisms of accumulation and of the unjust sharing of power. And, in general, theology is accused of obscuring the true recognition of the human condition by producing an illusory consciousness. The most extreme perversion of religion, then, consists in the exploitation once again of the angst of existence and the desperation of human beings by a religious system interested in exerting its power. The fundamentalistic regressions, which presently can be observed even inside the major churches, sufficiently illustrate the danger of this perversion. Theology, then, must first always prove itself anew as a critical endeavor. The attempts of a new "political theology," of a "theology of liberation," or of a "theology of the public realm" must be counted as attempts in the great tradition of theology to develop and bring to bear the critical potential of religion even within theology itself.[3]

But this same suspicion also applies to the Enlightenment, and, indeed, has been sharpened in the radical critique of reason within our century.[4] The critique of reason by reason belongs itself to the tradition of the Enlightenment. What is new, however, is the assumption that our enlightened rationality does not measure up to the consequences of its actions, so that, in the end, the repercussions of the expanding, competing and accelerating systems of action on a finite world cannot be comprehended, much less controlled. The critical theory of the Frankfurt School, whose own origin and development bears the imprint of the self-destructive effects of social-cultural processes, can be counted as one of the most important attempts to continue the project of Enlightenment— exactly because it itself underwent a radical self-criticism. This is true both of its original form and of its reconstruction by Jürgen Habermas with his theory of communicative action.

Both projects, theology as well as Enlightenment, need to enter into public conversation with each other to continue. This is clear for the project of theology insofar as it makes a claim to speak in a way that is understandable and reasonable to all. And, to my mind, this claim constitutively belongs to theology which then, however, must become engaged in the argumentative discourse. But my thesis is that the Enlightenment also handicaps itself if it does not face the challenge of the religious traditions of humanity and their reflective formulations in theologies in which the basic human condition has been reflected upon in a radical way.

I would like to expound these theses in the following steps. First, I present the basic approach of the first generation of critical theory and its relationship to theology. Second, I try to explain Jürgen Habermas's criticism of this approach and his reconstruction of critical theory in his theory of communicative action. This reconstruction is carried out in a double way: on the one hand, as a systematic analysis of the structure of human communication and its ethical implications, and, on the other hand, as a reconstruction of the genesis of the modern process of rationalization in which religion is replaced by a communicative ethics. In the third section, with respect to this claim I ask how a theology can be devised that can do justice both to its historical tradition and to the questions of critical theory. Finally, I consider what conclusions relevant for the public realm can be drawn from the discourse between critical theory and theology.

The First Generation of Critical Theory and Theology

The beginnings of critical theory date back more than two generations. The historians and interpreters of critical theory have shown that it is not possible to give a single theory or a homogeneous system that would have united so diversely creative thinkers from their different disciplines. Yet there were experiences from the first decades of the century that all of them found disturbing. To them belonged the rise of authoritarian movements and eventually of fascist systems in Southern and Central Europe. There was also the splitting up of the labor movement into social-democratic and communist factions. On the one side, this made workers susceptible to authoritarian movements in Western countries; on the other side, it led to the degeneration of the Russian Revolution into Stalinism. Further, there was the development of a new mass culture with new media that clearly tended to neutralize the potential of art for generating fundamental change. This then contributed to the stilling of protest and to the numbing of consciousness. For an explanation of these developments, obviously neither the theories of Marx on the development of capitalistic societies nor Max Weber's interpretation of the rise of modern societies from processes of rationalization and the expansion of administrative-bureaucratic power would be sufficient. The basic focus of their inquiry was to investigate how authoritarian structures of society were transformed into intrapsychic mechanisms in such a way that even the suffering borne under these structures could contribute to their stabilization. If one wants to speak of a hard core of the research program of critical theory in its first phase, this was found in a social-psychological approach that linked Marx's theory of society to Freud's psychoanalysis. This was expected to explain precisely this interdependence of psychic and social foundational structures. When Horkheimer took over the direction of the Institute of Social Research in 1931, he declared its goal to be the exploration of "the interconnection between the economical life of society, the psychic development of the individual and transformations in the realm of culture."[5]

The methodology of this program of research that linked analytical psychology, a critical theory of society, and dialectical philosophy was indeed the same "hermeneutics of suspicion" of which Paul Ricoeur later spoke. For these thinkers, consciousness itself is no longer an absolute. Instead now the Cartesian doubt is carried "to the very heart of the Cartesian stronghold."[6] But with this methodology, through a "hermeneutics of retrieval," a more encompassing concept of reason and the conception of a transformative praxis were supposed to be gained. This transformative praxis would make possible an overcoming of these social and psychic mechanisms and the realization of this broader idea of reason.[7]

It has always been considered to be the most frustrating moment in the development of critical theory when at least Adorno and Horkheimer gave up the hope of reaching a broader concept of reason through a research project that brought together empirical sciences and dialectical philosophy. In the preface to their *Dialectic of Enlightenment* they wrote: "However, the fragments united in this volume show that we were forced to abandon this conviction."[8] In the meantime, the Second World War and the Holocaust had begun. In 1944, near the end of the war, at the highest point of the industrialized extermination of human beings on the battle fields and in the concentration camps, they characterized their project in the following way: "It turned out, in fact, that we had set before ourselves nothing less than the discovery of why humanity, instead of entering into a truly human condition, is sinking into a new kind of barbarism."[9] The suspicion had become more radical; it was now directed against the concepts of Enlightenment and of reason themselves.

The *Dialectic of Enlightenment*, which Habermas describes as the "blackest book" of critical theory,[10] actually remained a fragment. Horkheimer and Adorno attempted to reconstruct the history of human culture as a history of Enlightenment and thereby as a history of reason. For them, reason signifies the ability to free oneself from a prereflective bond with nature and to be differentiated from it. This capacity of distancing, however, contains within it at the same time the possibility of transforming nature into an object of domination; things become "the substrate of domination." The motive for this domination is the "will of self-assertion" and, ultimately, the fear of being dominated onself.[11] That is why the will of self-assertion as a will of domination over nature also becomes a will of domination over fellow-human beings. "For those in positions of power, however, human beings become raw material just like the whole of nature is for society."[12] This can only succeed when those who seek to dominate others, also have dominion over themselves. Human beings dominate themselves, in order to be able to dominate others as well as nature, in order not to be dominated themselves. Reason thus degenerates into an instrument of domination.

For Horkheimer and Adorno, the inner contradiction in the concept of reason can be traced through history:

> reason comprises the idea of a free, human social life in which men organize themselves as the universal subject and overcome the conflict between pure and empirical reason in the conscious solidarity of the whole. This represents the idea of true universality: utopia. At the same time, however, reason constitutes the court of judgment of calculation, which

adjusts the world for the end of self-preservation and recognizes no function other than the preparation of the object from mere sensory material in order to make it the material of subjugation.[13]

For Adorno, this contradiction cannot be overcome. Twenty years later, in one of the gloomiest passages of the *Negative Dialectics*, he wrote:

Universal history must be construed and denied. After the catastrophes that have happened, and in the view of the catastrophes to come, it would be cynical to say that a plan for a better world is manifested in history and unites it. Not to be denied for that reason, however, is the unity that cements the discontinuous, chaotically splintered moments and phases of history—the unity of the control of nature, progressing to rule over men, and finally to that over man's inner nature. No universal history leads from savagery to humanitarianism, but there is one leading from the slingshot to the megaton bomb.[14]

This is the famous construction of a universal context of delusion in the face of which the question arises how it can be broken through at all. For Adorno, one possibility seems to appear in art. "That works of art do exist, indicates that non-being could come into existence."[15] I do not want here to go into Adorno's aesthetic theory, but it seems to me that at this point the theological motifs also show their relevance.

Theological elements of the Jewish tradition appear as undercurrents throughout the history of critical theory. Prime advocate for this tradition was Walter Benjamin. Inspired by his friend Gershom Scholem, Benjamin had intensively studied Jewish mysticism since the 1920s. In 1929 he had a number of conversations with Adorno on the relationship between avant-garde art, historical materialism, and theology. From then on the relationship of critical theory to theology became a central topic in the personal relations between Benjamin and Adorno, and later on, also between Benjamin and Horkheimer. After Adorno himself had met Scholem in 1938, he wrote to Benjamin that he liked Scholem most "where he makes himself the advocate of the theological motif in your, and perhaps I may also say in my philosophy, and it will not have escaped you that a number of his arguments concerning the task of the theological motif, above all, that it is in truth as little eliminated in your method as in mine, converge with my San Remo discussions. . . ."[16] Of course it was unthinkable for them to directly adopt the current theological language. For in their minds the Hebrew Bible's ban on images was linked very closely with a radical critique of any objectifying metaphysics. Here also the motif of historical materialism prevailed: that one must consider the historical process from the perspective of its victims. For them the point was to link theological and materialistic thinking to each other and thereby to conceive both more clearly in their interrelatedness:

"A restoration of theology, or better, a radicalization of the dialectic into the very glowing core of theology, would at the same time have to mean an utmost intensification of the social-dialectical, indeed economic, motifs."[17] This "radicalization of the dialectic into the very glowing core of theology," however, would also transform theology and its expressions. Through his dealing with surrealism, Walter Benjamin had found the formula that "religious illumination" had to be transformed into "a profane illumination of materialist and anthropological inspiration."[18] Adorno called such profane illumination "inverse theology."[19]

Yet, this transformation of theology also had to signify a transformation of the profane and could therefore leave neither theology nor historical materialism unchanged. This is illustrated in Benjamin's concept of time. In his "Theses on the Philosophy of History"[20] he tried to show that truly revolutionary action, in which not only the conditions but also the subjects are changed, breaks through the linear time of the victor's history of progress and challenges the conclusiveness of the past. It thus puts into question the definitiveness of the fate of the victims of the historical process. The possibility of such a mode of action is not simply given, it must be prepared. Benjamin's concept of the "now-time" (*Jetztziet*) thereby tries to join together both the apocalyptic-messianic discourse about the radical transformation in the moment of redemption with the conception transformed through negative dialectics of a revolutionary mode of action that breaks through the historical context of coercion and through delusive consciousness.[21]

It cannot be said that Benjamin or Adorno or any other representative of critical theory was able to realize this transformation of theology beyond outlining these approaches. In addition, it is a question whether the conceptual tools with which especially Adorno worked were not inadequate in themselves. This, anyway, is the criticism from Jürgen Habermas which stimulated him to reconstruct critical theory. It remains open whether this reconstruction preserves the cutting edges of the radical questions of the first generation of critical theory, and whether it is able to show from the new foundation of a theory of communicative action what a transformation of theological discourse might mean.

The Reconstruction of Critical Theory by Jürgen Habermas and Theology

While Habermas's thinking essentially has to be understood as a continuation of the work of the first generation of critical theory, this continuation is equally an independent basic "reconstruction" of the whole approach. In this reconstruction, Habermas proceeds on the assumption that the statement of a universal context of delusion is not just an historical diagnosis, but has also been caused by the theoretical means employed. For him, the older critical theory could conceive modern rationality only as a technical-instrumental rationality because it starts from a philosophy of consciousness within which the subject was primarily taken as a subject that dominates. In order to attain a concept of transformative praxis which would be relevant for our historical and social situation, it also seemed crucial to explicate another, equally important mode of human action. This mode is anchored just as deeply in the natural history of the human species and in the structure of human competences like instrumental action. It does not, however, aim at objectification and domination, but at the autonomous responsibility [*Mündigkeit*] of the individual in an intersubjectivity of unconstrained agreement.

This ability, which is founded in the history of the species, is that of interaction mediated through language. Language is the starting point for the history of the species and for anthropology. It constitutes the connection of subjectivity and intersubjectivity and through it a relationship towards reality as a whole. Habermas still finds the sentences he formulated in 1965 fundamentally valid: "The human interest in autonomy and responsibility is not mere fancy, for it can be apprehended *a priori*. What raises us out of nature is the only thing whose nature we can know: language. Through its structure autonomy and responsibility are posited for us. With the first sentence the intention of a universal and unconstrained consensus is unmistakably expressed."[22] With this interconnectedness of linguistic action, the autonomy of the individual and a general, unconstrained consensus, the basic idea of a theory of communicative action has been formulated.

I consider this approach as fundamentally correct in its central intuition—not only because it aims at a human praxis that breaks through the constraint of self-assertion accomplished through the accumulation of power, but also because theoretically this kind of approach seems to be the one most likely to solve the limit problems of a theory of the natural sciences and the human sciences.[23] Of course, the sentences quoted also call attention to the problems of the theoretical status of this approach: it asks for a new kind of association between philosophical reflection and the empirical sciences. It is in need (1) of a philosophical foundation that starts from the presuppositions which necessarily have to be made in communicative action. Yet, it also asks for an embodiment of these insights in an analysis of both (2) the architectonic and the ontogenesis of the competences of a subject capable of action, and (3) in an analysis of the rise of these competences in phylogenesis, in the history of the species. It should be clear that crucial problems in scientific theory are present in this connection.

In order to understand correctly the status of this approach, and thus its possible relationship to theology, one has to consider as well the philosophical-historical background from which Habermas argues. In 1954, Habermas in his dissertation *Das Absolute und die Geschichte. Von der Zwiespältigkeit in Schellings Denken* ("The Absolute and History. On the Conflict in Schelling's

Thinking") had treated the basic problems of modernity's critique of meta-physics.[24] This critique in postwar Germany had been articulated on the one side by Heidegger and his pupils, and on the other side by thinkers within the Marxist tradition, above all, by representatives of critical theory. This philo-sophical critique, inasmuch as it joined the self-critique within classical phi-losophy, considered itself at the culmination of a dramatic development. It wanted to show that metaphysical thinking would inevitably be full of aporias, because it had always tried to grasp the whole of reality and, as its ground, an Absolute. Yet this Absolute, in becoming the object of thinking, was subjected to this thinking and could not be the Absolute anymore. It thus had to be dis-tinguished again from the object of thought as something still more original, but only to appear thereby once again as a product of thinking.[25] This aporia within modern metaphysics that made everything into an object—an aporia which stimulated the subsequent philosophical development—had been most acutely analyzed by Schelling.[26] Starting from Schelling's analyses, Habermas tried to show that Feuerbach and Marx in their critique of metaphysics and theology had voiced a major suspicion: namely, that the construction of an absolute is the projection of a human being who is not yet free from illusion and able to find a place in a contradictory historical and social reality. Habermas's conclusion from this critique, taken in opposition to Heideggerian thought, is the turn to a "philosophy of history with a practical intent." Here, indeed, he saw himself in accord with radical Jewish mysticism. In 1971 Habermas charac-terized the relation of postmetaphysical thinking to theology in this way: "Post-metaphysical thought does not challenge any specific theological assertions; rather it asserts their meaninglessness. It wants to prove that, in the basic con-ceptual system in which the Judeo-Christian tradition is dogmatized (and hence rationalized), theologically meaningful statements cannot be asserted."[27] He adds: "This critique . . . strikes at the roots of religion."[28] This philosophical background must be considered if one wants to understand Habermas's ap-proach to the theory of communicative action, as well as his position with respect to the history of religion and to theology.

At first, Habermas tries to demonstrate the structure and the normative implications of communicative action by examining the genesis of human competences for action. For this, he refers to the theories of developmental psychology that explain the acquisition of different capabilities: theories of the development of cognitive (Jean Piaget) and interactive abilities (George Herbert Mead; John H. Flavell; Robert Selman); of the abilities of moral judgment and action (Lawrence Kohlberg); and theories of the development of individual psychological drives, following Freud. Looking at a child's development it is possible to see each successive step towards greater autonomy and independence as being accompanied by a corresponding step towards greater mutual interac-tion in human relationships, reaching steadily outward. The entire development seems to progress according to an inherent tendency: an individual identity initially dependent on the simple physical attention of others, gradually, through a long, drawn-out, and painful process of transformation, becomes an identity which does not depend simply on certain inculcated rules, but is itself capable of assuming responsibility for shaping and formulating the rules of communal life. Similarly, the goal of the development of moral consciousness would then be the ability to build a communicative world in which human beings can find ways of living together which enable every individual to work out his or her own lifestyle based on the recognition and respect of others, and to do so ultimately in a universal perspective not confined to small groups or nations. Individual freedom and universal solidarity would then be harmonious rather than contradictory concepts.

This form of communicative action includes a normative core which defines the basis of ethics. The attempts to formulate this core concur, it seems to me, in the following basic thesis: If I enter into communication with another person at all, I accept that person in principle as someone who is able to speak and make herself or himself understood and to contradict me. I accept that person as an equal partner and am prepared in what I say to expose myself to that person's criticism and response and to attempt to reach agreement with her or him on the truth of statements or the correctness of norms. These fundamental and inescapable suppositions depend primarily on the recognition and acceptance of the other person, an acceptance which must prove itself in jointly worked out norms of behavior. This mutual acceptance, in principle, can exclude no one as a partner in communication. The moment I begin to speak I enter a universal dialogue.

It is at this point of the reconstruction of the human competences of action and the corresponding forms of social agreement on the scale of the history of the human race that religion finds its significant role. Large parts of Habermas's *Theory of Communicative Action* can thus also be read as a dialogue with religion.[29] The first volume is focused on a discussion of Max Weber's analysis of western rationalization and its religious presuppositions. The second volume treats the thesis that in social evolution religion, which according to Durkheim guaranteed the social integration of a society, is replaced by communicative ethics.

Max Weber's reconstruction of the history of religion and Western rationalization is directed by the intention of highlighting in its genesis the final result of this development, namely the loss of meaning and of freedom in modern society. This reconstruction contains a double critique: (1) of the direction of this rationalization, thus also of the Enlightenment; (2) of the development of religion and its rationalization by its transformation into an individualizing ethics in which people set out to prove themselves in a capitalistic society of competition and turn against an original ethics of brotherliness. Weber, therefore, is also interested in the critique of a state of society: precisely the meaningless and freedom-threatening rationalized world of economics, of politics and of science. Weber's demonstration of the shortcomings of religion can therefore be interpreted as a critique of society; he shows that social conditions only allow a certain way of realizing religion and dooms other ways of realization to failure or to mere particularity.[30]

In opposition to Weber, Habermas wants to put forward another understanding of the social processes of modernization and rationalization. With the earlier critical theorists, he also accuses Weber of only introducing a concept of rationality that is limited to purposive reason (*Zweckrationalität*). In contrast, Habermas conceives the processes of modernization precisely as the release of communicative rationality. He explains the pathologies of modern societies from the functional constraints and the inner dynamics of the economical and political-administrative systems themselves. These "colonize" areas that constitutively depend upon the priority of unconstrained communicative action, for example, socialization, social integration and cultural reproduction.[31] Pathological developments in the individual can then be explained as appropriations of the pathologies of society.

At the same time Habermas tries to show in his treatment of Durkheim that with the spreading of communicative ethics in society the integrating function of religion becomes superfluous. Durkheim had conceived religion as the social bond of a normative consensus that receives the character of the sacred and is renewed in ritual.[32] In this way, religion can camouflage and legitimize unjust conditions of violence behind the veil of the holy. When in the course of the development of social forms of agreement the normative consensus is joined to discursive agreement, the authority of the sacred is dissolved. Religion loses not only its ability to protect structural violence by curtailing communication, but to a large degree is itself dissolved.[33] As Habermas explains, "to the extent that language becomes established as the principle of sociation, the conditions of socialization converge with the conditions of communicatively produced intersubjectivity. At the same time, the authority of the sacred is converted over to the binding force of normative validity claims that can be redeemed only in discourse."[34]

Yet recently Habermas has stressed that communicative reason cannot simply take over the role of religion. Above all, it cannot console. This results in the ambivalent position of a tolerant standing next to each other, a skeptical but peaceful coexistence:

Communicative reason does not enact itself in an aesthetic theory as the colorless negative of consoling religions. Neither does it announce the disconsolateness of a god-forsaken world, nor itself pretend to console. It also renounces exclusivity. As long as it does not find any better words in the medium of reasoned speech for that what religion can say, it will, without supporting it or combating it, abstinently co-exist with it.[35]

This is no longer simply the position that claims to have overcome religion and theology in a meta-communicative way.[36] Nevertheless, in public *argumentative* discourse neither of them has a real place. But then are not religion and theology once again suspected of falling away from communicative reason?

Theology and the Theory of Communicative Action

Theology, if it does not want to abandon itself, obviously cannot renounce making a claim to truth. Moreover, in a pluralist society it must attempt to formulate its subject matter in an intersubjectively understandable and communicative way. The first requirement for it is then that it does not evade the aporias and contradictions of the common historical situation.[37] Theology cannot break away from the extreme experiences of suffering and annihilation of our century into a beyond calmly speculated upon. In the "solidarity of all finite beings" (Horkheimer), the setting for theology's discourse remains wherever there can be individual and communal historical action in protest against extermination. It cannot suppress the question of theodicy through an amnesia that represses world history, nor, like conservative political theologies, leave the answer to innerworldly political or religious sovereigns. Theology, remembering this finiteness and death and in historical solidarity with humanity, must first of all hold the question of theodicy open. It also cannot use dialectic in theology to put itself in the position of the "totally Other"; by holding on to the historical negativity, rather, it must insist on that "radicalization of the dialectic into the very glowing core of theology."

For Habermas the claim to communicative reason is itself already a transcending power. "Again and again this claim is silenced; and yet in fantasies and deeds it develops a stubbornly transcending power, because it is renewed with each act of unconstrained understanding, with each moment of living together in solidarity, of successful individuation, and of saving emancipation."[38] Communicative reason then aims at both freedom and reconciliation at the same time: "The utopian perspective of reconciliation and freedom is ingrained in the conditions for the communicative sociation of individuals; it is built into the linguistic mechanism of the reproduction of the species."[39] The question then becomes whether theology can appropriate the talk of reconciliation, of saving emancipation and of the transcending power of communicative action in Habermas's sense; or, rather, having been freed itself from the mechanisms of self-assertion and competing accumulation of power, theology has to make itself understandable as the theory of a communicative action which in remembrance and anticipation lays claim to God in God's acting here and now as the prevenient absolute love for the other and for oneself.

Concretely, the dialogue between theology and the reconstructed critical theory will have to be carried on: (1) with respect to the interpretation of the history of religion against the background of a theory of development of modern societies; (2) as an attempt of an independent, systematic reconstruction of its approach as a critical, society-related theology that considers it possible to start from a theory of intersubjectivity.

Interpretation of the Role of Religion in a Theory
of the Development of Modern Societies

The interpretation of history is by no means secondary for theology; it touches its very core. Theology will thus pay attention to the way in which historical development as a whole and, within this development, its own traditions are interpreted. These interpretations shape the fundamental understanding of religion and especially of the world religions. For Habermas their prime task is clear: "Whereas mythical narratives interpret and make comprehensible a ritual praxis of which they themselves are part, religious and metaphysical worldviews of prophetic origin have the form of doctrines that can be worked up intellectually, and that explain and justify an existing political order in terms of the world-order they explicate."[40]

The question, however, is whether, historically, the task of religion, and especially the world religions, has been adequately described. With good reasons one can support the thesis that the basic problem in the development of advanced civilizations since the Neolithic revolution—and until today—is the accelerating accumulation and systematic organization of power.[41] The world religions by no means have reacted to this development and to the social injustice of class-divided societies only by legitimizing them. Indeed, in their origin and in their core, they are often protest movements against the basic trend of a society's development and attempt to ground other ways for human beings to relate to one another and to reality as a whole. This could be shown, for example, in early Buddhist texts. Here, I just want to point out some results of research in the Jewish and Christian traditions.

Max Weber had already conceived the ancient Israelitic union of tribes as a "confederation" (*Eidgenossenschaft*). Research has shown that responding to the accumulation of power in the neighboring ancient Near Eastern empires was fundamental for the whole of Jewish tradition. In contrast, the Israelite confederation of tribes constituted itself as an egalitarian society.[42] The experiences from this conflict were a driving force in the development of the understanding of that reality which can be called "God" and in what way their confession of God includes a specific societal communicative practice. The original profession of faith of Judaism is that of liberation from the slavery of Egypt. This experience is intensified during the period of exile and finally in the fight against the Seleucid empire in the second century, B.C.E. The latter was a totalitarian system that not only practiced external repression, but also tried to control the consciences of individuals. The apocalyptic originates as an answer to this exterminating power of the state. In an ever more radical way, God is confessed as the one who, intervening eschatologically, robs this untamable power of its force. God deprives this eschatological animal, with its continually reappearing new heads, of its ability to exterminate human beings, and in a way that extends even beyond the grave: God is the saving power whose range of action does not end at the threshold of death. God can call even the dead to life and make up for past injustice.[43] The knowledge of God includes the knowledge that a communal existence is possible, an existence that is not dominated by the mechanisms of power accumulation.

Viewed historically, Jesus is the one who decisively changes this apocalyptical understanding of history. For him also, of course, God is the one who in an eschatological intervention ultimately transforms the world through its completion. But the evil nexus has already been broken. ("I watched Satan fall from the sky like lightning," Luke 10:18.) God has begun to reign in unconditioned goodness and to restore creation. It is now not only possible, but necessary, indeed a matter of course, that one should realize this prevenient goodness of God practically: in the unconditioned affirmation of the other, even the one who may be an enemy. For this person, too, has been affirmed unconditionally. The execution of Jesus becomes the starting point for the experience and the confession that this is also true for his own person: that precisely in his death, he is saved and that, from now on, an intersubjective mode of conduct has become possible for all, in which we progress toward God as the saving reality even in death. Intersubjectivity is qualified in a new way; God's dominion means the abandonment of the domination of human beings over each other.

The fundamental problem of the history of Christianity is that, once it achieved the possibility of sharing power, it did not follow in an unequivocal way this claim to which it owes its existence. Seen historically, the problem of the relationship between religion and power has not been solved in Christianity. But this does not mean that theology was not able to or was not called to continually formulate this claim across the history of religions again and again. On the contrary, theology acts against the ground of its existence when it becomes an ideology of oppression; "theology of liberation" does not have to be a self-contradicting term.

The Task of Reconstructing Theology from a Theory of Intersubjectivity

How can a theology then be developed which is equal both to the claims of its tradition and to its own historical situation, and which thus faces up to the Enlightenment critique and its own self-critique? The project of Christian theology is yet unfinished. I would like, however, to point out at least the dimensions of this task and some basic problems.[44]

1. Theology must develop its expressions in discussions with the formal sciences, the natural sciences, with the human sciences in their genetic-reconstructive method, and with philosophy. Here the question of the foundation of ethics plays a decisive role. The classical transcendental foundation of ethics, as with Kant, obtains its evidence precisely from the circularity of its argumentation. Freedom only develops fully in the affirmation of another's freedom; by negating in principal another freedom, it destroys itself. Karl-Otto Apel's transformation of the Kantian ethics on the level of a theory of communication is also dependent upon such circular evidence when it falls back upon the procedure of argumentation: If I ask for reasons at all, I have always already acknowledged the other as a communication partner who is able to contradict me with reasons. Yet the starting point for this reasoning is the conception of the already fully developed autonomous subject. On the basis of its competences it interprets reality and acts in mastery over it. In this presupposition, however, lie the limits of this conception. For example, in situations of inequality and oppression, but also in therapeutic and pedagogical action, it is precisely the point that there must first be created for someone the possibility to agree with me or contradict me in freedom.

It therefore seems necessary to establish the ground of ethics on a deeper level. To intend the free recognition of the other in that person's freedom means to want the other person to *become* himself or herself by way of an intersubjectively reflected self-determination. Such action aims at the genesis of subjects; it wants to make life possible and recognizes itself as responsible for its preconditions. Such a radicalization of ethics aims at helping possible freedom realize itself as real freedom. This kind of ethics also changes the concept of intersubjective action. This can be illustrated in the understanding of language. From what we know from the foundations of logic, scientific theory, linguistics and philosophical pragmatics, to speak implies the creative projection of an interpretation of subjective, social and objective reality on to my conversation partner in a way that both opens up an understanding to that person and invites my partner to share her or his own creative interpretation with me. Thereby, we enter into a mutual process of *finding* a possible consensus which is not unequivocally preformed by conventions, but which preserves its character of being an innovative process for all participants. This way of provoking freedom through freedom is the condition of the possibility of an intersubjectively reflected commitment to agreements. In such a radicalized ethics, I also see the possibility of a discussion with "postmodern" theories of language.[45]

2. The character of this ethics, however, only becomes fully apparent when one takes into account that communicative action is always situation-related, temporal action; as this action changes present situations, it remembers things past and projects the future. An ethics that proceeds from the implications of the conversations about validity claims is always in danger of losing sight of the

temporality of human activity.[46] The practical recognition of the freedom of the other in communicative action, which means the willing of his or her genesis as a subject, aims, however, at the future realization of possibilities of freedom which, in part, can only first be disclosed in mutual activity. This recognition affirms in an unconditioned way a developing, yet still presumed integrity of the other which does not lie within the power of the one initiating the communication. This mode of communicative action that sets out from the freedom and the integrity of the other trusts in more than what it could achieve by itself.

3. Such an ethics of intersubjective creativity, admittedly, makes the tragical and antinomical character of ethical activity even more obvious. A person who orients herself or himself toward the freedom of the other as an end in itself, exposes herself or himself. That person becomes all the more vulnerable the more she or he is oriented to the freedom of the other and abandons without limitation any strategic-manipulative action directed toward the preservation of her or his own existence or social system. Freedom reaches its fulfillment only in being freely recognized through the other; yet it is precisely this acknowledgement that is not at its own disposal. Innovative freedom thus exposes itself to the danger of being futile, indeed, of being extinguished. The paradox in the founding of practical reason consists in that freedom, by accepting an unconditional interest in the realization of freedom and reconciliation, takes on the risk of itself being destroyed.[47]

4. This discussion about the destruction and annihilation of freedom is not merely metaphorical; it characterizes real historical experiences. The tradition of all great religions centers around the memory that men and women have perished in their attempts to act ethically in an unconditioned way. The remembrance of those just men and women who suffered and were destroyed, the "*memoria passionis et mortis*" belongs to the core of both the Jewish and the Christian traditions. For these traditions, the Holocaust, *the* experience of annihilation in our century, has proved an extreme challenge.[48] Its remembrance is not simply exhausted in the moral demand that this must never be repeated. For communicative action, which in the face of the annihilated victims still anticipates the communicative realization of possible freedom in a practical way and in this exposes itself to the risk of failure, the question of the salvation of the annihilated victims arises: the quest for an absolute freedom, saving even in death. The analytics and dialectics of communicative action point beyond themselves to the question of the foundation of theology.

5. The question that emerges here is the question about that which in the Jewish and Christian traditions is called "God." The "concept" of God which is outlined in temporal, finite, self-transcending intersubjective action in the form of a question encouraged by hope is not the concept of an absolute that we could have demonstrated through the drives of our objectifying thought. It is the concept of an absolute freedom, a freedom before which we hope that in the mortally-finite surpassing of ourselves it shows its true self, namely, as

absolutely liberating and saving love. Is such an analysis of intersubjective action and its structure illusionary?[49] It certainly would be, if it led us out of the concrete dialectic of our historical action. Yet, it does not lead us outside of our situation, but, rather, more radically into it.

6. I realize that here all the classical questions of a philosophical doctrine of God and of the relationship between metaphysical thought and theology reappear. Yet, to refuse to give up at this point the task of reflection does not necessarily mean a relapse into an objectifying metaphysics.[50] A way of thinking which has untangled itself from the compulsion to objectify in grasping reality as a whole—a "postmetaphysical" thinking in this sense—does not also have to be a "post-theological" thinking. It can, however, draw attention to experiences which cannot simply be reduced to a mythical consciousness. Along these lines I understand Adorno's sentences in the *Negative Dialectics:* "What demythologization would not affect . . . is . . . the experience that if thought is not decapitated, it will flow into transcendence, down to the idea of a world that would not only abolish extant suffering but revoke the suffering that is irrevocably past."[51]

7. I believe that a hermeneutics both of the interpretation of the praxis and preaching of the historical Jesus and of speech about resurrection (if this is not simply to be presented as something miraculous) can only be developed from a prior analysis of the dialectic of finite, temporal, and intersubjective action. For this speech, the common advance towards death is the hopeful advance towards God: a God who is that reality which in the midst of a death-bringing historical-social context reveals itself as liberating and as making conversion possible, and which proves itself as saving in death. In this discourse, it is clear that affirmation in solidarity as the assertion of the reality of God for the other person cannot be limited. It always already proceeds from the assertion of the salvation of the past, of the annihilated, from the "death of death." Then, however, a fundamental-theological hermeneutics of the reality of resurrection can make the resurrection of Jesus understandable as an event that is not completely isolated from us, but rather an event which first makes possible an existence in unconditional and unlimited solidarity and which is the ground of that ecstatic joy which belongs to the heart of Christianity.[52] This means, conversely, that this salvation in death has only been grasped if it holds good in the unconditioned acknowledgment of the other here and now. Then communicative action, in which human beings drawing from this experience expect from each other an existence in illimitable solidarity, is constitutive for Christian existence which works in a concrete society for its transformation.[53]

Final Remarks

I have started from the thesis that in our historical situation both the projects of theology and that of Enlightenment (and within this, the project of critical theory) are proved to be unfinished. This situation is characterized by a heretofore unknown expansion of human possibilities of action and by the tendency to organize these possibilities into competing systems of power accumulation, whose repercussions again threaten us. Today we know more about the conditions of our common existence than all previous generations, but we seem a long way off from being able to conceive it as a whole, much less to fundamentally change it. In addition, the plurality of languages and the ambiguity of interpretations continue to grow.[54]

Religion and the Enlightenment represent attempts to grasp the *condition humaine* as a whole, whether it be in mythical images or, also in theology, in argumentative discourse. The Enlightenment tried to determine the kind of rationality that would make a universal discourse possible in which a consensus of *all* as a basis for transformative action could be achieved. To do this it had to determine the limits of rationality and to exclude certain modes of self-interpretation. The question remains, however, whether this must lead to the conclusion that the religious traditions of humanity and their theological argumentation must be altogether excluded from the universal discourse.

It could be that we grasp the dimensions of crucial themes in our common public discourse only when we include these traditions and forms of argumentation, that only then can we completely grasp what this involves: the integrity and inviolable dignity of human beings; human rights in the wider social context in addition to the codified basic rights and the rights to political participation; justice that is more than the equal treatment of unequals, but that seeks to make individual integrity really possible; forms of discourse that enable the voiceless to speak; innovative conciliatory action that opens up the possibility for peace; and a solidarity which also includes the dead and the generations to come.[55]

Notes

1. Søren Kierkegaard, *Philosophical Fragments*, 2d ed., trans. David F. Swenson with revision by Howard V. Hong (Princeton, NJ: Princeton University Press, 1962), 11ff.
2. Carl Friedrich von Weizsäcker, *Bewußtseinswandel* (Munich: Hanser, 1988), 179.
3. See Johann Baptist Metz, *Faith in History and Society* (New York: Seabury, 1980); Gustavo Gutiérrez, *A Theology of Liberation* (Maryknoll, NY: Orbis, 1973); Clodovis Boff, *Theology and Praxis* (Maryknoll, NY: Orbis, 1987); David Tracy, *Plurality and Ambiguity: Hermeneutics, Religion, Hope* (San Francisco: Harper & Row, 1987).
4. See Helmut Peukert, *Bildung und Vernunft* (Frankfurt am Main: Suhrkamp, in press); Peukert, "Über die Zukunft von Bildung," in *Frankfurter Hefte*, FH-extra 6 (1984):129–37.
5. Max Horkheimer, "Die gegenwärtige Lage der Sozialphilosophie und die Aufgaben eines Instituts für Sozialforschung," in *Sozialphilosophische Studien* (Frankfurt am Main: Athenäum Fischer Verlag, 1972), 43; see Helmut Dubiel, *Wissenschaftsorganisation und politische Erfahrung. Studien zur frühen kritischen Theorie* (Frankfurt am Main, 1978); Martin Jay, *The Dialectical Imagination: A History of the Frankfurt School and the Institute of Social Research, 1923–1950* (Boston: Little Brown, 1973); see David Held, *Introduction to Critical Theory: Horkheimer to Habermas* (Berkeley: University of California Press, 1980), 33.
6. Paul Ricoeur, *Freud and Philosophy: An Essay in Interpretation*, trans. Denis Savage (New Haven, CT: Yale University Press, 1970), 33.

7. See Max Horkheimer, *Traditionelle und kritische Theorie. Vier Aufsätze* (Frankfurt am Main: Fischer Verlag, 1970); Herbert Marcuse, *Kultur und Gesellschaft*, vol. 1 (Frankfurt am Main: Suhrkamp, 1965), partially translated in *Negations: Essays in Critical Theory* (Boston: Beacon Press, 1968).
8. Max Horkheimer and Theodor W. Adorno, *Dialectic of Enlightenment*, trans. John Cumming (New York: Seabury Press, 1975), xi.
9. Ibid., translation slightly modified.
10. Jürgen Habermas, *The Philosophical Discourse of Modernity: Twelve Lectures*, trans. Frederick G. Lawrence (Cambridge, MA: MIT Press, 1987), 106.
11. Horkheimer and Adorno, *Dialektik der Aufklärung* (Amsterdam: Querido, 1947), 79. This has been republished by Fischer Verlag (Frankfurt am Main, 1969).
12. Ibid.
13. Horkheimer and Adorno, *Dialectic of Enlightenment*, 83–84.
14. Theodor W. Adorno, *Negative Dialectics*, trans. E. B. Ashton (New York: Seabury Press, 1973), 320.
15. Theodor W. Adorno, *Ästhetische Theorie*, in *Gesammelte Schriften* (Frankfurt am Main: Suhrkamp, 1970), 17:200. [ET: *Aesthetic Theory* (London: Routledge Methuen, 1986).]
16. Letter, Adorno to Benjamin, May 4th, 1938, Adorno Estate; see Susan Buck-Morss, *The Origin of Negative Dialectics: Theodor W. Adorno, Walter Benjamin and the Frankfurt School* (Hassocks, Sussex: Harvester Press, 1977), 284 n. 49.
17. Letter, Adorno to Benjamin, August 2, 1935, in Theodor W. Adorno, *Über Walter Benjamin*, ed. Rolf Tiedemann (Frankfurt am Main: Suhrkamp, 1975), 117; translated in Buck-Morss, *Origin*, 144.
18. Walter Benjamin, "Der Sürrealismus. Die letzte Momentaufnahme der europäischen Intelligenz," in *Angelus Novus: Ausgewählte Schriften* (Frankfurt am Main: Suhrkamp, 1966), 213; translated in Buck-Morss, *Origin*, 125.
19. Letter, Adorno to Benjamin, November 6, 1934, Adorno Estate; see Buck-Morss, *Origin*, 282 n. 34.
20. Walter Benjamin, "Über den Begriff der Geschichte," in *Gesammelte Schriften*, ed. Rolf Tiedemann and H. Schweppenhäuser (Frankfurt am Main: Suhrkamp, 1980), 1:691–704.
21. See Richard Wolin, *Walter Benjamin: An Aesthetic of Redemption* (New York: Columbia University Press, 1982), 263.
22. See Jürgen Habermas, *Knowledge and Human Interests*, trans. Jeremy J. Shapiro (Boston: Beacon Press, 1971), appendix, 314.
23. See H. Peukert, *Science, Action and Fundamental Theology: Toward a Theology of Communicative Action*, trans. James Bohman (Cambridge, MA: MIT Press, 1984).
24. Dissertation, Bonn 1954; see J. Habermas, "Dialektischer Idealismus im Übergang zum Materialismus — Schellings Idee einer Contraction Gottes," in *Theorie und Praxis. Sozialphilosophische Studien* (Frankfurt am Main: Suhrkamp, 1971), 172–227.
25. Walter Schulz, *Der Gott der neuzeitlichen Metaphysik*, 3rd ed. (Pfullingen: Neske, 1957).
26. Walter Schulz, *Die Vollendung des deutschen Idealismus in der Spätphilosophie Schellings* (Pfullingen: Neske, 1955).
27. Jürgen Habermas, "Wozu noch Philosophie?" in *Philosophisch-politische Profile*, enlarged edition (Frankfurt am Main: 1981) 29 [ET: *Philosophical-Political Profiles*, trans. Frederick Lawrence (Cambridge, MA: MIT Press, 1985); translation found in Peukert, *Science, Action and Fundamental Theology*, 162.
28. Ibid.
29. Jürgen Habermas, *The Theory of Communicative Action*, 2 vols., trans. Thomas McCarthy (Boston: Beacon Press, 1985, 1987).; see Rudolf J. Siebert, *The Critical Theory of Religion: The Frankfurt School* (New York: Mouton, 1985), 108–334); Klaus-Michael Kodalle, "Versprachlichung des Sakralen? Zur religionsphilosophischen Auseinandersetzung mit Jürgen Habermas' Theorie des kommunikativen Handelns," in *Allgemeine Zeitschrift für Philosophie* 12 (1987):39–66.
30. See Karl W. Dahm, Volker Drehsen, and Günter Kehrer, *Das Jenseits der Gesellschaft. Religion in Prozebsozialwissenschaftlicher Kritik* (Munich: Claudius Verlag, 1975), 325.
31. See Habermas, *The Theory of Communicative Action*, 2:119ff.
32. Ibid., 43ff.

370 • The Frankfurt School on Religion

33. Ibid., 188ff.
34. Ibid., 93–94.
35. Jürgen Habermas, "Die Einheit der Vernunft in der Vielheit ihrer Stimmen," in *Nachmetaphysisches Denken* (Frankfurt am Main: Suhrkamp, 1988), 153–86, 185.
36. Peukert, *Science, Action and Fundamental Theology*, 160–62.
37. See Tracy, *Plurality and Ambiguity*.
38. Jürgen Habermas, "A Reply to my Critics," in John B. Thompson and David Held, eds., *Habermas: Critical Debates* (Cambridge, MA: MIT Press, 1982), 219–88, 221.
39. Habermas, *The Theory of Communicative Action*, 1:398.
40. Habermas, *The Theory of Communicative Action*, 2:188.
41. See Peukert, "Universale Solidarität—Verrat an Bedrohten und Wehrlosen?" in *Diakonia* 8 (1978) 3–12.
42. See Norman K. Gottwald, *The Tribes of Yahweh: A Sociology of the Religion of Liberative Israel 1250–1050 B.C.E.*, 3rd ed. (Maryknoll, NY: Orbis 1985), esp. Part X: "The Religion of the New Egalitarian Society: Idealist, Structural-Functionalist, and Historical Cultural-Materialist Models," 591–663.
43. Klaus Müller, "Apokalyptik, Apokalypsen III. Die jüdische Apokalyptik," in *Theologische Realenzyklopädie III*, 202–51.
44. Peukert, *Science, Action and Fundamental Theology*, 143ff.; Helmut Peukert, "Fundamentaltheologie," in Peter Eicher, ed., *Neues Handbuch theologischer Grundbegriffe* (Munich: Kösel, 1984), 2:16–25; see also Edmund Arens, ed., *Habermas und die Theologie* (Düsseldorf: Patmos, 1989); Rudolf Siebert, *From Critical Theory to Communicative Political Theology* (New York: Peter Lang, 1989).
45. See Helmut Peukert, "Intersubjektivität—Kommunikationsgemeinschaft—Religion. Bemerkungen zu einer höchsten Stufe der Entwicklung moralischen Bewußtseins durch K.-O. Apel," in *Intersoggetività—Socialità—Religione*, ed. Marco M. Olivetti (Padova: Cedam, 1986), 167–78.
46. See Habermas, *Vorstudien und Ergänzungen*, 553.
47. See Thomas Pröpper, *Erlösungsglaube und Freiheitsgeschichte*, 2d ed. (Munich: Kösel, 1988), 165–71.
48. See Johann Baptist Metz, "Im Angesicht der Juden. Christliche Theologie nach Auschwitz," in *Concilium* (Ger.) 20 (1984):382–89.
49. See Thomas McCarthy, "Philosophical Foundations of Political Theology: Kant, Peukert and the Frankfurt School," in *Civil Religion and Political Theology*, ed. Leroy S. Rouner (Notre Dame, IN: University of Notre Dame Press, 1986) 23–40.
50. See Klaus Schäfer, *Hermeneutische Ontologie in den Climacusschriften Sören Kierkegaards* (Munich: Kösel, 1968), esp. pp. 112ff. on the relation between Kierkegaard and Schelling. Precisely from Kierkegaard's critique of the "metaphysical" could the discussion about metaphysics begin again.
51. Adorno, *Negative Dialectics*, 403.
52. See Karl Rahner, "Grundlinien einer systematischen Christologie," in Karl Rahner and Wilhelm Thüsing, *Christologie — systematisch und exegetisch* (Freiburg: Herder, 1972), 17–78; Francis Schüssler Fiorenza, *Foundational Theology: Jesus and the Church* (New York: Crossroad, 1984), esp. 5–55).
53. See Matthew L. Lamb, *Solidarity with Victims: Toward a Theology of Social Transformation* (New York: Crossroad, 1982).
54. See Tracy, *Plurality and Ambiguity*.
55. Helmut Peukert, "Praxis universaler Solidarität. Grenzprobleme im Verhältnis von Erziehungswissenschaft und Theologie," in Edward Schillebeeckx, ed., *Mystik und Politik. Theologie im Ringen um Geschichte und Gesellschaft* (Mainz: Matthias-Grünewald Verlag, 1968), 172–85; Francis Schüssler Fiorenza, "Politische Theologie und liberale Gerechtigkeits-Konzeptionen," in ibid., 105–17.

XI
Edmund Arens

25

Religion as Ritual, Communicative, and Critical Praxis

Edmund Arens
Translated by Chad Kautzer

Religion is first and foremost not a "view of life," but rather a "way of life." In this respect, it is not primarily about a *Weltanschauung*, i.e., a particular epistemological claim on or a particular view of reality, but fundamentally about a praxis of life. It is in this sense that the principle of the theological theory of action formulated by Helmut Peukert is to be taken: "Faith is itself a practice that, as a practice, asserts God for others in communicative action and attempts to confirm this assertion in action."[1] To what extent this claim, formulated from a theological perspective, holds religio-theoretically, and if and to what extent it can be made fruitful for the understanding of religion—thus to what extent religion can be understood as communicative praxis—will be discussed in this chapter.

Religion, as is argued in this chapter, has essentially to do with communication. Communication is, however, the basis of human life and social existence. There is no human existence without communication. Without communication, community is unthinkable. No society can manage without communicative exchange, without discursive dispute and understanding. Religion is also linked to communication in various respects. Religion and communication are profoundly connected with one another. Religious speech and action disclose reality and create community. Religion makes use, moreover, of different forms of communication and ways of enactment [*Handlungsvollzüge*]. It expresses itself in texts and traditions, taking place in diverse communication processes in ritual and communicative enactments. Whether proclamation or instruction, prayer or worship, prophesy or ministry, ritual or reflection—communication and action are always essentially at work. Religion is an action whose subjects, objects, contexts, media, and goals are implied. Religion is a ritual, communicative, and critical praxis. This can and shall be considered, but it must be done.

In the following, three positions come up for discussion with respect to a practical theory of religion, which grants religion a practical function and capacity. First, an understanding of religion as a praxis coping with contingency, which is manifest in systems-theoretic and functionalist approaches, is presented and criticized. The second section is concerned with positions that comprehend religion as essentially ritual praxis. The third section examines the relationship of religion and communicative praxis and attempts to answer the question of whether and under what circumstances religion can itself be understood as communicative praxis. Finally, in the fourth section, perspectives on a practical understanding of religion are addressed and developed.

I. Religion as Praxis Coping with Contingency

In the modern age, the experience of, as well as dealings with, the contingency of reality—as the contingency of one's own life—has become one of the basic problems of scientific theory construction and philosophical reflection. The German theologian Ernst Troeltsch already observed at the beginning of the twentieth century that the problem of contingency contained all philosophical problems *in nuce* and simultaneously concerned religious questions.[2] The American philosopher Richard Rorty sees the problem of contingency as decisive for his position, which he self-ironically describes as that of a postmodern bourgeois liberalism.[3] According to Rorty, it is the experience that we are ourselves contingent, that we are how we are only by chance—be it through luck or unluck and from no rational ground and without general meaning or purpose—which is typical for our postmodern times. "Our language and our culture," he pithily asserts, "are as much a contingency, as much a result of thousands of small mutations finding niches (and millions of others finding no niches), as are the orchids and the anthropoids."[4] This simply means that there is no general purpose, direction, universal conditions, or aims of human existence. Everything that we know and have accepted is the "sheer contingency"[5] of existence.

Rorty denies that there is any possibility of getting beyond our contingent existence, and he claims that whoever nowadays seeks to do so by means of religious or philosophical foundation "is still, in his heart, a theologian or a metaphysician."[6] For him, freedom consists essentially in our acceptance of contingency. Such acceptance is the chief virtue of members of a liberal society and the culture of such a society should be directed toward healing us from our "deep metaphysical need."[7] Rorty shows, in just as brilliant and provocative a fashion, that the problem of contingency does not merely affect questions limited to those connected with sickness, suffering, and death, but rather that the experience of contingency encompasses the whole of modern, or postmodern, life. Whereas Rorty as a liberal ironist strictly denies every type of religious or philosophical comfort, other social theorists and philosophers see the dealings and coping with contingency as the primary function (now more than ever) for religion. Included among them are Niklas Luhmann and Hermann Lübbe, whose approaches toward developing a practical theory of religion are as important as they are provocative.

Within the framework of his systems-theory of religion, Luhmann assigns to religion—whose achievements for the social system he locates in diaconal work and the care of souls—this function: "to transform the world, which is indeterminate because it is outwardly (environment) and inwardly (system) inconclusive, into a determinate one in which system and environment—which on both sides exclude the arbitrariness of change—can be related."[8] If religion could fulfill its function (making the world determinate) in the early stages of human social development—through the immediate sacralization and subsequent ritual treatment of the problem—then it would need more sophisticated mechanisms of coping with contingency, as society becomes more complex and reality is thereby increasingly experienced as contingent. Religion develops with it the contingency formula "God," which for the system of religion achieves the "transformation from indeterminate to determinate complexity,"[9] and thus not only explains contingent reality, but, with the help of a "good" God, simultaneously conducts "moral regulation of contingency."[10] As Peukert summarizes Luhmann's position, religion has "the function, which for a society is fundamental, of explaining the contingent reality of the possible with contingency formulas, and of absorbing destabilizing irritations that come from the experience of contingency in personality and societal systems."[11] Such religion comprises a professional praxis referring to salvation and grace that in a certain respect constitutes a transformative praxis—in so far as it transforms uncertainty into certainty—which supports its clients by coping with contingency and, in turn, helps them to do so. For Luhmann it is admittedly questionable, in view of the established degree of social differentiation and of the thereby given demands of reflection on the parts of the system under contemporary conditions, whether the problem of contingency can still find a satisfactory religious answer at all.

If for Luhmann the future of religion—which has for a long time integrated society into the world and up to now coped with contingency—is open, then for Hermann Lübbe the relevance, necessity, and future demand of religion coping with contingency are beyond doubt. In his work on the philosophy of religion, *Religion after the Enlightenment*,[12] Lübbe pointedly maintains that in the process of modernization and secularization, religion does not just fundamentally fade and finally vanish, but merely changes its forms of cultural expression. Lübbe holds that religion, in the course of this process, basically rids itself of its political and social restrictions in order to be able to adequately fulfill the task that its genuine contribution constitutes, which is namely to cope with contingency. Lübbe describes the task thereby posed for religion as "praxis coping with contingency." Colloquially, this would mean the praxis of overcoming contingency. According to Lübbe, however, contingency in reality just cannot be overcome. He notes: "What shall then 'coping' mean? The answer is: Coping with contingency is accepting contingency."[13]

According to Lübbe, religion deals with any contingency that bears on life's "indisposabilities." These indisposabilities, according to him, are neither affected by some form of enlightenment nor are they laid hold of through some form of emancipation: They are resistant to enlightenment and emancipation. They are simply there, as we too are simply there. Lübbe emphasizes (agreeing with Rorty throughout) that it is nothing but sheer chance that we exist instead of not existing, that we are what we are and nothing else. This contingent fact is not capable of being transformed into any meaning of action. It must simply be taken as such and that means being accepted. This is precisely what takes place in the praxis of religious life, which Lübbe conceives as intrinsically ritual. Rituals change nothing: They are in essence there to confirm that which exists, to sanction and bless it. Lübbe refers to ritual ceremonies like the consecration of a new house, a new highway, or a new president. In such ritual-religious praxis, nothing is added to what the builder of the house or the highway have created: rather it is simply affirmed in the face of technical or institutional accomplishments that the event of the moment is nothing other than an island lapped by an ocean of contingencies and indisposabilities. According to Lübbe, the question does not concern whether such praxis contains or refers to truth. He regards the question of truth as irrelevant in view of religion. What matters is whether religion really fulfills its function of coping with contingency through its acceptance of contingency.

Lübbe can even speak decisively of religion as a placebo.[14] He does not do this in order to criticize or unmask religion, but rather to demonstrate its function. Religion functions like a placebo, which means: Even though we know religion only pretends to be a heavenly medicine, that it *de facto* does not, of course, lead us beyond our contingent existence and to salvation and redemption, it works as if it does. It helps people stay healthy in the face of their contingent lives; it keeps us in shape and functioning, and it will exist so long as the sheer contingency of human existence does, and thus so long as there are people at all. This is, in fact, a pragmatic answer and simultaneously a cynical one.

On the one hand Lübbe rightly calls religion a praxis, a life praxis, and he recognizes that it manifests itself above all in ritual. On the other hand he strictly separates it from any moral, social, or political praxis. He emphasizes that religion has nothing to do with action, but rather takes place in our head, in the spiritual acceptance of our sheer contingency. Such a conceptualization is obviously not simply analytic and certainly not value free. It affirms a bodiless, alienated "bourgeois religion"[15] separated from real life and action—neither putting it in question nor changing anything. Quite the reverse, its function consists precisely in that it leaves everything as it was, preserves, legitimates, and sanctions the given status quo. In this respect, the apparent reaffirmation of religion after the Enlightenment proves to be a distortion of at least prophetic, biblical religion. This is needed for the maintenance of the social-political status quo. Religion is not affirmed for its own sake, but rather functions with the civil-religious intention to promote its social usefulness in the stabilization of existing relations.

In any systems-theoretic and functionalist approach, which—regardless of their internal differences—conceive of religion as (praxis) coping with contingency as Luhmann and Lübbe do, religion is functionalized and instrumentalized. Religion is made empty with regard to content and has no claims to truth; its intentionality is left out of consideration. It is meta-theoretically tailored to be responsible for residual problems and is at the same time reduced to a (merely) life-ordering religion [*Ordnungsreligion*]. If there is talk of religious praxis, it is strangely understood impractically and uncoupled from everyday praxis to the greatest possible extent. Such a theory of religion reduces practiced religion to a lubricant in the service of system's support and management.

Nevertheless, it must not be underestimated that systems-theoretic and functionalist theories of religion represent a temptation for existing religions— namely in view of their controversial claims not only of the secularization of the social sphere, but also in the name of deinstitutionalized postmodern religiosity—to willingly take up the position, which is, if anything, the only thing still demanded by their society, to become the very administrators and agents of contingency management.

II. Religion as Ritual Praxis

Religion is seen as ritual praxis in Anglo-American social anthropology in particular.[16] Of interest to theories of religion are above all the works of Victor Turner, who—following the classic studies of Arnold van Gennep on the "rites de passage"—studied the rites or rituals of passage and their characteristic features of what he calls the "ritual process."[17] From these rites of passage Turner determines three phases of ritual process, in which the religious dimensions and meanings of rituals simultaneously become evident.

For Turner, the ritual process exhibits three phases: the separation, margin, and aggregation phase.

The first phase (of separation) comprises symbolic behavior signifying the detachment of the individual or group either from an earlier fixed point in the social structure, from a set of cultural conditions (a "state"), or from both. During the intervening "liminal" period, the characteristics of the ritual subject (the "passenger") are ambiguous; he passes through a cultural realm that has few or none of the attributes of the past or coming state. In the third phase (reaggregation or reincorporation), the passage is consummated. The ritual subject, individual or corporate, is in a relatively stable state once more and, by virtue of this, has rights and obligations vis-à-vis others of a clearly defined and "structural" type; he is expected to behave in accordance with certain customary norms and ethical standards binding on incumbents of social position in a system of such positions. [18]

The rituals of passage—which Turner studied and documented largely with the Central African people of Ndembu in order to work out their general characteristics—are, first, always about one's removal of one from a given position in the group, community, or society; second, about a transitional phase in which the ritual subject no longer has the old, abandoned position, but does not yet have a new status; and, third, about the condition in which the passage is fulfilled, a new place or status reached, a new fixed position inside the group, community, or society is gained and occupied.

The middle or "margin" phase provides the key to understanding the ritual process, which Turner designates as "liminality." The characteristics of the "marginal condition" or "marginal person" are necessarily amorphous or undetermined. Marginal beings are neither here nor there; they are situated between socially fixed positions and are not integrated into the social structure. From this perspective they appear as outsiders, as transgressors. In the condition of liminality, however (and that is the point of Turner's investigations), something fundamental happens for ritual subjects. They have the experience of an alternative form of human relations that is opposed to the social structure, which Turner designates as "communitas." While the social structure represents a structured, differentiated, hierarchically arranged system of fixed political, legal, and economic positions, the communitas is an unstructured and relatively undifferentiated "communion of equal individuals who submit together to the general authority of the ritual elders." [19] In the ritual communitas there is no top and bottom: In the intermediate stage of statuslessness, an egalitarian community is experienced and practiced. The "margin" condition of spontaneous, immediate, concrete communitas comes into opposition with the status system of the norm-regulated social structure.

Turner discovers a religious, sacred quality in the margin phase. According to him, the religious quality of the marginal position in complex societies is conserved in definite religious enactments [*Vollzügen*] and institutions, although the liminal is here increasingly substituted by a secular liminality. According to Turner, the quality of transitional religious life appears nowhere "more clearly marked and defined than in the monastic and mendicant states in the great world religions."[20] The monastic communities and orders would therefore be something like institutionalized liminality, or attempts to, in the long run, set up communitas. Turner is, in this context, expressly alluding to the rule of the order of the holy Benedict; and he treats Francis of Assisi's movement of voluntary poverty under the rubric of permanent liminality. For St. Francis, religion was, according to Turner, communitas. The boundaries and paradigmatic destiny of spontaneous communitas are exhibited in the Franciscan movement. What is present in the mind of the founder as an ideal communitas requires structure in order to survive; it needs norms and rules, a concrete rule and organization of the Order, which soon after the death of St. Francis, fall into dispute and result in the schism of the Order, splitting into "Spirituals" and "Conventuals."

The existential or spontaneous communitas, as it is manifest in the ritual process, simply does not stand the test of time. It changes, as Turner says, into either normative communitas or ideological communitas. Both, however, are already a part of the social structure. In apocalyptic and millenarian movements, according to Turner, the realization of forms of existential communitas was constantly attempted. It is, however, necessary to resist the temptation of utopia and to find the suitable relationship, prevailing circumstances permitting, between ordinary structure and extra-ordinary communitas. Communitas occurs still today, according to Turner, in processes, actions, and enactments [*Vollzüge*], which express and realize the marginal character and transitional quality of religious life. It is these ritual actions—like the religious rites of passage, for example, the Christian sacrament and many others—be they determined by life phases, be they the calendrical [*kalendarischen*] rites of all religions—which are found in the praxis of pilgrimage[21] and liturgy of all religions of the world. "In complex industrialized societies, we still find traces in the liturgies of churches and other religious organizations of institutionalized attempts to prepare for the coming of spontaneous communitas."[22]

Bobby Alexander subjects the work of Victor Turner to a re-reading, in order to differentiate in particular Turner's understanding of ritual—as human action that is just as essential as it is transformative—from false and narrow interpretations. Alexander conceives ritual as an action in which "the experience of community validates the ideal of social structure—serving the common good, and it infuses community values into everyday social-structural life."[23] The innovative potential of ritual is constitutive for Turner's theory of ritual, according to Alexander. For him it is essentially a matter of highlighting the generative character of ritual, which Turner does by considering liminality and communitas as dimensions in which the existing social structure is suspended, criticized, and confronted with the alternative form of egalitarian relations, which, in contrast to existing relationships, reveal and make experienceable the innovative potential of possible coexistence. That is precisely why rituals represent a potential for social transformation; they are potentially subversive and do not have to, as in the structuralist-functionalist interpretation, be grasped as cathartic phenomena, which because of their "venting function" [*Ventilfunktion*] support and strengthen the social status quo.

For Tom Driver, the issue is essentially one of explicating ritualization as a fundamental human activity and analyzing (religious) ritual as human enactments, which together with confessional and ethical enactments constitute the basic form of human performance.[24] He understands rituals as performative actions that, as the rituals of sacrifice show, are admittedly religiously and morally equivocal; that is why he pleads for a connection of ritual performance with the confessional and the ethical. According to Driver, it is necessary to link the ritual mode with the confessional, which is for him essentially existential, since it discloses and communicates one's identity to others. According to Driver, the confessional propels the ethical mode, which he conceives as attested to and as itself both communal and social, as well as political, and aimed immediately at political action.

As social offerings of rituals, Driver sets out first the order that extends from the liturgical up to the order of a collectively shared "world"; second, that of community and solidarity; and third, the "magical" transformation of individuals, society, and nature.

The relationship of ritual theory and ritual praxis is reflected in methodological respects in the work of Catherine Bell, in which she analyzes ritual action by way of the concept of ritualization and thematizes the correlation between ritual and power.[25] Ritualization as the production of ritual acts represents, in her view, a strategic procedure aimed at ritualizing the social agent itself, by which the agent is endowed with different degrees of ritual competence and is granted "perceptions and experiences of a redemptive hegemonic order."[26]

Against structural-functionalist positions, which conceive of ritual as a means of social control, Bell insists that ritual constitutes not a controlling, but rather just a defining dynamic of social empowerment: ritual is itself a power and is, in part, an expression of power. Ritualization empowers not only those who control the ritual: it simultaneously restricts their power and gives space to those dominated for protest and resistance.

Bell makes clear through her keen awareness of Foucault that ritual both empowers and exercises power at the same time. From her formulation it is highly doubtful, as Alexander claims, that everyday social life impregnates all rituals with communitarian values. Against Alexander one must (with Driver) start from a dialectics of ritual ordering and ritual transformation. On the one hand, Bell's approach to ritual praxis goes theoretically further; on the other hand, her one-sided strategic conception of ritualization appears somewhat problematic. If ritual praxis is reduced to strategic action, its communicative dimension remains obfuscated. In addition to rituals of power and of empowerment, however, there are also rituals of understanding, in which an agreement, a shared conviction—be it pre- or post-discursive—reveals and manifests itself.

For theistic religions, worship is a particularly central ritual praxis. The worship form of ritual action comes up in the philosophical-theological literature, for the most part, under the concept of the cult. Richard Schaeffler emphasizes three distinctive features of cultic action. The cult is first, according to him, the action of worship; second, ritual action; and third, religious celebration.[27] Viewed phenomenologically, the cult is a community action in which groups, by means of external actions, come into relation with supernatural powers. The cult is, therefore, basically an event of communication. It is, first, a community of action, whose members communicate with a materially or personally represented supernatural power and simultaneously interact with each other. This happens, as a rule, in the form of a regulated, ritualized action in which the areas of authority and roles of the participants are carefully distributed and also require regulated preparations. Cultic community action is, second, spatially and temporally bound; it takes place in particular situations at fixed times in designated places. The cult, third, makes use of definite media in which, among other things, language and music, gestures and gesticulations are in play, and now and then join together in highly complex rituals and dramas. Fourth, the objects of cultic action are supernatural powers, to whom worship or veneration are shown; they are communicated with, in the case of personally presented powers, through prayer and sacrifice. The goals of such cultic action are, fifth, the magical influence and steering of material powers on the one hand, and on the other, personal communication with the deity. Face to face with the deity, the cultic community experiences itself; it is thus constituted and articulated in worship, sacrifice, pleas, and gratitude.

The cult is a constitutive dimension of religion and as such is indispensable for a practical theory of religion. Religion always takes place in the cultic realm: It needs ritual action as it needs the liturgical ceremony. The cult is thus in no way only expressive; it is not only the expression of human experiences with, or the encounter with, divinity. It is merely the expression of the participant's experiences of community. Cultic action, rather, is, like religion in general, *effective* in a determinate way. The cult gives divine reality space and time; gives it presence in the celebrating community; and thereby reveals, opens, and qualifies reality itself. Cultic action is at the same time communicative. It creates, strengthens, and transforms community.

Religious-ritual action can, of course, not only establish communitas, but also become neurotically compulsive in the Freudian sense; it can degenerate into magical effective-thinking [*Effektivitätsdenken*] and spiritless ritualism. The cult is constantly threatened with corruption and can degenerate into the demonstration of religious claims to power. The question of power is deeply connected with ritual action. Ritual action structured as or shaped by power brings about the critique of ritual. Similarly, the cult is from time immemorial connected with critiques of the cult, whose legitimacy, effectiveness, as well as morality are put into question. The critique of the cult contests either the very possibility and validity of cultic action in general, or it aims directly—like the prophetic critique of the cult—at "true worship," at the proper relation of cultic-ritual and ethical-communicative action. When the critique of the cult is no longer religious-theologically or ethically motivated to advocate for a better, more comprehensive and consequential worship, but rather becomes absolute, it turns into a critique of religion.[28] Prophetic ritual and cultic critique is an intrinsic moment of religion, and is, to that extent, indispensable for a practical-critical theory of religion. Prophetic critique aims at tying ritual-religious action back to, and thereby integrating it into a more comprehensive and integral religious praxis concerning the whole life of human life.

III. Religion as Communicative Praxis

The Frankfurt philosopher Jürgen Habermas has developed, in ever new attempts in his extensive work, a highly differentiated and globally discussed communicative theory of action.[29] The basic distinctions of the theory elaborated by Habermas—such as the opposition of agreement-oriented or communicative and result-oriented or strategic (or rather, instrumental) action, of action and action-relieved discourse, of real and ideal communication communities; the differentiation of validity claims of truth, truthfulness, and rightness; the analysis of the polarity of lifeworld and system, as well as communicative and instrumental rationality—yield not only essential elements for contemporary social, action-, and communications-theoretic theory-formation, but can also be made religion-theoretically fruitful.

Jürgen Habermas has, for a long time, taken the view that religion and communication are incompatible.[30] In his main systematic work, *The Theory of Communicative Action*, Habermas develops a sophisticated theory of society, action, communication, and rationality alongside an admittedly rudimentary theory of religion. His both religion-theoretical and religion-critical position contains the central thesis of the "linguistification of the sacred."[31] According to this thesis, the religious-metaphysical conceptions of the world become untenable in the process of social rationalization and the formation of modern structures of consciousness; they become, as he calls it, "obsolete." This stage of social evolution reached with modernity differentiates the once combined dimensions of moral-practical rationality in religion into right [*Recht*] and morals.

In his view, the religious ethic of brotherliness cultivated especially in the Judeo-Christian tradition, entered into "a communicative ethic detached from its foundation in salvation religion,"[32] and thereby is both superseded and preserved in secular form.

Besides its ethical orientation, religious praxis understood essentially as ritual praxis should have become obsolete, in that it passes its social functions of social integration and expression, fulfilled by ritual praxis, over to communicative action. The authority of the sacred is, according to Habermas, thereby progressively substituted by the authority of a justifiably held consensus—whereby communicative action is separated and released from sacredly protected normative contexts. The result of this sketched outline of his understanding of religion is that religion belongs to a historically obsolete developmental stage of humanity, which has in the meantime been superseded by modernity. Religion thereby loses its cognitive, expressive, and moral-practical content; it resolves itself into a communicative ethic. Free communication, in its intention to be unrestricted, thus takes the place of religion.

There are now, and have been for some time, remarks by Habermas on religion that contradict this systematic position. Already in his collected essays on postmetaphysical thinking, a notably clear change has come about in his interpretation, which no longer claims that religion is obsolete. Indeed, although it speaks more of the necessary appropriation of religious thought, it nevertheless does so without maintaining their supercession and dissolution. As the Frankfurt philosopher points out, he does not believe that "we, as Europeans, can seriously understand concepts like morality and ethical life, persona and individuality, or freedom and emancipation, without appropriating the substance of the Judeo-Christian understanding of history in terms of salvation."[33] The rhetorical power of religious speech retains its privilege so long as there is found no more convincing expression for those experiences and innovations which it still preserves. Whether philosophy or communicative reason can find better words is, since the end of the 1980s, evidently for Habermas again an open question.

In an essay from 1991, "Transcendence From Within, Transcendence in This World," Habermas enters, for the first time, into an explicit discussion with the theological recipients and critics of his theory.[34] The discussion centers around the concept of transcendence that Habermas understands as the vanishing point of an unending agreement and communications process, which in the advancement of the unbounded communications community, transcends the limitations of historical time and social space of the world. A transcendence so composed must in principle remain open. Through the "scrupulous questions about the salvation of the annihilated victim" advanced by Helmut Peukert and Johann Baptist Metz, we become, says Habermas, "conscious from within of the boundaries of each transcendence, which is directed toward this world;

but this kind of transcendence is unable to make us sure of the countermovement of a compensating [*ausgleichenden*] transcendence from the hereafter."[35] Since then the theorist of communicative action has constantly rubbed up against "anamnestic solidarity" (Peukert) or "anamnestic Reason" (Metz). [36]

According to Habermas's sensational acceptance talk for the Frankfurt Peace Prize on "Faith and Knowledge,"[37] the question of the relationship of religion and communication could, for him, be posed anew. The master thinker of contemporary enlightenment has by no means gone through a clandestine conversion. He, who now as ever before, still distances himself from religion and regards himself as "religiously unmusical," had, in the long-secularized St. Paul's Church in Frankfurt, made it plainly and simply clear that religion also represents a factor to be taken seriously in today's secularized society. One whose menacing dimension had become conspicuous with September 11, 2001, when the "tension between secular society and religion . . . exploded."[38] Nevertheless, in contrast to a fundamentalism that has become terroristic, there are also religious forms and religious communities that are entitled to "the predicate 'rational'."[39] Habermas now acknowledges, not only that the egalitarian law based on reason has expressly religious roots, but that it is understood moreover that the boundary between secular and religious reasons is after all fluid. Thus, according to him, "the fixing of this controversial boundary should be understood as a cooperative task, which requires of both sides that each take the perspective of the other."[40]

Cooperation, to be sure, presupposes communication. Indeed, the philosopher of communication reiterates that the philosophical translation of the apparent resources of religious perceptions and religious speech containing a considerable semantic potential has to be done. But even if he remains cautiously opposed to theology, he nevertheless accepts, in the meantime, that faith and knowledge, religion and reason, theology and philosophy are not simply antipodes of which one pole belongs to the future, while the other is now obsolete and disappearing into the Hades of history. Both are rather dependent on the reciprocal communication of each other, as well as on the productive dispute with one another, in which the issue is above all the basic questions of human life and survival. Religion is connected with, and directly about, communication. "The voice of God calling into life, from the outset, communicates within a morally tangible universe."[41] Even those who, like Habermas, do not believe in the theological premises of the concept of creation, can nevertheless understand and approve of its consequences. The discourse between religious and secular forms of communication essentially concerns a socially pressing agreement about humane praxis.

Habermas now decisively opposes an "unfair exclusion of religion from the public sphere,"[42] and at the same time firmly holds that "even the secular side retains a sense of the expressive power [*Artikulationskraft*] of religious speech."[43]

Inherent in religion is, thus, a communicative potential that—in the post-secular age of globalization and genetic technology, in which fundamentalist regression on the one side and scientific-technological transformation on the other are grappled with—is of undeniable importance. When it is about the clash of social worlds that must develop a common language, and when the reproduction and possibly also bio-technological production of "human nature"[44] are at stake—there it is evident that religion is in no way merely a private matter. Religion belongs, according to the peace prize winner's message, in public social discourse. It is introduced into such discourse and, in that respect, must be examined in a thorough Pauline manner. It can, if necessary, here demonstrate its argumentative power of persuasion and its performative power of change, which in this respect consists not in coming to terms with past injustice and suffering, but rather in calling into question "immutables," for example, through the speech and acts of memory, forgiveness and the promise of salvation and reconciliation.

IV. Perspectives on a Practical Understanding of Religion

The basic distinctions and intentions of the communicative theory of action elaborated by Habermas provide not only a productive social- and action-theoretic apparatus. They are also fundamentally significant from a religion-theoretic view, and are, in various respects, capable of being linked to a practical theory of religion.

In this respect, one should reject the confrontation of communicative reason and religion, which Habermas admittedly put forth several times prior to his Frankfurt Peace Prize speech. A contrasting of the two is from his own understanding of communicative rationality untenable, because communicative reason cannot *eo ipso* exclude religion and distance itself from something which belongs to it. Within the bounds of a procedural communicative rationality alone can what religion has to bring to it be proved—from participation in the procedure of argumentation and in conversation, or discourse, with those taking part. This could, thus, be found in a discourse with the members or representatives of various religions and mutually clarified in a cooperative search for truth. This cooperative search for truth appears to Habermas to be open when he calls for the establishment of an already fluid, disputed boundary between secular and religious reasons to be understood as a cooperative task, which has to be taken up in discourse by both sides.

From an action-theoretic approach, to which the insights of Charles S. Peirce's foundational pragmatic semiotics, of Ludwig Wittgenstein's theory of language games, of John L. Austin and John R. Searle's theory of speech acts, as well as of Karl-Otto Apel's transcendental pragmatic philosophy of communication, and Jürgen Habermas' theory of communicative action are dedicated,[45] an action-theoretically conceptualized theory of religion can be formulated. Such a theory understands religion as action between subjects, who, using particular types of texts and media in particular situations and contexts, articulate *something* to be understood for which *they* raise a truth-claim, make themselves *understandable,* and seek to come to an agreement.

Within the framework of a communicative action-theoretic approach, the following claim is to be explicated: Religion is itself at its core a constitutive communicative praxis, which, although there exist quite "privatized" limit-types of religious praxis throughout,[46] is genuinely intersubjective and agreement-oriented. As such it integrates in a religion—through various weightings and classifications—a variety of forms of communication, that is, speech acts enacted by its members. These speech acts go along with non-linguistic actions (e.g., gestures and gesticulations, as well as types of behaviour like walking, eating, drinking, and so forth), and these together are embedded in a comprehensive life praxis. Such life praxis—from its subjects, contents, texts, and contexts to its intentions as (religiously traceable) praxis—is carried out on the part of, as well as within, a communications community, which in these actions gives expression to its obligation to and responsibility in view of a transcendent reality, and by doing so creates, maintains, and changes community.

If the agreement-orientation represents the distinctive feature of communicative praxis, then religious praxis itself can be viewed as communicative—if and insofar as it is directed at a reality in which people do not deal with one another strategically (i.e., in a manner determined by power), functionalize, and instrumentalize each other, but rather mutually recognize, associate with, and experience each other solidaristically and in so doing act in concert. From the community-related and agreement-oriented character of religion, however, arises a significant difference from magic, which Durkheim has already made clear.[47] In Habermas's terminology, the decisive difference can be formulated in this manner: Whereas religion represents an intersubjective, consensus-dependent, and agreement-oriented praxis originating in previously established communalization and community organization, magic has a tendency toward monological, strategic-instrumental dealings with the external, social, or rather inner "world."

In communicative-religious praxis, definite semantic content is always at any given time brought forth, and it, as Habermas has since conceded, serves not only its own inspiring and motivationally stimulating rhetorical power, but also discloses and names a reality—which for human life and coexistence brings forth an inextricable semantic dimension, namely, the dimension of promise. It is the promise of a relieving and reconciling liberation from political, social, physical and psychic bondage and mortality's grip. In such religious speech and concerted praxis lies a semantic or rather performative-practical surplus, which is translated—admittedly only at the cost of thinning or emptying it—into philosophical speech, but cannot be transformed without residue. In such communicative-religious speech and praxis, according to my understanding, is shown: a *creative*, (that is, a reality-disclosing); an *innovative*, (namely reality-transforming); as well as an *anamnestic* potential, which becomes aware of and does justice to the reality of the victims of history. It is an action- and rationality-potential,[48] that communicative reason could disregard only at the price of its own impoverishment and "self-amputation"—which serves as a resource for the lifeworld and cultural capital (already in short supply) and that must make them fruitful. From the perspective of its members within the religious community, such innovative-anamnestically cultivated religious praxis would be understood, determined, and developed as a communicative praxis of faith.[49]

In Habermas's own systematic conception of his "theory of communicative action," a communicative action-theoretic understanding of religion is, in the end, missed, because contrary to the basic insights of his communicative theory of action he does not perceive religion as also present in diverse forms and enactments of actual praxis, but narrows it down to at most two of its dimensions—the semantic content and rhetorical function. For an action-theoretic understanding of religion, Habermas's concept of ritual action employed in his reconstruction of Durkheim is of great importance, but is certainly missing from his catalogue of action-types in which teleological, norm-regulating, dramaturgical and communicative action are distinguished.[50]

Habermas's understanding of ritual action is archaically restricted, although it follows Durkheim, whose intentions emphasize the actuality and contemporary relevance of ritual. Against Habermas stand newer ritual-theoretic conceptions that he has not engaged (as for instance those developed by Victor Turner, Clifford Geertz, and Catherine Bell),[51] which unfold decisive dimensions and elements of ritual-religious praxis. They are valid for both archaic and modern societies and are thus of significance. They show that ritual action refers to community and that it is communal, world-disclosing, reality-ordering, and reality-changing; and they explicate it as a precarious engagement and use of power that works to empower while also raising claims to power. An understanding of religion as agreement-oriented, as well as communicative praxis, appears to me to be able to incorporate the insights of these theories of ritual, on the one hand, thereby carrying the ambiguity of ritual praxis as a communicative-communal, transformative, but also latently power-determined action on the other, and, from there, to again ethically-critically reflect on and integrate it.

A communication- or action-theoretic understanding of religion takes up the communicative theory of action. A communicative action-theoretic understanding especially reveals itself in religion in the performative execution of various speech-actions of communicative events, or rather in the communicative praxis of subjects, who in their communicative, communal, and critical actions, which take place in their respective situations and contexts and by means of particular texts and media, communicate either *with* or *about a* reality—or in the theistic religions, with or about *a* reality called "God." This reality communicates to others through its own praxis of determinate communicative, and, therefore, action-forms.

Within the monotheist religions of Abrahamic origin, two basic forms of agreement-oriented religious-communicative action are recognizable: the act of witnessing and of confessing. Whereas the first form refers deictically to the reality of God aimed at in the prevailing religion, made accessible via the witness of the person, that discloses in kerygmatic, diaconal, prophetic, or pathic Praxis, and communicates with the goal of convincing others of this reality, confessing aims not at persuasion; rather, it publicly and obligingly gives expression to an already realized common conviction. Confessing means achieving consensus, or rather, presupposing it: confessing can only be done on the basis of an agreement, which manifests itself in the religious or confessional texts and is actualized in the speech-acts of confessing.[52]

Besides the elementary acts characteristic of monotheistic religions, namely that of witnessing (and of confessing), four religion-specific, contexualized action forms can be traced across all (major) religions at any one time, which in the case of Abrahamic religions are interwoven with witnessing and confessing and therefore overlapping. They are the speech-acts of: (1) *narrative accounts* of Gods, God, and faith; (2) ritual-worship *celebration*; (3) missionary, *parenetic* and prophetic *preaching*; as well as (4) the *sharing* of spiritual and material goods in the praxis of love of one's neighbor, of charity, pity, compassion, or solidarity.

Religions speak not only of God or of Gods, but also of the founders and paradigmatic figures of their religious traditions, whose actions they recount in stories. The cosmic event "in the beginning," the creation of the world and of people, primeval times, the origin of death, as well as the beginnings of separate traditions, are the subjects of religious narratives, from creation-myths and myths of primeval times to foundational stories,[53] which in the communicative-religious praxis of narrating are carried on and repeated. It is the telling in religion(s) of the beginning and end of the world, or of the cosmos from within one's own religious story. It is imaginatively anticipated, be it in the myths of the end of days, or in eschatological, or apocalyptic stories. What occurs at the end of the world and humanity is recounted in a multitude of illustrated stories, which, like the stories of primeval times, stand before the court of reason (including communicative reason) in the course of religious rationalization, correspondingly becoming de-mythologized, rationalized, and intellectualized. However, in the advanced phase of such a rationalization process, there becomes apparent, at the same time, the understanding that religiously relevant past, or rather, future "events" lacking imaginative narrative are not accessible and do not involve all de-mythologization necessary to completely transfer narratives into rational argumentation. It is rather important to: (1) realize and acknowledge the semantic picture contents and picture stories of narratives as necessarily imaginary-metaphoric, as anthropological, and also religiously indispensable and, therefore (2) to disclose and interpret the narratives in their semantic-cognitive meaning as well as in their aesthetic- and moral-practical intentions.[54]

A second fundamental form of communicative-religious praxis is the celebration.[55] Service to the divinity or divinities in all religions has the character of celebration. Worship of God must be celebrated and, in this respect, celebration is the suitable form of worshiping action. To the characteristics of cultic action belong these "memory- and –making-present-signs of a foundation effected beforehand by the divinity,"[56] in which the divine original event appears effective. In cultic worship, the divine origin and, at the same time, the epiphanic presence of the divinity are liturgically celebrated.

Worshiping, cultic-ritual action as celebration is a constitutive dimension of religion and, as such, indispensable for an action-theoretically conceived theory of religion. Religion is also always enacted within a cultic framework; it requires ritual action as liturgical celebration. Worshiping-celebration is not only about the expression of human experiences and being deeply touched by the divinity. It is likewise not by itself the expression of the participant's experiences of community, although it is admittedly this in part, in so far as it always also represents celebration in and of the community. Worshiping action is rather in a determinate and indeed performative way effective: Namely it imagines the self-understanding of the particular religious community and brings about that which it expresses and celebrates.

A third basic form of communicative-religious praxis is proclaiming. Through proclaiming, religious meaning is communicated in order that they be shared. Proclaiming is the praxis of religious subjects, which can be performed by priests, prophets, and official, charismatic Preachers.[57] Proclaiming makes known the meaning of a religion and is, in this respect, informative. This happens, of course, in the sense of an engaged and evocative communication, which intends that the addressees make what is communicated their own. Proclaiming is at the same time always communicative and situated. It emphasizes impressing the prevailing religious message upon the addressees while taking into account the situation of its listeners, and is thereby cable of being fruitful. There is a missionary element within proclaiming. Proclaiming aims at persuading people into a religion or—in the case of those who already possess religious conviction—at reinforcing, defending, strengthening, or perfecting such conviction.

Missionary proclaiming belongs to the communicative praxis of every religion. In fact, individual religions have certainly developed very different conceptions and styles of missionary praxis. Monotheistic-prophetic religions are more explicitly missionary, whereas the polytheistic or non-theistic religions of the East do not essentially recognize a mission. The "mystical religions"[58] coming from Indian culture are set in contrast to the prophetic religions of Semitic cultures, and do not aim at conversion or at confession, but rather at the experience and inspiration, at the understanding of the constitution and transitory and devoid nature of human, worldly, as well as cosmic existence. Indeed, these understandings are also codified in sacred texts. It is these, the insights, which have been proclaimed by the founders of religion and wise men and have been proclaimed, disseminated, and carried on by their followers, by mystics and monks, and by religious teachers and preachers.

In addition to the missionary, a second moment of proclaiming is above all encountered in the Semitic-Western religions. This aspect has brought the Abrahamic religions under a common description as prophetic religions. In fact, prophetic preaching is an important element for Judaism, Christianity, and Islam. The prophet is first of all the one who preaches God's words and instructions, God's revelations and holy word—the one who authoritatively-charismatically carries forth and spreads God's word of judgment.

Prophetic proclamation takes place above all where people raise objections against the prevailing conditions in the name of God, where they intervene in God's "lawsuits" with the world or with idols and take God's side. Prophetic preaching sets these conditions before God's court, acting as the prosecutor against injustice and preaching not only God's objection, but also his promise of a new, just, and benevolent order as well. Prophetic preaching comprises opposition to the political, social, economic, and religious injustice taking place. It accompanies the "condemnation of sinful conditions" with the "heralding of a new world."[59] Prophetic preaching places the "world" before God's court and charges it, suing for justice for the victim. This prophetic element of preaching is characteristic for the Abrahamic religions, although analogies are also found in the Eastern traditions.[60]

The fourth action-form of communicative-religious praxis is, finally, sharing. This is a general term for what in biblical Christian terminology means diaconal praxis. Such praxis of benevolence, compassion, pity, solidarity is central for all religions; it belongs everywhere to the ethical, communicative core of religion. The praxis of sharing creates, strengthens, and transforms community in particular ways. Sharing as practicing charitableness (*Zakat*) is one of the five "pillars of Islam." *Karuna* as pity, practical sympathy, and compassion is one of the basic characteristics of Buddha and one of the principal virtues of Buddhism. Judaism, like Christianity, emphasizes the obligation to share solidaristically the goods of the world, to eradicate inequality, to assume responsibility for one's neighbor, and to stand by those in need, distress, and to whom injustices are being committed.

All religions have their ideas about how the goods of the earth—the material as the spiritual, the social as the communal goods—are to be shared. Sharing "is here not meant in the sense of occasional conduct, but rather as a definite form of living and dealing with each other. It is the expression of a deep-reaching consciousness of solidarity. Consciousness distinguishes itself from other (pre)forms of solidaristic action, as for instance 'helping,' since 'helping' requires that one possesses and exercises power over something which the other lacks, allowing the former to be of benefit to the latter; whereas 'sharing' means recognizing in the encounter with the other in need that one's own needs and one's own fate is caught up in theirs. Thus, one in the first place experiences oneself as standing in reciprocal relationship to another, and, in giving the respective share of one's (not only material) fortune, one is enabled to mutually form a life praxis. Sharing, thus understood, is the most radical form of communicative praxis, in that those involved share with and participate in one another."[61]

The propositional-performative communication of the ultimate and, finally valid reality in theistic religions, as well as of the reality of God, in narrating, celebrating, proclaiming, and sharing (and the latter is, as a rule, unexpressed and, therefore, non-verbalized), occurs in the communicative intention that the narratively thematized and liturgical-ritual experience of each reality be shared and appropriately handled. The communication of the reality of God pursues the goal that people will be persuaded of this redemptive and liberating reality that is experienced and attested to, and that the human, worldly, as well as cosmic reality will (hopefully) be transformed in the direction of this reality (of God), with the participation of their devout witnesses and confessors.

Religion would, in an action-theoretic perspective, need to be analyzed and determined essentially as transformative praxis that embraces an intersubjective, an objective, a contextual, a media-related, and an intentional dimension, whereby these dimensions would be explicated in an action-theoretically conceived theory of religion as interlocking elements of religion, irreducible to each other. In view of such a theory of religion, four tasks appear to me as pressing.

First, it would be important to state more precisely the controversial concept of "religion"[62] with regard to its usefulness and scope, that it is neither an attempt to substantially investigate the nature of religion, nor to reduce religion functionally-operationally to an empty form of communication. A communications or action-theoretic concept of religion that integrates ritual-theoretical insights offers an alternative, in my view. From an understanding of religion formulated on this basis, it can be expected that it neither isolates nor reduces the elements (i.e., the subjects, content, places/contexts, texts/media, and intentions) that are differentiated in the pragmatic theory construction and have to, likewise, be considered in the analysis of religion. It must rather take them into common consideration and attempt to do justice to all of them in order to gain from the co-operative interaction of these elements a differentiated access to such phenomena to which it is sensible to apply the term "religion."

Second, the elaboration of the empirically rich and logical criteria of a relevant concept of religion would reflect precisely the normative core of religion or religious praxis. This concept, as far as it would be communicable and acceptable today, should not, on the one hand, undercut these normative standards of universality qua universalization, or more specifically of equality and reciprocity—worked out by a communicative action theory and reflected in discourse ethics—without, on the other hand, being able to raise the claim that these standards are "out bid" metaphysically, for example. Such a normative core may be investigated within the framework of the principles and procedures of communicative reason, and should be defined in the context of the self-understanding of the respective religious communities, from which their own traditions and resources are substantially enriched and at the same time the particular forms of ethos are applied to the general principles of communicative action.[63]

Third, one would have to explicate how and why the functionalist, as well as the ritual-theoretic and action-theoretic sides of religion, are rightly regarded as transformative. Thus the question of whether and to what extent such a transformation (also in pluralistic theories of religion as centrally religious matters of concern) is taking place at all would have to be thoroughly examined, especially in view of the fact that religious, as well as human, action is susceptible to power and to power abuse—an examination in which we are also inextricably involved. It would be necessary in this context to especially work out what occurs in this transformation, what is happening in it, with what is it happening, and upon what it is happening.

Fourth, this theory of religion would demonstrate how religious praxis appears under the present social-cultural conditions of various contexts: if, and how, it is today conducted as ritual; communicative, communal, and critical praxis and happening in the face of a globalized de-traditionalization, de-ritualization, de-institutionalization and individualization. In the process, it would investigate if from such processes, for instance, new traditions, rituals, communities, as well as new or rather contextually revitalized forms of "public religions"[64] come about. In every case, it would examine how religious praxis—be it in defensive-traditional or fundamentalist;[65] in postmodern-eclectic;[66] or in intentionally universal, creative-critical and transformative ways—applies to such processes and experiences. Thereby, it could be shown whether and how religion or religions succeed in narratively and discursively bringing the resources, practices, and visions of religious traditions into the present processes of social analysis and understanding; and therein show their validity and relevance.

Notes

1. Helmut Peukert, *Science, action and fundamental theology: Toward a theology of communicative action* (Cambridge, MA: MIT Press, 1984), 241. Translated by James Bohman. Cf. T. W. Tilley, *The Wisdom of Religious Commitment* (Washington, DC: Georgetown University Press, 1995).
2. Ernst Troeltsch, "Art" and "Contingency" in *Encyclopedia of Religion and Ethics*, Volume IV (1911) 87–89.
3. Cf. Richard Rorty, "Postmodern Bourgeois liberalism," in *Objectivity, Relativism and Truth* (New York: Cambridge University Press, 1991), 197–202.
4. Richard Rorty, *Contingency, irony, and solidarity* (New York: Cambridge University Press, 1989), 16.
5. Ibid., 22.
6. Ibid., xv.
7. Ibid., 46.
8. Niklas Luhmann, *Funktion der Religion* (Frankfurt: Suhrkamp, 1979), 26. Cf. Niklas Luhmann, *Die Religion der Gesellschaft* (Frankfurt: Suhrkamp, 2000).
9. Ibid., 20.
10. Ibid., 205.
11. Helmut Peukert, "Kontingenzerfahrung und Identitätsfindung. Bemerkungen zu einer Theorie der Religion und zur Analytik religiös dimensionierter Lernprozesse," in J. Blank and G. Hasenhütt, eds., *Erfahrung, Glaube und Moral* (Düsseldorf: Patmos, 1982), 76–102, 81.
12. Hermann Lübbe, *Religion nach der Aufklärung* (Graz: Styria, 1986).
13. Ibid., 166.
14. Cf. Lübbe, *Religion nach der Aufklärung*, 219–228; See also H.J. Schneider, "Ist Gott ein Placebo? Eine An-merkung zu Robert Spaemann und Hermann Lübbe," in *Zeitschrift für evangelische Ethik* 25 (1981), 145–47.
15. Cf. J. B. Metz, *Jenseits bürgerlicher Religion* (München: Matthias Grünwald Verlag 1980); Cf. Metz, *Glaube in Geschichte und Gesellschaft. Studien zu einer praktischen Fundamentaltheologie* (Mainz: Matthias Grünwald Verlag, 1977).
16. Cf. Clifford Geertz, *The Interpretation of Cultures. Selected Essays* (New York: Basic Books 1973); M. Douglas, *Ritual, Tabu und Körpersymbo-lik. Sozialanthropologische Studien in Industriegesellschaft und Stammeskul-tur* (Frankfurt: Fischer, 1981).
17. Victor Turner, *The ritual process: Structure and anti-structure* (Chicago: Aldine Publishing Co., 1969).
18. Ibid., 94–95.
19. Victor Turner, *The ritual process: Structure and anti-structure* (Chicago: Aldine Publishing Co., 1969), 96.
20. Ibid., 107.
21. Cf. Turner, "Pilgrimage and Communitas," in *Studia missionalia* 23 (1974) 305–27; Victor Turner and Edith Turner, *Image and Pilgrimage in Christian Culture: Anthropological Studies* (New York: Columbia University Press, 1978).
22. Turner, *Ritual*, 138; See also Turner's critique of the liturgical form of the second Vatican, that has destroyed the ritual character of the Roman Mass, in Turner, "Ritual, Tribal, and Catholic," *Worship* 50 (1976) 504–26.
23. B. C. Alexander, *Victor Turner Revisited: Ritual as Social Change* (Atlanta: Scholars Press, 1991), 9.
24. Cf. T. F. Driver, *The Magic of Ritual: Our Need for Liberating Rites that Trans-form Our Lives and Our Communities* (San Francisco: HarperCollins, 1991).
25. Cf. C. Bell, *Ritual Theory, Ritual Practice* (New York: Oxford University Press, 1992); Bell, *Ritual: Perspectives and Dimensions* (New York: Oxford University Press, 1997).
26. Bell, *Ritual Theory*, p. 141.
27. Cf. R. Schaeffler, "Der Kultus als Weltauslegung," in B. Fischer, E. J. Lengeling, and R. Schaeffler (eds.), *Kult in der säkularisierten Welt* (Regensburg: Friedrich Pustet, 1974), 9–62; Schaeffler, "Kultisches Handeln. Die Frage nach Proben seiner Bewährung und nach Kriterien seiner Legitima-tion," in R. Schaeffler and P. Hünermann, eds., *Ankunft Gottes und Handeln des Menschen* (QD 77), Freiburg 1977, 9–50.

28. In the same way in which work has an understanding of itself. Cf. A. Lorenzer, *Das Konzil der Buchhalter. Die Zerstörung der Sinnlichkeit. Eine Religionskritik* (Frankfurt: Suhrkamp, 1981).
29. Cf. Jürgen Habermas, *The theory of communicative action: Reason and the rationalization of society, Vol. I.* (Boston: Beacon Press, 1984); *The theory of communicative action: Lifeworld and system: a critique of functionalist reason, Vol. II.* (Boston: Beacon Press, 1989), *On the Pragmatics of Social Interaction: Preliminary Studies in the Theory of Communicative Action* (Cambridge, MA: MIT Press, 2002); Habermas, *Moral consciousness and communicative action* (Cambridge, MA: MIT Press, 1990); Habermas, *Justification and application: remarks on discourse ethics* (Cambridge, MA: MIT Press, 1993); Habermas, *Postmetaphysical thinking* (Cambridge, MA: MIT Press, 1992); Habermas *Truth and justification* (Cambridge, MA: MIT Press, 2003). For a discussion of Habermas' work, see Thomas McCarthy, *The critical theory of Jürgen Habermas* (Cambridge, MA: MIT Press, 1978); R. Roderick, *Habermas and the Foundations of Critical Theory* (New York: Macmillan, 1986).
30. Cf. E. Arens, "Kommunikative Rationalität und Religion," in E. Arens, O. John, and P. Rottländer, *Erinnerung, Befreiung, Solidarität. Benjamin, Marcuse, Habermas und die politische Theologie* (Düsseldorf: Patmos, 1991), 145–200; Arens, "Vom Kult zum Konsens. Das Religionsverständnis der Theorie des kommunikativen Handelns," in H. Tyrell, V. Krech, and H. Knoblauch, eds., *Religion als Kommunikation* (Würzburg: Ergon, 1998), 241–72; See also G.M. Simpson, *Critical Social Theory: Prophetic Reason, Civil Society, and Christian Imagination* (Minneapolis: Fortress Press, 2001).
31. Cf. Habermas, *The theory of communicative action,* II, 77–111.
32. Habermas, *The theory of communicative action,* I, 242.
33. Habermas, *Postmetaphysical thinking,* 15.
34. In Habermas, *Texte und Kontexte* (Frankfurt: Suhrkamp, 1991), 127–56. The essay refers to an article in E. Arens, ed., *Habermas und die Theologie. Beiträge zur theologischen Rezeption., Diskussion und Kritik der Theorie kommunikativen Handelns* (Düsseldorf: Patmos, 1989); See also E. Arens, ed., *Kommunikatives Handeln und christlicher Glaube. Ein theologischer Diskurs mit Jürgen Habermas* (Paderborn: Schöningh, 1997).
35. Habermas, *Texte und Kontexte,* 142.
36. See J. Habermas, "Israel or Athens: Where does Anamnestic Reason Belong? Johannes Baptist Metz on Unity amidst Multicultural Plurality" and the interview with Eduardo Mendieta "A Conversation About God and the World: Interview with Eduardo Mendieta," in Jürgen Habermas, *Religion and Rationality: Essays on Reason, God, and Modernity,* edited with an introduction by Eduardo Mendieta (Cambridge: Polity, 2002), 129–38, and 147–67, respectively.
37. Habermas, *Glauben und Wissen — Friedenspreis des Deutschen Buchhandels* (Frankfurt: Suhrkamp, 2001).
38. Ibid., 9.
39. Ibid., 13.
40. Ibid., 22.
41. Ibid., 30f.
42. Ibid., 22.
43. Ibid., 22.
44. Cf. Habermas, *The future of human nature* (Cambridge: Polity Press, 2003).
45. Cf. C. S. Peirce, *Schriften zum Pragmatismus und Pragmatizismus,* edited by K.-O. Apel (Frankfurt: Suhrkamp, 1976); Ludwig Wittgenstein, *Philosophical investigations* (Oxford: Blackwell 1963). Translated by G. E. M. Anscombe; John Austin, (1962). *How to do things with words* (Cambridge: Harvard University Press, 1962); John Searle, *Speech acts: An essay in the philosophy of language* (London: Cambridge University Press, 1969); Karl-Otto Apel, *Towards a transformation of philosophy* (Boston: Routledge 1980); See also E. Arens, *The Logic of Pragmatic Thinking: From Peirce to Habermas* (Atlantic Highlands, NJ: Humanities Press, 1994).
46. Cf. Durkheim's thesis of the "cult of the individual" toward the end of his *Elementary Forms of the Religious Life* (New York: Free Press, 1995) or the explanations of "Sheilaism" in R. N. Bellah, R. Madsen, W. M. Sullivan, A. Swidler, and S. M. Tipton, *Habits of the Heart: Individualism and Commitment in American Life* (Berkeley: University of California Press, 1996).

47. Cf. Durkheim, *Elementary Forms* 69 ff; See also H. G. Kippenberg and B. Luchesi, eds., *Magie. Die sozialwissenschaftliche Kontroverse über das Verstehen fremden Denkens* (Frankfurt: Suhrkamp, 1987); H.-G. Heimbrock and H. Streib, eds., *Magie. Katastrophentheorie und Kritik des Glaubens. Eine theologische und religionstheoretische Kontroverse um die Kraft des Wortes* (Kampen: Kok Pharos, 1995).

48. Habermas recognizes an "innovative world-disclosing power" of religion, which is imminent in prophetic speech and also in art which has become autonomous. Cf. Habermas, "Transcendence from within, transcendence in this world," 146f, Cf. his answer to D. Tracy's objections in Tracy, "Theology, Critical Social Theory, and the Public Realm," in D. Browning, F. Schüssler Fiorenza, eds., *Habermas, Modernity, and Public Theology* (New York: Crossroad, 1992), 19–42. He also accepts the innovative dimension of religious speech, particularly in his replies to Peukert's critique of his understanding of religion; Cf. H. Peukert, *Wissenschaftstheorie*; H. Peukert "Sprache und Freiheit. Zur Pragmatik ethischer Rede," in F. Kam-phaus and R. Zerfaß, eds., *Ethische Predigt und Alltagsverhalten* (München: Chr. Kaiser, 1977), 44–75; Peukert, "Kontingenzerfahrung"; Peukert, "Kommunikatives Handeln, Systeme der Machtsteigerung und die un-vollendeten Projekte Aufklärung und Theologie," in E. Arens, ed., *Habermas und die Theologie*, pp. 39–64; Cf. Habermas' replies in his *On the Pragmatics of Social Interaction;* Habermas, *The Philosophical Discourse of Modernity: Twelve Lectures* (Cambridge, MA: MIT Press, 1990), 25ff; Habermas, "Transcendence." 141ff.

49. Cf. E. Arens, ed., *Gottesrede - Glaubenspraxis. Grundzüge theologischer Handlungstheorie* (Darmstadt: Wissenschaftliche Buchgesellschaft 1994).

50. Cf. J. Habermas, *The theory of communicative action*, I, 126–51. The absence of ritual action in the typology might be based on the fact that Habermas understands such action as structured by power, compulsive, and irrational, and is therefore understood as non-communicative in the sense that in it a free communication about the things that need to be done is refused particularly by acts that are dictated obligatorily. On the other hand, one could understand the way Habermas views ritual action by drawing a parallel with the dramaturgical and its collective counterpart, in which it is not about a single actor presenting himself to an audience, but about a community representing itself to their members and also—in the case of religious-ritual action—to a transcendental reality.

51. Cf. Turner, *Ritual*; Geertz, *The Interpretation of Cultures*; Bell, *Ritual Theory*; See also E. Arens, "Religion und Ritual," in *Theologische Revue* 91 (1995) 105–114.

52. Cf. E. Arens, *Christopraxis: A Theology of Action* (Minneapolis: Fortress Press 1995).

53. Cf. the extensive work of M. Eliade, *A history of religious ideas*, 3 Volumes (Chicago: University of Chicago Press, 1978–1985).

54. Cf. The theoretical work on narrative by Paul Ricoeur, *Interpretation Theory: Discourse and the Surplus of Meaning* (Fort Worth: Texas Christian University Press, 1976); Paul Ricoeur, *Time and narrative*, 3 Volumes (Chicago: University of Chicago Press, 1984–1988); A. LaCocque and P. Ricoeur, *Thinking Biblically: Exegetical and Hermeneutical Studies* (Chicago: University of Chicago Press, 1998).

55. Cf. V. Turner (ed.), *Celebration: Studies in Festivity and Ritual* (Washing-ton, D.C.: 1982); J. Assmann and T. Sundermeier (eds.), *Das Fest und das Heilige. Religiöse Kontrapunkte zur Alltagswelt* (Gütersloh: Gütersloh Verlag, 1991).

56. Schaeffler, *Kultus*, p. 21.

57. Cf. the representation of diverse religious protagonists in Max Weber, *Economy and society: an outline of interpretive sociology* (Berkeley: University of California Press, 1978) edited by Guenther Roth and Claus Wittich; translators, Ephraim Fischoff et al., 335–37, 346–60.

58. F. Heiler, *Das Gebet* (München: E. Reinhardt, 1923), 255–58; Cf. the typological differentiation between the world-oriented prophetic-esthetic redemptive religions of the Occident and the world-rejecting mystical religions of the Orient in Max Weber "Zwischenbetrachtung: Theorie der Stufen und Richtungen religiöser Weltablehnung," in his *Aufsätze zur Religionssoziologie I*, (Stuttgart: UTB, 1988), 536–73, 536ff; See also Habermas, *The theory of communicative action*, I, 86–215.

59. J. Comblin, *Das Bild des Menschen* (Bibliothek Theologie der Befreiung) (Düsseldorf: Patmos, 1987), 37; Cf. D. Batstone, E. Mendieta, L. A. Lorentzen, and D. N. Hopkins, eds., *Liberation Theologies, Postmodernity, and the Americas* (New York: Routledge, 1997); R.

K. Fenn, *Liturgies and Trials: The Secularization of Religious Language* (Oxford: Pilgrim Press, 1982), 49: "In its prophetic language, then, religion places the world on trial."

60. Cf. On the person and praxis of M. Gandhi; See also R. Iyer, *The Moral and Political Thought of Mahatma Gandhi* (Oxford: Bookpeople, 1973); I. Jesudasan, *A Gandhi-an Theology of Liberation* (Maryknoll, NY: Orbis Books, 1984), or the Thai Buddhists Buddhadasa Bhikkhu; See also S. Sivaraksa, *A Buddhist Vision for Renewing Society* (Bangkok: Parallax Press, 1986); Sivaraksa., *A Socially Engaged Buddhism* (Bangkok: Parallax Press, 1988).

61. N. Mette, "(Religions-)Pädagogisches Handeln," in E. Arens, ed., *Gottesrede*, 164–84, 182.

62. Cf. W. C. Smith, *The Meaning and End of Religion* (New York: Fortress Press, 1962); N. Smart, *Worldviews: Crosscultural Explorations of Human Belief* (New York: Prentice Hall, 1983); T. Asad, *Genealogies of Religion: Discipline and Reasons of Power in Christianity* (Baltimore: Johns Hopkins University Press, 1993); D. L. Pals, *Seven Theories of Religion* (New York: Oxford University Press, 1996).

63. If the normative core of today's religious praxis is no longer allowed to undermine the normative niveau of discourse ethics, then this particular praxis positively distinguishes itself, not simply through "supererogatory acts" (See Habermas, *Justification and application*, 137), but this praxis opens it up and enlarges the communicative ethic, on the one hand, anametically, and on the other hand, innovatively going beyond it. Such ethical and religious praxis has to pass its definitive test today, particularly in view of the necessities and requirements of intercultural as well as inter-religious communication. Cf. R. Schreiter, "Theorie und Praxis interkultureller Kommunikationskompetenz in der Theologie," in E. Arens, ed., *Anerkennung der Anderen. Eine theologische Grunddimension interkultureller Kommunikation* (Freiburg: Herder, 1995), 9–30; Schreiter, *The New Catholicity: Theology Between the Global and the Local* (Maryknoll, NY: Orbis Books, 1997); T. Sundermeier, *Den Fremden verstehen. Eine praktische Hermeneutik* (Göttingen: Vandenhoeck & Ruprecht, 1996).

64. Cf. J. Casanova, *Public Religions in the Modern World* (Chicago: University of Chicago Press 1994); Robert N. Bellah et al., *Gewohnheiten des Herzens*; Bellah, *The Good Society* (New York: Vintage Books, 1991); See also E. Arens and J. Manemann, "Wie sollen wir zusammen leben? Zur Diskussion über den Kommunitarismus," in J. Manemann, ed., *Demokratiefähigkeit* (Jahrbuch Politische Theologie 1) (Münster: Lit Verlag, 1995), 155–87.

65. Cf. B. B. Lawrence, *Defenders of God: The Fundamentalist Revolt Against the Modern Age* (Columbia: University of South Carolina Press, 1995); M. Riesebrodt, *Fundamentalismus als patriarchalische Protestbewegung*, (Tübingen: Mohr Siebeck, 1990); Gilles Kepel, *Die Rache Gottes. Radikale Moslems, Christen und Juden auf dem Vormarsch* (München: Piper, 1994); T. Ali, *The Clash of Fundamentalisms: Crusades, Jihads and Modernity* (London: Verso, 2002).

66. Cf. H. Knoblauch, "Die Verflüchtigung der Religion ins Religiöse" in T. Luckmann, ed., *Die unsichtbare Religion* (Frankfurt: Suhrkamp, 1991), 7–41; P. Berry and A. Wernick, eds., *Shadow of Spirit: Postmodernism and Religion* (London: Routledge, 1993); T. W. Tilley, ed., *Postmodern Theologies: The Challenge of Religious Diversity* (Maryknoll, NY: Orbis Books, 1995).

Permissions

Part 1. Ernst Bloch

1. Bloch, Ernst. "On the Original History of the Third Reich." In *Heritage of Our Times*, trans. Nevill and Stephen Plaice, 1990, 117–144. Courtesy of the University of California Press.
2. Bloch, Ernst. "Not Hades, But Heaven on Earth." In *Heritage of Our Times*, trans. Nevill and Stephen Plaice, 1990, 117–144. Courtesy of the University of California Press.
3. Bloch, Ernst. "Hunger," "Something in a Dream," and "God of Hope, Thing-For-Us." In *Atheism and Christianity*, trans. J. T. Swann (New York: Herder and Herder, 1972), 265–273. Courtesy of Crossroads Publishing Company.
4. Bloch, Ernst. "Marx and the End of Alienation." In *Atheism and Christianity*, trans. J. T. Swann (New York: Herder and Herder, 1972), 265–273. Courtesy of Crossroads Publishing Company.

Part 2. Erich Fromm

5. Fromm, Erich. "The Dogma of Christ." In *The Dogma of Christ: And Other Essays on Religion, Psychology, and Culture,* trans. James Luther Adams (New York: Holt, Rinehart, and Winston, 1963), 9–71. Courtesy of Holt, Rinehart, and Winston.

Part 3. Leo Löwenthal

6. Löwenthal, Leo. "The Demonic: Project for a Negative Philosophy of Religion." In *Gabe Herr Rabbiner Dr. Nobel zum 50*; Kauffmann Verlag, 1921. Translation courtesy of Matthias Fritsch.

Part 4. Herbert Marcuse

7. Marcuse, Herbert. Luther, Calvin, Kant from "A Study of Authority." In *Studies in Critical Philosophy*, trans. Jorrs des Bres, 1972, 50–94. Courtesy of Beacon Press.

Part 5. Theodor W. Adorno

8. Adorno, Theodor W., "Reason and Sacrifice." In *Kierkegaard: Construction of the Aesthetic*, trans. Robert Hullot-Kentor, 1989, 106–122. Courtesy of the University of Minnesota Press.
9. Adorno, Theodor W., "Reason and Revelation." In *Critical Models: Interventions and Catchwords*, trans. Henry W. Pickford, 1998, 135–142. Courtesy of Columbia University Press.
10. Adorno, Theodor W. "Meditations on Metaphysics." In *Negative Dialectics*, trans. E. B. Ashton, 1983, 361–408. Courtesy of Continuum Books.

Part 6. Max Horkheimer

11. Horkheimer, Max. "Theism and Atheism." In *Critique of Instrumental Reason*, trans. Matthew J. O'Connell, 1974, 34–50. Courtesy of Continuum Books.
12. Horkheimer, Max. "The Jews and Europe." In *Critical Theory and Society*, Routledge 1989. Courtesy of Taylor and Francis Publishing.
13. Horkheimer, Max. "Religion and Philosophy." In *Gesammelte Schriften*, Vol. 7, trans. Mark Ritter, Fischer Verlag, 1985. Courtesy of Fischer Verlag; translation courtesy of Eduardo Mendieta.
14. Horkheimer, Max. "Observations on the Liberalization of Religion." In *Gesammelte Schriften*, Vol. 7; Fischer Verlag, 1985. Courtesy of Fischer Verlag; translation courtesy of Eduardo Mendieta.

Part 7. Walter Benjamin

15. Benjamin, Walter. "Capitalism as Religion (Fragment 74)." In *Gesammelte Schriften*, Vol. 6, 1985, 100–103. Courtesy of *Gesammelte Schriften*; translation courtesy of Chad Kautzer.
16. Benjamin, Walter. "Theological-Political Fragment." Excerpt from *Reflections: Essays, Aphorisms, Autobiographical Writings*, trans. Edmund Jephcott, 1978, 312–313. Courtesy of Harcourt Publishing.
17. Benjamin, Walter. "Theses on the Philosophy of History." In *Illuminations*, trans. Harry Zohn, 1968, 255–266. Courtesy of Harcourt Publishing.

Part 8. Johann Baptist Metz

18. Metz, Johann Baptist, "Productive Noncontemporaneity." In Jurgen Habermas, ed., *Observations on the Spiritual Situation of the Age*, trans. Andrew Buchwalter, 1984, 169–177. Courtesy of MIT Press.

19. Metz, Johann Baptist, "Anamnestic Reason: A Theologians Remarks on the Crisis of the Geisteswissenshaften." In Axel Honneth, Thomas McCarthy, Clauss Offe, and Albrecht Wellmer, eds., *Cultural-Political Interventions in the Unfinished Project of the Enlightenment*, trans. Barbara Fultner, 1992, 189–194. Courtesy of MIT Press.

Part 9. Jürgen Habermas
20. Habermas, Jürgen. "Israel and Athens, or to Whom Does Anamnestic Reason Belong? On Unity in Multicultural Diversity" by Jürgen Habermas, in David Batstone, et al. eds., *Liberation Theologies, Postmodernity, and the Americas* (New York: Routledge, 1997), 243–252. Courtesy of Taylor and Francis Publishing.
21. Habermas, Jürgen. "Transcendence from Within," "Transcendence in this World." In Don S. Browning and Francis Schüssler Fiorenza, eds., *Habermas, Modernity, and Public Theology* (New York: Crossroads, 1992), 226–250. Courtesy of Crossroads Publishing.
22. Habermas, Jürgen. "Faith and Knowledge," in *The Future of Human Nature*, trans., Hella Beister and William Rehg, Polity Press, 2003. Courtesy of Polity Press.
23. Habermas, Jürgen. "On the Relation between the Secular Liberal State and Religion." Courtesy of the author; translation courtesy of Matthias Fritsch.

Part 10. Helmut Peukert
24. Peukert, Helmut. "Enlightenment and Theology as Unfinished Projects." In Don S. Browning and Francis Schüssler Fiorenza, eds., *Habermas, Modernity, and Public Theology* (New York: Crossroads, 1992), 43–65. Courtesy of Crossroads Publishing.

Part 11. Edmund Arens
25. Religion as Ritual, Communicative, and Critical Praxis Couresy of the author; translation courtesy of Chad Kautzer.

Index

A

Abraham 27, 122, 153
Adam 170, 336
Adler 162
Adorno, Theodor W. 1, 3, 6, 7, 9, 10, 12, 13,
  14n4, 14n5, 15n13, 15n17, 15n18, 16n23,
  16n25, 16n26, 16n34, 289n4, 289n5, 297,
  308, 320, 334, 335, 337n13, 337n14, 355-
  357, 367, 369n8, 369n9, 369n11–17,
  370n51
Alexander 22, 23
Alexander, Bobby C. 379, 380, 393n23
Ali, Tariq 396n65
Alighieri, Dante 28
Amalrich of Bena 27
Antoninus 23
Apel, Karl-Otto 311, 317, 365, 385, 394n45
Aquinas, Saint Thomas 128, 144n41, 171,
  295
Archelaus 71
Arendt, Hannah 10
Arens, Edmund 13, 323n3, 370n44, 394n30,
  395n49, 395n51, 395n52, 396n64
Aristotle 238
Asad, Talal 396n62
Asoka, King 213
Augustine, Saint 10, 32, 33, 125, 213, 295
Augustus 22, 23
Austin, John L. 385, 394n45

B

Baader, Franz 56, 297
Bach, Johann Sebastian 201
Ball, Hugo 311
Barthe, Karl 307, 312

Baudelaire, Charles 215
Beckett, Samuel 176, 180, 189, 190
Beethoven, Ludwig van 193, 201
Bell, Catherine 380, 381, 387, 393n25,
  393n26
Bellah, Robert N. 396n64
Bengel, Johann Albrecht 304
Benhabib, Seyla 317–319, 324n31
Benjamin, Walter 9, 10, 12, 13, 15n18, 167,
  173n1, 178, 187, 261n1, 262n2–4, 273n5,
  289n4, 295, 308, 309, 322, 334, 356, 357,
  369n16–20
Berg, Alban 185
Bergson, Henri 187
Bernstein, Jay M. 14n4
Bernstein, Richard J. 325n38
Beyerhaus, Peter 144n28, 144n33, 144n35,
  144n36
Beza, Théodore de 126
Bin Laden, Osama 327
Blanqui, Louis Auguste 270
Bloch, Ernst 7, 11–13, 16n24, 16n27, 16n37,
  111, 112n5, 112n6, 185, 263, 289n4, 297,
  308, 334
Bloom, Alan 289n7
Böckenförde, Ernst Wolfgang 339, 341–343,
  346, 348n1, 348n5
Boesen, Pastor Emil 161
Boff, Clodovis 368n3
Bohman, James 14n6
Böhme, Jakob 56, 297
Bonald, Louis Gabriel de 232, 241n4
Bonaparte, Napoleon 25
Bonss, Wolfgang 14n8
Borradori, Giovanna 17n45

Brecht, Bertolt 44, 39n10, 267
Briggs, Sheila 317, 318
Bruck, Moeller van den 22, 30
Brunkhorst, H. 348n4
Bruno, Giordano 217, 253
Buber, Martin 37, 308
Buck-Morss, Susan 16n31, 369n16, 369n17,
    369n19
Buddha 103, 390
Bultmann, Rudolf Karl 307

C
Caesar, Julius 97n39, 110, 213
Calhoun, Craig 14n3
Calvin, John 117, 124–132, 144n25–27,
    144n34
Carnap, Rudolf 192
Casanova, Jose 396n64
Celsus (Platonist) 76–77
Charlemagne 24–25
Charybdis 322
Chesterton, Gilbert Keith 281
Churchland, Paul M. 337n4
Comblin, Joseph 395n59
Constantine 85, 86, 213
Copernicus, Nicolaus 252, 330
Coulanges, Fustel de 267
Cumont, Franz 96n32
Cusa, Nicholas of 216

D
Dahm, Karl W. 369n30
Dallmayr, Fred 303, 320–323, 323n5,
    325n36–38
Daniel 24
Darwin, Charles 262n3, 330
Davidson, Donald 322
Davis, Charles 314, 315, 324n25
Dehn, Günther Karl 36, 40n25
Delekat, Johann Heinrich 132
Derrida, Jacques 7, 307, 335, 337n16
Descartes, Rene 181, 245, 253, 255
Detel, W. 337n6, 337n7
Dewey, John 307
Dietzgen, Josef 269, 270
Dimitrov, Georgi 35, 40n23
Diocletian (Valerius Diocletianus) 86
Döbert, Ranier 311
Domitian (Titus Flavius Domitianus) 97n39
Don Juan 152, 159
Dostoevsky, Fyodor 30
Drehsen, Volker 369n30
Drew, David 12, 16n33
Driver, Tom F. 380, 393n24
Dubiel, Helmut 368n5
Durkheim, Emile 360, 361, 386, 387, 394n46,
    395n47

E
Eckermann, Johann Peter 200
Eder, Klaus 348n7
Eicher, Peter 324n12
Eliade, Mircea 395n53
Eliezer, Rabbi 70
Empedocles 24
Engels, Frederick 54, 219, 222
Epicurus 187
Erasmus (Desiderius) 245
Euripides 151
Eusebius of Caesarea 97n39
Eve 336

F
Faust 203
Feenberg, Andrew 14n7
Felix, Governor 72
Feuerbach, Ludwig 54, 149, 334, 345, 359
Fichte, Johann Gottlieb 216, 288n3, 304
Fiorenza, Francis Schüssler 305, 306, 323n6,
    323n7, 370n55
Flavell, John H. 359
Flaubert, Gustave 267
Flavius, Titus 75
Forst, Rainer 14n6, 337n2
Foucault, Michel 7, 380
Fourier, Charles 34, 40n18, 269
Francis of Assisi, Saint 379
Freud, Sigmund 3, 7, 13, 62–67, 95n2, 95n3,
    95n4, 97n47, 247, 295, 354, 359
Friedrich I (Barbarossa) 24
Friedrich II 24–25, 226
Fromm, Erich 12, 16n39
Fuchs, Bruno Archibald 262n7

G
Gadamer, Hans-Georg 7
Galilei, Galileo 252
Gandhi, Mohandas 396n60
Gay, Peter 14n2
Geertz, Clifford 387, 393n16
Gennep, Arnold van 377
Geyer, Florian 57
Geyer, Hans-Georg 323n2
Gilligan, Carol 319
Goebbels, Joseph 30
George, Stefan 202
Goethe, Johann Wolfgang von 109, 112n3–4,
    193, 200, 203, 208, 217, 225
Gollwitzer, Helmut 305
Göring, Hermann 30
Gottwald, Norman K. 370n42
Grimmich, Virgil 143n16
Groethuysen, Bernhard 199
Günter, Klaus 324n32
Gutiérrez, Gustavo 368n3

H

Habermas, Jürgen 3, 7, 8, 12, 13, 14n4,
  15n14, 15n18, 16n30, 16n31, 16n36,
  17n44, 286, 299, 321, 323n1, 323n3,
  323n4, 324n15, 324n16, 324n18, 324n20–
  22, 324n26, 324n28, 324n33, 324n40,
  324n41, 348n2, 348n3, 348n10, 353, 355,
  357-363, 369n22, 369n24, 369n27–29,
  369n31, 369n32, 370n33–35, 370n38–40,
  370n46, 382–387, 394n29, 394n31–45,
  395n48, 495n50, 396n63
Haecker, Theodor 156
Hamann, Johann Georg 322
Hanussen, Jan Erik 37, 40n27
Harnack, Adolf V. 79, 95n21, 95n24–25,
  96n29, 96n33, 96n38, 97n41–44, 97n46,
  285
Hegel, Georg Wilhelm Friedrich (G.W.F) 5,
  10, 40n13, 145n68, 149, 162, 168, 178, 179,
  185, 188, 191–193, 198, 204, 206, 207,
  209n2, 216, 266, 295, 297, 304, 308, 309,
  318, 333, 334, 336, 337n12, 345
Heidegger, Martin 180, 181, 200, 288, 303,
  320, 322, 335, 344, 359
Heiler, Friedrich 395n58
Held, David 368n5
Henry the Lion 25
Herod 71
Hippoytus, Saint 96
Hitler, Adolf 25, 30, 32, 34, 36, 39n1, 39n7,
  41, 42, 178, 235, 239
Hobbes, Thomas 170, 241n10
Holbach, Paul Henri Thiry d' 217, 218
Hölderlin, Friedrich 195
Honneth, Axel 7, 14n9, 15n12, 15n14,
  337n9
Horkheimer, Max 1, 3, 9, 11–13, 14n5,
  15n18, 16n23, 16n29, 289n5, 320, 333,
  337n15, 354–356, 362, 368n5, 369n7–9,
  367n11–13
Horus 23
Hudson, Wayne 16n32
Hullot-Kentor, Robert 17n40
Humboldt, Wilhelm von 322
Hume, David 245
Husserl, Edmund 103

I

Ibsen, Henrik 30
Isaiah 32, 101
Iwand, Hans Joachim 305
Iyer, Sri Raghavan 396n60

J

Jacobi, Friedrich Heinrich 188
James 78
Janowski, Hans-Norbert 323n2

Jay, Martin 14n1, 14n11, 15n18, 16n22,
  368n5
Jellinek, Georg 341
Jeremiah 98n49
Jesudasan, Ignatius 396n60
Jesus 23, 24, 32, 61, 77, 78, 80, 83, 84, 88–90,
  92–95, 95n23, 154, 218, 286, 364, 367
Joachim of Fiore (abbot) 24, 26–30, 39
Job 159, 295
Jochanan, Rabbi 70
John the Baptist 24, 75, 76
John, Saint 30
John XXIII 215
Jonas, Hans 289n4
Josephus, Flavius 69, 72, 95n6–9, 95n13,
  95n14, 95n17
Just, Saint 236

K

Kafka, Franz 178, 205
Kant, Immanuel 10, 115, 118, 132–142,
  145n68–111, 171, 178, 182, 183, 190–201,
  205, 207, 208, 209n1, 216, 232, 233,
  241n5–6, 245, 246, 248, 253, 254, 304, 315,
  317, 318, 322, 333, 334, 337n10, 337n11,
  341, 345, 365
Karaganis, Joseph 14n3
Kaufmann, David 9, 12, 15n15, 16n21,
  16n28, 16n35
Kautsky, Karl 78, 95n5, 95n21, 96n27, 96n33,
Kehrer, Günter 369n30
Keller, Gottfried 266
Kellner, Douglas 14n4
Kelsen, Hans 341
Kepel, Gilles 396n65
Keppler, Johannes 252
Keyserling, Hermann Graf 37, 40n26
Kierkegaard, Søren 13, 111, 149–165, 165n1–
  8, 166n9–41, 168, 169, 176, 186, 215, 308,
  311, 345, 368n1, 370n50
Kirchheimer, Otto 1, 3
Klee, Paul 268
Kluke, Paul 324n13
Knoblauch, Herbert 396n66
Kodalle, Klaus-Michael 369n29
Kohlberg, Lawrence 7, 319, 359
Kraus, Karl 186, 203, 206, 271
Krupp and Thyssen 229
Kusche, Karl-Josef 294

L

Laband, Paul 341
LaCocque, A. 395n54
Lamb, Matthew 306, 323n9, 370n53
Landauer, Gustav 261, 262n10
Lassalle, Ferdinand 273n3
Lawrence, Bruce B. 396n65

Lazarus 78
Leibniz, Gottfried Wilhelm von 49, 175, 205, 245, 253, 262n3
Lenin, Vladimir 35, 38, 46
Lessing, Gotthold Ephram 29, 30
Levinas, Emmanuel 289n4
Liebknecht, Karl 273n4
Liebknecht, Wilhelm 273n3
Lobstein, Jean-Frederic 127, 144n37–39
Locke, John 219, 322
Lorenzer, Alfred 394n28
Lotze, Rudolf Hermann 265
Löwe, Heinrich der 39n11
Löwenthal, Leo 1, 13
Löwith, Karl 323n4
Löwry, Michael 14n11
Lübbe, Hermann 375–377, 393n12, 393n13
Ludwig II 25
Luhmann, Niklas 7, 317, 341, 375, 377, 393n8–10
Lukács, Georg 6, 7, 12, 13, 15n12, 45, 107, 108, 112n1, 112n2, 161, 186, 200
Luther, Martin 22, 31, 50, 117–121, 123–134, 136, 139, 142, 143n1–15, 143n17–21, 144n22–25, 144n42–44, 144n47–63, 145n64, 171, 216, 245, 246, 250n1, 252
Lützow, Adolf von 44
Luxemborg, Rosa 273n4

M
Machiavelli, Nicolo 232
Mandeville, Bernard de 231
Manemann, Jürgen 396n64
Mann, Thomas 170
Marcuse, Herbert 1, 3, 13, 145n68, 145n84, 162, 369n7
Marquard, Odo 320, 324n34
Marshall, Alfred 262n3
Marx, Karl 1, 7, 9, 15n20, 37, 38, 40n31, 43, 44, 49, 50, 53–56, 103, 123, 143n19, 149, 178, 196, 219, 222, 255, 260, 269–271, 273n3, 304, 334, 345, 354, 359
Mary 93–94, 98n49
McCarthy, Thomas 324n23, 370n49
Mead, George Herbert 7, 319, 359
Meister Eckhart 37, 40n30
Mendieta, Eduardo 15n18, 394n36
Methodius, Saint 23, 24
Mette, Norbert von 396n61
Metz, Johann Baptist 13, 17n42, 288n2, 293–300, 308, 309, 314, 324n14, 368n3, 370n48, 383, 384, 393n15
Meyer, Eduard 95n5, 97n40
Mieses, Jacques 192
Mohammed 24
Möller, Jens Glebe 311, 312, 315, 324n17
Moltmann, Jürgen 13, 17n42

Monrad, Olaf Peder 151, 165n1
More, Thomas 38
Mornet, Daniel 241n9
Moses 22, 24, 72, 80, 131, 295, 336
Müller, Adam 261, 262n12
Müller, Klaus 370n43
Munch, Edvard 107
Münzer, Thomas 22, 31, 37, 38, 143n21

N
Nero 97
Newmann, Franz 1, 3
Newton, Isaac 252
Niebuhr, Reinhold 307
Nietzsche, Friedrich 7, 183, 188, 191, 206, 215, 260, 270, 288
Noerr, Guzelin Schmid 15n18

O
Oetinger, Friedrich Christoph 304

P
Pals, Daniel L. 396n62
Pannenberg, Wolfhart 286
Parsons, Talcott 7
Paschal, Pope Rainerius 143n19
Pascal, Blaise 169
Paul, Saint 30, 80, 84, 85, 87, 96n39, 97n39, 118
Pensky, Max 17n45
Peter, Saint 30
Peukert, Helmut 13, 17n43, 306, 307, 310–315, 317, 323n8, 324n19, 324n24, 368n4, 369n23, 370n36, 370n41, 370n44, 370n45, 370n55, 373, 375, 384, 393n1, 393n11, 393n48, 395n48
Philo of Alexandria 105
Piaget, Jean 359
Pierce, Charles S. 307, 313, 316, 317, 324n29, 324n30, 385, 394n45
Plotinus 285
Pollack, Fredrick 1
Prantl, Heribert 337n1
Prester John 23, 24
Proper, Thomas 370n47
Proust, Marcel 184, 187, 188
Pryzwara, Erich 36, 40n24

Q
Quine, Willard von Orman (W.V.O.) 322

R
Radó, Sándor 94
Rahner, Karl 281, 370n52
Ranke, Leopold von 267
Raphael 215
Ratzinger, Cardinal Joseph 286, 288n1

Raulet, Gerard 16n38
Rawls, John 299, 337n2, 339, 347, 348n8
Reik, Theodor 62, 65, 82, 95n1
Richelieu, Cardinal Armand Jean du Plessis 235
Ricoeur, Paul 354, 368n6, 395n54
Riesebrodt, Martin 396n65
Rimbaud, Arthur 203
Robespierre, Maximilien 222, 236, 271
Robinson, John 220
Rorty, Richard 7, 307, 374-376, 393n3-7
Rosenzweig, Franz 289n4
Rostovtzeff, Michael Ivanovich 95n5
Rousseau, Jean Jacques 199, 219, 222

S

Sade, Marquis de 232, 241n3
Sakkai, Rabbi Jochanan ben 70, 74
Sanchez, Juan José 17n41
Sartre, Jean-Paul 303
Schäfer, Klaus 370n50
Schaeffler, Richard 381, 393n27, 395n56
Schelling, Friedrich Wilhelm Joseph von (F.W.J.) 12, 30, 297, 304, 358, 359, 370n50
Schiller, Friedrich 193
Schindler, Norbert 14n8
Schirmacher, Wolfgang 14n1
Schleiermacher, Friedrich 305, 307, 345
Schmidt, Alfred 323n2
Schmitt, Carl 341, 344
Scholem, Gerlard 268
Scholem, Gershom 15n19, 356
Schönberg, Arnold 202
Schopenhauer, Arthur 7, 177, 187, 193, 200, 205, 209n3, 221, 246, 248, 250n2-5, 250n7-8, 254, 255
Schreiter, Robert J. 396n63
Schubert, Gotthilf Heinrich von 96n28
Schulz, Walter 369n25, 369n26
Schürer, Emil 95n15
Searle, John R. 385, 394n45
Seel, Martin 316
Sellars, Wilfrid 330, 331, 337n3
Selman, Robert 359
Shaftesbury, Earl of 106
Siebert, Rudolf J. 15n18, 17n41, 369n29, 370n44
Simmel, George 7
Simon, Saint 191
Simpson, Gary M. 307, 324n11
Singer, Wolf 348n9
Sivaraksa, Sulak 396n60
Smart, Ninian 396n62
Smith, Adam 241n11
Smith, Jonathan Z. 15n16
Smith, Wilfrid Cantwell 396n62

Socrates 111, 335, 345
Sölle, Dorothy 13
Sorel, Georges 262n5
Spengler, Oswald 170, 199
Spinoza, Baruch 10
Steinbüchel, Theodor 308
Strauss, Leo 344
Sundermeier, Theo 396n63
Suso, Heinrich 37, 40n30

T

Tauler, Johann 37, 40n29
Telesphorus of Cosenza 28
Tertulian, Nicolae 14n10
Theudas 72, 75
Theunissen, Michael 297
Tillich, Paul 13, 220, 243, 244, 246, 250n6, 308
Tolstoy, Leo 171, 202, 248
Tracy, David 306, 310, 312, 314, 316, 323n10, 368n3, 370n37, 370n54, 395n48
Trajan, Emperor 23
Troeltsch, Ernst 126, 144n29-32, 145n66, 261, 262n9, 374, 393n2
Turner, Victor 377, 379, 387, 393n17-22, 395n51

U

Unger, Erich 262n6
Uzziah (King) 101
Vanini, Lucilio 217
Vetter, August 163
Virgil 22-23
Vogel, Steven 14n7
Voltaire, François-Marie Arouet de 36, 175, 217, 223, 226, 246, 248, 250n9, 250n10

W

Weber, Max 95n5, 129, 130, 144n46, 259, 261, 262n8, 313, 330, 352, 354, 360, 361, 363, 395n57, 395n58
Weissenberg, Joseph 37, 40n28
Weitling, Wilhelm 34, 38, 40n17
Weizsäcker, Carl Friedrich von 368n2
Wellmer, Albrecht 7, 316, 324n27
Wiggerhaus, Rolf 14n1, 16n39
Wilhelm I, Kaiser ("The Great") 24, 39n6, 235
Wittgenstein, Ludwig 205, 385, 394n45
Wolin, Richard 369n21
Wundt, Wilhelm 104
Wuthnow, Robert 303, 319, 320, 324n34

X

Xenocrates 105
Xenophanes 208